DOMESTIC JUDICIAL REVIEW
OF TRADE REMEDIES

Trade remedies, namely anti-dumping, countervailing measures and safeguards, are one of the most controversial issues in today's global trading environment. When used, such measures effectively close the markets of the importing countries to competition from outside for a certain period of time. Exporters that are faced with such measures can try either to convince their government to bring a case against the government of the importing country in the WTO or to use, themselves, the judicial review mechanism of the importing country. This second path, until now, has been largely unexamined. *Domestic Judicial Review of Trade Remedies* is the first book of its kind to examine in detail how the judicial review process has functioned, and considers the experiences in the domestic courts of the twenty-one WTO members that are the biggest users of trade remedies.

MÜSLÜM YILMAZ works as a Counsellor in the Rules Division of the WTO. He functions as legal officer to WTO panels handling disputes on trade remedies and as Secretary to the WTO Committee on Subsidies and Countervailing Measures. Before joining the WTO in 2001, Mr Yilmaz worked as counsel and investigator at the Turkish Anti-Dumping and Anti-Subsidy Investigating Authority.

As the processes of regionalization and globalization have intensified, there have been accompanying increases in the regulations of international trade and economic law at the levels of international, regional and national laws.

The subject matter of this series is international economic law. Its core is the regulation of international trade, investment and cognate areas such as intellectual property and competition policy. The series publishes books on related regulatory areas, in particular human rights, labour, environment and culture, as well as sustainable development. These areas are vertically linked at the international, regional and national level, and the series extends to the implementation of these rules at these different levels. The series also includes works on governance, dealing with the structure and operation of related international organizations in the field of international economic law, and the way they interact with other subjects of international and national law.

Series Editors

Dr Lorand Bartels, *University of Cambridge*

Professor Thomas Cottier, *University of Berne*

Professor William Davey, *University of Illinois*

Books in the series

Trade Policy Flexibility and Enforcement in the WTO: A Law and Economics Analysis
Simon A. B. Schropp

The Multilaterization of International Investment Law
Stephan W. Schill

The Law, Economics and Politics of Retaliation in WTO Dispute Settlement
Edited by Chad P. Bown and Joost Pauwelyn

Non-Discrimination in International Trade in Services: 'Likeness' in WTO/GATS
Nicolas Diebold

Processes and Production Methods (PPMs) in WTO Law: Interfacing Trade and Social Goals
Christiane R. Conrad

African Regional Trade Agreements as Legal Regimes
James Thuo Gathii

The Law and Politics of WTO Waivers: Stability and Flexibility in Public International Law
Isabel Feichtner

DOMESTIC JUDICIAL REVIEW OF TRADE REMEDIES

Experiences of the Most Active WTO Members

Edited by

MÜSLÜM YILMAZ

CAMBRIDGE
UNIVERSITY PRESS

CAMBRIDGE UNIVERSITY PRESS
Cambridge, New York, Melbourne, Madrid, Cape Town,
Singapore, São Paulo, Delhi, Mexico City

Cambridge University Press
The Edinburgh Building, Cambridge CB2 8RU, UK

Published in the United States of America by Cambridge University Press, New York

www.cambridge.org
Information on this title: www.cambridge.org/9781107022232

© Cambridge University Press 2013

First published 2013

Printed and bound in the United Kingdom by the MPG Books Group

A catalogue record for this publication is available from the British Library

Library of Congress Cataloguing in Publication data
Domestic judicial review of trade remedies : experiences of the most active WTO
members / Edited by Müslüm Yilmaz.
p. cm.
1. Foreign trade regulation. 2. Judicial review 3. World Trade Organization.
I. Yilmaz, Müslüm.
K3943.D655   2012
343.08′7–dc23
2012024807

ISBN 978-1-107-02223-2 Hardback

CONTENTS

CONTRIBUTORS

MAZHAR BANGASH Partner, Rizvi, Isa, Afridi & Angell Advocates and Corporate Counsellors, Islamabad, Pakistan

GUSTAV BRINK Extraordinary Lecturer in Mercantile Law, University of Pretoria and Research Associate, Trade Law Centre of Southern Africa

ERRY BUNDJAMIN Founding Partner, Bundjamin & Partners Law Offices, Jakarta, Indonesia

LUCIANA B. COSTA Senior Associate, Nasser Sociedade de Advogados, São Paulo, Brazil

MERCEDES DE ARTAZA Counsel, M. & M. Bomchil Abogados, Buenos Aires, Argentina

STEPHEN GAGELER Solicitor-General of Australia

HENRY GAO Professor of Law, Law School, Singapore Management University, Singapore

MADHURENDRA NATH JHA Advocate, Law Chambers of Madhurendra Nath Jha, New Delhi, India

PATTANAN KALAWANTAVANICH Associate, Apisith & Alliance Ltd., Bangkok, Thailand

CHRISTOPHER J. KENT Founding Partner, Cassidy Levy Kent (Canada) LLP

FAIZULLAH KHILJI Former Head of the National Tariff Commission, Pakistan

ANDREW M. LANOUETTE Associate, Cassidy Levy Kent (Canada) LLP

JAEMIN LEE Professor of Law, Hanyang University Law School, Seoul, Republic of Korea

LUIS ALBERTO LEÓN Technical Secretary of the Anti-Dumping and Countervailing Duties Commission INDECOPI (National Institute for the Defence of Competition and the Protection of Intellectual Property), Peru

MARÍA CLARA LOZANO Counsel, Lozano & Abogados Derecho, Competencia & Globalización, Bogotá, Colombia

MICHELE D. LYNCH Senior Counsel for Litigation, Office of the Chief Counsel for Import Administration, US Department of Commerce

JOHN D. MCINERNEY Chief Counsel for Import Administration, US Department of Commerce

HUGH MCPHAIL Independent consultant, former head of New Zealand's trade remedies investigating authority, Wellington, New Zealand

MARÍA ANTONIETA MERINO Executive 1 (Legal Assistant) of the Anti-Dumping and Countervailing Duties Commission INDECOPI (National Institute for the Defence of Competition and the Protection of Intellectual Property), Peru

JORGE MIRANDA Principal International Trade Advisor, International Trade Group, King & Spalding LLP, Washington DC, USA

GILL NADEL Founding Partner, Gill Nadel Law Office, Israel

RABIH A. NASSER Founding Partner, Nasser Sociedade de Advogados, São Paulo, Brazil; Professor of International Trade Law, Fundação Getúlio Vargas Law School, São Paulo (Direito GV)

JUAN CARLOS PARTIDA Partner, Rubio Villegas y Asociados, Mexico City, Mexico

ARIE REICH Dean and Professor of Law, Faculty of Law, Bar-Ilan University, Israel

EDMUND SIM Partner, Appleton Luff, Singapore

JUHI SUD Counsel, VVGB Advocaten, Brussels, Belgium

APISITH JOHN SUTHAM Partner, Apisith & Alliance Ltd., Bangkok, Thailand

OSAMU UMEJIMA Local partner, White & Case LLP, Tokyo Office, Japan

SAKKAPOL VACHATIMANONT Associate, Apisith & Alliance Ltd., Bangkok, Thailand

EDWIN VERMULST Founding Partner, VVGB Advocaten, Brussels, Belgium

MÜSLÜM YILMAZ Counsellor, World Trade Organization, Rules Division, Geneva, Switzerland

FOREWORD

The scope of rules that regulate international trade expanded significantly with the emergence of the present international trading system following the conclusion of the Uruguay Round of trade negotiations in 1995 that led to the creation of the World Trade Organization (WTO). The WTO is an organization that seeks to implement a rules-based, open trading system. A rules-based system is one that offers predictability in terms of the regulatory framework within which trade takes place. Maintaining a predictable trading environment in turn requires transparency and rule of law.

Within the WTO system, transparency is achieved mainly through the peer review of the notification obligations contained in the WTO Agreement and the rule of law through the dispute settlement mechanism. Since 1995 WTO dispute settlement has proved most helpful in resolving trade disputes between WTO members and thereby providing the security and predictability needed to ensure a well-functioning international trading system. This mechanism has received extensive attention in academia and in government circles.

However, in today's highly complex world, the WTO alone cannot tackle all the legal issues that arise from the implementation of its many different agreements, each dealing with a different aspect of international trade. There is a great deal that governments which are WTO members can do at the domestic level which may contribute to the common ultimate objective: creating as seamless and as predictable as possible an environment in which commercial entities can conduct their commerce. Thus, the involvement of domestic courts in the resolution of legal disputes affecting international trade is an important element of providing the ideal rules-based trading environment.

This book represents the first major attempt to shed light on judicial review at domestic level, a singularly important issue in connection with trade remedies that, despite its potential importance, has unfortunately received little notice so far. The book offers an in-depth analysis of how the domestic courts of 21 WTO members review the determinations of their own investigating authorities in trade remedy proceedings. The fact that roughly half of the disputes raised so far in the WTO concerned trade remedies underlines the importance of this study.

The results obtained in this research project, which are summarized in the overall conclusion, deserve the attention of all stakeholders in trade remedy proceedings. First, in terms of numbers, the book shows that there have been many more judicial review cases before domestic courts compared with the disputes raised at the WTO. Arguably, judicial review of trade remedy determinations by domestic courts could be potentially more significant than WTO dispute settlement. Second, the book identifies a number of common problems faced by many of the countries studied and suggests ways in which such problems may be addressed. The commonality of these problems across countries from different parts of the globe is notable, and underlines the need to take timely and appropriate steps to address these issues. As always, the WTO is ready to play the role that its members deem appropriate in addressing this particular aspect.

I believe that this book will fill an important gap in academic research on international trade law, besides meeting the needs of practitioners, and pave the way for further, more detailed, studies on judicial review at domestic level and its inter-linkages with WTO dispute settlement.

Pascal Lamy
Director-General
World Trade Organization

ACKNOWLEDGEMENTS

I am indebted to many colleagues and friends who supported this major research project with their invaluable ideas and comments. First, I would like to offer my deepest thanks to the authors who agreed to participate. Without their efforts, this book would not have seen the light of day.

I have also benefited greatly from the ideas and support offered by many colleagues in the WTO Secretariat. Mark Koulen provided never-ending intellectual support throughout this project, which contributed significantly to the quality of the outcome. Johann Human, Director of the Rules Division, provided comments that helped ensure that the book would prove useful to practitioners and academics specializing in trade remedies. Jesse Kreier helped to define the scope of the work at a formative stage. Graham Cook read through some of the draft texts and provided helpful comments.

Thanks are also due to Professor Hélène Ruiz Fabri for her encouragement at an early stage of the project. Anthony Martin and Keith Rockwell provided invaluable administrative support, and Nélida Varela was most helpful in ensuring a coherent textual style. Finola O'Sullivan and Kim Hughes of Cambridge University Press guided the project to its completion with professional competence.

Finally, I would like to thank my wife, Figen, and the two other crew members, Baran and Alp, who have endured my overexcitement about judicial review for such a long time. It is to them that I dedicate my work on this book.

1

Introduction

MÜSLÜM YILMAZ[*]

This book represents a research project on the judicial review of trade remedy determinations by the competent tribunals of the members of the World Trade Organization (hereinafter WTO) which are the most active users of trade remedies. The main objective of this project is to shed light on how judicial review of trade remedy determinations is conducted by WTO members. In terms of its substantive scope, the book covers the judicial review of the determinations made in the three trade remedy proceedings: anti-dumping, countervail and safeguards.

In terms of the selection of countries, we generally looked at the level of trade remedies activity in order to cover countries that are active users of these measures. However, in order to observe a certain geographical balance, we have also covered countries such as Japan that are not very active users. Thus, our list contains countries from North America (Canada, Mexico and the United States), Latin America (Argentina, Brazil, Colombia, Peru), Europe (European Union, Turkey), Middle East (Israel), Africa (South Africa), Asia (China, India, Indonesia, Japan, Korea, Malaysia, Pakistan, Thailand) and Oceania (Australia and New Zealand). We have also covered not only developed countries that are traditional users of trade remedies and which also have well-established judicial review systems, but also developing countries that started using trade remedies relatively late, but which quickly became active users of such measures. The authors have been selected from among the top practitioners, government officials or academics who are trade remedies experts in their respective jurisdictions. This has contributed significantly to the depth of the analysis provided in the chapters.

* The author thanks Mark Koulen, Graham Cook and authors of country chapters in this book for their valuable comments on earlier drafts.

In this book, we use the term "trade remedies" when referring to anti-dumping, countervailing and global safeguard measures. The General Agreement on Tariffs and Trade (GATT) has always contained specific provisions (Article VI for anti-dumping and countervail and Article XIX for safeguards) allowing these measures, and thus rendering them consistent with its principles. In addition to the GATT provisions that authorize the use of trade remedies, today there are also three agreements attached to the WTO Agreement, each elaborating the rules that apply to the investigative processes which lead to the imposition of a specific trade remedy measure. These are the Agreement on Implementation of Article VI of the GATT 1994 (dealing with anti-dumping measures, hereinafter AD Agreement), the Agreement on Subsidies and Countervailing Measures (hereinafter SCM Agreement) and the Agreement on Safeguards (hereinafter SG Agreement).

Much has been said about the impact of trade remedies on international trade. Many consider these measures to fly in the face of the principles of free trade and efficient allocation of resources at the global level.[1] Others take the view that trade remedies ensure a level playing field by protecting domestic industries against unfair practices in international trade and that, by functioning as a safety valve, they actually encourage countries to engage in trade liberalization.[2] We will not revisit this long-standing debate here. Our starting point in this regard is a pragmatic one: no matter what effect trade remedies have on international trade, the reality is that WTO members use these measures, provided that certain conditions are met. What matters is whether trade remedy measures are applied in a WTO-consistent fashion. Taking this for granted, we look into the domestic

---

[1] See, for instance, Claude Barfield, "Anti-dumping Reform: Time to Go Back to Basics" 28 (2005) *The World Economy*, 720; Bernard M. Hoekman and Michael P. Leidy, "Dumping, Antidumping and Emergency Protection" 23(5) (1989) *Journal of World Trade* 27; Bernard Hoekman and Petros C. Mavroidis, "Dumping, Antidumping and Antitrust", 30(1) (1996) *Journal of World Trade* 49.

[2] For the positive economic effects of trade remedies, in particular anti-dumping, see Terry Collins-Williams, "The Evolution of Anti-dumping in a Globalizing Economy", in Terence P. Stewart (ed.), *Opportunities and Obligations: New Perspectives on Global and US Trade Policy* (Kluwer Law International, 2009), p. 119; Thomas R. Howell, "The Trade Remedies: A U.S. Perspective", in Geza Feketekuty and Bruce Stokes (eds), *Trade Strategies for a New Era* (Brookings Institute, 1998), p. 299; Dan Ciuriak, "Anti-dumping at 100 Years and Counting: A Canadian Perspective" 28 (2005) *The World Economy* 644–9; Jorge Miranda, "Should Antidumping Laws Be Dumped?" 28 (1996) *Law and Policy in International Business* 255.

judicial review of the determinations made in the course of trade remedy proceedings.

Regardless of the point of view taken with respect to the utility of trade remedies, all academics, experts and stakeholders in trade remedy proceedings would certainly support the idea of promoting effective judicial review of the investigating authorities' determinations made in the course of such proceedings. After all, effective judicial review is a cornerstone of good governance[3] and is therefore to be promoted. Together with transparency, effective judicial review is probably the most important tool in ensuring the rule of law in the conduct of trade remedy investigations. It aims to ensure that the rules of the game are observed. In today's highly complex trading environment, judicial review of trade remedy determinations is conducted at three different levels: multilateral, regional and domestic.

At the multilateral level, there is the WTO dispute settlement mechanism.[4] As an inter-governmental organization, the WTO allows its members to challenge the measures taken by other members if the complaining member is of the view that such measures violate the obligations assumed under the WTO Agreement. If the complaining member prevails in the dispute settlement process, the non-compliant member will have no option but to bring its measure into compliance with its WTO obligations or to negotiate compensation with the complaining member, failing which the latter can suspend an equivalent level of concessions against the non-compliant member.

WTO dispute settlement differs from other international dispute settlement systems in that its panels and the Appellate Body have compulsory jurisdiction. Much has been written on the functioning of WTO dispute settlement, as well as on panel or Appellate Body reports

---

[3] Christopher Forsyth et al., *Effective Judicial Review: A Cornerstone of Good Governance* (Oxford University Press, 2010).

[4] The title of this book was determined through the collective thinking of all of the authors. However, it must be underlined that considerably diverging views were expressed in this process. The most important issue was the use of the concept of "judicial review". Certain authors expressed the view that the title "domestic *judicial* review of trade remedy determinations" would give the wrong impression that we see WTO dispute settlement as also being a judicial review mechanism and that the only difference between these two types of judicial review was the kinds of tribunals conducting the review. Ultimately, however, it was decided to go ahead with this title, mainly because it gives the reader the intended impression that the book concerns the review conducted by the courts of the WTO members examined. This, of course, is without prejudice to the authors' views on whether WTO dispute settlement is also of a judicial nature.

resolving individual disputes. These reports usually attract considerable attention from academics, government officials and legal practitioners. This area is also taught academically at many universities across the globe. Whatever its shortcomings, WTO dispute settlement has been described as "the most successful system for international dispute settlement in the history of the world"[5] and is one of the most commonly used international dispute resolution mechanisms.[6]

It has been generally observed that the WTO dispute settlement mechanism aims to establish the rule of law in the functioning of the organization in the exercise of the rights and the enforcement of the obligations set forth in the WTO Agreement.[7] One area in which WTO dispute settlement has contributed significantly to the strengthening of the rule of law is the application of trade remedy measures. Since 1995, this system has been used frequently with respect to trade remedy measures imposed by various WTO members. In fact, trade remedies top the list in terms of the distribution of WTO disputes on the basis of their subject matter. Between 1995 and 2011, around 40 per cent[8] of all disputes initiated in the WTO concerned trade remedies, with anti-dumping being the most frequent, followed by safeguards and counter-vailing measures.

Judicial review at the regional level takes place under the rules agreed in the regional trade agreements signed between two or more countries. Many of these agreements incorporate a dispute settlement mechanism; yet not all of these mechanisms are used very frequently. Perhaps the most important example of judicial review at the regional level is the mechanism contained in Chapter 19[9] of the North American Free Trade Agreement (hereinafter NAFTA). NAFTA dispute settlement has been

---

[5] James Bacchus, "Open Doors for Open Trade: Shining Light on WTO Dispute Settlement", 2004, available at www.worldtradelaw.net/articles/bacchusopendoors.pdf (last visited 15.3.2012).

[6] Jeffrey L. Dunoff, "The WTO's Legitimacy Crisis: Reflections on the Law and Politics of WTO Dispute Resolution" 13 (2002) *American Review of International Arbitration* 197.

[7] Bacchus, "Groping Toward Grotius: The WTO and the International Rule of Law", 2002, available at www.worldtradelaw.net/articles/bacchusgrotius.pdf (last visited 15.3.2012), p. 9; Amin Alavi, "African Countries and the WTO's Dispute Settlement Mechanism" 25(1) (2007) *Development Policy Review*, 25; Swedish International Development Co-operation Agency, "The WTO Dispute Settlement", April 2004, available at www9.georgetown.edu/faculty/mlb66/SIDA.pdf (last visited 15.3.2012), p. 1.

[8] This percentage is based on the number of disputes examined by panels; it excludes disputes that were resolved through consultations.

[9] Chapter 19 of the NAFTA covers the determinations made in anti-dumping and counter-vailing duty investigations, but not safeguards.

used frequently between Mexico, Canada and the United States, the three NAFTA parties. Similar to the WTO, trade remedies figure high on the list of substantive issues that have given rise to NAFTA disputes.[10] Given its importance and the frequent use made by the NAFTA parties, a considerable body of academic literature has evolved over the years which analyses different aspects of NAFTA dispute settlement.

Finally, there is judicial review at the domestic level, which is the subject matter of this book. Unlike WTO and regional judicial review systems such as NAFTA, domestic judicial review of trade remedy determinations has not attracted much academic attention thus far except, of course, in countries like the United States, Canada and Australia, where judicial review has been used frequently and is a traditional component of the trade remedies system.

There is no doubt that domestic judicial review supplements WTO dispute settlement and any other regional dispute settlement mechanisms in terms of the objective to ensure the rule of law in the application of trade remedy measures. Typically, the tribunals conducting domestic judicial review apply their domestic trade remedies legislation[11] in resolving the disputes brought before them. However, the provisions in domestic trade remedies laws and regulations by and large mirror the provisions of the relevant WTO agreement. Hence, domestic judicial review and WTO dispute settlement are clearly supplementary. It is therefore important to study domestic judicial review systems of the active users of trade remedies, identify any potential problems and discuss how such problems may be addressed.

We started this research project with the assumption that domestic judicial review had certain advantages compared to WTO dispute settlement, and that providing in-depth analysis of it would therefore help further the observance of the rule of law in the implementation of the WTO agreements on trade remedies.

---

[10] See the list of cases on NAFTA's website, www.nafta-sec-alena.org/en/DecisionsAnd Reports.aspx?x=312 (last visited 15.3.2012).

[11] Strictly speaking, the AD and SCM Agreements do not require WTO members to enact national laws in order to conduct investigations and impose measures. Interestingly, the SG Agreement provides, in its Article 3.1, that members willing to conduct safeguard investigations first have to establish procedures and make such procedures public. However, in order to establish fully operational investigative systems, members do need to have laws and regulations on all three trade remedies, because the WTO agreements on trade remedies do not address all issues that pertain to trade remedy investigations.

The first and perhaps most important difference between domestic judicial review and WTO dispute settlement pertains to standing. Unlike WTO dispute settlement, which is an inter-governmental mechanism,[12] domestic judicial review is typically available to private entities which are affected by trade remedy measures. Whereas governments set the rules of international trade, trade takes place between companies. Naturally, these companies, which are direct stakeholders in trade remedy investigations, follow the conduct of the investigations much more closely and carefully than foreign governments whose commercial interests are affected. Importantly, domestic judicial review is also open to domestic producers who seek the imposition of measures. Foreign exporters at least have the opportunity to try to convince their governments to file a WTO dispute settlement proceeding against the country imposing the measures. Obviously, domestic producers have no such option. Thus, the quality of domestic judicial review is particularly important for domestic producers in the importing country.

The second difference is that the number of judicial review cases with respect to trade remedy determinations filed before domestic tribunals is considerably higher than the number of trade remedies-related disputes brought before the WTO. Thus, we considered that any improvements to domestic judicial review systems of WTO members could bring about significant benefits to the international trading system.

The third difference is the wider scope of requests that can be directed to domestic tribunals, and the greater powers that these tribunals have. Unlike WTO panels and the Appellate Body, domestic tribunals generally have powers that go further than a declaration that the challenged measure is inconsistent with the applicable rules. Typically, domestic tribunals have the power to annul the determinations that they find to be inconsistent with them. In addition, in some countries, these tribunals have the authority to order the compensation of damage caused by legal flaws in the conduct of trade remedy investigations and to suspend the implementation of the challenged measure pending the judicial review proceedings.

---

[12] A WTO member initiating a dispute settlement proceeding against another member acts in order to protect the economic interests of its producers/exporters and vis-à-vis the producers/exporters of the defendant member. Thus, in reality, WTO dispute settlement also protects the rights of private entities, but it does so in an indirect fashion, with the involvement of governments.

Each chapter in this book provides a concise description of the judicial review of trade remedy determinations in the relevant country. Each describes: (a) the scope of determinations subject to judicial review, (b) the tribunal(s) responsible for judicial review, (c) parties that have standing to bring a case, (d) the main procedural steps involved in a judicial review proceeding, (e) appeals, and (f) powers of the tribunals. After describing the judicial review of trade remedy determinations in a given country, each chapter also identifies problems encountered in that system and, in its concluding part, suggests ways to address such problems.

We hope this book will be useful to a wide audience. The country chapters are intended as guides for parties affected by the determinations made in trade remedy proceedings. It is intended that exporters whose products are subjected to trade remedy measures will use the book to make an informed decision as to the feasibility of bringing a case before the national tribunals of the importing country in order to challenge the imposition of such measures. It will also be useful for governments to acquaint themselves with the judicial review systems of other countries and, in case of a legal conflict, decide whether it would be feasible to pursue a domestic judicial review proceeding in the importing country.

In addition to depicting the judicial review of trade remedy determinations in a given country, most chapters in the book also generally describe the judicial review of administrative actions in that country. In this sense, the book offers a comparative analysis of administrative judicial review in 21 jurisdictions, which scholars specializing in administrative law may find interesting. Although the structure and operation of domestic judicial review varies from one country to another in certain regards, each system must comply with the minimum requirements set forth in the WTO agreements on trade remedies. It is therefore useful to highlight these requirements before proceeding to the country chapters.

Generally speaking, WTO members are under an international obligation to maintain a judicial review system for their investigating authorities' determinations made in the course of trade remedy proceedings. However, each of the three WTO agreements on trade remedies contains different provisions regarding this issue. At the outset, it should be noted that only the AD and SCM agreements explicitly address judicial review, whereas the SG Agreement is silent on this matter.

Article 13 of the AD Agreement reads:

Judicial Review
Each Member whose national legislation contains provisions on anti-dumping measures shall maintain judicial, arbitral or administrative tribunals or procedures for the purpose, *inter alia*, of the prompt review of administrative actions relating to final determinations and reviews of determinations within the meaning of Article 11. Such tribunals or procedures shall be independent of the authorities responsible for the determination or review in question.

Thus, the AD Agreement imposes an obligation to maintain a judicial review system for the review of the determinations made by the investigating authorities of an importing WTO member in the course of an anti-dumping investigation or review. However, Article 13 limits that obligation in certain regards. First, the obligation applies only to members who have anti-dumping legislation. Second, the scope of judicial review is limited to administrative actions relating to final determinations and reviews of determinations. Consequently, other determinations, such as decisions to initiate or not to initiate an investigation or review, as well as the imposition of provisional measures and acceptance or rejection of undertakings, are not required to be subject to judicial review. With respect to reviews, Article 13 references Article 11; therefore determinations undertaken in all reviews addressed under Article 11 are also required to be subject to judicial review.

With regard to institutional aspects of judicial review, the AD Agreement recognizes that members may have different institutional schemes and legal traditions. Under Article 13, the body that conducts judicial review may be a judicial, arbitral or administrative tribunal. Thus, domestic judicial review does not necessarily have to be conducted by courts; tribunals of different nature may also undertake this function. Naturally, the agreement requires that the bodies responsible for judicial review be independent of the investigating authorities or other decision-making bodies in the context of investigations or reviews. Finally, it is important to note that Article 13 provides that judicial review has to be prompt.

Judicial review in the context of countervailing duty investigations is addressed in Article 23 of the SCM Agreement. This provision reads:

Judicial Review
Each Member whose national legislation contains provisions on counter-vailing duty measures shall maintain judicial, arbitral or administrative tribunals or procedures for the purpose, inter alia, of the prompt review of administrative actions relating to final determinations and reviews of

determinations within the meaning of Article 21. Such tribunals or procedures shall be independent of the authorities responsible for the determination or review in question, *and shall provide all interested parties who participated in the administrative proceeding and are directly and individually affected by the administrative actions with access to review* (emphasis added).

Article 23 contains provisions identical to those of Article 13 of the AD Agreement with respect to judicial review. Therefore, our explanations with respect to Article 13 of the AD Agreement also apply here. However, unlike Article 13 of the AD Agreement, Article 23 of the SCM Agreement also contains an extra phrase that addresses the issue of standing in judicial review proceedings with respect to countervailing duty determinations. It provides that in the context of a countervailing duty investigation or review, WTO members are required to make judicial review available only to interested parties who participated in the relevant investigation or review and who are directly and individually affected by the challenged administrative action. This could mean, for instance, that interested parties such as foreign exporters or domestic producers who do not cooperate with the investigating authority during the relevant investigation or review cannot challenge the authority's determinations because of non-participation.[13]

Depending on the interpretative approach taken, Article 23 of the SCM Agreement may be construed as allowing WTO members to deny standing to importers that are not related to foreign exporters or producers subject to the relevant countervailing duty proceeding. This is because, unlike importers that are related to foreign producers subject to the same proceeding, unrelated importers may be seen as not being directly and individually affected by countervailing duty proceedings.[14]

The negotiating history of the SCM and AD Agreements does not clarify why this additional text on standing was incorporated in the former but not in the latter. It should be noted, however, that both the AD Agreement and

---

[13] This does not necessarily imply that under the AD Agreement WTO members are required to provide non-cooperating interested parties with standing to initiate a judicial review proceeding. As noted above, Article 13 of the AD Agreement does not specifically address the issue of standing.

[14] We note that the European Union's law on judicial review also stipulates that parties which initiate a judicial review proceeding are required to show that the challenged act is of direct and individual concern to them. The chapter on the European Union explains that, pursuant to this provision, the Court of Justice of the European Union (formerly known as the European Court of Justice) has generally denied standing to unrelated importers, while also noting that there have been some exceptions to this.

the SCM Agreement set the minimum requirements with respect to judicial review. WTO members are free to adopt rules that go beyond the requirements set forth in these agreements. For instance, members may subject the imposition of provisional measures to judicial review. Or, in the case of countervailing duty investigations, they may omit the extra phrase in Article 23 of the SCM Agreement and allow all interested parties in an investigation or review to resort to judicial review.

As for the judicial review of determinations made in safeguard investigations, it is interesting to note that, contrary to the AD and SCM Agreements, the SG Agreement does not contain any provision on judicial review. It would not be unreasonable, therefore, to argue that WTO members do not have an international obligation to provide for the judicial review of determinations made in the course of safeguard investigations.[15] However, no WTO panel or Appellate Body has yet addressed this issue.

The negotiating history of the SG Agreement does not reveal any reason why negotiators in the Uruguay Round did not consider adopting a provision similar to Article 13 of the AD Agreement or Article 23 of the SCM Agreement. Two possible explanations suggest themselves. First, the provisions of the SG Agreement explaining the procedural aspects of investigations are much more general in nature compared with the AD and SCM Agreements. Given this, it may be argued that members simply omitted the inclusion of a provision on the judicial review of safeguard determinations. Alternatively, one could argue that this was not a simple omission and that negotiators willingly chose not to include a judicial review provision in the SG Agreement because of the political nature of safeguard measures.

As we noted with respect to the AD and SCM Agreements, however, it should be recalled that the SG Agreement contains the minimum requirements with respect to the conduct of safeguard investigations. WTO members are free to go beyond such requirements and subject their investigating authorities' determinations in safeguard investigations to judicial review. In fact, as explained in various chapters of this book, there are a number of members who have followed this approach.

---

[15] Our observation here is without prejudice to Article X.3(b) of the GATT 1994, which requires the institution of "judicial, arbitral or administrative tribunals or procedures for the purpose, *inter alia*, of the prompt review and correction of administrative action relating to customs matters". Thus, any customs matter that arises from a trade remedy proceeding would fall within the scope of the obligation set forth in this provision, and WTO members would be required to provide for the judicial review of such matter.

Canada: high deference, stark reality

ANDREW M. LANOUETTE AND CHRISTOPHER J. KENT

I Introduction

This chapter will discuss the review of trade remedy determinations in Canada. First, we will provide an overview of Canada's trade remedy regime and the types of determinations made pursuant to Canada's trade remedy laws. Second, we will provide an overview of Canada's system of administrative law, which governs the review of administrative decisions including those made in trade remedies proceedings. We will then provide a detailed discussion and commentary on key Canadian court, Canada–US Free Trade Agreement (CUFTA) and North American Free Trade Agreement (NAFTA) bi-national panel decisions involving trade remedy determinations made by the Canadian International Trade Tribunal (CITT) and the Canada Border Services Agency (CBSA). Based on this discussion and commentary, we will offer some concluding remarks on the implications of Canada's legal system, from both a domestic and comparative legal perspective.

II Canada's trade remedy law regime

Similar to the trade remedy regimes of many industrialized countries, Canada has a complex web of domestic trade remedy laws embodied in multiple statutes. The principal domestic trade remedy regimes in Canada are anti-dumping/countervail, set out in the Special Import Measures Act (SIMA), global safeguards, contained in the Canadian International Trade Tribunal Act (CITT Act) and China-specific safeguard remedies for market disruption and trade diversion under the CITT Act. Given that the large majority (i.e. well over 95 per cent) of Canadian trade remedy cases of the past two decades have involved anti-dumping and countervail, the focus of this chapter is on the review of Canadian anti-dumping and countervailing duty determinations, although the principles discussed are applicable to the review of safeguards determinations as well. Under Canada's anti-dumping and countervailing duty laws, investigative jurisdiction is bifurcated, with the CBSA responsible for investigating and making determinations regarding dumping and subsidization and the CITT responsible for making determinations regarding injury/threat of injury. The investigative process in Canada runs approximately 210 days from beginning to end, with the key determinations by investigative authorities being: initiation of investigation by the CBSA (Day 0),[1] preliminary determination of injury/threat of injury by the CITT (Day 60),[2] preliminary determination of dumping and/or subsidization by the CBSA (Day 90),[3] final determination of dumping/subsidization by the CBSA (Day 180)[4] and final determination of injury by the CITT (Day 210).[5]

The CBSA and the CITT are also responsible for conducting expiry reviews (i.e. sunset reviews) to determine whether to extend an injury finding past the five-year automatic expiry limit. In this process, the CITT can initiate an expiry review at the request of the Minister of Finance, the CBSA, any government, or at the request of any other person who satisfies the CITT that a review is warranted.[6] If the CITT initiates a review, the CBSA conducts an investigation within 120 days to determine if the dumping or subsidizing of the goods is likely to continue or resume if the finding expires.[7] If the CBSA makes an affirmative finding, the CITT then determines whether the expiry of the order or finding is likely to result in injury or retardation.[8] The CITT may either rescind the order or finding, or continue it with or without amendment.[9] Additionally, the CITT may carry out an inquiry to determine if the imposition of anti-dumping or countervailing duties following an investigation is in the public interest.[10] The CITT will conduct a public interest inquiry upon application by a party to the investigation, or any other group or person affected by the investigation, and if it is of the opinion that there are reasonable grounds to act on the request.[11] If the CITT determines that it is in the public interest to reduce or eliminate

---

[1] SIMA, RSC 1985, c. S-15, s. 31.   [2] SIMA, RSC 1985, c. S-15, s. 37.1.
[3] SIMA, RSC 1985, c. S-15, s. 38.   [4] SIMA, RSC 1985, c. S-15, s. 41.
[5] SIMA, RSC 1985, c. S-15, ss. 42, 43(1).   [6] SIMA, RSC 1985, c. S-15, s. 76.03(2), (3).
[7] SIMA, RSC 1985, c. S-15, s. 76.03(7).   [8] SIMA, RSC 1985, c. S-15, s. 76.03(10).
[9] SIMA, RSC 1985, c. S-15, s. 76.03(12).   [10] SIMA, RSC 1985, c. S-15, s. 45(1).
[11] Canadian International Trade Tribunal, *Guideline on Public Interest Inquiries* (Ottawa: Canadian International Trade Tribunal, 2000), at p. 1, online: www.citt-tcce.gc.ca/doc/english/Publicat/PubInt_e.pdf.

duties, it will issue a report to the Minister of Finance, who will ultimately make the decision.[12]

The CITT may also conduct interim reviews of findings or orders while they are still in effect.[13] The CITT itself, the Minister of Finance, the president of the CBSA, or any person of any government can initiate the review if there are reasonable grounds to act on the request.[14] The CITT may rescind, amend or continue the finding or order because of the interim review.[15] The CBSA also conducts re-investigations to update normal values, export prices or amounts of subsidy under a finding or order. Interestingly, there are no statutory provisions in Canada that govern such re-investigations. SIMA also provides for assessments and re-determinations of anti-dumping duty liability for given entries.[16] Finally, SIMA empowers the CITT to make rulings as to who is the importer of goods subject to anti-dumping findings, which can be important given that liability for anti-dumping duties falls on the importer for SIMA purposes.[17]

Findings or orders made in any of these proceedings are subject to various appeal and review mechanisms, discussed in the balance of this chapter.

III   Administrative law in Canada

1   Introduction

As statutorily created and governed administrative bodies, the CITT and the CBSA are both subject to Canada's administrative law regime. Administrative law deals with the legal constraints placed upon administrative decision-makers[18] who exercise statutory power.[19] The purpose of administrative law is to ensure that agencies remain within the bounds of the rule of law.[20]

---

[12] SIMA, RSC 1985, c. S-15, s. 45(4), (5).   [13] SIMA, RSC 1985, c. S-15, s. 76.01(1).
[14] SIMA, RSC 1985, c. S-15, s. 76.01(1), (3).   [15] SIMA, RSC 1985, c. S-15, s. 76.01(5).
[16] SIMA, RSC 1985, c. S-15, ss. 55–9.
[17] SIMA, RSC 1985, c. S-15, s. 89. Note that in Canada the importer for SIMA purposes is not necessarily the importer for customs purposes.
[18] For the purposes of this chapter and for ease of reference, the chapter will use the terms "agency" or "agencies" to refer to all administrative bodies or administrative decision-makers, unless quoting directly from a source which uses other terminology.
[19] *Canadian Encyclopedic Digest*, 3rd edn, vol. I (Toronto: Carswell, 1973), "Title 3: Administrative Law", § 1.
[20] Colleen M. Flood, "An Introduction to (the Effervescence of) Administrative Law", in Colleen M. Flood and Lorne Sossin (eds), *Administrative Law in Context* (Toronto: Emond Montgomery Publications Limited, 2008), at p. 10.

The sources of administrative law, as they pertain to CITT and CBSA decisions, include SIMA, the Federal Courts Act[21] (FCA) and the common law.[22] As a general legal matter, these sources provide that where an agency has acted outside its authority, that decision is invalid.[23] More specifically, an agency acts outside its authority when it makes a decision which violates procedural fairness (whether the agency used the proper procedures in reaching a decision) or substantive validity (whether the agency made an error in the decision of sufficient magnitude that the court is willing to remedy it).[24] The most important questions in seeking review of an agency's decision are the proper review mechanisms to invoke, the grounds of review and the standard of review (i.e. the level of deference given to the agency's decision).

2   Mechanisms for review

The above-discussed determinations made by administering authorities under Canada's anti-dumping and countervailing duty laws fall into three categories for purposes of review under Canada's administrative law regime. First, SIMA provides a statutory right of appeal for a very small number of determinations made under it, namely re-determinations of actual anti-dumping liability made by the CBSA.[25] A second category of determinations, namely, certain final determinations, orders and/or findings of dumping, injury/threat of injury, likelihood of dumping and likelihood of injury in investigations, expiry reviews and interim reviews, are subject to a **statutory right of judicial review** at Canada's Federal Court of Appeal or a bi-national panel (if the goods at issue are eligible). Third, certain determinations which are neither "final", nor qualify as "orders or findings", are in theory reviewable pursuant to the Federal Court's supervisory jurisdiction over all federal boards, commissions or tribunals, which has been codified in Canada's Federal Courts Act.[26] Interestingly, for this third

---

[21] FCA, RSC 1985, F-7.

[22] See generally, Cristie L. Ford, "Dogs and Tails: Remedies in Administrative Law", in Flood and Sossin (eds), *Administrative Law in Context*, at p. 64.

[23] *Canadian Encyclopedic Digest*, "Title 3: Administrative Law", § 2.

[24] Flood, "An Introduction to (the Effervescence of) Administrative Law" in Flood and Sossin (eds), *Administrative Law in Context*, at p. 11.

[25] SIMA, RSC 1985, c. S-15, s. 60. Note that the appeal lies to Canada's Federal Court of Appeal and that, prior to such an appeal being made, the party in question must follow the procedure of requesting re-determinations and appeal to both the CBSA and the CITT, as set out in ss. 55 to 59 of SIMA.

[26] FCA, RSC 1985, F-7, ss. 18(1), 18.1, 28(1).

category of determinations, jurisdiction for judicial review would appear to be split between the Federal Court for CBSA determinations and the Federal Court of Appeal for CITT determinations.[27] Notably, while the jurisdiction for review and the standards governing review of the second and third categories of decisions are different (see discussion in the next section), the permitted grounds of applications for judicial review of these categories of decisions are identical. Specifically, applications for judicial review may be made on the ground that the CBSA or the CITT, as the case may be:

- acted without jurisdiction, acted beyond its jurisdiction or refused to exercise its jurisdiction;
- failed to observe a principle of natural justice, procedural fairness or other procedure that it was required by law to observe;
- erred in law in making a decision or an order, whether or not the error appears on the face of the record;
- based its decision or order on an erroneous finding of fact that it made in a perverse or capricious manner or without regard for the material before it;
- acted, or failed to act, by reason of fraud or perjured evidence; or
- acted in any other way that was contrary to law.[28]

3 Standard of appeal or review

Although an exhaustive history of the standard of review for administrative decisions in Canada is beyond the scope of this chapter, an understanding of the basic history and evolution of standard of review analysis is necessary to understand how Canadian courts currently treat CBSA and CITT decisions. At its core, the standard of review analysis is the means through which a court determines how much deference to give to an agency's decision.

3.1 Privative clauses and questions of jurisdiction

An issue at the core of early Canadian judicial decisions discussing standards of review pertained to the use of privative clauses to "thwart

---

[27] See FCA, RSC 1985, F-7, s. 28(1). See also *Whirlpool Corporation v. Camco Inc. et al.* [2000] 2 SCR 107; 2000 SC 67.

[28] SIMA, RSC 1985, c. S-15, s. 96.1(2). FCA, RSC 1985, F-7, s. 18.1(4). See also Annex 1911 of the NAFTA, which defines the standard of review for purposes of review of qualifying final determinations of Canadian investigative authorities as "the grounds set out in subsection 18.1(4) of the *Federal Court Act*, as amended".

attempts by the judiciary to trespass on the administrative domain".[29] The legislature established these statutory provisions – which deemed the agency's decision final and not subject to review – to remove agency decisions from the purview of the courts.[30] Courts, uncomfortable with the consequence that an "inferior tribunal" would essentially be the sole judge of the validity of its own acts, developed the concept of jurisdictional error to circumvent the privative clause protection.[31] The definition of jurisdictional error included any interpretation of a statute made by an agency, and the court would substitute its own opinion of the correct interpretation of the statue for the agency.[32] Essentially, the agency would have to get the "right" or "correct" answer on the jurisdictional question before it was entitled to protection from the privative clause, since privative clauses only protected decisions within the agency's jurisdiction.

3.2   The patently unreasonable decision

The Supreme Court of Canada issued one of the most influential decisions in Canadian administrative law in 1979 in *C.U.P.E.* v. *N.B. Liquor Corporation*,[33] in which, among other things, it criticized the arbitrariness of the above approach. Dickson J., writing for the Court, noted that it is difficult to determine what is "jurisdictional" and easy to label a question as jurisdictional, subjecting the agency to broader review.[34] Moreover, Dickson J. recognized that agencies were often specialized, administering highly technical statutory schemes and that courts should recognize their lack of relative expertise in reviewing decisions of such specialized agencies.[35]

In light of these criticisms, Dickson J. set out a second tier of analysis to be conducted in addition to assessment of jurisdictional errors: evaluation of specialized agencies' decision against a standard of "patent unreasonableness". In short, where the specialized agency acts within its jurisdiction, courts may interfere with that decision where the agency did "something which takes the exercise of its powers outside the protection of the privative or preclusive clause".[36] Examples of such an error would be acting in bad faith, basing the decision on extraneous matters, failing

---

[29] Guy Régimbald, *Canadian Administrative Law* (Markham: LexisNexis, 2008), at p. 393.
[30] David Philip Jones and Anne S. de Villars, *Principles of Administrative Law* (Toronto: Carswell, 2009), at p. 14.
[31] *Canada (Attorney General)* v. *P.S.A.C* [1993] 1 SCR 941, at para. 23.   [32] Ibid.
[33] *C.U.P.E.* v. *N.B. Liquor Corporation* [1979] 2 SCR 227.   [34] Ibid., at 233.
[35] Ibid., at 235.   [36] Ibid., at 237.

to consider relevant factors or making an interpretation that the relevant legislation cannot rationally support.[37]

This analysis also gave rise to the notion that there is more than one "right" decision. The Court recognized that there are often many different interpretations to a statutory provision or factual situation, such that "[t]here is no one interpretation which can be said to be 'right'".[38] So long as the agency comes to an interpretation that is not patently unreasonable, then its privative clause should protect that decision from review.

The result of *C.U.P.E.* v. *N.B. Liquor Corporation* is that courts review questions of jurisdiction on a standard of "correctness" while they evaluate questions within jurisdiction against the standard of "patent unreasonableness".

3.3   The pragmatic and functional analysis

The Supreme Court further refined the analysis of the standard of review in *U.E.S., Local 298* v. *Bibeault*.[39] Writing for the Court, Beetz J. noted, "[t]he formalistic analysis [. . .] is giving way to a pragmatic and functional analysis, hitherto associated with the concept of the patently unreasonable error".[40] The central question is whether the legislature intended the question asked to be within the jurisdiction conferred on the agency.[41] A court must look at this question and factors such as the wording of the statute conferring jurisdiction, the purpose of the statute, the reason for the agency's existence, the agency's area of expertise and the nature of the problem confronting the agency, in order to determine whether the standard of correctness or patent unreasonableness applies to the decision.[42] Thus, the pragmatic and functional analysis became the governing framework to determine the standard of review to apply, and the Court relegated jurisdictional error to a lesser role.

3.4   Deference and statutory appeals: the "spectrum" of standards

However, courts had difficulty in applying this approach to agencies not protected by privative clauses or to those subject to statutory appeal. In such cases, there was no legislative direction to defer to the agency's

---

[37] Ibid.   [38] Ibid.   [39] *U.E.S., Local 298* v. *Bibeault* [1988] 2 SCR 1048.
[40] Ibid., at para. 122.   [41] Ibid., at para. 119.   [42] Ibid., at para. 122.

decision. In *Pezim* v. *British Columbia*, the Supreme Court created the concept of a "spectrum of standards" to address this issue.[43] The Court was clear that despite the absence of a privative clause, "the concept of the specialization of duties requires that deference be shown to decisions of specialized tribunals on matters which fall squarely within the tribunal's expertise".[44] Accordingly, Iacobucci J. held that:

> the courts have developed a spectrum that ranges from the standard of reasonableness to that of correctness. Courts have also enunciated a principle of deference that applies not just to the facts as found by the tribunal, but also to the legal questions before the tribunal in the light of its role and expertise.[45]

To determine which standard on the spectrum applies, the Court noted that courts should examine factors such as the agency's specialized duties and policy development role, as well as the nature of the problem under consideration.

Canada v. *Southam Inc.* clarified the spectrum's breadth.[46] In that case, Iacobucci J. held that when dealing with agencies that are subject to statutory appeals, there are three standards of review: the deferential standard of patent unreasonableness, the non-deferential standard of correctness and a middle standard of reasonableness *simpliciter*.[47] The difference between patent unreasonableness and reasonableness *simpliciter* lies "in the immediacy or obviousness of the defect. If the defect is apparent on the face of the tribunal's reasons, then the tribunal's decision is patently unreasonable. But if it takes some significant searching or testing to find the defect, then the decision is unreasonable but not patently unreasonable."[48] Thus, courts now had a pragmatic and functional framework to assess the applicable standard of review.

3.5   Harmonization: the pragmatic and functional analysis

The next development was to harmonize the pragmatic and functional analysis in the statutory appeals context with the pragmatic and functional analysis in the context of statutes that provided no statutory right

---

[43] *Pezim v. British Columbia* [1994] 2 SCR 557.   [44] Ibid., at 591.   [45] Ibid., at 590.
[46] *Canada (Director of Investigation and Research) v. Southam Inc.* [1997] 1 SCR 748.
[47] Interestingly, Iacobucci J. retroactively claims that the standard of review chosen in *Pezim* was that of reasonableness *simpliciter*. See ibid., at para. 58.
[48] Ibid., at para. 57.

of appeal or review, but rather, included a privative clause. This occurred in *Pushpanathan* v. *Canada*.[49]

First, Bastarache J., writing for the majority, clarified the position of jurisdictional errors in the context of the pragmatic and functional approach. He held that a jurisdictional error is "simply an error on an issue with respect to which, according to the outcome of the pragmatic and functional analysis, the tribunal must make a correct interpretation and to which no deference will be shown".[50] Thus, jurisdiction remains a very small element in the analysis. Second, he categorized the factors to be taken into account when determining the standard of review, subsuming the presence of a privative clause as merely one factor for consideration. Drawing from *Southam*, Bastarache J. identified the following categories of factors to determine what standard to apply:

- the absence or presence of a privative clause;
- the expertise of the agency;
- the purpose of the Act as a whole and the provision in particular; and,
- the nature of the problem.[51]

A court is to consider each individual factor and balance them to determine the appropriate standard of review. It is to do so in every case, at every instance.

3.6 Revision: the standard of review analysis

The Supreme Court reformed all of this jurisprudence in *Dunsmuir* v. *New Brunswick* in response to judicial and academic criticism that the pragmatic and functional approach lacked predictability, workability and coherency.[52] The Court expressly noted that the analytical problems which arise in trying to apply the different standards undercut any conceptual usefulness created by the inherently greater flexibility of having multiple standards of review.[53]

To address these issues, the Court first collapsed reasonableness *simpliciter* and patent unreasonableness into one deferential standard of reasonableness.[54] This leaves only two standards of review: reasonableness and correctness. Reasonableness is the deferential standard,

---

[49] *Pushpanathan* v. *Canada (Minister of Citizenship and Immigration)* [1998] 1 SCR 982.
[50] Ibid., at para. 28.   [51] Ibid., at paras. 30–3, 36–7.
[52] Jones and de Villars, *Principles of Administrative Law*, at pp. 520–2.
[53] *Dunsmuir* v. *New Brunswick*, 2008 SCC 9; [2008] 1 SCR 190, at para. 44.   [54] Ibid.

concerned mostly "with the existence of justification, transparency and intelligibility within the decision-making process" and "whether the decision falls within a range of possible, acceptable outcomes which are defensible in respect of facts and law".[55] Correctness, on the other hand, means that "the reviewing court will not show deference to the decision maker's reasoning process; it will rather undertake its own analysis of the question".[56] The two standards simplify the analytical process.

Bastarache J. also established a two-step approach to the now termed "standard of review analysis", overriding the previous "pragmatic and functional approach".[57] First, the court will ascertain whether jurisprudence has already established a standard to apply to a particular category of question. In that respect, questions of fact, discretion, policy or mixed fact and law "will usually" be reviewed on the reasonableness standard.[58] On the other hand, the court reviews questions of law relating to the constitution or true jurisdiction and questions relating to procedural fairness on the standard of correctness.[59]

If jurisprudence has not already settled which standard to choose, the court must proceed to an analysis of the standard of review factors to determine the proper standard. These are the *Pushpanathan* factors: "(1) the presence or absence of a privative clause; (2) the purpose of the tribunal as determined by interpretation of enabling legislation; (3) the nature of the question at issue, and; (4) the expertise of the tribunal."[60] Moreover, Bastarache J. notes that in applying these factors, reasonableness "will usually result" where an agency is interpreting its own statute or a statute close to its function, or where the agency has developed a particular expertise in the application of a general common law or civil law rule in relation to a specific statutory context.[61] Correctness will likely apply to other legal issues.[62]

In sum, the evolution of the standard of review analysis began with little deference, characterized by the jurisdictional error analysis, and then shifted to a variable and case-specific pragmatic and functional analysis with spectrums of deference at its core. Standards of review in Canada have reached their current evolution in *Dunsmuir*, with jurisprudence and the category of question driving whether to defer with a standard of reasonableness or not to defer with a standard of correctness. The above evolution has also naturally governed judicial review of CBSA and CITT decisions.

---

[55] Ibid., at para. 47.   [56] Ibid., at para. 50.   [57] Ibid., at para. 62.   [58] Ibid., at para. 53.
[59] Ibid., at paras. 58–60.   [60] Ibid., at para. 64.   [61] Ibid., at para. 54.   [62] Ibid., at para. 51.

IV   Judicial review of CITT decisions

1   Procedure

With the exception of CITT appeal decisions of anti-dumping and/or countervailing duty liability under section 59 of SIMA, which are subject to a formal statutory appeal process discussed in section V below, decisions and determinations made by the CITT are subject to judicial review. Under SIMA, a person directly affected by the determination, decision order or finding may make an application for judicial review by filing a notice of application in the Federal Court of Appeal (or Federal Court, in the limited circumstances discussed above).[63] This application must be made by a person who is directly affected by the decision within 30 days of the decision in question, and such applications are heard in a summary way in accordance with the rules made in respect of applications for judicial review pursuant to the FCA.[64] For decisions concerning goods from NAFTA countries, this is extended to 40 days because of the prohibition on seeking review until 30 days after a decision (the NAFTA option for review is discussed in more detail below).[65] The Federal Court of Appeal may dismiss the application, set aside the final determination, order or finding, or refer the matter back to the CITT for reconsideration in accordance with its directions.[66]

2   Standard

2.1   Evolution of the standard

To understand the current approach to the standard of review applied to CITT decisions, it is important to trace the evolution of their treatment before the Federal Court of Appeal and, in particular, to examine how they fit within that era of administrative law generally. In addition, it is important to note that, in practice, after the harmonization of standard of review approaches in *Pushpanathan*, courts no longer distinguish between cases under the statutory appeal and those under the judicial review procedure for the purposes of determining the standards of review.

First, in the pre-*Pushpanathan* era of review, the Court accorded a high degree of deference to the CITT. At the time, a strong privative

---

[63] SIMA, RSC 1985, c. S-15, s. 96.1(3).   [64] SIMA, RSC 1985, c. S-15, s. 96.1(3), (5).
[65] SIMA, RSC 1985, c. S-15, s. 77.012(1).   [66] SIMA, RSC 1985, c. S-15, s. 96.1(6).

clause protected the CITT's jurisdiction. As such, the Court followed the *Bibeault* analysis, and where the issue was not one going to the jurisdiction of the CITT, it would apply a standard of patent unreasonableness. Otherwise, it would apply a standard of correctness. As the Court noted in *LNK Manufacturing Agencies Inc.* v. *Canadian International Trade Tribunal*:

> Courts should exercise caution and deference in reviewing the decisions of specialized administrative tribunals . . . This deference extends both to the determination of the facts and the interpretation of the law. Only where the evidence, viewed reasonably, is incapable of supporting a tribunal's findings of fact, or where the interpretation placed on the legislation is patently unreasonable, can the court interfere.[67]

The Court, therefore, accorded a high degree of deference to CITT decisions and was less searching in its review.

In 1994, the legislature amended SIMA, removing its privative clause and replacing it with a right of judicial review for various CITT decisions. This led the Court to switch from the *Bibeault* framework to the *Pezim* framework to determine the appropriate standard of review. Although one would expect that the removal of the privative clause would lead to less deference to CITT decisions and a more probing review, this was not the case. In fact, the Court continued to apply the standard of patent unreasonableness to the CITT's decisions notwithstanding the removal of the privative clause. For example, in *Canadian Pasta Manufacturers' Association*, the Court noted that:

> It should be noted that Gonthier J.'s reasoning [in *National Corn Growers* v. *Canadian Import Tribunal*] turned in part on the then current wording of section 76 of the Special Import Measures Act (SIMA). That section was amended with effect 1 January 1994, and no longer contains a privative or finality clause. However, the other factors which point towards a need for judicial deference, most particularly the scheme of the statute, the subject matter of the inquiry and the specialized and expert nature of the Tribunal, are still in place.[68]

---

[67] *LNK Manufacturing Agencies Inc.* v. *Canadian International Trade Tribunal* [1990] FCJ No. 843, at para. 1 (QL) (FCA), citing *United Association of Journeymen and Apprentices of the Plumbing and Pipefitting Industry, Local 740* v. *W.W. Lester Ltd.* [1990] 3 SCR 644, at 669.

[68] *Canadian Pasta Manufacturers' Association* v. *Aurora Importing & Distributing Ltd.*, 1997 CanLII 4726 (FCA) np.

Thus, despite the privative clauses' removal, the Court continued to apply a high standard of deference by using the *Pezim* factors.

With such a high level of deference accorded to the CITT, but with the legislative signal of no privative clause, the Court had a difficult time determining which standard to apply after *Southam* established the three standards of review. In fact, the Court created a fourth standard to deal with the CITT, which:

> falls between reasonableness simpliciter and patent unreasonableness which is reserved for those cases where a decision has been rendered by an expert tribunal on an issue within its field or expertise and has arrived at a higher Court by way of application for judicial review. This fourth standard of review requires more deference to a tribunal's findings than that given to expert tribunals containing a statutory right of appeal but slightly less deference than that given to tribunals protected by a true privative clause.[69]

Adding a fourth standard shows that the Court was willing to accord the highest level of deference possible, despite the fact that the legislature, by removing the privative clause, could have been sending a signal of legislative intent that the Court should show less deference to the CITT.

The move to the pragmatic and functional approach in *Pushpanathan* did not change this position. The Court, now with clear guidance that there were only three standards of review, consistently applied the standard of patent unreasonableness to the CITT's decisions.[70] Also during this period, the Court began using section 18.1(4)(d) of the FCA as the standard to apply to review the CITT's findings of fact, combining section 18.1(4)(d) with that of the pragmatic and functional approach.[71] This provision states that the Court may grant relief if the agency based its decision or order on an erroneous finding of fact that it made in a perverse or capricious manner or without regard to the material before it.[72] Rather than creating a more searching review given the larger range of discretionary considerations under the pragmatic and functional approach, even more deference was accorded to the CITT. In *Stelco Inc.* v. *British Steel Canada Inc.*, the Court held that

---

[69] *British Columbia Vegetable Marketing Commission* v. *Washington Potato and Onion Association*, 1997 CanLII 5694, at para. 3 (FCA).

[70] See, e.g., *GRK Fasteners* v. *Leland Industries Inc.*, 2006 FCA 118, at para. 20; *Dofasco Inc.* v. *Macsteel International (Canada) Ltd.*, 2002 FCA 419, at para. 6.

[71] *Stelco Inc.* v. *British Steel Canada Inc.* [2000] 3 FC 282, at paras. 14–15 (FCA).

[72] FCA, RSC 1985, F-7, s. 18.1(4)(d).

section 18.1(4)(d), when interpreted in light of the *Pushpanathan* factors, leads to a conclusion that:

> the Court should be very reluctant to set aside a decision by virtue of the inferences drawn by the Tribunal from the material before it or to insist that the Tribunal's reasons canvass all the material on which the applicant and the interveners relied, when that which the Tribunal regarded as particularly important, and on which it evidently based its decision, was sufficient to provide a rational basis for it.[73]

Thus, even during the *Pushpanathan* era of standards of review, when one would expect a more detailed and searching standard, given the malleability of the *Pushpanathan* factors, the CITT remained relatively impervious to review on a standard lower than patent unreasonableness.

With *Dunsmuir*, the Court has become more transparent regarding the standards of review. Relying on precedent, the Court has conclusively held that it will review all questions, except for questions of jurisdiction, on a standard of reasonableness. As the Court stated most recently in *Owen & Company Limited* v. *Globe Spring & Cushion Co. Ltd.*:

> [t]he tribunal is highly specialized and is entitled to significant deference. Only questions related to its jurisdiction are reviewed on a standard of correctness. All other questions attract a standard of reasonableness.[74]

Therefore, the Court remains and has remained throughout the entire tenure of the CITT, reluctant to interfere with the CITT's decisions, despite the changes in administrative law and in the SIMA statute itself.

2.2   Implications

(a) Correctness on questions of jurisdiction only   As the Court only reviews jurisdictional questions on a standard of correctness, this itself gives rise to queries over what constitutes jurisdictional questions and whether anything before the CITT is jurisdictional. Notably, the CITT has been reviewed on questions of jurisdiction only in extremely rare circumstances. In the 1993 case of *Australian Meat & Live-stock Corp.* v. *Canada*,[75] the Court considered whether the CITT erred in law and exceeded its jurisdiction by conducting a safeguard inquiry where it

---

[73] *Stelco Inc.* v. *British Steel Canada Inc.*, at para. 21 (FCA).

[74] *Owen & Company Limited* v. *Globe Spring & Cushion Co. Ltd.*, 2010 FCA 288, at para. 4. See also *MAXX Bath Inc.* v. *Almag Aluminum Inc.*, 2010 FCA 62, at para. 31.

[75] *Australian Meat & Live-stock Corp.* v. *Canada (Canadian International Trade Tribunal)* (1993), 106 DLR (4th) 733 (FCA).

excluded from its consideration whether imports of boneless beef from the major source, United States, together with all other sources of imports, were such as to cause or threaten to cause serious injury to Canadian producers of like or directly competitive goods.[76] The Court found that there was no error in jurisdiction, as the CITT acted within the Order in Council setting out the mandate for its safeguard inquiry.[77]

Based on recent jurisprudence, it is clear that the reviewing Court would consider very little to be jurisdictional. For example, the question of whether the CITT chose the right products to be "subject goods" was not a question of jurisdiction, but a question of law within the CITT's expertise. The Court noted in *Maxx Bath Inc. v. Almag Aluminum Inc.* that:

> The applicant (and others) argued that certain goods fell outside the ambit of the preliminary determination and asked the Tribunal to draw the line, a task which is unquestionably within the Tribunal's jurisdiction ... Properly understood, the issue raised by the applicant does not go to jurisdiction but to the exercise of that jurisdiction. As with the other issues which the applicant has raised, the Tribunal will have committed a reviewable error only if its interpretation and application of the Agency's definition of the subject goods can be shown to be unreasonable.[78]

Typically, "line-drawing" by its very nature is a jurisdictional question, as it establishes what is and is not in an agency's scope. If "line drawing" falls within CITT jurisdiction, then not much would fall without, and very little would be determined on a standard of correctness.

(b) Errors that would not affect the outcome   One implication of the standard of reasonableness is that courts have found that unless the CITT commits an error that would change the outcome of the decision, the Court will not overturn the decision and remit it to the CITT for re-determination. *Stelco Inc. v. British Steel Canada Inc.* best expresses this principle. In that case, the Court held that "even if the Tribunal committed a reviewable error on some of its findings of fact, its decision to rescind will still be upheld if there were other facts on which it could reasonably base its ultimate conclusion".[79] This approach to the CITT is found throughout the Court's jurisprudence.[80]

---

[76] Ibid., at para. 14 (FCA).   [77] Ibid., at paras. 18 and 20 (FCA).
[78] *MAXX Bath Inc. v. Almag Aluminum Inc.*, at para. 33.
[79] *Stelco Inc. v. British Steel Canada Inc.*, at para. 22.
[80] See *Stelco Inc. v. Canada (Canadian International Trade Tribunal)* [1995] FCJ No. 832, at para. 4 (QL) (FCA); *British Columbia Vegetable Marketing Commission v.*

The result is that reviewing courts and bi-national panels (which, as discussed below, are required to apply Canadian law in their review of CBSA and CITT decisions) have arguably resorted to *post-facto* justifications for CITT decisions in spite of findings of error. For example, in *Certain Malt Beverages*, the bi-national panel, reviewing the CITT's negative likelihood of injury determination in an expiry (sunset) review on the basis that there was no longer a "regional market", found as follows:

> We agree that the figures from *Solid Urea* and *Reinforcing Bars* were misinterpreted or erroneously applied by the Tribunal. However, the Panel is uncertain what effect this misinterpretation had on the Tribunal's conclusion that:
>
>> In no case, where flows into and out of a market were of the magnitude of the flows in the present case, given the consistent pattern of significant movement of packaged beer both into and out of British Columbia, the Tribunal is of the view that there is no longer a regional industry in packaged beer in British Columbia.
>
> It is not clear to the panel whether the Tribunal based its conclusion regarding inflows on the evidence before it and found that it did not meet the "not to any substantial degree" test, or whether the Tribunal simply measured the level of inflows against the numbers used in the *Solid Urea* and *Reinforcing Bars* cases which it misinterpreted. The Panel is of the opinion that the Tribunal has not fulfilled its statutory obligation under section 45(1) of SIMA to provide ". . .a statement of facts and reasons that caused it to be of [an] opinion. . ." The Panel believes that pivotal issues, such as inflow and outflow determinations in the context of a regional industry determination, must be handled with enough depth for this Panel to understand the steps the Tribunal made in arriving at its findings.[81]

Notwithstanding the above acknowledgement that it did not understand the CITT's reasoning, the panel went on to determine that the errors in question were "immaterial to the result", because the CITT's negative regional market finding could be based exclusively on its determination that outflows were too significant for a regional market to exist.[82] Thus, not only on the reasonableness standard is the CITT not required to

---

Washington Potato and Onion Association, at para. 9 (FCA); *Infasco Division of Ifastgroupe and Company LP* v. *Canada (Canadian International Trade Tribunal)*, 2006 FCA 130, at paras. 13–14; *Owen & Company Limited* v. *Globe Spring & Cushion Co. Ltd.*, at para. 9.

[81] *Certain Malt Beverages from the United States of America (Injury)*, CDA-95–1904–01, p. 23.

[82] Ibid., at p. 24.

make the "correct decision", but it may also make an erroneous one, so long as that error would not have changed the eventual outcome, in the opinion of the reviewing court.

(c) Chances of success   There have been very few successful reviews of CITT decisions. In fact, since the formation of the CITT, of 28 judicial reviews, courts quashed and remanded only five cases in whole or in part.[83] All of those cases dealt with the review of a decision taken in the context of an investigation. Of those, only two cases involved a remand of a final decision, and both were because the CITT made patently unreasonable findings of fact leading to erroneous determinations of injury.[84] Two of the cases dealt with whether the CITT erred in denying a product exclusion, and the Court only quashed and remanded the CITT's decision on that narrow issue.[85] The final case was actually before the Federal Court on a procedural issue regarding the disclosure of confidential information.[86] In all of the cases, the Court either failed to identify the standard of review being applied, or applied the standard of patent unreasonableness or reasonableness.

The low remand rate is likely a direct result of the extremely deferential standard of review applied to CITT decisions. This view is bolstered by the fact that the Court only reviews questions of jurisdiction on a standard of correctness. Moreover, the principle, as discussed above, that the Court only quashes and remands CITT decisions on reviewable errors, such that errors that would not affect the outcome of the decision are not grounds for a remand, also supports this trend. The high level of deference and low success rate provide a bleak picture for those who wish to challenge a decision of the CITT at the Federal Court of Appeal. From the perspective of counsel, it is extremely difficult to advise a client to seek review of CITT decisions, even in the face of blatant and material errors. From a policy perspective, given the high economic stakes of trade remedy cases, it can legitimately be asked whether the courts have shed too much of their supervisory role and

---

[83] *LNK Manufacturing Agencies Inc. v. Canadian International Trade Tribunal; Canada (Director, Investigation and Research Competition Act) v. Canadian International Trade Tribunal* (1991), 48 FTR 50 (FC); *Canadian Pasta Manufacturers' Association v. Aurora Importing & Distributing Ltd.; GRK Fasteners v. Leland Industries Inc.*, 2006 FCA 118; *MAXX Bath Inc. v. Almag Aluminum Inc.*

[84] *LNK Manufacturing Agencies Inc. v. Canadian International Trade Tribunal; Canadian Pasta Manufacturers' Association v. Aurora Importing & Distributing Ltd.*

[85] *GRK Fasteners v. Leland Industries Inc.; MAXX Bath Inc. v. Almag Aluminum Inc.*

[86] *Canada (Director, Investigation and Research Competition Act) v. Canadian International Trade Tribunal.*

whether assumptions which underlie the rationale for deference (e.g. relative expertise of the administrative decision-maker) should be examined on a case-by-case basis.

Even in cases where remands have occurred, since the CITT has existed in its present form (1989), we are aware of only one case where it changed its ultimate finding because of a remand by the Federal Court of Appeal or a NAFTA panel in the context of either an investigation or an expiry review. In *Machine Tufted Carpeting* (1991), the CITT changed its finding from an affirmative finding of injury to a negative finding of injury and threat of injury.[87] This further supports the view that successful outcomes from appeals either to the Federal Court of Appeal or to NAFTA panels have very little effect on the ultimate outcome of a CITT trade remedy case.

V   Judicial review of CBSA decisions

1   Procedure

The timelines and procedures for review of CBSA decisions, other than for re-determinations, are the same as those of the CITT (as outlined above). For re-determinations of anti-dumping and/or countervailing duty liability, a person aggrieved by a decision may appeal to the CITT by filing a notice of appeal within 90 days of the re-determination.[88] The CITT is permitted to make any order or finding as may be required.[89] The person who appealed, the CBSA, or any individual who entered an appearance in the CITT appeal, may appeal the CITT's decision within 90 days to the Federal Court of Appeal. The Federal Court of Appeal may make such order and finding as required.[90]

The importance of using the proper procedure for seeking re-determinations and appeals of duty liability has been highlighted in the recent case of *Toyota Tsusho America Inc.* v. *Canada*. In that case, the applicant immediately sought judicial review of a CBSA re-determination at the Federal Court rather than first filing an appeal of re-determination at the CITT. The Court concluded that:

> In my view, the scheme of re-determinations and appeals provided by the SIMA is complete and, in enacting it, Parliament has clearly expressed its

---

[87] *Machine Tufted Carpeting*, NQ-91–006 Remand (2) (CITT).
[88] SIMA, RSC 1985, c. S-15, s. 61(1).   [89] SIMA, RSC 1985, c. S-15, s. 61(3).
[90] SIMA, RSC 1985, c. S-15, s. 62.

intention to oust the jurisdiction of this Court to review decisions taken under the authority of that statute ... The only way to have such a determination "quashed" or "set aside" is to follow the procedures set out in the SIMA itself.[91]

The Court considered the SIMA procedures to be adequate alternative relief and exercised its jurisdiction to decline to hear the judicial review application, since the applicant had not exhausted all adequate remedies. Thus, it is important to set the proper route to ensure the Court hears the application. However, while the **procedure** for challenging anti-dumping/countervailing duty re-determinations is different and involves filing appeals at the CITT and then the Federal Court,[92] for reasons discussed above, there is little substantive difference between the standards of review applied to Federal Court appeals of CITT decisions on appeal and Federal Court judicial reviews of other CITT and CBSA decisions and determinations.[93]

An issue of interest with respect to the review of both CBSA and CITT decisions is whether duties can be re-imposed retroactively if a matter involving a negative determination is remanded back to the CBSA or the CITT. SIMA appears to provide for retroactive application of duties in the case of a referral back from a NAFTA panel. Section 9.4 states that the importer is liable for duties as if the CITT's order had never been rescinded by the NAFTA panel. On the other hand, there are no provisions which govern retroactive application of duties on referral back by the Federal Court of Appeal. This discrepancy has yet to be tested in the case law.

2   Standard

2.1   Evolution of the standard

There have been considerably fewer reviews of CBSA decisions than of CITT decisions: in total, there have been eight decisions subject to review. Nevertheless, it would appear that the standard of review applicable to CBSA decisions, whether pursuant to statutory appeal or judicial review, would follow the framework outlined in *Dunsmuir*. With respect to findings

---

[91] *Toyota Tsusho America Inc.* v. *Canada (Canada Border Services Agency)*, 2010 FC 78, at para. 20, aff'd 2010 FCA 262. See also *GRK Fasteners* v. *Canada (Attorney General)*, 2011 FC 198.

[92] The processes for appeals and applications for judicial review are likewise governed by separate rules under the Federal Court Rules.

[93] See, e.g., *Commissioner for the Canada Customs and Revenue Agency* v. *M & M Footwear*, A-339–03, 28 April 2004 (Fed. CA).

of fact, the Court has applied section 18.1(4)(d) of the FCA such that the "Court cannot intervene unless it is shown that the CBSA based its decision on an erroneous finding of fact that it made in a perverse or capricious manner or without regard to the material before it."[94] In our view, in any case filed today, the Court would likely choose the deferential standard and apply reasonableness. The Court would review errors of mixed fact and law on a standard of reasonableness, as indicated in *Dunsmuir*. In this respect, the Court has found that errors such as the calculation of dumping margins remain legal, and that factual determinations deserve "more, and considerable, deference".[95] Lastly, the Court has applied the standard of correctness when faced with questions of procedural fairness.[96] It remains to be seen how the Court will review questions of law decided by the CBSA, as there have been no cases analysing the standard to apply to such an error, and the Court will have to conduct a full standard of review analysis to determine the applicable standard.

2.2   Implications of the standard

Because of the relatively few cases involving the CBSA, it remains difficult to discern any significant trends in the case law. Of the eight decisions, the Court quashed and remanded only one because the CBSA made an error of law by not allowing counsel access to confidential information.[97] As this was a preliminary, procedural decision, the Federal Court and not the Federal Court of Appeal heard it. In respect of the other cases, applicants have been unsuccessful in reviewing factual findings,[98] procedural fairness violations[99] and errors of law.[100] It is therefore possible to draw the conclusion that an applicant's likelihood of success, regardless of the standard applied, remains very low.

In addition, in the context of procedural rights and procedural fairness, the Court accords a high degree of deference to the CBSA's choice of procedures. The Court has done so because of the tight timelines

---

[94] *Tianjin Pipe (Group) Corporation v. Tenarisalgomatubes Inc.*, 2009 FCA 164, at para. 3.
[95] *Uniboard Surfaces Inc. v. Kronotex Fussboden GmbH and Co. KG*, 2006 FCA 398, at para. 60.
[96] *Uniboard Surfaces Inc. v. Kronotex Fussboden GmbH and Co. KG.*
[97] *Canadian Steel Producers Assn. v. Canada (Commissioner of Customs and Revenue)*, 2003 FC 1311.
[98] *Tianjin Pipe (Group) Corporation v. Tenarisalgomatubes Inc.*
[99] *Uniboard Surfaces Inc. v. Kronotex Fussboden GmbH and Co. KG; Shaw Industries Inc. v. Deputy Minister of National Revenue (Customs & Excise)* (1992), 51 FTR 304.
[100] *Shaw Industries Inc. v. Deputy Minister of National Revenue (Customs & Excise)* (1992), 53 FTR 15.

facing the CBSA in dumping investigations. In *Uniboard Surfaces*, the Court held that:

> One has to accept that notwithstanding the diligence of the Agency and of all the parties, incidents are likely to occur which, in this particular context, will be seen as being inescapably inherent to the process. Investigations of that magnitude (360,000 pages, six countries, three continents, five or six different languages) can simply not be completed within the maximum allotted time (225 days) unless the duty of procedural fairness is set at a low threshold. There can be no legitimate expectation of a higher threshold. Perfection or near-perfection is simply not in sight.[101]

A challenge regarding procedural fairness, therefore, would likely be met with little success.

VI   Bi-national panel reviews

1   Introduction

Where goods of a NAFTA or CUFTA country are the subject of a CBSA or a CITT decision, a person may access a review procedure involving bi-national panels as an alternative to the statutory appeal or judicial review procedures.[102] Canada and the United States signed the CUFTA in 1988 and it came into force in 1989.[103] The CUFTA was effective until the NAFTA came into force between Canada, the United States and Mexico in 1994.[104] The provisions in the NAFTA, however, generally left the panel review regime under the CUFTA untouched, with some small but significant exceptions. As such, the following section will describe the experiences of the panel review regimes under both the CUFTA and NAFTA together, but the discussion of procedure will focus on the NAFTA only.

2   Procedure

SIMA, NAFTA Article 1904 and the *Rules of Procedure for Article 1904 Binational Panel Reviews* govern panel reviews. A Minister of

---

[101] *Uniboard Surfaces Inc. v. Kronotex Fussboden GmbH and Co. KG*, at para. 45.
[102] SIMA, RSC 1985, c. S-15, s. 77.011(1), (2), (4).
[103] Foreign Affairs and International Trade Canada, "Canada-United States Free Trade Agreement", online: Foreign Affairs and International Trade Canada www.international.gc.ca/trade-agreements-accords-commerciaux/agr-acc/fast-facts-US.aspx?lang=en&view=d.
[104] Ibid.

International Trade, or any person who would be entitled to apply under the FCA or section 96.1 of SIMA may, within 30 days of a "definitive decision", request a review of that decision if the goods are from a CUFTA or NAFTA country (i.e. United States or Mexico).[105] A definitive decision is essentially any of the decisions subject to a statutory right of judicial review under section 96.1 of SIMA.[106] An applicant commences the process by filing a request for panel review to the NAFTA Secretariat.[107] Filing a request for a panel review removes any right to judicial review at the Federal Court.[108]

The grounds for a panel review are limited to:

- the allegations of error of fact or law, including challenges to the jurisdiction of the investigating authority; and
- procedural and substantive defences raised in the panel review.[109]

Thus, the grounds are essentially the same as those under the FCA and SIMA. Regarding remedies, the panel may either confirm the decision or refer the matter back for reconsideration.[110]

Although panel decisions are final and not subject to any judicial review, the panel, on its own initiative or that of an applicant, may request a review of a remanded determination.[111] Further, the minister or the government of a country to whom the order relates may request an extraordinary challenge proceeding against a panel decision.[112] The grounds for such a proceeding relate to the conduct of the panel from a procedural standpoint.[113]

3   Standard

3.1   Evolution of the standard

Pursuant to NAFTA Article 1904(3), a panel must apply the standard of review set out in Annex 1911 and the general legal principles that a court

---

[105] SIMA, RSC 1985, c. S-15, ss. 77.011(1), 77.011(2), 77.11.
[106] SIMA, RSC 1985, c. S-15, s. 77.01(1).
[107] Rules of Procedure for Article 1904 Binational Panel Reviews, r. 6.
[108] SIMA, RSC 1985, c. S-15, s. 77.011(7).
[109] Rules of Procedure for Article 1904 Binational Panel Reviews, r. 7.
[110] SIMA, RSC 1985, c. S-15, s. 77.015(3).
[111] SIMA, RSC 1985, c. S-15, ss. 77.02, 77.015(4).
[112] SIMA, RSC 1985, c. S-15, s. 77.017(1).
[113] North American Free Trade Agreement Between the Government of Canada, the Government of Mexico and the Government of the United States, 17 December 1990, Can. T.S. 1994 No. 2, Article 1904(13).

of the importing party otherwise would apply to a review of a determination.[114] Annex 1911 states that the standard of review, in the case of Canada, is the "grounds set out in subsection 18.1(4) of the *Federal Courts Act*".[115] In applying standards of review, therefore, panels apply the same common law principles and statutes as the Federal Court of Appeal would in review decisions, and the same case law relied on by the Federal Court of Appeal.[116] Thus, the evolution and experience described above applies equally to panel reviews.

3.2 Implications

Ten of the 26 CUFTA and NAFTA panel reviews have resulted in remands either in whole or in part, all of which were in the context of an investigation.[117] Seven of the panels were regarding determinations by the CBSA, while three involved determinations by the CITT. Of the 10 remands, most were extremely limited in scope and did not affect the overall outcome of the case. Therefore, overall it would appear that CUFTA and NAFTA panels have generated a slightly higher remand rate than the Federal Court of Appeal.

VII Conclusions

As the above discussion should make clear, Canada's framework of review of trade remedy determinations is complex in terms of both procedure and the evolving body of law governing the standard of review. Yet for all of this complexity, the stark reality for parties seeking redress against CBSA and/or CITT determinations is that the level of deference applied by reviewing courts in Canada is extremely high. From a policy perspective, one could legitimately ask whether Canadian courts

---

[114] Ibid., Article 1904(3).   [115] Ibid., Annex 1911.

[116] See, e.g., *Certain Iodinated Contrast Media used for Radiographic Imaging, originating in or exported from the USA (including the Commonwealth of Puerto Rico)*, CDA-USA-2000-1904-01 (Ch. 19 Panel).

[117] *Certain Cold-Rolled Steel Sheet* (1994), CDA-USA-1993-1904-08 (Ch. 19 Panel); *Certain Beer* (1992), CDA-USA-1991-1904-01 (Ch. 19 Panel); *Certain Carpets* (1993), CDA-USA-1992-1904-02 (Ch. 19 Panel); *Certain Beer* (1992), CDA-USA-1991-1904-02 (Ch. 19 Panel); *Gypsum Board* (1993), CDA-USA-1993-1904-01 (Ch. 19 Panel); *Certain Corrosion-Resistant Steel* (1995), CDA-USA-1994-1904-03 (Ch. 19 Panel); *Refined Sugar* (1996), CDA-USA-1995-1904-04 (Ch. 19 Panel); *Certain Iodinated Contrast Media* (2003), CDA-USA-2000-1904-01 (Ch. 19 Panel); *Synthetic Baler Twine* (1995), CDA-USA-1994-1904-02 (Ch. 19 Panel); *Certain Hot-Rolled Carbon Steel Plate* (1999), CDA-MEX-1997-1904-02 (Ch. 19 Panel).

have shed too much of their supervisory role, given what is at stake in trade remedy disputes, and whether Canada's trading partners such as the United States got what they thought they were getting when they agreed to bi-national panel review of anti-dumping and countervailing duty determinations for goods of the other party under the CUFTA and the NAFTA. From a practical perspective, it will be interesting to see whether greater future use is made of mechanisms such as state-to-state dispute resolution under the WTO Agreements, in which less deference appears to be applied in the assessment of conformity of CBSA and CITT determinations and other measures of Canadian authorities with the obligations in those agreements.

United States: judicial review: a cornerstone of trade remedies practice

JOHN D. MCINERNEY AND MICHELE D. LYNCH*

I Introduction

Judicial review is a cornerstone of trade remedies practice in the United States. Over the last century, US anti-dumping and countervailing duty laws have evolved to provide detailed procedures governing agency determinations, and also to provide a framework for judicial review. Anti-dumping and countervailing duty determinations made by the Import Administration, the US Department of Commerce (Commerce) and the US International Trade Commission (ITC, or the Commission) are the most common forms of trade remedy relief in the United States, and are statutorily subject to judicial review. Safeguard actions, on the other hand, which are implemented at the discretion of the president of the United States, are much less frequently used as a means of trade remedy relief and are generally judicially reviewable only on procedural grounds and not on their merits.[1] Because judicial review of anti-dumping and countervailing duty determinations in the United States is more developed than that of safeguard actions, this chapter focuses on the former.

The US Government consists of three branches: the legislative branch (the US Congress), the executive branch (the president and administrative agencies), and the judicial branch (US federal court system). Each branch is vested under the US Constitution with authority separate and distinct from the others. Although the principle that the federal courts

---

* Many thanks to Jessica Forton, Svetlana Matt, Martin Harms and Christopher Lamar for their assistance. This work presents the authors' views. It is not an official document of the US Department of Commerce.
[1] Safeguard or escape clause provisions address fair trade practices that may have a harmful effect on US domestic industries. See Vivian C. Jones, *Cong. Research Serv.*, RL 32371, *Trade Remedies: A Primer* 1 (2008).

can review the determinations of administrative agencies is well established, the scope of such review is not unlimited. "Federal courts . . . have only the power that is authorized by Article III of the Constitution and the statutes enacted by Congress pursuant thereto."[2]

The United States has a rich history of trade remedy legislation and judicial review. The first general US countervailing duty law was in the Tariff Act of 1897.[3] Since at least 1916, the United States has had a general law addressing dumping of imported merchandise,[4] and since the late 1930s, has generally included some form of escape clause in trade agreements that permits it to escape from its obligations with respect to a product when increased imports of the product cause or threaten to cause serious injury to domestic producers of the like or a directly competitive product.[5] Review of early trade actions can best be viewed in the anti-dumping statutes. Five years after the Anti-dumping Act of 1916, the Anti-dumping Act of 1921 was enacted, pursuant to which an administrative agency, the US Department of Treasury, was authorized to make dumping determinations, and dumping duties were imposed, rather than criminal penalties or damages.[6] Under the 1921 Act, review of agency action was conducted by a Board of General Appraisers,[7] the precursor to the United States Customs Court. The Board settled controversies over appraisals of imported merchandise and tariff classifications, and judicial review of the Board's decisions was vested in the US circuit courts. In 1909, judicial review of the Board was transferred to the US Court of Customs Appeals.[8]

---

[2] *Bender* v. *Williamsport Area School Dist.*, 475 US 534, 543 (1986) (*Bender*); US Const. Art. III. US federal courts are organized under Article I or Article III of the Constitution. Article III courts have general jurisdiction to hear all types of federal cases, while Article I courts have specialized jurisdiction to hear only certain cases.

[3] See Tariff Act of 1897, 30 Stat. 151 (repealed 1909). The US countervailing duty law has been amended numerous times. See Payne-Aldrich Tariff Act of 1909, ch. 6; Tariff Act of 1913, ch. 16; Fordney-McCumber Tariff Act of 1922, 19 USC § 127; Tariff Act of 1930, Pub. L. No. 71–361; Trade Act of 1974, Pub. L. No. 93–618, 88 Stat. 1978, 19 USC ch. 12.

[4] Anti-dumping Act of 1916, 15 USC § 72 (repealed 2004) (dumping was a criminal offence punishable by fine, imprisonment, or both).

[5] See, e.g., Agreement on Reciprocal Trade, Dec. 23, 1942, United States–Mexico, Art. XI, 57 Stat. 833, 845–46, EAS. No. 311.

[6] 42 Stat. 11, Sec. 201–202; 19 USC §§ 160–71 (repealed 1979); *supra* note 4.

[7] Established as part of Treasury in 1890. See Customs Administration Act of 1890, ch. 407. In 1926, the Board became the United States Customs Court: Act of 28 May 1926, ch. 411.

[8] Payne-Aldrich Tariff Act of 1909 (ch. 6, 36 Stat. 11).

Between 1947 and 1994, the world's trade remedy arena expanded with the General Agreement on Tariffs and Trade (GATT) and the multiple negotiating rounds that ensued. The United States variously amended or not[9] its anti-dumping, countervailing duty and safeguard statutes[10] during this time. One such amendment occurred in 1979 to conform US trade remedy laws to the Tokyo Round Codes. Significantly, the Trade Agreements Act of 1979 repealed the 1921 Act and enacted the revised anti-dumping and countervailing duty laws as a new Title VII to the Tariff Act of 1930, as amended[11] (the Act) where those laws are found today. The statutes were further amended in 1984,[12] 1988[13] and, most substantively in 1994, when Congress passed the Uruguay Round Agreements Act (URAA) for the primary purpose of implementing the multilateral agreements generated by the Uruguay Round negotiations and the creation of the World Trade Organization (WTO).[14] The current authority and procedures for the implementation of safeguard measures are found in sections 201–4, 406 and 421 of the Trade Act of 1974, as amended.[15]

Throughout these successive statutory amendments, judicial review of trade remedies practice has evolved in the United States. Significantly, the Customs Court Act of 1980 expanded and clarified

---

[9] See generally, 82 Stat. 1347, Sec. 201 (1968 law providing that the Kennedy Round Anti-dumping Code would apply only to the extent it did not conflict with existing US law); the Trade Act of 1974, 19 USC § 2101.

[10] For safeguard amendments, generally, see section 7 of the Trade Agreement Extension Act of 1951, ch. 141 (containing first statutory procedures and criteria); sections 301, 351 and 352 of the Trade Expansion Act of 1962, Pub. L. No. 87–794; sections 201–3 of the Trade Act of 1974; section 1401 of the Omnibus Trade and Competitiveness Act of 1988, Pub. L. 100–418; sections 315 and 317 of the North American Free Trade Agreement Implementation Act of 1993, Pub. L. No. 103–182; sections 301–4 of the URAA, Pub. L. No. 103–465; section 103 of the US–China Relations Act of 2000, Pub. L. No. 106–286.

[11] 19 USC § 1671 *et seq.* Administration of the laws was transferred in 1980 from Treasury to Commerce: Reorganization Plan No. 3: Reorganization of Functions Relating to International Trade, 44 FR 69273, 69724–25 (Dec. 3, 1979).

[12] The Tariff and Trade Act of 1984, 19 USC § 1677, 98 Stat. 3034, Sec. 612(a)(2)(A).

[13] The Omnibus Trade and Competitiveness Act of 1988, 19 USC § 1677, 102 Stat. 1192, Sec. 1321.

[14] URAA, Pub. L. No. 103–465,108 Stat. 4809 (1994).

[15] See sections 201–4 of the Trade Act of 1974 (19 USC §§ 2251–2254, global safeguard provision); section 406 of the Trade Act of 1974 (19 USC § 2436, market disruption from communist countries); section 421 of the Trade Act of 1974 (19 USC § 2451, market disruption from imports from China). Section 302 of the NAFTA Implementation Act (19 USC § 3355) provides transitional safeguard authority for imports from Canada and/or Mexico that generally has lapsed.

the authority of the US Customs Court[16] under the newly created United States Court of International Trade (CIT). Judicial review of trade remedies cases continues to be the exclusive province of the CIT (located in New York City),[17] with appeals exclusively vested in the US Court of Appeals for the Federal Circuit (Federal Circuit) (located in Washington DC).[18] Importantly, the United States is also a party to the North American Free Trade Agreement (NAFTA), and as such, certain determinations involving Mexico or Canada may be subject to bi-national panel review.

II   Framework for judicial review

Article III of the US Constitution vests jurisdiction over "Controversies to which the United States shall be a Party" in the federal courts.[19] However, to sue the United States, a number of requirements must be satisfied. Discussed below is the process of obtaining judicial review of various trade remedy determinations made by Commerce and the Commission, the two US agencies charged, respectively, with making anti-dumping and countervailing duty determinations and injury deter-minations. Review of safeguard actions is also briefly discussed. Broadly speaking, once the US Congress enacts and the president signs a statute authorizing a US federal agency such as Commerce or the Commission to administer a law, review of agency action is vested in the judicial branch. Judicial review includes review of agency determinations made pursuant to a statute or the implementing rules and regulations, and review of those rules and regulations.[20] As a threshold issue, judicial review of actions by the United States is limited by the doctrine of sovereign immunity.[21] With respect to many US federal agency

---

[16] Initially an Article I court, in 1956 Congress elevated the Customs Court to Article III status. Act of 14 July 1956, ch. 589 (codified at 28 USC § 251(a)). See also *supra* note 2.

[17] For a detailed history, see Edward D. Re, "Litigation Before the United States Court of International Trade" 26 (1981) *N.Y.L. Sch. L. Rev.* 437 (1981).

[18] 28 USC § 1295(a) (5) ("The United States Court of Appeals for the Federal Circuit shall have exclusive jurisdiction ... of an appeal from a final decision of the United States Court of International Trade").

[19] US Const. Art. III sec. 2.

[20] See, e.g., *Chevron, USA v. Natural Resources Defense Council, Inc.*, 467 US 837, 865–66 (1984) (*Chevron*).

[21] See *Hans v. Louisiana*, 134 US 1, 16 (1890) ("The suability of a State, without its consent, was a thing unknown to the law. This has been so often laid down and acknowledged by courts and jurists that it is hardly necessary to be formally asserted").

actions, a general waiver of sovereign immunity is contained in the Administrative Procedure Act (APA)[22] at 5 USC § 702.[23] With respect to certain trade remedy actions, including Commerce's anti-dumping and countervailing duty determinations and the Commission's injury determinations, section 516A of the Act expressly waives sovereign immunity and provides for judicial review.[24]

Consent by the United States to be sued is not sufficient, however, to ensure that a federal court will hear a case. Pursuant to US law, a federal court must have authority over all of the parties and the subject matter of the lawsuit. For a federal court to have jurisdiction, a party filing an action must establish that there is a "case or controversy" as required by Article III of the Constitution. To satisfy constitutional standing, a person must allege (1) injury-in-fact (that the injury is concrete and particularized and actual or imminent); (2) that the injury is fairly traceable to the challenged action; and (3) that a favourable court decision will likely redress the injury.[25] If constitutional standing is not established, the case will be dismissed because the court lacks subject matter jurisdiction.[26]

Trade remedy actions arising under section 516A of the Act are the exclusive domain of the CIT,[27] except where parties are challenging a trade remedy determination involving Canadian or Mexican merchandise under NAFTA Chapter 19, which provides an alternative, mutually exclusive, forum.[28] In addition to the general grant of jurisdiction

---

[22] The APA establishes procedures governing US administrative agency conduct including rule making, adjudications and hearings: 5 USC § 551 *et seq.* Significantly, however, "actions of the President cannot be reviewed under the APA because the President is not an 'agency' under that Act". *Dalton v. Specter*, 511 US 462, 476 (1994).

[23] "A person suffering legal wrong because of agency action, or adversely affected or aggrieved by agency action within the meaning of a relevant statute, is entitled to judicial review thereof . . . . The United States may be named as a defendant in any such action." 5 USC § 702.

[24] Section 516A, codified at 19 USC § 1516a, lists reviewable agency actions. As discussed below, challenges to certain agency actions arise pursuant to the APA.

[25] US Const. Art. III; *Allen v. Wright*, 468 US 737, 749–50 (1984).

[26] "The requirement of 'actual injury redressable by the court,' serves several of the 'implicit policies embodied in Article III.' It tends to assure that the legal questions presented to the court will be resolved not in the rarified atmosphere of a debating society, but in a concrete factual context conducive to a realistic appreciation of the consequences of judicial action." *Bender*, 475 US, at 542 (internal citations omitted).

[27] 28 USC § 1581(c).

[28] Such parties may request bi-national panel review in lieu of US court review. There are, however, statutory exceptions to panel exclusivity: NAFTA Ch. 19, Art. 1904(1), (2); 19 USC § 1516a(g)(2) and (3).

covering anti-dumping and countervailing duty determinations, section 1581(i)[29] grants exclusive residual jurisdiction to the CIT over other trade-related matters.[30] The jurisdictional basis for review of safeguard actions is less clear. Section 1581(i) does not explicitly cover such actions, although the Federal Circuit determined that it had jurisdiction under section 1581(i) to consider a procedural challenge to a safeguard action.[31] Significantly, section 1581(i) does not confer jurisdiction over determinations reviewable either by the CIT under section 516A or by a NAFTA panel.[32] Consequently, if a party could or should have sued the United States under section 1581(c), it will not be allowed to avail itself of section 1581(i) jurisdiction.[33] The statutes of limitations differ for section 1581(c) and (i) cases. Under the former, there is a 60-day, while under the latter, a two-year limitations period.[34]

In all cases in federal courts, personal jurisdiction over the defendant must also exist. Absent personal jurisdiction, a defendant is not required to honour a court's judgment. Traditionally, the standard for determining personal jurisdiction is whether "maintenance of the suit does not offend 'traditional notions of fair play and substantial justice'".[35] "Where the United States is the defendant, such notions are not offended so long as the United States is properly served with notice of suit".[36] In trade remedy cases where the US Government is always the defendant,[37] service of the summons and complaint upon the United States is governed by CIT Rule 4.[38]

---

[29] Section 1581(i), in part, vests jurisdiction with the CIT "over any civil action . . . that arises out of any law of the United States providing for" (i) revenue from imports; (2) tariffs, duties, fees, or other taxes on imports other than for revenue; (3) certain embargoes or other quantitative restrictions; or (4) the administration and enforcement of any of these matters or matters arising under other subsections of section 1581 including 1581(c).

[30] See 28 USC §§ 1581–1584 (2006) (jurisdiction of the CIT).

[31] See *Corus Group PLC v. ITC*, 352 F.3d 1351, 1358 (Fed. Cir. 2003) (*Corus Group PLC*) ("Because no other statute specifically vests the court with jurisdiction over duties imposed pursuant to the escape clause provision and because there is no other statute precluding the court's jurisdiction in this case, section 1581(i)(2) vested the court with statutory jurisdiction over this case").

[32] 28 USC § 1581(i).

[33] *International Custom Prods., Inc. v. United States*, 467 F.3d 1324, 1327 (Fed. Cir. 2006).

[34] 28 USC § 1581(i); 19 USC § 1516a(a)(2)(A); 28 USC § 2636(i).

[35] *International Shoe Co. v. Washington*, 326 US 310, 316 (1945) (quoting *Milliken v. Meyer*, 311 US 457, 463 (1940)).

[36] *Burton v. United States*, 668 F. Supp. 2d 86, 93 (DDC 2009) (citations omitted).

[37] 28 USC § 1581.

[38] See USCIT R. 4. "The USCIT Rules govern whether service is proper in cases before this Court." *United States v. Wilfran Agricultural Indus.*, 716 F. Supp. 2d 1352, 1356 (CIT 2010). See also 28 USC § 2633(c) ("When the United States, its agencies, or its officers

III   Eligible parties

In addition to the constitutional requirements and the jurisdictional limitations imposed by the courts, the Act limits those who are eligible to sue the United States. Statutory eligibility is similar to constitutional standing discussed above. Section 516A of the Act identifies a person who may sue the United States as an "interested party who is a party to the proceeding".[39] "Interested party" is defined, in part, to mean: foreign manufacturers, producers, or exporters; US importers; a business association the majority of members of which are producers, exporters or importers of subject merchandise or an association the majority of members who manufacture, produce or wholesale the domestic like product in the United States; the government of a country; the domestic manufacturer, producer or wholesaler of the domestic like product; a certified union or recognized union or group of workers representative of a US industry; and an association comprised of interested parties.[40] A "party to the proceeding" is defined in Commerce's regulations, in relevant part, as "any interested party that actively participates, through written submissions of factual information or argument, in a segment of a proceeding".[41] So a party to the proceeding must have participated in the agency's administrative action to be entitled to sue the agency in court.[42]

NAFTA Article 1904(5) permits bi-national panel review in cases involving Canadian or Mexican imports upon "request of a person who would otherwise be entitled under the law of the importing Party to commence domestic procedures for judicial review of that final determination".[43] Thus, if a person is an "interested party" within 19 USC § 1677(9), Article 1904(5) allows that person to request review by a NAFTA panel so long as the request is timely filed and properly served.[44]

---

are adverse parties, service of the summons shall be made upon the Attorney General and the head of the Government agency whose action is being contested").

[39] 19 USC § 1516a(a)(1); see also 28 USC 2631(c) (similar language).

[40] 19 USC § 1677(9).

[41] 19 CFR § 351.102(36). The Commission's regulations permit "[p]ersons entitled to judicial review under section 516A ... to seek judicial review in the CIT" 19 CFR § 207.50(a).

[42] See *Miller & Co. v. United States*, 824 F.2d 961, 964 (Fed. Cir. 1987) (importer that did not participate before agency lacked standing to invoke 1581(c) jurisdiction).

[43] NAFTA Art. 1904(5).

[44] 19 USC § 1516a(g)(8)(A); see also NAFTA Rule 34(1)(b); 73 Fed. Reg. 19458, 19464 (10 Apr. 2008).

The statute also permits certain parties to intervene in CIT cases. To intervene as of right in a trade remedies case, a proposed intervener must be "an interested party who was a party to the proceeding".[45] A party seeking to intervene in other types of actions may do so, by leave of court, if the party can establish that it "would be adversely affected or aggrieved" by a decision in the case. However, the CIT "shall consider whether the intervention will unduly delay or prejudice the adjudication of the rights of the original parties".[46] Intervention has been permitted in a safeguard challenge.[47]

IV   Competent courts

The CIT is distinguishable from other federal courts, in that it is one of the only federal courts of specialized jurisdiction organized under Article III of the US Constitution instead of Article I.[48] Despite its specialized subject matter, the CIT "possess[es] all the powers in law and equity of . . . a district court of the United States".[49] The CIT consists of nine active judges, including a chief judge, who, similar to all federal judges, are appointed by the president with the advice and consent of the Senate.[50] Most CIT actions are assigned by the chief judge to a single judge; however, a three-judge panel may also be assembled.[51] Decisions of the CIT are appealable directly to the Federal Circuit,[52] and ultimately to the United States Supreme Court.[53]

The Federal Circuit is similar to the CIT in that it is also a court of national jurisdiction by virtue of the various areas within its jurisdictional grant. By the court's statistics, in fiscal year 2010, international

---

[45] 28 USC § 2631(j)(1)(B). "Interested party" has the same meaning as in 19 USC § 1677(9); 28 USC § 2631(k)(1). An intervener may support the original parties' positions; it may not expand them. See *Laizhou Auto Brake Equip. Co.* v. *United States*, 477 F. Supp. 2d 1298, 1300–01 (CIT 2007) (citations omitted).

[46] 28 USC § 2631(j)(2).

[47] See *Corus Group PLC*, 352 F.3d, at 1353 (domestic industry intervened).

[48] 28 USC § 251(a); see *supra* note 2.

[49] 28 USC § 1585. US district courts are the trial level courts.

[50] 28 USC § 251(a). CIT judges enjoy Article III privileges including lifetime tenure and removal by congressional action only: 28 USC § 252. No more than five CIT judges may be of the same political party: 28 USC § 251(a).

[51] 28 USC §§ 253–255.

[52] 28 USC § 1295(a)(5) ("The United States Court of Appeals for the Federal Circuit shall have exclusive jurisdiction . . . of an appeal from a final decision of the United States Court of International Trade").

[53] 28 USC § 1254; see, e.g., *United States* v. *Eurodif S.A.*, 555 US 305 (2009) (*Eurodif*).

trade cases represented only 4% of appeals filed.[54] The Federal Circuit, which currently has 12 active judges, generally sits in three-judge panels and follows the same appellate rules and procedures as other US courts of appeal, with certain local modifications.[55]

V Procedural steps

Although the CIT is unique in that it is the only lower federal court with exclusive jurisdiction over trade remedy determinations, procedurally it is similar to other federal courts reviewing agency action. There are five main segments of a CIT proceeding: Summons and Complaint, Filing of Agency Record, Briefing Stage, Oral Arguments, Judgment and/or Remand. On average, a CIT proceeding may take 15 months, but that varies significantly depending upon case complexity. A party seeking judicial review of a trade remedy determination made pursuant to section 516A must file a summons with the CIT within 30 days of publication of the final agency decision.[56] Within 30 days of the summons, the plaintiff must file a complaint, "contesting any factual findings or legal conclusions upon which the [agency] determination is based".[57] As discussed above, in section 1581 cases, parties may have up to two years to file a case from the time the party knew or should have known of the agency action.[58]

Generally, once a complaint has been filed, the agency has 40 days to submit to the court the official record or certified list of the items in the record of the challenged administrative proceeding.[59] Section 1581(c) actions differ from other court actions, because the defendant United States is not required to answer the complaint;[60] rather, it files the administrative record or certified list, and briefing ensues. The record

---

[54] www.cafc.uscourts.gov/images/stories/the-court/statistics/Caseload_by_Category_Appeals_Filed_2010.pdf.

[55] United States Court of Appeals for the Federal Circuit, *Rules of Practice* (June 2011).

[56] 19 USC § 1516a(a)(2)(A). See generally, USCIT R. 3. Other 28 USC § 1581 actions have different filing requirements.

[57] 19 USC § 1516a(a)(2)(A); USCIT R. 3(a)(2). In some cases, the summons and complaint must be filed concurrently: 19 USC § 1516a(a)(1); USCIT R. 3(a)(3).

[58] 28 USC § 2636(i). Generally, "[a] cause of action accrues when 'all events' necessary to state the claim, or fix the liability of the Government, have occurred". *Mitsubishi Elecs. Am. Inc. v. United States*, 44 F.3d 973, 977 (Fed. Cir. 1994) (citations omitted).

[59] 28 USC § 2635(b); USCIT R. 73.2(a) and (b).

[60] 28 USC § 2635(b). Section 1581(i) actions differ from 1581(c) actions because, for example, in 1581(i) cases the United States must answer the complaint before briefs are filed. See USCIT R. 7(a)(2).

contains any and all information presented to or obtained by the agency during the course of the proceeding,[61] including the determination and the facts and conclusions of law upon which the determination was made, all transcripts or records of conferences or hearings, and all *Federal Register* notices.[62] Within 30 days of the record filing, a joint briefing schedule should be filed.[63] Typically, within 60 days thereafter, the plaintiff's opening brief is due.[64] The agency generally responds within 60 days and the plaintiff has 25 days to submit its rebuttal. The court would be expected to have a hearing (if at all) a few months after the last brief is filed, and issue its opinion within 90 days of the hearing. Once the final judgment (after all remands) is issued, a party may appeal to the Federal Circuit. When the United States is a party, the time to appeal is 60 days after the entry of the final judgment rather than the standard 30 days.[65] The approximate time from docquetting to a merits decision is 10 months.

Because the CIT has "all the powers in law and equity" as other federal district courts,[66] it may order injunctive relief.[67] In trade remedy cases, injunctive relief is statutory[68] and arises when a party moves for a preliminary injunction prohibiting the agencies from collecting duties on the merchandise subject to the anti-dumping (AD) or countervailing duty (CVD) orders. This is referred to as enjoining "liquidation" of the entries.[69] Generally, the agency will not object to the preliminary injunction.[70] The injunction remains valid until the final and conclusive judgment in the case.[71]

NAFTA Chapter 19 contains dispute settlement procedures if panel review is selected in disputes involving Canada or Mexico.[72] A party must first determine whether to challenge the agency's determination in the CIT or before a NAFTA panel. If the party selects the CIT, within 20 days of the *Federal Register* publication of the final determination the party must file a notice of intent to seek judicial review with the CIT, with

---

[61] 28 USC § 2635(b)(1)(A).   [62] 28 USC § 2635(b)(1)(B).   [63] USCIT R. 56.2(a).
[64] USCIT R. 56.2(d).   [65] 28 USC § 2107(b); Fed. R. App. P. 4(a)(1)(A) and (B).
[66] 28 USC § 1585.   [67] 28 USC § 2643.   [68] 19 USC § 1516a(c)(2).
[69] 19 USC § 1516a(c)(1).
[70] See *Zenith Radio Corp* v. *United States*, 710 F.2d 806, 810 (Fed. Cir. 1983) (liquidation constitutes irreparable harm).
[71] 28 USC § 2645(c) ("A decision of the [CIT] is final and conclusive, unless . . . an appeal is taken to the Court of Appeals for the Federal Circuit"); *Yancheng Baolong Biochem. Prods. Co.* v. *United States*, 406 F.3d 1377, 1381–82 (Fed. Cir. 2005) (preliminary injunction lasts through all appeals).
[72] See generally, NAFTA Ch. 19, Art. 1904.

copies to the NAFTA Secretariat and other parties.[73] If the party selects NAFTA, it may initiate a challenge by filing a request for panel review (in place of a summons) within 30 days after publication of the agency's final determination[74] and a complaint within 30 days of the first request for panel review.[75]

A NAFTA panel consists of five individuals drawn from rosters of judges, trade experts and lawyers.[76] Panellist selection is decided by the two governments involved.[77] A panel reviewing US agency action must determine whether that action is consistent with US law.[78] The NAFTA briefing schedule is similar to the CIT's, except reply briefs are due within 15 days of the opposition brief rather than 25 days.[79] Also, similar to the CIT, a panel may alter the briefing schedule.[80] Ideally, the panel process should take no more than 315 days,[81] although the reality is that many proceedings take much longer.

Although NAFTA panels may not order injunctive relief, US law provides for continued suspension of liquidation in administrative review proceedings subject to a NAFTA challenge.[82] The NAFTA does not provide private parties with the right to challenge panel decisions; however, a government may request review by an extraordinary challenge committee (ECC).[83] The ECC roster contains only 15 names (five

---

[73] 19 USC § 1516a(g)(3)(B) and NAFTA Ch. 19, Art. 1904(15)(c)(i). See *Desert Glory, Ltd.* v. *United States*, 368 F. Supp. 2d 1334 (CIT 2005) (dismissed for lack of jurisdiction where no notice of intent to seek judicial review). Other parties thus have time to request a NAFTA panel. If one party timely requests panel review, the case is heard by a NAFTA panel. See 19 USC § 1516a(g)(3) (permitting judicial review if a bi-national panel has not been requested and timely notice of intent to commence judicial review has been given); NAFTA Ch. 19, Art. 1904(15)(c) (same). Removal to US courts would be permitted if a constitutional question is raised (§ 1516a(g)(4)) or one of the exceptions under section 1516a(g)(3) is satisfied.

[74] NAFTA Ch. 19, Art. 1904(2), (4).

[75] NAFTA Rule 39(1). The administrative record is due 60 days after the first request for panel review: NAFTA Rule 41(1).

[76] NAFTA Ch. 19, Annex 1901.2 paras. 1, 2. Each country maintains a roster.

[77] NAFTA Ch. 19, Annex 1901.2 paras. 2, 3.

[78] NAFTA Ch. 19, Art. 1904(2). A party may request panel review "to determine whether such determination was in accordance with the anti-dumping or countervailing duty law of the importing Party;" see also Art. 1904(3).

[79] NAFTA Rule 57(1), (2), and (3); 73 Fed. Reg. 19458, 19468 (10 April 2008).

[80] NAFTA Ch. 19, Art. 1904(14).   [81] Ibid.

[82] 19 CFR § 356.8. The regulations do not provide for administrative suspension in investigations.

[83] NAFTA Ch. 19, Art. 1904(13). A party must allege that: (1) a panellist was guilty of gross misconduct, bias, or a serious conflict of interest, or otherwise materially violated the rules of conduct; (2) the panel seriously departed from a fundamental rule of procedure;

nominees from each country), all of whom are judges or former judges of a federal court.[84] An ECC may overturn a panel only if the underlying decision or an action of the panel "materially affected the panel's decision or threatens the integrity" of the NAFTA bi-national process[85] – a standard that the six ECCs constituted in the United States have never found to be satisfied.[86]

VI   Standard of review

In almost all anti-dumping and countervailing duty cases, the standard of review is whether the agency's decision is supported by substantial evidence on the record, or is otherwise in accordance with law.[87] When applied to the agencies' factual determinations, this standard requires the CIT to decide whether the determination is supported by "such relevant evidence as a reasonable mind might accept as adequate to support a conclusion".[88] The court may not substitute its judgment for that of the agency, or allow parties to re-try factual issues.[89] Moreover, the possibility of drawing two inconsistent conclusions from the same evidence does not preclude a finding of substantial evidence.[90] An agency's determination will not be overturned solely because a complaining party points to contrary evidence in the record.[91] As long as

or (3) the panel manifestly exceeded its Chapter 19 powers, authority or jurisdiction, for example by failing to apply the appropriate standard of review.

[84] NAFTA Ch. 19, Annex 1904 para. 13(1).   [85] NAFTA Ch. 19, Art. 1904(13).

[86] See *Pure Magnesium from Canada*, ECC-2003–1904–01USA, at 11 (7 Oct. 2004) ("[T]he ECC concludes that (a) the Panel manifestly exceeded its powers by failing to apply the correct standard of review and (b) such action materially affected the Panel's decision, but (c) that the Panel's action did not threaten the integrity of the bi-national panel review process"). See also *Gray Portland Cement and Clinker Cement from Mexico*, ECC-2000 1904–01USA (30 Oct. 2003); *Certain Software Lumber Products from Canada*, ECC-2004–1904–01USA (10 Aug. 2005); *Fresh, Chilled or Frozen Pork from Canada*, ECC-91–1904–01USA (14 June 1991); *Live Swine from Canada*, ECC-93–1904–01USA (8 Apr. 1993); *Certain Softwood Lumber Products from Canada*, ECC-94–1904–01USA (3 Aug. 1994).

[87] 19 USC § 1516a(b)(1)(B)(i) (applicable to 1516a(a)(2) actions) ("The court shall hold unlawful any determination, finding, or conclusion found … to be unsupported by substantial evidence on the record, or otherwise not in accordance with law"). See also 28 USC 2640(b). For section 1516a(a)(1) actions, an arbitrary, capricious or abuse of discretion standard applies: 19 USC § 1516a(b)(1)(A).

[88] See, e.g., *Steel Authority of India, Ltd.* v. *United States*, 146 F. Supp. 2d 900, 903 (CIT 2001); *Timken Co.* v. *United States*, 865 F. Supp. 881, 883 (CIT 1994).

[89] *Inland Steel Industries, Inc.* v. *United States*, 188 F.3d 1349, 1359 (Fed. Cir. 1999).

[90] See, e.g., *Mitsubishi Heavy Indus., Ltd.* v. *United States*, 275 F.3d 1056, 1060 (Fed. Cir. 2001).

[91] *Chefline Corp.* v. *United States*, 170 F. Supp. 2d, 1320, 1323 (CIT 2001).

the agency's decision was reasonable given the record as a whole, it should be upheld.

The agency's determination must also be in accordance with law.[92] The US Supreme Court established a two-step process to examine agency decisions in *Chevron*.[93] Pursuant to *Chevron*, the initial task is to determine "whether Congress has directly spoken to the precise question at issue".[94] If Congress has spoken, that is the end of the matter and the agency "must give effect to the unambiguously expressed intent of Congress".[95] If, however, the court finds that "the statute is silent or ambiguous with respect to the specific issue", the second step of *Chevron* is triggered, and the court will uphold the agency's determination if it is "based on a permissible construction of the statute".[96] The court should not impose its interpretation of a statute on the agency and should give the agency considerable deference when reviewing its interpretation of the statute. The Supreme Court recently reaffirmed this in *Eurodif*, holding that courts should defer to an administrative agency when that agency is interpreting a statute, so long as the decision is reasonable.[97]

When parties appeal to the Federal Circuit, the appellate court reviews the agency's determination by applying "anew" the standard of review applied by the CIT.[98] In other words, the Federal Circuit decides whether the agency's determination is supported by substantial evidence on the record. As for questions of law, the Federal Circuit also applies anew the same standard as the CIT; the agency determination must be in accordance with law.[99] A different standard of review applies, however, in both the CIT and the Federal Circuit for cases under 28 USC § 1581(i). Such cases are reviewed in both courts under an "arbitrary, capricious, an

---

[92] 19 USC § 1516a(b)(1).   [93] *Chevron*, 467 US, at 842–3.

[94] Ibid.   [95] Ibid.   [96] Ibid.

[97] *Eurodif*, 555 US, at 317 ("This is the very situation in which we look to an authoritative agency for a decision about the statute's scope, which is defined in cases at the statutory margin by the agency's application of it, and once the choice is made we ask only whether the Department's application was reasonable"). The Supreme Court held further that "the whole point of *Chevron* is to leave the discretion provided by the ambiguities of a statute with the implementing agency". Ibid., at 314 (quoting *Smiley* v. *Citibank*, 517 US 735, 742 (1996)).

[98] *Atlantic Sugar, Ltd.* v. *United States*, 744 F.2d 1556, 1559 (Fed. Cir. 1984). The Federal Circuit's *de novo* standard of review for findings of fact in trade remedy cases is not typical for US appellate review. Cf. *United States* v. *United States Gypsum Co.*, 333 US 364, 394 (1948) (findings of fact should not be set aside by an appellate court unless clearly erroneous); but see *Pierce* v. *Underwood*, 487 US 552, 555 (1988) (a court of appeals should review questions of law *de novo*).

[99] *NSK, Ltd.* v. *Koyo Seiko Co.*, 190 F.3d 1321, 1326 (Fed. Cir. 1999).

abuse of discretion, or otherwise not in accordance with law" standard of review.[100]

The standard of review applied in safeguard actions is extremely limited.[101] In the absence of any statutory language on standard of review, the Federal Circuit has held that "for a court to interpose [in a safeguard action], there has to be a clear misconstruction of the governing statute, a significant procedural violation, or action outside delegated authority".[102]

Finally, Article 1904(3) of the NAFTA requires NAFTA panels to apply the "standard of review" and "general legal principles" that a US court would apply in its review of a Commerce or Commission determination.[103] Thus, Chapter 19 NAFTA panels must apply the same substantial evidence or otherwise in accordance with law standard of review applied by the CIT.[104]

VII   Reviewable determinations

Most, but not all trade remedy actions undertaken by Commerce and the Commission are subject to judicial review by the CIT. Section 516A specifically identifies the anti-dumping and countervailing duty determinations that may be reviewed with subsection (a)(1) covering "Review of certain determinations" and subsection (a)(2) "Review of determinations based on record". The typical trade remedy lawsuit against the United States involves challenges to (i) a final affirmative or negative anti-dumping or countervailing duty investigation determination by Commerce, (ii) the final results of an administrative review of an order, (iii) an affirmative or negative final injury determination by the Commission, or (iv) a negative preliminary

---

[100] 5 USC § 706(2)(A). See *Conoco, Inc.* v. *United States Foreign Trade Zones Bd.*, 855 F. Supp. 1306, 1311 (CIT 1994).

[101] See *Corus Group PLC* v. *Bush*, 217 F. Supp. 1347, 1352 (CIT 2002) (*Corus Group*) (citing *Maple Leaf Fish Co.* v. *United States*, 762 F.2d 86, 89 (Fed. Cir. 1985)), aff'd *Corus Group* ("Because the Act vests the President and [Commission] with 'very broad discretion' and does not specifically provide for judicial review, the court's review is extremely limited"). In *Corus Group*, the ITC's vote was divided with respect to certain steel products, and the president imposed safeguard measures. Foreign producers challenged the ITC's determination and the president's action. The CIT granted the Government's summary judgment motion and parties appealed. The Federal Circuit dismissed the action against the president, and affirmed the CIT in all other respects, applying the *Maple Leaf* standard of review: 352 F.3d, at 1353.

[102] *Maple Leaf*, 762 F.2d, at 89.   [103] NAFTA Art. 1904(3).

[104] See 19 USC § 1516a(b)(1)(B).

determination by the Commission.[105] However, reviewable determinations also include: Commerce determinations to suspend an anti-dumping or countervailing duty investigation, Commission injurious effect determinations undertaken during suspended investigations, Commerce scope determinations, determinations by either agency pursuant to 19 USC § 3538 (section 129 of the URAA) to act consistently with adopted WTO Dispute Settlement Body (DSB) reports, and Commission injury determinations with respect to imports that were not eligible for an injury determination at the time the countervailing order was originally issued.[106]

Reviewable determinations pursuant to NAFTA are a subset of those for which federal judicial review is available. Pursuant to NAFTA Article 1904(2), a person may seek review of "a final anti-dumping or countervailing duty determination".[107] A "final determination" is defined in NAFTA as: final dumping margin and subsidy determinations by Commerce or the Commission, final injury determinations by the Commission, final results of administrative reviews of an AD or CVD order, determinations by the Commission not to review a decision based on changed circumstances, and final scope determinations by Commerce.[108]

As noted above, as a general matter, actions of the Commission and the president in safeguard matters are reviewable on procedural grounds, but not on the merits.[109] The principal safeguard laws administered by the Commission are in sections 201–4 (the global safeguard law – imports from all country sources)[110] and section 421 (imports from China) of the Trade Act of 1974.[111]

---

[105] 19 USC §§ 1516a(a)(2)(B)(i)–(iii), (a)(2)(B)(v), and (a)(1)(C) and (D).
[106] See 19 USC § 1516a(a)(2)(B)(iv), (a)(2)(B)(vi)–(viii).   [107] NAFTA Art. 1904(2).
[108] NAFTA Annex 1911.
[109] See also *Sneaker Circus, Inc. v. Carter*, 566 F.2d 396, 402 (2nd Cir. 1977) (a challenge to the mandatory procedures employed by the executive in concluding orderly marketing agreements to provide import relief for non-rubber athletic footwear is within the supervision of the federal courts, but a challenge to the substance of the agreements would be non-justiciable because it involves political questions) (interesting jurisdictional decision finding district court and not US Customs Court was proper venue); *Sneaker Circus, Inc. v. Carter*, 457 F. Supp. 771, 790 (EDNY 1978), aff'd 614 F.2d 1290 (2nd Cir. 1979) (the president's choice of the most representative period for purposes of an orderly marketing agreement is not reviewable because it was left to his discretion by Congress and is a political question).
[110] 19 USC §§ 2251–2254.
[111] 19 USC §§ 2451–2451a. The United States is a party to a number of free trade agreements that permit an FTA party, generally during a transitional period, to apply a safeguard measure against imports from the other FTA party when certain criteria are satisfied.

Article 2005 of the NAFTA provides that disputes regarding any matter arising under both the NAFTA and the GATT, any agreement negotiated thereunder, or any successor agreement, may be settled in either forum. In 1998, Mexico successfully challenged a US global safeguard action on imports of corn brooms under the dispute settlement provisions in NAFTA Chapter 20.[112] Mexico was the principal supplier of US imports of such brooms.

VIII   Applicable law

When US courts review determinations by Commerce and the Commission, their substantive analyses are governed by US law. As previously discussed, the US anti-dumping and countervailing duty statutes have been amended over the years, but the current statutes are in Title VII of the Tariff Act, as amended.[113] The most recent substantive amendments to Title VII occurred in 1994 as a consequence of the Uruguay Round Agreements which created the WTO. That year, Congress passed the URAA for the primary purpose of implementing the multilateral agreements. Specifically, through the URAA, Congress conformed existing US law to the WTO Anti-dumping (AD) and the Subsidies and Countervailing Measures (SCM) Agreements. International obligations are not US law unless and until enacted by Congress through implementing legislation, in this case the URAA. As such, the United States did not adopt the AD and SCM Agreements. Rather, the URAA expresses Congress's understanding that US laws as amended by the URAA are consistent with the AD and SCM Agreements.[114] Thus, US courts reviewing trade remedy determinations are required to apply the US statutes, which are not the AD and SCM Agreements, and in the event of a conflict, the statutes prevail.[115]

In addition to the statutes, the agencies' implementing regulations, found in Title 19 of the Code of Federal Regulations, also constitute US law, with agency actions made pursuant to the regulations subject to judicial review.[116] Precedential court opinions from the Supreme Court

---

[112] *Broom Corn Brooms*, USA-MEX-1997–2008–01, Article 2008 (30 Jan. 1998).

[113] 19 USC §§ 1671 *et seq.*

[114] See URAA Statement of Administrative Action (SAA), HR Doc. 103–316, vol. 1, at 807, 819, 846.

[115] 19 USC § 3512(a)(1).

[116] See 19 CFR Chapter II (Commission) and Chapter III (Commerce). See also *Royal Thai Government* v. *United States*, 436 F.3d 1330, 1340 (Fed. Cir. 2006) (deferring to Commerce's reasonable interpretation of its regulation).

and Federal Circuit constitute US law and are binding upon not only the agencies, but also upon the courts.[117] However, a NAFTA decision is only controlling in the case in which issued[118] and is not binding on the courts, but "may be take[n] into consideration".[119] Legislative history, as well as the administration's intent, may be relied upon by the courts reviewing agency action.[120] Finally, agency practice may also be considered by the courts.

Since the United States joined the WTO and enacted the URAA, the effect, if any, that WTO panel and Appellate Body reports – i.e. adopted by the WTO DSB – have on US courts has been a recurring issue in domestic cases.[121] Although private parties have argued that the United States must follow DSB reports, Congress[122] and the US courts consistently have held that they are not binding upon the United States. The Federal Circuit addressed this in *Corus Staal BV* v. *Department of Commerce*, holding that neither the GATT nor any of the enabling agreements such as the AD Agreement, "trump domestic legislation".[123] US statutes, the appellate court held, direct Congress and the executive branch to decide when and how to implement adverse WTO rulings.[124]

The Federal Circuit was referencing the two procedures in the URAA by which an adverse WTO report may be implemented in US domestic law. The first, in section 123 of the URAA, establishes a procedure for amending or rescinding an agency regulation or practice to implement a DSB report finding that the regulation or practice (within the meaning of US law) is

---

[117] *Strickland* v. *United States*, 423 F.3d 1335, 1338 n.3 (Fed. Cir. 2005) (citing *Bankers Trust NY. Corp.* v. *United States*, 225 F.3d 1368, 1372 (Fed. Cir. 2000)) (Federal Circuit decisions are binding upon the CIT); *Hometown Fin. Inc.* v. *United States*, 409 F.3d 1360, 1365 (Fed. Cir. 2005) (Federal Circuit is "bound to follow our own precedent as set forth by prior panels"). But see *Algoma Steel Corp.* v. *United States*, 865 F.2d 240, 243 (Fed. Cir. 1989) (no court rule suggests that the CIT's opinions are binding in other CIT cases).

[118] NAFTA Art. 1904(9).   [119] 19 USC § 1516a(b)(3).

[120] *Chevron*, 467 US, at 843–5.

[121] DSB reports are not binding on other WTO panels or WTO members not parties to the dispute in which the report is issued. See Understanding on Rules and Procedures Governing the Settlement of Disputes Art. 1, Annex 2, 33 ILM 1226, Art. 3(2), 19(1–2) (1994) (DSU).

[122] 19 USC § 3512(a)(1) ("No provision of any of the Uruguay Round Agreements, nor the application of any such provision to any person or circumstance, that is inconsistent with any law of the United States shall have effect"). Moreover, "[o]nly Congress and the Administration can decide whether to implement a WTO panel recommendation and, if so, how to implement it." SAA, *supra* note 114, at 659.

[123] *Corus Staal BV* v. *Department of Commerce*, 395 F.3d 1343, 1348 (Fed. Cir. 2005) (*Corus Staal*).

[124] Ibid., at 1349; 19 USC §§ 3533, 3538.

inconsistent with the agreements.[125] The second, in section 129, applies when a particular action by Commerce or the Commission is not in conformity with the obligations of the United States under the WTO agreements.[126] Both of these statutory procedures provide for consultation between the United States Trade Representative (USTR), an executive branch agency, Congress and relevant stakeholders before the USTR determines whether, and Commerce or the Commission determines how, to implement the DSB report.[127] The United States, similar to other WTO members, is not required to implement DSB rulings.[128] Unlike US court decisions, WTO reports are not self-executing and it is for the executive branch to decide, after proper consultation, whether a change in US law, policy or methodology is appropriate.

Findings in DSB reports are not automatically accepted under US law as "the law of nations" according to Congress and the US courts.[129] It does not "violate the law of nations" for an agency to interpret the US statute in a manner that is inconsistent with a WTO report. US courts have recognized that WTO reports have no precedential value, even within the WTO,[130] and the WTO agreements recognize that WTO members may choose not to implement reports domestically, instead accepting the consequences under the WTO.[131] Thus, if the United States ultimately determined not to implement a DSB report, the adherence of Commerce or the Commission to an interpretation of the US statute found to be inconsistent with the AD or SCM Agreements in the DSB report would not "violate" the "law of nations as understood in this country". The Federal Circuit has continually refused to hold that WTO decisions are binding upon the agencies in trade remedy cases. As instructed by Congress, it has left the decisions as to whether and how to comply with WTO reports to the political branches.[132] Once the

---

[125]   19 USC § 3533(f) and (g).   [126]   19 USC §§ 3533(f)(3), 3538(b)(1).

[127]   19 USC § 3538(b)(3) and (d).   [128]   DSU, *supra* note 121, Art. 22.

[129]   In *Arc Ecology* v. *Air Force*, 411, F.3d 1092, 1102–03 (9th Cir. 2005), the Ninth Circuit Court of Appeals held that "In Charming Betsy, the Supreme Court had to determine whether a ship could be seized for violating an American embargo against France. The Court interpreted the relevant statute so as to avoid embroiling the nation in a foreign policy dispute unforeseen by either the President or Congress". The Ninth Circuit was referring to *Murray* v. *The Charming Betsy*, 6 US 64 (1804), in which the Supreme Court held that "an Act of Congress ought never be construed to violate the law of nations if any other possible construction remains ... further than is warranted by the law of nations as *understood in this country*" (emphasis added).

[130]   *Corus Staal BV* v. *United States*, 259 F. Supp. 2d 1253, 1264 (CIT 2003).

[131]   DSU, *supra* note 121.

[132]   *Corus Staal*, 395 F.3d, at 1349 ("We give Commerce substantial deference in its administration of the statute because of the foreign policy implications of a

United States implements a DSB report, the actual implementation is treated as part of US law and is subject to judicial review.[133] In *US Steel Corp.* v. *United States*, the CIT held a WTO Appellate Body decision to be relevant where a federal agency determination implemented the DSB report.[134]

At this time, 24 CIT and Federal Circuit cases mention the WTO. More than half address the issue of WTO panel and Appellate Body reports and US law, all of which have held that WTO decisions are not binding precedent on US courts.[135] Of these, seven of the CIT cases provide that although WTO reports are not precedential, US courts may consider their persuasive reasoning.[136] However, any persuasive reasoning must be balanced against the deference owed the political branches' authority to respond to WTO reports in conducting foreign relations.

IX   Remedies

One of the most interesting aspects of the CIT's role in reviewing trade remedy determinations is that the court essentially is prohibited from directing a new outcome.[137] Rather, US law provides that an agency's decision be sustained or remanded by the CIT for further findings consistent with the law or opinion of the court.[138] The court's ability to

dumping determination. We will not attempt to perform the duties that fall within the exclusive province of the political branches"; *Koyo Seiko Co.* v. *United States*, 551 F.3d 1286, 1291 (Fed. Cir. 2008) (*Koyo Seiko*) ("The determination whether, when, and how to comply with the WTO decision ... involves delicate and subtle political judgments that are within the authority of the Executive and not the Judicial Branch").

[133] 19 USC 1516a(a)(2)(B)(vii) (section 129 determinations subject to judicial review but no comparable provision for 123 determinations). *US Steel Corp.* v. *United States*, 637 F. Supp. 2d 1199, 1212 (CIT 2009) ("The deference accorded to Commerce's interpretation is at its highest when that agency acts under ... a Congressional mandate to harmonize US practices with international obligations, particularly when it allows the Executive Branch to speak on behalf of the United States to the international community on matters of trade and commerce").

[134] *US Steel Corp.* v. *United States*, 621 F.3d 1351 (Fed. Cir. 2010).

[135] Space precludes referencing all, but see, e.g., *Koyo Seiko*, 551 F.3d, at 1290–1; *Corus Staal*, 395 F.3d, at 1348; *Adaman Seafood Co.* v. *United States*, 675 F. Supp. 2d 1363, 1373 (CIT 2010).

[136] See, e.g., *Timken Co.* v. *United States*, 240 F. Supp. 2d 1228, 1239 (CIT 2002).

[137] *Nippon Steel Corp* v. *ITC*, 345 F.3d 1379, 1381 (Fed. Cir. 2003) (*Nippon Steel*) ("Despite its express dissatisfaction with the fact-finding underlying the [agency]'s remand decision, the [CIT] abused its discretion by not returning the case to the [agency] for further consideration").

[138] 19 USC § 1516a(c)(3). *Altx* v. *United States*, 370 F.3d 1108, 1111 n.2 (Fed. Cir. 2004) ("Section 1516a limits the [CIT] to affirmances and remand orders; an outright reversal

craft a remedy is closely aligned with the standard of review, i.e. the court is not to usurp the agency's decision-making function.[139] Therefore only in "rare circumstances"[140] may the court direct an outcome. Generally, it must remand the case and await the agency's response, and either affirm or remand the case again. There is no limit to how many times a case may be remanded to an agency.

Depending upon the scope of the remand and any limitations imposed by the CIT, the agency may provide a further explanation of its findings, change its determination, and/or reopen the record and collect additional information. In Commerce's actions, a draft of the remand results is usually released to the parties for comment, with those comments addressed in the final remand results. In ITC actions, the parties are typically provided an opportunity to comment, and the Commissioners vote and issue a new determination with accompanying views explaining the Commission's reasoning. The final remand results are submitted to the CIT, and must either be sustained or remanded again.[141] After the CIT has issued its final judgment (affirming the agency's original determination or the results of remand),[142] a party may appeal to the Federal Circuit.[143]

As discussed above, the Federal Circuit reviews decisions of the CIT *de novo*, applying the same standard of review as the court below.[144] The Federal Circuit may either affirm or reverse the CIT's final judgment, and where appropriate remand the proceeding back to the CIT, which may result in a remand to the agency.

X Concluding remarks

Judicial review is so fundamental to the United States that the judiciary is established in the US Constitution. When applied to trade remedies, the processes and procedures established by the US statutes, the agencies' regulations and practices, and the courts' rules create a transparent system that is accessible to all parties affected by the anti-dumping and countervailing duty laws.

---

without remand is not contemplated by the statute"). NAFTA panels are similarly constrained: NAFTA Ch. 19, Art. 1904, para. 8.

[139] *Nippon Steel*, 345 F.3d, at 1381 ("The [CIT] ... went beyond its statutorily-assigned role to 'review'"). The CIT does have authority to enter money judgments for or against the United States, and "order any other form of relief that is appropriate in a civil action, including, but not limited to, declaratory judgments, orders of remand, injunctions, and writs of mandamus and prohibition". 28 USC 2643 (a)(1) and (c)(1).

[140] *Florida Power & Light Co. v. Lorion*, 470 US 729, 744 (1985).

[141] 19 USC § 1516a(c)(3).   [142] 19 USC § 1516a(e).   [143] 28 USC § 1295(a)(5).

[144] *PPG Indus., Inc. v. United States*, 978 F.2d 1232, 1236 (Fed. Cir. 1992).

Mexico: quasi-judicial review of trade remedy measures by NAFTA panels

JORGE MIRANDA AND JUAN CARLOS PARTIDA*

I Introduction

In this chapter, we survey the review of Mexican anti-dumping and coun-tervailing definitive determinations by bi-national panels under Chapter 19 of the North American Free Trade Agreement (hereinafter NAFTA).[1] As we explain in the chapter, such review is only quasi-judicial because bi-national panels are not fully equivalent to domestic courts. As the relevant context for discussing NAFTA panel review, we also discuss administrative appeals as the prelude to judicial appeals, as well as proper judicial appeals.

II Application of trade remedy measures under Mexican law

Until the Mexican economy was liberalized in the period from the mid-1980s to the early 1990s, including its foreign trade regime,[2] there was little need for protection against imports in the form of

---

* The opinions expressed in this chapters are ours alone and do not represent in any way the official views of King & Spalding LLP, Rubio Villegas y Asociados, or their respective clients.

[1] The panel review mechanism foreseen under Chapter 19 of the NAFTA does not apply to safeguard determinations because, under paragraph 1 of Article 802 of the NAFTA, imports originating in a NAFTA Party are generally exempted from safeguard measures applied by another NAFTA Party under Article XIX of the General Agreement on Tariffs and Trade (GATT). It is important to note that, for reasons of space, we limit our discussion to bi-national panels involving challenges of Mexican anti-dumping and countervailing measures on imports of US goods.

[2] For a comprehensive account of Mexico's trade liberalization process, see Jaime Zabludovsky, "Trade Liberalization and Macroeconomic Adjustment in Mexico", in Dwight S. Brothers and Adele E. Wick (eds), *Mexico's Search for a New Development Strategy* (Westview Press, 1990). A detailed description of Mexican trade policy prior to the trade liberalization process is presented in Bela Balassa, "Trade Policy in Mexico" 11(9) (1983) *World Development* 795–811.

trade remedy measures.[3] A legal framework allowing the conduct of trade remedy investigations was put into place in 1986. In that year, Mexico adopted its first law specifically addressing foreign trade[4] (the Regulatory Law of Article 131 of the constitution[5]) and subsequently a set of regulations governing trade remedy investigations (the Regulations Against Unfair Trade Practices).[6] In 1986, Mexico also joined the General Agreement on Tariffs and Trade (GATT) 1994 and became a signatory to the Tokyo Round Anti-Dumping Code (formally known as the Agreement on Implementation of Article VI of the General Agreement on Tariffs and Trade).[7] Given that under Mexican law international agreements are self-executing once ratified by the Senate, upon ratification the Anti-Dumping Code became domestic law.

In 1993, as part of the institutional reforms predating the NAFTA, both the Regulatory Law of Article 131 of the Constitution and the Regulations Against Unfair Trade Practices were revoked in their entirety. The former was replaced by the Foreign Trade Law[8] (hereinafter the FTL), while the latter was replaced by the Regulations to the Foreign Trade Law[9]

---

[3] By "trade remedy measures", we refer to anti-dumping, countervailing and safeguard measures.

[4] Prior to the adoption of the first foreign trade law in 1986, activities relating to foreign trade were regulated on the basis of Article 131 of the Mexican Constitution (formally known as *Constitución Política de los Estados Unidos Mexicanos*). In particular, Article 131 of the constitution provides that the Executive Branch may be authorized by Congress to increase, decrease, eliminate or institute duty rates on imports and exports, as well as to restrict or prohibit imports or exports, in cases of urgency, with a view, *inter alia*, to protecting the stability of domestic production, or any other purpose that benefits the country.

[5] *Ley Reglamentaria del Artículo 131 de la Constitución Política de los Estados Unidos Mexicanos en Materia de Comercio Exterior*, published in the *Diario Oficial de la Federación* (Mexico's *Official Gazette*) on 13 January 1986. Unless otherwise specified, legislation in Mexico becomes effective on the day following the date of publication.

[6] *Reglamento contra Prácticas Desleales de Comercio Internacional*, published in the *Official Gazette* on 25 November 1986.

[7] As is well known, as there was no "single undertaking approach" prior to the Uruguay Round, the contracting parties of the GATT were free to join individual codes of conduct as they saw fit. Thus, while Mexico became a signatory to the Tokyo Round Anti-Dumping Code, it did not join the Tokyo Round Subsidies Code (formally known as the Agreement on Interpretation and Application of Articles VI, XVI and XXII of the General Agreement on Tariffs and Trade).

[8] *Ley de Comercio Exterior*, published in the *Official Gazette* on 27 July 1993, although it did not become effective until 1 January 1994. The FTL was amended on 22 December 1993, 13 March 2003, 24 January 2006 and 21 December 2006.

[9] *Reglamento de la Ley de Comercio Exterior*, published in the *Official Gazette* on 30 December 1993. The Regulations were amended on 29 December 2000.

(hereinafter the Regulations). According to Article 85 of the FTL, where it is silent as regards a procedural matter, Mexican trade remedy proceedings should be governed, where applicable, by the Fiscal Code.[10] As a matter of practice, where both the FTL and the Fiscal Code are silent as regards a procedural matter, the Regulations to the Fiscal Code[11] and the Federal Code on Civil Procedure[12] are followed.[13] The constitution, by implication, is also part of Mexican trade remedy legislation. Although the Federal Law on Administrative Litigation[14] is sometimes referred to as part of Mexican trade remedies legislation, formally speaking such law only governs appeals of trade remedy actions filed before the Federal Tribunal on Tax and Administrative Matters (hereinafter the Tax Court).[15]

The Senate ratified the Uruguay Round package on 13 July 1994 and on 30 December 1994 all of the resulting agreements (including GATT 1994, the Anti-dumping (AD) Agreement,[16] the Agreement on Subsidies and Countervailing Measures,[17] the Agreement on Safeguards and the Agreement on Agriculture) were published in the *Official Gazette*. In addition, the "transitional safeguard" under paragraph 16 of China's Protocol of Accession was published on 21 April 2005. The corresponding regulations were published on 23 August 2005. In addition, there are a number of regional trade and investment treaties signed by Mexico (including the NAFTA, first and foremost) that feature provisions on

---

[10] *Código Fiscal de la Federación*, published in the *Official Gazette* on 31 December 1981, as amended.

[11] *Reglamento del Código Fiscal de la Federación*, published in the *Official Gazette* on 7 December 2009, as amended.

[12] *Código Federal de Procedimientos Civiles*, published in the *Official Gazette* on 24 February 1943, as amended.

[13] See, for example, Preliminary Determination, *Anti-dumping Investigation on Coaxial Cables from China*, *Official Gazette*, 30 December 2011, para. 81.

[14] *Ley Federal de Procedimiento Contencioso Administrativo*, published in the *Official Gazette* on 1 December 2005, although it did not become effective until 1 January 2006. Portions of this law replaced Title VI of the Fiscal Code (to which explicit reference is made under Chapter 19 of the NAFTA).

[15] *Tribunal Federal de Justicia Fiscal y Administrativa*. The statute instituting this tribunal is the *Ley Orgánica del Tribunal de Justicia Fiscal y Administrativa*, published in the *Official Gazette* on 6 December 2007.

[16] Formally known as the Agreement on Implementation of Article VI of the General Agreement on Tariffs and Trade 1994 and commonly referred to by the acronym "AD Agreement".

[17] Commonly referred to by the acronym "SCM Agreement".

trade remedy proceedings. Such provisions are also part of the Mexican trade remedies legislation.[18]

Under Mexican law, the Ministry of the Economy (Economía, previously known as the Ministry of Industrial Development and Trade, or SECOFI) serves as the investigating authority for anti-dumping, countervailing and safeguard proceedings and, in the case of anti-dumping and countervailing proceedings, is responsible for conducting the aspects of investigations relating to dumping, subsidization and injury.[19] Over the years, the specific administrative branch within Economía/ SECOFI directly responsible for the conduct of trade remedy proceedings has grown from a small office within a general directorate dealing with a variety of foreign trade matters to a separate general directorate, and then to an independent trade remedies unit (formally known as *Unidad de Prácticas Comerciales Internacionales*, or UPCI) reporting directly to an under-secretary. Although Economía is responsible for initiation, the preliminary determination, and the final determination, it has to submit all draft final determinations to the Foreign Trade Commission (*Comisión de Comercio Exterior*, or COCEX) and obtain the Commission's opinion.[20] COCEX is an inter-ministerial body whose membership includes Banco de México (the Central Bank), the Ministry of Finance and the Competition Commission, which traditionally have been opposed to all sorts of trade remedy protection. However, as COCEX's opinion is not actually binding upon Economía, any objections raised by Banco de México, Finance and the Competition Commission cannot prevent Economía from issuing a final determination as it sees fit.

The first Mexican trade remedy case was an anti-dumping case filed in 1986 against imports of caustic soda from the United States. During the period 1987–2011, Mexico conducted 190 anti-dumping investigations, 14 countervailing investigations, and four safeguard investigations.[21] Exports originating in 54 countries have been subject to investigation, although the United States, China and Brazil have been the exporting countries most frequently targeted.[22]

---

[18] A list of the treaties involved and their corresponding dates of publication can be found in *Sistema Mexicano de Defensa contra Prácticas Desleales de Comercio Internacional y Salvaguardias: Legislación Nacional e Internacional*, published by the Ministry of the Economy in 2006.

[19] Thus, unlike its NAFTA partners, Mexico adopted a unitary rather than a bifurcated approach to the conduct of unfair trade investigations.

[20] Article 58 of the FTL.   [21] UPCIPEDIA Bulletin No 15, 2011.   [22] Ibid.

III   Administrative appeal (*recurso de revocación*)

Articles 94–8 of the FTL provide for the administrative appeal of determinations in trade remedy proceedings. Any interested party may file the appeal. In particular, according to Article 94, affirmative final determinations imposing definitive measures, in addition to negative preliminary and final determinations, may be subject to an administrative appeal. Article 94 also foresees the mechanism of administrative appeal for final determinations concerning annual reviews, sunset reviews, and anti-circumvention proceedings. Administrative appeal is formally known as *recurso de revocación*, or "appeal for revocation", which is a misnomer because, according to Article 95 of the FTL, as a result of the appeal the challenged determination may not only be revoked or confirmed, but also modified. Thus, a more apt name for administrative appeal would have been *recurso de reconsideración*, or "appeal for reconsideration".

Economía (UPCI) itself hears the administrative appeal. Unsurprisingly, in the overwhelming majority of cases the outcome of the administrative appeal has been the confirmation of the findings in the final determination. One of the few cases where the investigating authority reversed itself involved the administrative appeal filed by Conagra, Inc. and Monfort Food Distribution Company regarding the final determination in *Beef from the United States*.[23] In its determination concerning this administrative appeal, Economía conceded that it had improperly rejected the information submitted by these two companies, and recalculated the dumping margins and anti-dumping duty rates based upon the information concerned.[24]

A key problem is that the FTL does not outline proceedings for the administrative appeal, simply stating that it should be conducted by reference to the Fiscal Code, which has resulted in all administrative appeals being held behind closed doors. In fact, parties not pursuing an administrative appeal only become aware that Economía has had such appeal in its hands when the corresponding determination is published. In any event, transposing the deadlines set out in the Fiscal Code, a request for administrative appeal must be filed within 45 business days from the date the determination challenged was notified,[25] and

---

[23] Final determination concerning the administrative appeal filed by Conagra, Inc., *inter alia*, *Official Gazette*, 10 October 2000.

[24] Ibid., paras. 19 and 94.

[25] Article 121 of the Fiscal Code. According to paragraph III of Article 59 of the FTL, final determinations must be notified to all known interested parties subsequent to publication.

Economía is required to issue its determination on the administrative appeal within three months from filing.[26] If Economía fails to issue its determination within this time frame, it is understood that the findings in the challenged determination have been confirmed.[27] Notably, Article 95 of the FTL provides that challenges of trade remedy determinations before the Tax Court are contingent upon conclusion of the administrative appeal. Article 95 further provides that determinations concerning administrative appeals can also be challenged before the Tax Court.

According to Article 97 of the FTL, interested parties that have recourse to "alternative dispute settlement mechanisms" (regarding trade remedy actions) adopted in international trade treaties signed by Mexico cannot pursue administrative appeals, or appeals before the Tax Court. Article 97 also provides that those interested parties may not pursue administrative appeals, or appeals before the Tax Court against remand determinations arising from these mechanisms, and that such remand determinations are to be considered conclusive. It is interesting to note that in a recent dispute involving Economía's final determination in its joint annual and sunset review on *Stearic Acid from the United States*, the exporter at issue filed an administrative appeal, whereas the domestic producer sought a NAFTA panel. Apparently, this dual track is consistent with Article 97 of the FTL, since neither party pursued both an administrative appeal and a NAFTA panel.[28] Importantly, dispute settlement under the Dispute Settlement Understanding (hereinafter DSU) of the World Trade Organization (hereinafter WTO) does not fall under the scope of Article 97 of the FTL, given that it does not constitute an alternative dispute settlement mechanism for interested parties (since WTO litigation is only available to WTO members).

Article 98 of the FTL provides that, where a treaty signed by Mexico includes an alternative dispute settlement mechanism, the deadline for filing the administrative appeal does not start to run until the deadline for triggering such mechanism has lapsed. Article 98 further provides that a party pursuing an administrative appeal in this context additionally has to comply with all relevant formalities foreseen in the treaty at issue.

---

[26] Article 131 of the Fiscal Code.   [27] Ibid.

[28] However, a judicial appeal could not follow in the tracks of the administrative appeal concerned because, according to paragraph 11 of Article 1904 of the NAFTA, recourse to a bi-national panel forecloses judicial review.

IV   Appeals under the WTO dispute settlement mechanism

As the WTO is an intergovernmental organization, private parties do not have recourse to its dispute settlement mechanism.[29] For the purposes of our chapter, it is instructive briefly to recall three particular features of WTO dispute settlement.

1   Standard of review of WTO panels

The standard of review of WTO panels is set out in Article 11 of the DSU. However, disputes concerning anti-dumping measures are subject to a special standard of review established under Article 17.6 of the AD Agreement. Accordingly, WTO panels reviewing trade remedy measures other than anti-dumping, are tasked with assessing objectively the facts involved and with verifying compliance of the challenged measures with the relevant "covered Agreements" (in the context of the specific claims raised by the complainant). By contrast, the standard of review applicable to WTO panels reviewing anti-dumping measures is far more specific, at least in theory; they can overturn an anti-dumping measure only if they find that the investigating authority's establishment of the facts was not proper, or where the investigating authority's evaluation of those facts was not unbiased and objective. Additionally, where a provision of the AD Agreement admits more than one interpretation, WTO panels reviewing an anti-dumping measure cannot overturn such measure if they conclude that it was based on a permissible interpretation of the provision at issue.[30] While there is significant debate as to the degree

---

[29] As a matter of practice, however, they do so indirectly, because a member is unlikely to bring a dispute against another member unless an affected private party (e.g. an exporter) pushes the national government of that member into action.

[30] Panels and the AB have rarely found that a provision in the AD Agreement admits more than one interpretation. The AB report in *US–Hot Rolled* is one of those few cases. In particular, in that case, the AB upheld the practice by the US Department of Commerce to infer the home market price to unrelated parties on the basis of the resale price to the first unrelated customer, although Article 2.1 of the AD Agreement recognizes this approach explicitly only for purposes of determining export prices to unrelated customers. See Appellate Body Report, *United States – Anti-dumping Measures on Certain Hot-Rolled Steel Products from Japan*, WT/DS184/AB/R, adopted 23 August 2001, para. 172: "we find that the reliance by USDOC on downstream sales to calculate normal value rested upon an interpretation of Article 2.1 of the *Anti-Dumping Agreement* that is, in principle, 'permissible', following application of the rules of treaty interpretation in the Vienna Convention".

to which the standard of review actually applied by WTO panels reviewing anti-dumping measures has differed in fact from the general standard of review, it is clear that WTO panels, irrespective of their jurisdiction, are subject in principle to a relatively narrow standard of review. By contrast, as we will discuss below, the first panels under Chapter 19 of the NAFTA reviewing Mexican trade remedy measures had no reservations in interpreting the standard of review to which they are subject in an expansive manner that openly went well beyond the treaty text.

Another feature of the WTO dispute settlement process worth noting for purposes of comparison with judicial review and quasi-judicial NAFTA review in Mexico, is that under the DSU there is no need to demonstrate that a violation of WTO rules has an adverse economic impact upon the complainant.[31]

2   Appellate review

WTO panel reports, unlike NAFTA panel reports, may be appealed. Notably, Article 17.6 of the DSU provides that appeals before the WTO's Appellate Body (hereinafter AB) shall be limited to "issues of law covered in the panel report and legal interpretations developed by the panel".

3   Powers of WTO panels and the AB

Under Article 19.1 of the DSU, neither panels nor the AB have the power to vacate a trade remedy measure (or, for that matter, any trade measure by a member). All they can do is recommend, through the WTO Dispute Settlement Body (or DSB), that the member concerned brings its measure into conformity with the findings in the relevant reports. Notably, the power that panels and the AB have under Article 19.1 of the DSU to suggest specific ways in which implementation should take place is rarely exercised. In practice, trade remedy measures are brought into conformity by issuing a re-determination purportedly remedying the aspects of the original determination that were found not to be in compliance with WTO rules.

---

[31] In fact, Article 3.8 of the DSU provides that: "[i]n cases where there is an infringement of the obligations assumed under a covered agreement, the action is considered *prima facie* to constitute a case of nullification or impairment".

V   Appeals before domestic courts

1   Appeals on constitutional grounds (juicio de amparo)

A Mexican trade remedy measure may be challenged on the ground that the process leading to its application involved the violation of a provision in the constitution. For instance, as will be discussed in greater detail below in section VI, in the mid- to late 1990s many anti-dumping measures were challenged because they allegedly breached Article 16 of the constitution, which provides that no individual may be harassed as regards their person, place of residence, documentation or properties absent a written writ issued by a competent authority setting out the legal reasons justifying the action involved. In particular, the complainants argued that situations such as the receipt of notifications and the hosting of verifications constituted "nuisances", and that the officers who had sent the notifications concerned and conducted the verifications at issue had not been properly appointed. Thus, according to the complainants, the imposition of the challenged anti-dumping duties was in violation of Article 16 of the constitution. The appeal of a trade remedy measure on the ground that in the process leading to its application a constitutional provision was violated takes place through a *juicio de amparo*,[32] which is governed by the Ley de Amparo[33] and heard by a District Court. Decisions by a District Court in a *juicio de amparo* may be appealed, before either a Circuit Court or the Supreme Court, depending upon the circumstances involved.[34]

If an *amparo* is granted, "things revert to their state prior to the violation involved".[35] This implies that, if a constitutional provision was violated in

[32] The term *amparo* derives from the Spanish verb *amparar* meaning "to protect" (the rights of an individual). The *juicio de amparo* also has other modalities, one of which is equivalent to a *habeas corpus*. In addition, through a *juicio de amparo* it is possible to challenge on constitutional grounds not only administrative decisions (such as the imposition of trade remedy measures), but also judicial decisions and legislation. See "Amparo", in *Diccionario Jurídico Mexicano*, (Editorial Porrúa, S.A., 2009). More specifically, Mexican law distinguishes between "amparo directo" and "amparo indirecto". It is the "amparo indirecto" that is lodged before a District Court. However, the "amparo indirecto" requires a showing that an aspect of the law at issue is unconstitutional. By contrast, the "amparo directo" is, rather, a legal remedy of last resort based on the allegation that in the conduct of an administrative proceeding, certain constitutional rights were breached (even if the proceeding involved otherwise complied with the law).

[33] *Ley de Amparo, Reglamentaria de los Artículos 103 y 107 de la Constitución Política de los Estados Unidos Mexicanos*, published in the *Official Gazette* on 10 January 1936, as amended.

[34] See Articles 85 and 84, respectively, of the Amparo Law.

[35] Article 80 of the Amparo Law.

the course of a trade remedy proceeding, all of the steps subsequent to the violation, including the application of the resulting measure, become null and void. However, as will be discussed below in section VII.10, the investigating authority arguably remains free to reinstate the proceeding concerned as of the step prior to the violation, to repeat that step avoiding the violation at issue, and go on to complete the investigation. It is also important to underscore that, if an amparo is granted, the benefits thereof are limited to the complainants and not extended to non-complainants.[36]

2   Appeals on grounds other than constitutional grounds (juicio de nulidad)

Appeals on grounds other than constitutional grounds are heard by the Tax Court and are known as *juicios de nulidad* (or, appeal for annulment). Article 1 of the statute instituting the Tax Court characterizes it as a tribunal for administrative litigation and therefore makes it clear that the Tax Court lacks legal authority to hear appeals raising constitutional issues.[37] Decisions by the Tax Court are not final and may be appealed before a Circuit Court.[38]

2.1   Standard of review of the Tax Court

The standard of review of the Tax Court is set forth in Article 51 of the Federal Law on Administrative Litigation.[39] In particular, according to Article 51, an administrative decision is illegal in event of any of the following five circumstances.

(1) The official who issued, ordered or conducted the proceeding on which the challenged decision is based is (legally) incompetent.

(2) Omission of the formalities required by the law, provided that this has prejudiced the complainant and has had an effect upon the challenged decision.

(3) Procedural errors, provided they have prejudiced the complainant and have had an effect upon the challenged decision.

---

[36] Article 76 of the Amparo Law. See, for instance, the notice published in the *Official Gazette* on 13 December 2005, revoking anti-dumping duties on imports of US bond paper exported by International Paper Company.

[37] See Article 1 of the *Ley Orgánica del Tribunal de Justicia Fiscal y Administrativa* ("[E]l Tribunal Federal de Justicia Fiscal y Administrativa es un tribunal de lo contencioso-administrativo ...").

[38] Article 63 of the Federal Law on Administrative Litigation.

[39] Article 51 of the Federal Law on Administrative Litigation corresponds to Article 238 of the Fiscal Code which, as noted previously, was revoked in 2006.

(4) If the facts on which the challenged decision is based did not take place, were different, or were appreciated incorrectly, or where the challenged decision was issued contrary to or disregarding the relevant provisions.
(5) When a decision issued pursuant to discretionary powers is inconsistent with the purposes for which the law grants such powers.

The first three grounds described in Article 51 for declaring an administrative decision illegal are procedural in nature, whereas the remaining two are substantive. Importantly, ground (4) correlates with the WTO standard of review set out in Article 11 of the DSU and Article 17.6 of the AD Agreement, in the sense that the WTO standard of review also makes reference to the assessment (i.e. the establishment and evaluation) of the relevant facts and to consistency with the relevant legal provisions.

It is worth noting that, under the standard of review set out in Article 51, the Tax Court cannot declare a trade remedy measure illegal on account that Economía committed procedural errors, such as missing the deadlines for the different investigative stages provided for in both the AD Agreement and the FTL, unless the complainant can show that such errors had an impact upon the outcome of the challenged decision. As this requirement is difficult to satisfy, in practice Economía is free to conduct its trade remedy proceedings with great flexibility time-wise and without much concern as to whether the deadlines contemplated in the legislation are being met. By contrast, as the WTO standard of review does not require it to be shown that any violations of WTO rules, including procedural errors, have had an effect upon the outcome of a challenged decision, procedural errors, such as missing deadlines, do constitute grounds for a finding of inconsistency with WTO rules.[40]

2.2 Powers of the Tax Court

The powers of the Tax Court are set forth in Article 52 of the Federal Law on Administrative Litigation.[41] In particular, according to Article 52, the Tax Court may:

(i) confirm the challenged decision;
(ii) vacate the challenged decision;

---

[40] In fact, the WTO panel in *Mexico–Olive Oil* found that Mexico had violated Article 11.1 of the SCM Agreement because it took in excess of 18 months to complete the investigation. See Panel Report, *Mexico – Definitive Countervailing Measures on Olive Oil from the European Communities*, WT/DS341/R, adopted 21 October 2088, para. 8.1(a).

[41] Article 52 of the Federal Law on Administrative Litigation corresponds to Article 239 of the Fiscal Code, revoked in 2006.

(iii) vacate the challenged decision in certain aspects, giving precise instructions as to the manner in which the authority should comply and reinstating the proceeding, where applicable, from the time the violation involved took place;

(iv) in the event of either one of the violations referred to under paragraphs (ii) and (iii) of Article 51 (omission of the formalities required by law, and procedural errors, respectively), vacate the challenged decision so that the proceeding is reinstated or a new decision is issued; in other cases, instructions may be given as to the manner in which the authority should comply.

Thus, unlike WTO panels, the Tax Court has the power to vacate the entirety of a Mexican trade remedy determination.[42] Points (iii) and (iv) of Article 52 also foresee partial annulments, limited to particular aspects of a determination. In particular, point (iv) refers to partial annulments on account of procedural deficiencies relating specifically to the omission of the formalities required by law and procedural errors. Implicitly, point (iii) refers to partial annulments by reason of other procedural deficiencies (i.e. the incompetence of the officials involved) as well as by reason of substantive deficiencies. The architecture of points (iii) and (iv) of Article 52 is not ideal, however. While both provisions make reference to the reinstatement of certain aspects of a proceeding, which would normally lead to a remand determination reflecting the investigating authority's new findings, only point (iv) expressly requires the issuance of a remand determination.[43]

VI   Quasi-judicial review by NAFTA panels

1   General aspects of NAFTA panel review

Article 1904 of the NAFTA institutes a review mechanism of definitive anti-dumping and countervailing determinations by a NAFTA

---

[42] For example, on 15 April 2010, a re-determination was published in the *Official Gazette*, whereby Economía vacated the anti-dumping duties on paper sacks from Brazil exported by Kablin SA, pursuant to a decision by the Tax Court (which found that the verification of the questionnaire response had been ordered by an official who had not been properly appointed).

[43] For example, on 30 May 2006, Economía issued a re-determination pursuant to a ruling by the Tax Court that it had improperly rejected an administrative appeal filed by Distribuidora Liverpool, SA de CV, *inter alia*, concerning Economía's final determination in the sunset review of the anti-dumping duties on apparel from China.

Party[44] concerning imports originating in another NAFTA Party.[45] In particular, paragraph 1 of Article 1904 provides that "each Party shall replace judicial review of final anti-dumping and countervailing duty determinations with bi-national panel review".[46] Paragraph 1 is important not only for what it says, but also for what it does *not* say. In particular, it does not say that NAFTA panel review shall be fully equivalent to judicial review, or that NAFTA panels shall have the same jurisdiction, standard of review and powers as the domestic court that would otherwise have reviewed final anti-dumping and counter-vailing determinations. It only requires substituting NAFTA panel review, whatever its features, for judicial review in the event that the NAFTA dispute settlement mechanism is triggered.[47]

Paragraph 2 of Article 1904 sets out the mandate of NAFTA panels as follows:

> An involved Party may request that a panel review, based on the administrative record, a final antidumping or countervailing duty determination of a competent investigating authority of an importing Party to determine whether such determination was in accordance with the anti-dumping or countervailing duty law of the importing Party.

Paragraph 2 goes on to define what is to be understood as the relevant law of the importing Party:

> [T]he antidumping or countervailing duty law consists of the relevant statutes, legislative history, regulations, administrative practice and judicial precedents, to the extent that a court of the importing Party would rely on such materials in reviewing a final determination of the competent investigating authority.

Paragraph 3 of Article 1904 provides that, in discharging their functions, NAFTA panels:

---

[44] Meaning a signatory to the NAFTA, as opposed to an individual company with a commercial interest in the application (or not) of anti-dumping and countervailing duties.

[45] According to paragraph 1 of Article 1901, "Article 1904 applies only with respect to goods that the competent investigating authority of the importing Party, applying the importing Party's anti-dumping and countervailing duty law to the facts of a specific case, determines are goods of another Party."

[46] Unlike WTO panels, NAFTA panels are composed of five individuals (a majority of whom must be lawyers). Such individuals must be nationals of the two NAFTA Parties involved in the dispute at issue. See Annex 1901.2 of the NAFTA.

[47] Paragraph 12 of Article 1904 provides that Article 1904 does not apply where neither involved party seeks panel review of a final determination.

> shall apply *the standard of review* set out in Annex 1911 and *the general legal principles* that a court of the importing Party otherwise would apply to a review of a determination of the competent investing authority (emphasis added).

The definition of the term "standard of review" in Annex 1911 is reproduced below. According to Article 1911, the term "general legal principles" specifically "includes principles such as standing, due process, rules of statutory construction, mootness and exhaustion of administrative remedies".

Importantly, the term "final determination" (used in paragraph 1 of Article 1904 and defined differently for each NAFTA Party in Annex 1911) is limited in the case of Mexico to three specific proceedings: final determinations in anti-dumping and countervailing duty investigations; final determinations in annual administrative reviews; and final determinations in scope reviews. Given that, at the time the NAFTA was signed, the FTL already provided for sunset reviews and anti-circumvention proceedings, it is clear that NAFTA panels, in the case of Mexico, do not have jurisdiction over final determinations in either sunset reviews or anti-circumvention investigations. By contrast, under Article 51 of the Federal Law on Administrative Litigation (and its predecessor provision, Article 238 of the Fiscal Code), the Tax Court may review administrative decisions in general, which implies that it has jurisdiction to review all final determinations involving anti-dumping and countervailing proceedings, including those referring to sunset reviews and countervailing investigations. Thus, it is indisputable that NAFTA panels have a narrower jurisdiction than the Tax Court.

As noted above, if a WTO panel decision is adverse to the defendant, it should heed the recommendations of the DSB that it bring its measure into conformity. However, whether or not compliance actually takes place is entirely up to the defendant (although in the event of lack of compliance the complainant could gain authorization from the DSB to apply countermeasures). By contrast, paragraph 9 of Article 1904 provides that NAFTA panel decisions are binding: "[t]he decision of a panel under this Article shall be binding on the involved Parties with respect to the particular matter between the Parties that is before the panel". Another key distinction between WTO panels and NAFTA panels is that, as the NAFTA dispute settlement mechanism does not incorporate an appeal stage, NAFTA panel decisions cannot be appealed. The absence of an appeal mechanism also distinguishes NAFTA panel review from review by the Fiscal Court since, as explained above, decisions by the Fiscal Court may be appealed before either a District Court or the Supreme Court, depending upon the circumstances involved.

2 Standard of review of NAFTA panels

Annex 1911 provides NAFTA Party-specific definitions of the term "standard of review". In the case of Mexico, "standard of review" means:

> [T]he standard set out in Article 238 of the *Federal Fiscal Code* ("Código Fiscal de la Federación"), or any successor statutes, based solely on the administrative record.

As noted above, Article 238 of the Fiscal Code, subsequently superseded by Article 51 of the Federal Law on Administrative Litigation, sets out the standard of review for the Tax Court. Thus, NAFTA panels and the Tax Court do share a commonality in terms of the standard of review.

3 Powers of NAFTA panels

Paragraph 8 of Article 1904 sets out the powers of NAFTA panels as follows: "the panel may uphold a final determination, or remand it for action not inconsistent with the panel decision".

Article 1911 defines the term "remand" as a "referral back for a determination not inconsistent with the panel or committee decision". Thus, according to paragraph 8 of Article 1904, if a panel does not uphold a final determination, all it can do is refer it back to the investigating authority for the authority to issue a re-determination that is not contrary to the panel's decision. Notably, whereas NAFTA panels and the Tax Court share the same standard of review, because the definition of the standard of review for NAFTA panels provided in Annex 1911 makes reference to the standard of review to which the Tax Court is also subject, paragraph 8 of Article 1904 setting out the powers of NAFTA panels does not correlate at all with Article 52 of the Federal Law on Administrative Litigation, nor with its predecessor provision, Article 239 of the Fiscal Code. As explained above, under Article 52 of the Federal Law on Administrative Litigation, the Tax Court may confirm the decision challenged in its entirety, or vacate it in its entirety or in part, that is, with respect to only certain aspects thereof. By contrast, under paragraph 8 of Article 1904, the two avenues available to NAFTA panels are to confirm the challenged decision as a whole, or to remand it to the investigating authority so that it rectifies the decision in light of the panel's findings and issues a re-determination. There is a question as to whether a NAFTA panel could issue a remand instructing the investigating authority to vacate the challenged measure in its re-determination. We think not. If the drafters of the NAFTA had intended to grant NAFTA panels the power to vacate a challenged measure, albeit indirectly, they would have made specific reference in paragraph 8 of Article 1904 to Article 239 of the Fiscal Code which confers such power.[48]

To sum up, NAFTA panel review and judicial review are not equiv-alent. The reason for this distinction is that, although NAFTA panels and the Tax Court share the same standard of review, NAFTA panels have a narrower jurisdiction and weaker powers. In addition, unlike decisions by the Tax Court, NAFTA panel decisions cannot be appealed. Accordingly, NAFTA panel review is only a partial analogue to judicial review and, therefore, can best be described as quasi-judicial in nature.

VII   An assessment of NAFTA panel review

As decisions by District Courts and the Tax Court (irrespective of their subject matter) are only available to the parties that participated in the proceeding, we were unable to examine them in order to provide an overview of how appeals of trade remedy measures before domestic courts have worked in practice.[49] Moreover, the re-determinations issued by Economía pursuant to such court decisions are frequently cryptic as to the grounds underlying them (perhaps intended as a way to avoid a ripple effect). It is for these reasons that we have limited our overview to decisions by NAFTA panels that are publicly available.

1   Plate in Coils (1995)

Plate in Coils[50] was the first bi-national panel under Chapter 19 of the NAFTA. This was a split decision. The majority, composed of three panellists, found that the challenged anti-dumping determination was

---

[48] Of course, there might be cases where the findings of a NAFTA panel are so burdensome that the investigating authority is unable to implement the challenged measure in a manner not contrary to such findings, and ends up revoking the measure concerned. In this case, however, the NAFTA panel would not have instructed the investigating authority to take such action, consistent with its powers under paragraph 8 of Article 1904.

[49] The *Semanario Judicial de la Federación* publishes summaries of decisions, but the decisions included are only those that constitute jurisprudence under Mexican law.

[50] MEX-94-1904-02.

illegal in terms both of Article 16 of the constitution and paragraph I of Article 238 of the Fiscal Code, because some of the officials who had been involved in the investigation were not legally competent (as they had not been properly appointed).[51] The majority then went on to issue a remand instructing the investigating authority to revoke anti-dumping duties against the two US complainants. The majority reached its decision based on what it thought was a requisite analogy between NAFTA panels and the Tax Court, without feeling constrained by the strictures of the treaty text and domestic legislation.

The panel chastised the NAFTA drafters for having neglected to make an explicit reference to the constitution as a source of law relevant for NAFTA panel review.[52] But the point was not whether the constitution was part of Mexico's anti-dumping and countervailing duty law within the meaning of paragraph 2 of Article 1904 – obviously, it was – it was whether the panel was the proper venue for hearing a claim regarding the alleged violation of Article 16 of the Constitution. It was not, since Article 1 of the statute instituting the Tax Court made it clear that the court only dealt with matters relating to administrative litigation which meant, by implication, that the court lacked the legal authority to hear claims relating to constitutional issues.

As noted above, paragraph I of Article 238 of the Fiscal Code (the predecessor provision to Article 51 of the Federal Law on Administrative Litigation) provided that a final determination is illegal if "the official who issued, ordered or conducted the proceeding on which the challenged decision is based is incompetent". Importantly, the panel adopted a reading of this provision that was at odds with its ordinary meaning. In particular, it interpreted the term "proceeding" as if it meant "proceedings" in the plural, and subsequently interpreted "proceedings" to mean each of the intervening steps in the investigation (the issuance of notifications and the conduct of verifications, for instance) that led to the application of the challenged duties. As the panel did not even take notice that its reading of paragraph I of Article 238 was inconsistent with the actual wording of this provision, it did not explain why it

---

[51] It is interesting to note that the issue of improper appointments arose purely on account of Mexico's archaic bureaucratic structures. As higher grade professional positions were tied to seemingly managerial appointments in specific offices, irrespective of whether such offices existed only in theory and were actually meaningless, professional staff whose theoretical offices had not been included in the ministry's official organizational chart as at the time of the investigations concerned, arguably had not been properly appointed. Seldom has such a substantively inane issue generated so much litigation.

[52] *Plate in Coils*, Panel Report, p. 18 (in the Spanish original).

thought that it was appropriate to substitute "proceedings" for "proceeding", nor why each of the intervening steps in the investigation qualified as a separate "proceeding" (the issuance of a notification, for example, was most definitively not an individual "proceeding"). The panel then concluded that since, in its view, some of the officials who had been involved in certain investigative steps ("proceedings", in the panel's view) had not been properly appointed, the challenged determination was illegal in terms of paragraph I of Article 238 of the Fiscal Code. Interestingly, if the panel had adopted a reading of paragraph I of Article 238 based on the ordinary meaning of the terms therein, it would never have reached such a conclusion. In particular, the official who had issued, ordered or conducted the proceeding had been the Secretary of the then Ministry of Commerce and Industrial Development (the predecessor to Economía). This was evident, in that all of the corresponding notices (the notice of initiation, for instance) had been signed by the secretary himself. It was unquestionable that the secretary had the legal authority to do so because, according to Article 5 of the FTL, his ministry was responsible for trade remedy investigations.

Finally, the panel reasoned that the NAFTA drafters did not intend to exclude Article 239 of the Fiscal Code (which allowed the Tax Court to vacate administrative decisions) from the standard of review and expanded it to include such provision.[53] The panel used this as legal cover to justify issuing a remand instructing the investigating authority to revoke the challenged measure as regards the two complainants. One obvious problem with this approach is that it substituted what the panellists thought were the intentions of the NAFTA drafters for the actual treaty text. But this was a lesser problem. The more serious problem was that, incredibly, the panellists mistook the panel's standard of review for the powers granted to the panel. Needless to say, the failure to understand such a crucial distinction made it easier for the panel to adopt its legal theory that Article 239 was a lost sibling to Article 238.

In sum, to say that the flaws of the majority opinion in *Plate in Coils* were a teething problem of the NAFTA dispute settlement mechanism is an understatement. The findings by the majority in the *Plate in Coils* panel are much more in the way of an abomination. The minority in the panel issued a dissenting opinion, concluding that the final determination was not illegal, because it had found that the officials who had participated in the investigation had been properly appointed. It went

---

[53] Ibid., p. 27 (in the Spanish original).

on to examine the substantive claims involved and concluded that, if its views had prevailed, it would have issued a remand instructing the investigating authority to clarify its calculation of freight expenses, and reconsider its injury determination without considering a consultant's report to which the complainants had not had access.

2   Polystyrene *(1996)*

Polystyrene[54] was a split decision at several levels. However, all five panellists agreed that the challenged anti-dumping determination was not illegal in terms of paragraph I of Article 238 of the Fiscal Code because the official who had issued, ordered and conducted the proceeding leading to such determination had been the secretary of the ministry responsible under Mexican law for handling trade remedy investigations.[55] In addition, the majority of the panel upheld the challenged determination with respect to all other aspects of the dispute. For instance, the majority found that the investigating authority had discretionary authority under Mexican law (including the Regulatory Law of Article 131 of the constitution, subsequently superseded by the FTL) to assess the representativeness of domestic sales in the exporting country in order to establish whether such sales were comparable to export sales and thus an appropriate basis for normal value, as well as to apply a test for such purposes.[56] Conversely, one panellist found that the investigating authority's application of its test for representativeness had been defective, because it had neglected to inform the complainant about the specific test involved and that the complainant's domestic sales had been rejected as a result of having failed the test.[57] Accordingly, this panellist found that the challenged determination was illegal in terms of

---

[54] MEX-94-1904-03.

[55] See *Polystyrene*, Panel Report, pp. 64-7 (in the Spanish original), for the majority opinion (arrived at by three panellists) on the issue of legal competence. The other two panellists concurred with the majority opinion regarding this particular issue.

[56] See *Polystyrene*, Panel Report, pp. 26-31 (in the Spanish original). One should recall in this connection that, at the time the investigation concerned took place, the AD Agreement, which is self-executing under Mexican law and institutes a requirement to examine the sufficiency of domestic sales in terms of quantity, had not yet been adopted.

[57] Conversely, in the view of the investigating authority, the complainant should have known about the specific test involved and the consequences of failing it, given that the test was part of the investigating authority's practice and the questionnaire instructed respondents to report export sales to a third market in the event that home market sales failed the test. See *Polystyrene*, Panel Report, pp. xxi and xxii.

paragraph V of Article 238 of the Fiscal Code (declaring illegal any decisions issued pursuant to discretionary powers which are inconsistent with the purposes for which the law grants such powers).[58]

3   Coated Flat Steels (1996)

In Coated Flat Steels,[59] the panel found that, with respect to one of the complainants, the challenged anti-dumping determination was illegal in terms of paragraph I of Article 238 of the Fiscal Code, because the official who had participated in certain steps of the investigation concerning that complainant was legally incompetent, since he had not been properly appointed. The panel then remanded the decision, instructing the investigating authority to reinstate the steps concerned as regards that complainant. The panel made it very clear that, given its powers as set out in paragraph 8 of Article 1904, its legal authority was limited to remands and therefore could not vacate the challenged decision.[60] Conversely, the panel found that, with respect to the other complainants, the challenged decision was not illegal in terms of paragraph I of Article 238 of the Fiscal Code, because the officials who had participated in certain steps of the investigation concerning those complainants were legally competent, since they had acted on behalf of UPCI, which had been properly established.[61] Notably, although the panel in Coated Flat Steels properly interpreted its powers under paragraph 8 of Article 1904, and additionally rejected most of the claims alleging that the officials who had participated in the investigation had been legally incompetent, it addressed the issue of legal competence adopting a reading of paragraph I of Article 238 of the Fiscal Code that goes beyond the ordinary meaning of this provision, as the panel did in Plate in Coils. The panel also remanded several substantive aspects of the challenged determination, instructing the investigating authority, for instance, to undertake an extensive recalculation of the dumping margin for three complainants.[62] In some cases, in remanding some of the dumping aspects of the challenged determination, the panel had no reservations about substituting its judgment on technical issues for that of the investigating authority. For instance, it instructed the investigating authority to

---

[58] See ibid., pp. xcviii–xcix (in the Spanish original).   [59] MEX-94-1904-01.
[60] See Coated Flat Steels, Panel Report, paras. 120-1 (in the Spanish original).
[61] See, for instance, ibid., para. 145 (in the Spanish original).
[62] Ibid., pp. 140-3 (in the Spanish original).

exclude restructuring expenses from the calculation of the general expenses of one of the complainants on the basis of the argument that corporate restructuring expenses are not part of the cost of production of the subject product.[63] The panel also concluded that the cost of production of off-grade material was lower than the cost of production of standard materials (in spite of the investigating authority's protestations that prior to production it was impossible to distinguish one from the other), and instructed the investigating authority to recalculate the dumping margin of one complainant taking into consideration such distinction.[64]

4   High Fructose Corn Syrup (2001)

Probably bearing in mind the shortcomings of the panel in Plate in Coils, the panel in High Fructose Corn Syrup (HFCS)[65] found that, while the jurisdiction and the powers of the Tax Court were governed by the Fiscal Code, the jurisdiction and the powers of bi-national panels were governed by NAFTA in the first place and, where foreseen by NAFTA, by the Fiscal Code as well. Hence, one could expect the results of bi-national panel review to be different from the results of a review by the Tax Court.[66] Accordingly, the panel further found that bi-national panels did not have the power to vacate a challenged decision, nor to issue a remand instructing the authority to vacate a challenged decision.[67] Importantly, the panel found, in addition, that bi-national panels did not have the legal authority to review constitutional issues.[68]

The panel rejected the complainants' claim that the challenged anti-dumping determination was illegal by reason of the alleged legal incompetence of the officials involved in certain steps of the investigation.[69] However, in rejecting this claim, the panel oddly framed its analysis in terms of whether the investigative steps at issue had constituted "nuisances" within the meaning of Article 16 of the constitution,[70] which was at odds with its view that NAFTA panels were not empowered to address

---

[63] See ibid., para. 272 (in the Spanish original).
[64] See ibid., paras. 222, 224 and 227 (in the Spanish original).
[65] MEX-USA-98–1904–01.
[66] See HFCS, Panel Report, para. 261 (in the Spanish original).
[67] See ibid., para. 264 (in the Spanish original).
[68] See ibid., para. 265 (in the Spanish original).
[69] See ibid., para. 412 (in the Spanish original).
[70] See ibid., para. 413 (in the Spanish original).

constitutional issues.[71] In any event, the panel found that the investigative steps such as the receipt of notifications, extending deadlines and dispatching supplemental questionnaires, did not constitute "nuisances",[72] and proceeded to reject the claim.

Notably, the panel adopted the principle of comity and on this basis made the substantive findings of the concurrent WTO panel in *HFCS* its own.[73] This approach was enabled by the fact that, as the AD Agreement is self-executing under Mexican law, both the NAFTA panel and the WTO panel reviewed compliance with the AD Agreement, although the NAFTA panel visualized the AD Agreement as domestic law binding the investigating authority, while the WTO panel viewed the AD Agreement as an international treaty binding Mexico.

The panel did address on its own a number of substantive issues that had not been raised in the concurrent WTO panel. One such issue was whether the product produced by the domestic industry as configured by the petitioners (sugar) qualified as "like product" to the imported product (high fructose corn syrup) within the meaning of Article 2.6 of the AD Agreement.[74] The panel ruled in the affirmative, based upon the argument that, in spite of the differences in physical characteristics between both products, sugar and high fructose corn syrup were commercially substitutable.[75] This finding is a hard fit *vis-à-vis* the wording of Article 2.6 of the AD Agreement, particularly as interpreted by the WTO panel in *EC–Salmon*.[76] Interestingly, the panel would have

[71] Consistent with this view, one would have expected the panel to examine the claim of legal incompetence before it in paragraph I of Article 238 of the Fiscal Code.

[72] See *HFCS*, Panel Report, para. 432 (in the Spanish original).

[73] See ibid., para. 452 (in the Spanish original).

[74] This issue was important because the petitioners had configured the domestic industry excluding producers of domestic high fructose corn syrup (which evidently was identical to imported high fructose corn syrup) on the grounds that such producers were subsidiaries of US exporters.

[75] See *HFCS*, Panel Report, paras. 500 and 517–18 (in the Spanish original).

[76] See Panel Report, *European Communities – Anti-Dumping Measure on Farmed Salmon from Norway*, WT/DS337/R, adopted 15 January 2008, and Corr. 1, paras. 7.52 ("It is important to note that the assessment of whether goods are 'like' in the sense of Article 2.6 entails first, a consideration of whether goods are identical. Only if there are no goods which are identical to the product under consideration does Article 2.6 allow an investigating authority to consider whether there is some other good which 'has characteristics closely resembling those of the product under consideration'" and 7.56 ("[A]n assessment of whether products resemble one another is only permitted, however, in the absence of identity under Article 2.6"). Accordingly, inquiring whether domestic sugar was a commercial substitute for imported high fructose corn syrup was improper, in view of the existence of domestic high fructose

avoided focusing its decision on the issue of substitutability if it had described the distinction in physical characteristics between sugar and high fructose corn syrup as mainly having to do with the raw materials used in each case.

In its report, the panel also reviewed the re-determination issued pursuant to the findings of the WTO panel. The panel concluded that the investigating authority had failed to demonstrate the existence of threat or injury, and proceeded to instruct the investigating authority to revoke the challenged measure.[77]

5   Urea *(2002)*

Urea[78] was the first NAFTA panel reviewing a final anti-dumping determination issued by Mexico where the complainant was a domestic party, in particular, a domestic producer. The fact that a domestic producer took this step, as, subsequently, did certain domestic parties involved in *Liquid Caustic Soda* and *Pork Legs*, suggests that many domestic parties view NAFTA panels as a better venue to have their claims reviewed than the Tax Court. The background to the *Urea* NAFTA panel is that the investigating authority had terminated the proceeding, without imposing measures, based upon the argument that, as the petitioner had shut down its operations while the proceeding was ongoing, it had lost its legal standing to bring an anti-dumping investigation. To say the least, this argument was odd, because the petitioner had shut down its operations, at least in part, as a result of the commercial pressures exerted by the investigated imports. The panel found that the specific term used by the investigating authority to characterize the concept of "legal standing" (*legitimación procesal activa*) applied to judicial, but not to administrative proceedings.[79] The panel then ruled that the challenged final determination was inconsistent in terms of paragraph II of Article 238 of the Fiscal Code.[80] Interestingly, the panel also reached the conclusion that the concept of "standing" referred to by the investigating authority was more in the nature of a

---

corn syrup. It appears that the panel's inquiry would have been much better framed if it had focused on whether Article 4.1(i) of the AD Agreement (allowing exclusions from the domestic industry) could have any implications as regards the interpretation of Article 2.6 of the Agreement.

[77] See *HFCS*, Panel Report, para. 747 and pp. 113–14 (in the Spanish original).

[78] MEX-USA-00-1904-01.   [79] *Urea*, Panel Report, para. 13 (in the Spanish original).

[80] Ibid., para. 22 (in the Spanish original).

requirement that need be met for triggering an anti-dumping investigation,[81] which is equivalent to saying that the test of standing under Article 5.4 of the AD Agreement need only be met for purposes of initiation.

6   Beef *(2004)*

The panel in *Beef*[82] also rejected claims that the challenged anti-dumping determination was illegal on the ground that some of the officials who had participated in certain steps of the investigation had been legally incompetent. In particular, the panel concluded that the secretary of the ministry responsible had signed the challenged determination in compliance with Mexican trade remedy law; thus, the determination was issued by a competent authority.[83] Because this implied that the official who had "issued, ordered or conducted the proceeding", within the meaning of paragraph I of Article 238 of the Fiscal Code, had been legally competent to do so, the panel could then have dismissed the claim of legal incompetence directly on this basis, as the panel in *Polystyrene* did. Surprisingly, the panel went on to examine whether the investigative steps within the proceeding had constituted "nuisances" within the meaning of Article 16 of the constitution, as the panel in *HFCS* did. It ruled in the negative.[84]

The panel also addressed several substantive claims. For example, it found that there was no legal basis under the Mexican anti-dumping law to apply the "facts available rate" to export shipments that lacked an alleged sanitary certification.[85] The panel also remanded the determination to the authority instructing it to exclude un-dumped imports from its analysis of threat of injury,[86] and confirmed the investigating authority's finding that an affirmative determination of threat of injury does not require that all the factors considered attest to the existence of threat of injury.[87] The panel upheld all of the findings of the investigating authority in the remand determination.[88]

---

[81] Ibid., para. 19 (in the Spanish original).   [82] MEX-USA-00–1904–02.
[83] *Beef*, Panel Report, para. 8.9 (in the Spanish original).
[84] Ibid., paras. 8.16–8.17 (in the Spanish original).
[85] Ibid., para. 10.70 (in the Spanish original).
[86] Ibid., para. 20.10.2 (in the Spanish original).
[87] Ibid., para. 20.10.1 (in the Spanish original).
[88] *Beef*, Panel Remand Report, p. 11 (in the Spanish original).

7   Liquid Caustic Soda *(2006)*

Liquid Caustic Soda[89] was a split decision involving review of a final anti-dumping determination in a sunset review. The majority (composed of three panellists) properly found that, under Annex 1911, NAFTA panels lacked the jurisdiction to deal with sunset reviews.[90]

8   Welded Pipe *(2008)*

Welded Pipe[91] was a split decision where the majority (composed of four panellists) upheld all aspects of the challenged determination. Like *Plate in Coils*, *Welded Pipe* is a very good example of a very bad NAFTA panel review.

Two findings of the panel in *Welded Pipe* are clearly inconsistent with WTO case law. First, the panel upheld the investigating authority's injury determination, although it was based on a period of investigation that ended nearly 20 months before the date of initiation.[92] The panel was very emphatic that there was nothing wrong with this approach, because there was no rule in the AD Agreement concerning the selection of the period of investigation.[93] Unbeknown to the panel, this argument had been summarily dismissed in the WTO dispute in *Mexico–Rice*. In particular, in that case, the AB confirmed the WTO panel's finding that using an outdated period of investigation did not conform to the obligation under Article 3.1 of the AD Agreement that an injury determination should be based on "positive evidence".[94] Second, the panel upheld the investigating authority's analysis of other potential causes of injury, although such analysis treated other potential causes of injury as factors that added to the injury suffered by the domestic industry,[95] and the authority thus completely failed to disentangle the effects of dumped imports from those of the "other factors", as required by WTO case law.[96]

---

[89]   MEX-USA-2003–1904–01.
[90]   *Liquid Caustic Soda*, Panel Report, p. 23 (in the Spanish original).
[91]   MEX-USA-2005–1904–01.
[92]   *Welded Pipe*, Panel Report, p. 7 (in the Spanish original).
[93]   Ibid., p. 33 (in the Spanish original).
[94]   Appellate Body Report, *Mexico – Definitive Anti-Dumping Measures on Beef and Rice, Complaint with Respect to Rice*, WT/DS295/AB/R, adopted 20 December 2005, paras. 163–7.
[95]   *Welded Pipe*, Panel Report, p. 119 (in the Spanish original).
[96]   See Appellate Body Report, *United States – Anti-Dumping Measures on Certain Hot-Rolled Steel Products from Japan*, WT/DS184/AB/R, adopted 23 August 2001, para. 223.

In addition, the panel wrote off Article 43 of the Regulations, which makes cost investigations contingent upon the submission of information by petitioners, leading to the presumption that home market sales in the country of export are made at prices below cost. According to the panel, the investigating authority had the legal authority to request cost information from respondents, even absent allegations of sales below cost by petitioners, in view of Article 2.2.1 of the AD Agreement.[97] Unbeknown to the panel, Article 2 of the AD Agreement does not categorize sales below cost as sales in the ordinary course of trade, and leaves in the hands of each member whether to do so. As Article 32 of the FTL permits exclusion of sales below cost for purposes of determining normal value, and Article 43 of the Regulations lays the burden of proof for the corresponding cost investigation upon petitioners, under Mexican law the investigating authority clearly lacked the authority for requesting cost data from respondents on its own motion.

9   Pork Legs (2008)

In Pork Legs,[98] the panel found that the complainant (a domestic producer) did not have the standing to challenge the final anti-dumping determination at issue (which terminated the case without imposing measures) because it had not participated in the proceeding leading to such determination.[99]

10   Apples (2009)

In Apples,[100] the panel reviewed a re-determination issued by the investigating authority subsequent to having lost an appeal through a juicio de amparo. The juicio de amparo concerned had declared the proceeding that had led to the application of challenged measure null and void, as of the stage where a violation of a constitutional provision had occurred, but had not instructed the investigating authority to conduct a remand. The investigating authority revoked the challenged measure, and nevertheless proceeded to reinstate the proceeding as of the stage prior to which the violation occurred. Given that the appeal through the juicio de amparo had been filed pursuant to the application of definitive measures

[97] Welded Pipe, Panel Report, p. 74 (in the Spanish original).
[98] MEX-USA-2006-1904-01.
[99] Pork Legs, Panel Report, pp. 16–17 and 19 (in the Spanish original).
[100] MEX-USA-2006-1904-02.

subsequent to the termination of an undertaking that had lasted for nearly five years, the reinstatement of the proceeding as of the stage where the violation occurred meant that the investigating authority's new injury determination was based on data that was several years old. Unsurprisingly, the panel found that this approach was contrary to Article VI of the GATT 1994, Article 3 of the AD Agreement and Article 76 of the Regulations[101] and remanded the determination to the investigating authority, instructing it to rely on more recent data.[102] The panel rightly declined to address a number of claims regarding the determination of dumping and injury until the remand was concluded.[103] Conversely, the panel found, similarly to the panel in *Welded Pipe*, that the investigating authority had the legal authority to request cost data from respondents on its own motion,[104] suggesting, by implication, that the provisions in the FTL dealing generically with the authority's powers for obtaining any information deemed relevant, superseded Article 43 of the Regulations.

VIII   Conclusions

Parties affected by the application of trade remedy measures in Mexico have a multiplicity of options for challenging such measures. A first is a judicial appeal in the form of a *juicio de amparo* before a District Court, but this option requires demonstrating the violation of a constitutional provision. A second option is a judicial appeal before a specialized tribunal, the Tax Court. A third option consists of the dispute settlement mechanism under the NAFTA, which provides for bi-national panel review. But NAFTA panel review is only quasi-judicial because, while sharing the same standard of review with the Tax Court, NAFTA panels have a narrower jurisdiction and weaker powers. While a few decisions of the NAFTA panels have been less than exemplary, it appears that NAFTA panel review is increasingly perceived as an appeal mechanism preferable to judicial appeals, because NAFTA panels routinely deal more or less competently with issues of great procedural and substantive complexity.

---

[101] *Apples*, Panel Report, paras. 63–4 (in the Spanish original).
[102] Ibid., p. 30 (in the Spanish original).
[103] Ibid., paras. 76–7 (in the Spanish original).
[104] Ibid., para. 82 (in the Spanish original).

5

Colombia: a complex court system with the possibility of three instances

MARÍA CLARA LOZANO*

I Introduction

1 History of trade remedies in Colombia

Colombia signed the General Agreement on Tariffs and Trade (hereinafter GATT) in 1981. Under Colombian law, for an international treaty to become enforceable in Colombia, it requires approval from the Colombian Congress[1] and, after presidential endorsement, the treaty must be analysed by the Constitutional Court.[2] Law 49/81 ratified the protocol of Colombia's adherence to the GATT.

Colombia's economic liberalization started at the beginning of the 1990s when President Gaviria decided to open substantially the Colombian economy to imports, generating significant effects on Colombia's market competition. The former Colombian government, headed by President Barco, adopted the regulation necessary to provide national production with the tools to deal with practices such as dumping and subsidization.

The first Colombian regulation[3] on trade remedies was Decree 1500 of 1990. This decree regulated only anti-dumping and countervailing duties, leaving aside safeguards. It had a very short life, and was repealed a few months later. This initial decree had been replaced five times before the one currently in force came into effect. However, the main features of the

---

* Counsel, Lozano & Abogados Derecho, Competencia & Globalización, Bogotá, Colombia.
[1] Article 224, Political Constitution (hereinafter PC).
[2] Article 241.10, PC. The Constitutional Court was created by amendment made to the constitution in 1991.
[3] This regulation was issued by the National Government, represented by the president and the Minister of Economic Development (now Mincomercio).

investigating authority have remained unchanged over the years. Since the adoption of the first decree, the investigating authority has been the Colombian Institute of Foreign Trade (hereinafter Incomex). Although Incomex was abolished at the end of 2000, its functions were completely transferred to the Directorate General for Foreign Trade (hereinafter DGCE) of the Ministry of Commerce, Industry and Tourism (hereinafter Mincomercio). This has ensured stability in the institutional structure within which trade remedies have been implemented.

Since 2001, trade remedy investigations have been conducted by the Trade Practices Sub-Directorate (hereinafter SPC) of the DGCE. The SPC is in charge of conducting investigations, whereas the main procedural decisions are made by the DGCE's director. As an administrative agency, the DGCE conducts trade remedy investigations in the public interest. This implies that in providing an opinion as to whether or not a trade remedy measure should be imposed, the DGCE takes into account the interests of the nation, and its acts are to be of a general nature.[4] As explained in detail below, only those acts undertaken by the DCGE that are of a definitive nature are subject to judicial review and, due to their general nature, such acts may not previously have been appealed before the DGCE.[5]

In the case of safeguard measures, just days after signing[6] the Agreement Establishing the World Trade Organization (WTO), the Colombian government took the first initiative towards the regulation of safeguard investigations by issuing Decree 809 of 1994. This decree was intended to be a comprehensive[7] legal instrument regulating safeguard investigations to be conducted by Colombia, without prejudice to special rules set forth in international treaties. Decree 809/94 was partially amended by

---

[4] Regarding the judicial definition of general acts, see Council of State, Contentious Administrative Chamber, Fourth Section, Hugo Bastidas Barcenas, 3 June 2011, Docket: 11001-03-27-000-2006-00032-00-16090, complainant: Diana Caballero and Gloria Arango, defendant: DIAN.

[5] Since these are general administrative acts, trade remedy final decisions and other procedural acts are not appealable, as stipulated in Article 49 of the CCA: "Inadmissibility. There shall be no appeal against the acts of a general nature, or against procedural, preparatory or execution acts except as expressly provided in the relevant regulation."

[6] Signature took place on 15 April, and Decree 809 was issued on 25 April. It should be noted that no reference to the Agreement on Safeguards was made, due to the fact that the corresponding law ratifying the treaty had not yet been issued.

[7] Chapter III of Decree 809/94 governed agricultural safeguard measures. A textile safeguard regime was also in place at that time.

Decree 2038 of 1996, which provided for different periods of application for provisional safeguard measures, depending on whether they were imposed against WTO members or non-WTO members. Since Decree 809/94 did not provide for differential treatment between WTO members and other countries, the government issued Decree 2657 of 1994, which subjected safeguard investigations against non-WTO members to more lenient legal standards.[8]

On 15 December 1994, Law 170 was adopted, ratifying the WTO Agreement and supplementing Colombian anti-dumping and counter-vailing duty legislation. Law 170/94 incorporated the provisions of the WTO Agreement, including its annexes, into Colombian law, which rendered such provisions directly enforceable in Colombia. In 1995, Decree 299 was issued. This decree represented the first post-WTO initiative to regulate anti-dumping and countervailing duty investiga-tions in Colombia.

As the investigating authority's experience on anti-dumping and safeguard investigations grew, the need arose to improve the legal frame-work in these two fields, taking into consideration the national experi-ence and the relevant international developments. This led to the adoption of Decree 991/98[9] on anti-dumping investigations and Decree 152 of 1998 on safeguard investigations. However, given the investigating authority's limited experience on countervailing duty investigations, this area is still governed by the original Decree 299 of 1995. Finally, Decree 2550 was issued in 2010 in order to reflect in national legislation the changes that had occurred in the WTO jurispru-dence on anti-dumping.

2   Colombia's trade remedies laws and regulations in force

Colombian law on trade remedies consists of two sets of rules, namely, national legislation and the supranational rules of the Andean

---

[8] For instance, this decree provided that in the absence of a treaty requiring evidence of serious injury to a farming or fishing production branch, safeguard measures could be imposed on the basis of injury or threat thereof. Further, Decree 2259 of 1996 clarified that, under such circumstances, there was no need to demonstrate critical circumstances in order to impose provisional safeguard measures.

[9] Decree 991 of 1998 covers all relevant aspects of anti-dumping investigations against imports from WTO members and other free trade agreement partners, as well as against imports from non-WTO members and imports from other countries with special trade agreements on this matter.

Community.[10] It is important to bear in mind that anti-dumping investigations conducted at the Andean Community level concern imports
into Andean territory. Therefore, an Andean member may impose an
anti-dumping measure against a third country without having production in its territory of the subject product. The fact that the Andean
Community produces the product would suffice, under Andean
Community rules, for an Andean member to take action against dumped
imports of that product, even if the member taking the action does not
produce it.

Under this rule, a Colombian domestic industry filed a request with
the General Secretariat of the Andean Community that Peru be directed
to impose an anti-dumping duty on certain imports originating in the
United States.[11] All resolutions issued by the General Secretariat of
the Andean Community during this process were challenged by the
Peruvian government before the Andean Tribunal of Justice, which
decided[12] in favour of the General Secretariat of the Andean
Community, and ordered Peru to impose the requested anti-dumping
duty. However, the Andean Tribunal of Justice annulled articles 2 and 3
of Resolution 672, which required that Peru notify the WTO's Council
for Trade in Goods, and impose the anti-dumping duty immediately
after obtaining such approval.[13]

2.1 Anti-dumping

At the national level, anti-dumping investigations are currently governed by Decree 2550 of 2010. This decree was issued, among others,
in order to adapt the legislation to the new administrative structure of
Mincomercio after the abolition of Incomex. Like Decree 991 of 1998,
Decree 2550/10 regulates not only investigations on imports from WTO

[10] In the Andean Community, each member applies anti-dumping, countervailing and
safeguard measures to third countries under its own independent regulation. Contrary
to what happens in other regional integration blocs, the Andean Community decided to
allow the possibility of imposing anti-dumping, countervailing duty and safeguard
measures between Andean members. Andean Community rules also apply when the
practice originates in a third country and has an Andean border effect. It should be noted
that anti-dumping investigations conducted at the Andean Community level are governed by Decision 456.

[11] See Resolution 672 of 2002 issued by the General Secretariat of the Andean Community,
for the order directed at the Peruvian government to impose an anti-dumping duty on
the imports of the product under investigation.

[12] Andean Tribunal of Justice, Case 35-AN-2003, 25 August 2004.

[13] This particular provision paralleled Article 14.4 of the AD Agreement.

members, but also from non-WTO members and countries with which Colombia has signed treaties containing provisions with respect to anti-dumping investigations. In the case of WTO members, Decree 2550/10 should be read in conjunction with Law 170 of 1994 ratifying the WTO Agreement. Where there is a treaty between Colombia and another country containing anti-dumping provisions, Decree 2550/10 must be read in conjunction with the relevant provisions of that treaty.

Anti-dumping proceedings require the involvement of various administrative agencies. As already mentioned, under Decree 2550/10, the investigating authority is the DGCE. The DGCE has various sub-directorates, including the SPC, which is headed by a sub-director and is responsible for conducting anti-dumping, countervailing duty and safeguard investigations.

Led by its director, the DGCE is responsible for: (i) deciding whether an investigation should be initiated at the request of the domestic industry or on an *ex officio* basis; (ii) making preliminary determinations[14] and deciding whether provisional anti-dumping duties should be imposed; and (iii) making the final decision,[15] according to the final recommendation of the Trade Practices Committee (hereinafter the Committee), a body whose composition and functions are explained below.

Although the decisions on matters listed above are to be made by the head of the DGCE, the SPC – a technical unit – conducts the actual investigations. In doing so, the sub-director decides on: (a) assessment of the petition;[16] (b) dispatch of questionnaires to interested parties;[17] (c) collection of evidence in the process,[18] including verification visits to the premises of the exporters;[19] (d) hearings;[20] (e) receipt and assessment of final arguments of the parties;[21] (f) preparation of the technical report[22] to be submitted to the Committee, presentation thereof and invitation to the corresponding meeting;[23] and (g) preparation and transmission of the essential facts report after the inclusion of any information requested by the Committee.

---

[14] The preliminary determination must be issued within two months following the commencement of the investigation, but this period may be extended for 30 calendar days.
[15] The final resolution will also be published in the *Official Journal*.
[16] Article 26, Decree 2550/10.   [17] Article 29, Decree 2550/10.
[18] Article 32, Decree 2550/10.   [19] Article 34, Decree 2550/10.
[20] Article 35, Decree 2550/10.   [21] Article 37, Decree 2550/10.
[22] This is basically a draft report of essential facts, subject to the Committee's scrutiny.
[23] Article 37, Decree 2550/10.

The Committee[24] is a collegiate body whose members are: (i) the Deputy Minister of Foreign Trade, who chairs the meetings; (ii) the Deputy Minister of the public body which, in the opinion of the Committee's chairman, is most directly related to the domestic industry affected by dumped imports; (iii) the Director of National Customs Administration; (iv) the Director of Commercial Relations or the Director of Economic Integration in Mincomercio, depending on the country investigated, to be decided by the Committee's chairman; (v) the Deputy Director General of the National Planning Department; and (vi) two advisers from the Superior Council of Foreign Trade. The Deputy Superintendent for Consumer Protection and Metrology of the Superintendence of Industry and Trade[25] and the Director of DGCE may also participate, with a voice but no vote in the Committee's meetings.

Over the years, the Colombian authorities have developed a system to test the clarity of the reports of essential facts and the sufficiency of the evidence that supports the final decision.[26] The DGCE submits the draft of the essential facts report to the Committee, and the latter may request further information on the results of the investigation. Once the Committee approves the draft, the Sub-Director of the SPC, within three days, will send the report of essential facts to interested parties and give them the opportunity to comment. Interested parties' comments and the SPC's views will be forwarded to the Committee, which will make a final recommendation to the DGCE. Colombian legislation[27] provides that the final decision must be taken by the DGCE in light of the Committee's final opinion.

As the explanations show, the procedure provided for in Decree 2550 closely follows the AD Agreement and introduces a number of innovations aimed at improving interested parties' due process rights. One such innovation is the technical briefing[28] aimed at explaining to interested parties the methodology used for dumping margin calculations, as well as injury and causation determinations.

The final decision is not subject to appeal, because it is a general administrative act, which means that its issuance and notification exhaust the administrative procedure. Upon exhaustion of this procedure, the possibility

[24] Article 99, Decree 2550/10.
[25] The Superintendence of Industry and Trade is the antitrust agency of Colombia, but its representative is the Superintendent for Competition Protection.
[26] Among others, these refer to decisions on the imposition of anti-dumping duties, acceptance of undertakings, and their extensions and modifications.
[27] Article 99, Decree 2550/10.   [28] Article 40, Decree 2550/10.

of a judicial review is then open. The next section will explain the scope and procedural aspects of such a review.

All anti-dumping duties currently in force in Colombia have been imposed on imports from China as a result of eight investigations, and affect approximately 30 subheadings. Since 1990, Colombia has conducted around 50 anti-dumping investigations or reviews. Only three of these administrative procedures have been challenged before the contentious-administrative jurisdiction. While there have been other discussions, such as requests for direct revocation of the administrative acts issued during the administrative procedure, the explanations in this chapter pertain exclusively to discussions that arose in the context of judicial reviews in Colombia.

2.2   Countervailing measures

As noted above, Decree 299 of 1995 provides the legal basis for the conduct of countervailing duty investigations in Colombia. Decision 457 of the Commission applies to countervailing duty investigations conducted in the Andean Community. Decree 299 designated Incomex as the investigating authority in countervailing duty cases. After the abolition of Incomex, these functions were transferred to Mincomercio's DGCE. The procedure laid down in Decree 299/95 regarding countervailing duty investigations does not differ significantly from the procedure that applies in anti-dumping investigations. The only important difference pertains to the obligation to conduct consultations as provided for in the Agreement on Subsidies and Countervailing Measures (hereinafter SCM Agreement).

As far as the decision-making process is concerned, the main difference in countervailing duty investigations is that the final decision is made by the Minister of Mincomercio. The remaining procedural steps are similar, but not identical, to anti-dumping investigations. Despite being an active user of anti-dumping, Colombia so far has not initiated any countervailing duty investigations.

2.3   Safeguards

As for anti-dumping proceedings, Colombia has different sets of regulations with respect to safeguard investigations. Decree 152 of 1998 applies to safeguard investigations against WTO members. This decree has different sub-sets of rules concerning general safeguards under the WTO Agreement on Safeguards, safeguards on textile products[29] and the agricultural

---

[29]   The Agreement on Textiles and Clothing (ATC) expired in January 2005.

safeguard measures under the WTO Agreement on Agriculture. The chapter focuses exclusively on safeguards regulated by this decree.[30]

As in the anti-dumping and countervailing duty cases, various authorities are involved in the conduct of safeguard investigations. The main difference in such investigations concerns the authority that makes the final decision. Given their more complex nature as an escape clause, the final decision-making process in safeguard investigations consists of a recommendation issued by the Committee on Customs, Tariff and Foreign Trade (hereinafter AAA Committee, for its Spanish acronym) to the Senior Foreign Trade Council, which includes the President of the Republic.

The AAA Committee members[31] are: (a) Deputy Minister of Foreign Trade, who chairs the Committee; (b) Technical Deputy Minister of Finance and Public Credit; (c) Business Development Deputy Minister, Mincomercio; (d) Deputy Minister of Agriculture and Rural Development; (e) Deputy Minister of Mining and Energy; (f) Deputy Director General of National Planning Department; (g) National Customs Director; and (h) two advisers to the Senior Foreign Trade Council. This Committee makes a recommendation to the Senior Foreign Trade Council, the members[32] of which are: (a) the President of the Republic, who chairs the Council; (b) Minister of Mincomercio; (c) Minister of Foreign Affairs; (d) Minister of Finance; (e) Minister of Agriculture and Rural Development; (f) Minister of Mining and Energy; (g) Minister of Transport; (h) Minister of Environment, Housing and Territorial Development; (i) Director of the National Planning Department; and (j) Director of the Central Bank.

The Council's decisions are issued by a decree signed by the president and the ministers related to the affected domestic industry. Such decrees contain general rules and are not appealable administratively, but they are subject to judicial review.

There are no safeguard measures currently in force in Colombia. The most recent measure expired in June 2011.[33] Since 1990, Colombia has

---

[30] In the interest of completeness, it should be noted that Colombia also has specific rules with respect to: (a) safeguards in the context of bilateral treaties (Decree 1820 of 2010); (b) procedures whereby domestic industries may request a tariff increase below Colombia's bound rates in the WTO (Decree 1407 of 1999); and (c) safeguards on imports from China as provided for under China's Protocol of Accession to the WTO (Decree 1480 of 2005).

[31] Decree 2303/06.   [32] Decree 2553/99.

[33] The safeguard measure on *Imports of flexible PVC film from Brazil*, within the Andean Community – MERCOSUR Agreement.

conducted around 40 safeguard investigations, only one of which has been subject to judicial review.

II Legislative framework for judicial review

In Colombia, the judicial review of administrative acts imposing trade remedies is not subject to special rules. Such judicial review is conducted under general rules.[34]

The Colombian Constitution provides that "individuals are liable only to the authorities for violating the constitution and the laws. Civil servants are liable for the same cause and for their omission or for overreaching in the exercise of their functions."[35] Given this constitutional principle, the investigating authorities of Colombia are required to follow the substantive and procedural rules set forth in the relevant laws in the conduct of their investigations. Failing to do so may lead to their acts being challenged before the competent courts.[36] Above, we have explained the source of the substantive and procedural rules on trade remedy investigations in Colombia. In what follows, we will elaborate the procedural rules that apply to their judicial review.

At the outset, we must point out an important legislative change concerning judicial review that will come into effect in July 2012. The Contentious Administrative Code, Decree 01 of 1984, which is currently in force and which governs judicial review proceedings, has been amended by the Colombian Congress. These amendments are due to enter into force in July 2012. The new act[37] introduces some important amendments to the contentious-administrative procedure. The explanations in this chapter are based on the current law; however, where necessary, reference will be made to the relevant amendments in the new law. As explained in section IV below, in Colombia, only definitive trade remedy acts are subject to judicial review.

---

[34] Article 82, Contentious Administrative Code (CCA) (to be repealed by Article 104 Law 1437, 2010).

[35] Article 6, PC.

[36] In Colombia, civil servants may also be subject to an action that will hold them responsible for the payment of the punitive damages and sanctions that the administration had to pay due to their negligence.

[37] 1437 of 2010.

Colombia's administrative review system has three judicial instances: administrative judges,[38] contentious-administrative tribunals[39] or the Council of State.[40] Regarding territorial jurisdiction, since Mincomercio is a national authority, the cases against the DGCE's determinations must be brought before the courts in Bogotá. The competent court will be determined on the basis of the subject matter of the administrative act, its nature and the quantum at stake.

In the case of review of trade remedy acts, the identification of the competent court is complicated because of the nature of such acts. General acts are usually challenged before the Council of State through an action for annulment. However, under the theory of "determining motives or mobiles", depending on the interest of the complainant, Colombian courts accept the use of the action for annulment and reinstatement of rights, which may be filed before the three courts mentioned above, depending on the quantum at stake.

Any person is entitled to challenge definitive administrative acts related to trade remedy investigations.

III   Types of judicial review proceedings

Under Colombian law, administrative acts may be subject to various types of judicial review proceedings, depending on their nature and origin. As far as acts issued in the context of trade remedy investigations are concerned, these may be subject to two judicial review proceedings, namely, an "action for annulment" or an "action for annulment and reinstatement of rights".

1   Action for annulment

An action for annulment may be brought against a trade remedy act or a general trade remedy regulation.[41] In general, these two proceedings will

---

[38] Article 134B, CCA. This judicial authority was introduced by Act 446 of 1998 (Article 42).
[39] Article 131, CCA.   [40] Articles 128 and 129, CCA.
[41] That was the case in the action initiated by Materiales de Construcción Varlop against Article 10 of Decree 991 of 1998. The following are the actions for annulment initiated against the National Government for alleged violations of superior regulations: (a) annulment action against Decree 2444 of 1990, Council of State, First Section, Dossier: 1642 of 1992, speaker: Miguel González Rodríguez, complainant: Andrés Rodríguez Pizarro; (b) annulment action against Decree 150 of 1993, Council of State, Fourth Section, Dossier: 4834 of 1995, speaker: Delio Gómez Leyva, complainant: Hugo Palacios Mejía.

be brought separately, but there is always the possibility of conjoining different proceedings due to their relationship.[42]

The action for annulment[43] is intended to remove the challenged trade remedy act from the legal system. "The simple action for annulment seeks the restoration of legality to ensure lawful performance of the Administration; it encompasses an altruistic purpose as one who exercises the action cannot pursue any interest other than to restore the legal order violated by the act."[44]

This action may be brought by any person who intends to ensure the protection of the legal system. Further, anyone may join an action for annulment proceeding, either to support the complainant's case or to defend the administration's decision. Due to its nature, there is no statute of limitations for the initiation of an action for annulment; it may be filed at any time.[45] Therefore, there is a permanent possibility to file this action against a trade remedy act. However, four months after the service of the disputed action, the reviewing court, taking the complainant's objectives into consideration, may consider that the correct action would have been a proceeding for annulment and reinstatement of rights, apply the theory of "determining motives or mobiles" and reject the case on the ground that the statute of limitations has expired.

The decision made by the court in an annulment proceeding concerns whether or not the disputed administrative act is null and void. Such decision has *erga omnes* effect. It is also important to bear in mind that an action for annulment may seek partial or total annulment[46] of the disputed trade remedy act. In terms of the temporal effect of an annulment decision with respect to a trade remedy determination, we should underline that such decision will only have prospective effect, and will not affect past transactions. Thus, if an importer has paid an antidumping duty that has been annulled by the court, this will not entitle the importer to seek the reimbursement of such past payments.

The action for annulment has been used with respect to several trade remedy determinations. Two examples of this are the action filed by

---

[42] Article 145, CCA, to be read in conjunction with Article 82.3 of the Civil Procedure Code (hereinafter CPC).

[43] Article 84, CCA, to be replaced by Article 137 of Act 1437/2010 as of July 2012.

[44] Juan Angel Palacio, *Administrative Procedural Law*, 3rd edn (Sanchez R. Law Library Ltd., 2002), p. 203.

[45] Colombian law contains certain exceptions to this principle, but none of them applies to actions for annulment initiated with respect to trade remedy determinations.

[46] As in the aforementioned CAN case.

Comercializadora Internacional SA Invermec,[47] pending final decision, challenging Resolution 1665 of 2009 imposing anti-dumping duties on *Imports of Shovels, Hoes, Sticks and Pickaxes* originating in China; and the application filed against Decree 1153 of 1996,[48] which imposed a provisional safeguard measure on *Imports of Textiles and Clothing* originating in Chinese Taipei, North Korea, China and Panama, which were not then WTO members.

The action for annulment has been used not only with respect to individual determinations made in certain trade remedy investigations, but also with respect to general decrees that regulate the conduct of such investigations. One example of this is the case brought by Materiales de Construcción Varlop,[49] which sought the annulment of Article 10 of Decree 991 of 1998 on the determination of normal value with respect to exporters from countries with centrally planned economies. The Council of State rejected this complaint. There were also two other similar cases, one[50] with respect to Decree 2444 of 1990 and the other, presented by Hugo Palacios,[51] against Decree 150/93.

2 Action for annulment and reinstatement of rights

The action for annulment and reinstatement of rights[52] seeks to annul an administrative act and to reinstate the individual rights affected.

> The action for annulment and reinstatement of rights is directed not only to obtain the annulment of the administrative act, which seeks the restoration of legality to ensure lawful performance of the administration, but also the

---

[47] Council of State, Division of Administrative Litigation, Fourth Section, counsellor speaker: William Giraldo Giraldo, Docket: 11001–03–27–000–2009–00048–00 (18 033), actor: Comercializadora Internacional Invermec SA, respondent: Mincomercio, Order dated 25 February 2010.

[48] Council of State, Division of Administrative Litigation, First Section, counsellor speaker: Manuel S. Urueta Ayola, Docket: 3980, actor: Gabriel Hernández Villareal, respondent: National Government, Decision 4 March 1999.

[49] Council of State, Division of Administrative Litigation, Section One, counsellor speaker: Gabriel Mendoza Eduardo Martelo, Docket: 5708, actor: Building Materials SA Varlop, 1 June 2000.

[50] Council of State, Division of Administrative Litigation Section One, counsellor speaker: Miguel Gonzalez Rodriguez, Docket: 1642, actor: Andrés Rodríguez Pizarro, respondent: National Government, 28 May 1992.

[51] Council of State, Division of Administrative Litigation, Section Four, counsellor speaker: Delio Gómez Leyva, Docket: 4834, actor: Hugo Palacios Mejía, respondent: National Government, 31 March 1995.

[52] Article 85, CCA which will be replaced by Article 138, Act 1437/2010 in July 2012.

restoration of the violated right, compensation of damages, or have them returned as wrongly paid. It looks at all the private interests of its complainants.[53]

The action for annulment and reinstatement of rights has been brought against several administrative acts imposing trade remedy measures. Examples are the complaint filed by Ferretería la Campana SA[54] against the resolution which imposed definitive anti-dumping duties on *Imports of Cold Rolled Steel* originating in Ukraine, and the complaint filed by BASF AG, BASF ABT, BASF QUIMICA COLOMBIANA and Hugo Palacios Mejía[55] against Resolution 1609 of 1993, which imposed an anti-dumping duty on the *Imports of Chemical Compound Fertilizer* NPK-17-6-18-2 (grade coffee) originating in Belgium.[56]

Generally an action for annulment and reinstatement of rights must be filed within four months following service of the disputed trade remedy determination. The notification term is calculated from the day following the publication of the disputed determination in the Colombian *Official Journal*.

An important difference between an action for annulment and an action for annulment and reinstatement of rights is that, unlike in an action for annulment, the complainant in an action for annulment and reinstatement of rights is required to demonstrate legitimacy to invoke the action, which means that he or she must show the actual or potential damage caused by the disputed act. Typically in an action for annulment and reinstatement of rights, the complainant requests the court to order that the collection of duties be stopped or that their rate be reduced, or that duties paid in excess of the legally justified rate be refunded. Furthermore, the powers of the reviewing judge are wider in the context of actions for annulment and reinstatement of rights. In such cases, the judicial reviewer will be able not only to confront the challenged act, but also to establish "the rules that will govern in replacement of the act

---

[53] Palacio, *Administrative Procedural Law*, p. 233.
[54] Council of State, Contentious Administrative Chamber, Fourth Section, speaker: Ligia López Díaz, July 2003, Docket: 25000-23-24-000-1999-00481-01 (13619), complainant: Ferretería La Campana SA, defendant: Colombian Institute of Foreign Trade – Incomex and Mincomercio.
[55] Council of State, Administrative Litigation Division, Section Four, counsellor speaker: Delio Gómez Leyva, October 1996, Docket: 5449, actors: BASF AG, BASF ABT, BASF QUIMICA COLOMBIANA and Hugo Palacios Mejia, respondent: Mincomercio.
[56] In both cases, the Council of State refused the pleas of the demand, in the first case as a second-instance court, and in the fertilizers case as the only instance.

declared void and order how to reinstate the complainant's affected right or its compensation for the damages suffered".[57]

The decision on nullity has *erga omnes* effect; it deletes the administrative act declared void from the legal system. However, "if the court denies the requested annulment, it has *erga omnes* effect on the matter under litigation, that is, regarding the facts or grounds alleged in support of the nullity. This means that against the refusal of declaring an administrative act invalid, the action can be challenged but based on facts or reasons other than those initially alleged."[58]

In the case of trade remedy acts, this presents significant complexity, since there may be several people affected by the administration's acts. Therefore these cases are likely to lead to the combination of proceedings.[59]

IV   Reviewable determinations

Administrative acts in Colombia may be subject to various classifications. The most relevant in the case of trade remedy acts are: (i) general administrative acts and particular administrative acts, and (ii) final acts and merely procedural acts.

As already explained, in the case of anti-dumping and countervailing duty investigations, the outcome and the main administrative acts issued during an investigation are resolutions deciding whether or not to impose a final or provisional anti-dumping or countervailing measure. In safeguard cases, given their different nature and procedure, the administrative act that imposes a safeguard measure takes the form of a decree. If the decision is negative, it will be a simple communication.

In terms of the distinction between general and particular acts, the applicable rules clearly provide that since trade remedy investigations concern general interest, all administrative acts issued during the investigations are of a general nature,[60] and therefore usually challenged through an action for annulment. However, due to the theory of "determining motives or mobiles" already referred to, Colombian courts have considered that such acts are likely to be subject to both actions.

---

[57] Palacio, *Administrative Procedural Law*, p. 237.   [58] Ibid.

[59] Article 145, CCA, which must be read in conjunction with Article 157, CPC.

[60] In the case of a particular act, the action for nullity proceeds only in exceptional circumstances.

With regard to the classification between merely procedural acts[61] and final acts, it is important to note that the merely procedural acts are intended to drive the course of the proceedings, whereas the final acts are those that "directly or indirectly decide the merits of the case",[62] i.e. those that bring an administrative procedure to an end. Merely procedural acts may not be challenged on the grounds of simple nullity or annulment and reinstatement of rights, except where they put an end to an administrative action, i.e. "when they make it impossible to continue".[63] It should be noted, however, that under the new Law 1437/2010 due to come into force in 2012, procedural acts of this kind will be considered definitive and therefore be subject to administrative appeal and judicial review.

At this juncture, it may be useful to explain the legal nature and classification of the main administrative acts that are taken in the course of trade remedy investigations. Procedural decisions such as the initiation of an investigation, the writ (if any) ordering requested evidence to be collected, and fixing dates for hearings, are not subject to administrative appeal or judicial review. Turning to provisional measures, on one hand, a provisional measure drives the course of the investigative process but does not imply the imposition of a definitive measure, whereas, on the other hand, despite its temporary nature, it has undeniable immediate effects, such as collateral cost or other security for importers.

The court decision in the annulment proceeding before the Council of State with respect to the provisional safeguard measure imposed by Decree 1153 of 1996 on *Imports of certain subheadings for textiles and clothing* originating in Chinese Taipei, North Korea, China and Panama might shed some light on the nature of provisional measures under Colombian law. In this case, neither party raised the issue of the classification of the provisional measure as definitive or procedural. The Council of State did not analyse this specific subject, but ruled against the claims of the complainants using other legal arguments. While this particular issue was not raised, such a ruling may be interpreted to indicate that Colombian contentious-administrative courts treat provisional measures as final administrative acts.

The main determinations made in trade remedy investigations which constitute definitive administrative acts are the decision accepting

---

[61] Article 49, CCA.
[62] Article 50, CCA, final paragraph (to be replaced by Article 74 of Law 1437/2010).
[63] Ibid.

undertakings, the final decision on whether or not a definitive measure should be imposed, and the decision refusing to initiate an investigation. With respect to these determinations, interested parties may request judicial review before the competent court.

V   Parties eligible to bring a case

An action for annulment may be filed by anyone. The complainant in an annulment proceeding does not need to have a direct financial interest in the case; he or she may simply seek to restore the legal system. Further, anybody can join an ongoing action for annulment as co-defendant or co-complainant.

On the contrary, only those who suffered the effects of the disputed act may file an action for annulment and reinstatement of rights. Interested parties in a trade remedy proceeding may file an action for annulment and reinstatement of rights against an act undertaken by the investigating authority only if they can demonstrate that their rights have been affected by the act. If an action for annulment and reinstatement of rights is initiated, only third parties who are able to prove a direct interest in the outcome of the proceedings are entitled to join as co-complainants or co-defendants. A threat to a collective right does not suffice; the complainant also has to prove some direct interest (e.g. as a consumer) in order to join the action.

VI   Competent courts

As already mentioned, under the theory of "determining motives or mobiles", cases against trade remedy acts may be brought before one of three judicial authorities: administrative judges, contentious-administrative tribunals[64] and the Council of State.[65] Determination of the competent court in judicial review proceedings concerning trade

---

[64] Article 106, CCA sets forth the functions and members of the courts, indicating that each department will have an administrative court residing in the respective capital, with jurisdiction in that territory.

[65] Article 89, CCA provides that the Council of State will be composed of 27 judges, elected by themselves, for periods of eight years. Its functions are exercised through three chambers: (i) the full chamber, which consists of all of its members, (ii) the administrative chamber of 23 counsellors; and (iii) the Consulting and Civil Service chamber. The administrative chamber is divided into administrative sections. In judicial review proceedings involving trade remedy determinations, usually the first and fourth sections have heard the cases.

remedy acts will essentially depend on the type of action to be initiated (which depends on the interest of the complainant) and the quantum involved.

As authorities involved in the decision-making process of a trade remedy determination have national jurisdiction, the courts located in Bogotá will therefore have jurisdiction. The determination of which particular court has jurisdiction will depend primarily on the act in question, quantum involved and the action to be used.

If an action for annulment is filed, the only competent court is the Council of State, which is the highest judicial authority in administrative legal matters and the single-instance court with respect to actions for annulment. When an action for annulment and reinstatement of rights is raised, the Council of State will also be the single-instance jurisdictional authority if the complaint filed has no quantum.[66] The Administrative Tribunal of Cundinamarca plays the role of court of first instance when the action raised is for annulment and reinstatement of rights and the quantum of claims exceeds 300 legal minimum wages.[67] Finally, judges are the first-instance judicial reviewers in actions for annulment and reinstatement of rights, the quantum of which does not exceed 300 legal minimum wages.[68]

VII Procedural steps

As mentioned before, there is a four-month[69] statute of limitation for the filing of an action for annulment and reinstatement of rights, whereas there is no such limitation with respect to actions for annulment.

Once a complaint is filed,[70] the competent court with jurisdiction will proceed to rule on whether or not such complaint is admissible, depending on the fulfilment of the relevant substantive and procedural requirements. If the procedural deficiencies identified by the court are not remedied within five days from the service of the writ, the complaint will be rejected outright. This decision may be subject to appeal if issued by a court of first instance, or appeal for reconsideration[71] if issued by a

---

[66] Article 128.1, CCA.   [67] Article 132.3, CCA.

[68] Such was the case in the action for annulment and reinstatement of rights initiated by Ferretería la Campana against Incomex in 1999. Minimum monthly wage is 535,600 pesos, i.e. US$300.

[69] Article 136, CCA.

[70] The requirements for the complaint are set forth under Article 137.

[71] "*Recurso de súplica*" in Spanish.

single-instance court. The complainant may request the provisional suspension of the disputed administrative act in his or her complaint. According to Article 152 of the current Contentious Administrative Code (hereinafter CCA), for a successful provisional suspension the contested act must be ostensibly contrary to the relevant legal provisions.

It is usually very difficult to convince an administrative court to grant temporary suspension of the disputed administrative act. This was underlined by the Council of State in the judicial review proceeding initiated by Comercializadora Internacional SA Invermec[72] for annulment and temporary suspension of a definitive anti-dumping duty. The Council of State expressly stated:

> As it has been repeatedly argued by this Corporation, the temporary suspension of the effects of administrative acts is an exceptional measure, and as such its viability requires the strict and rigorous enforcement of each and all the requirements expressly provided by law, namely Article 152 of the CCA; the apparent breach of the rules invoked as the basis of the application must be of such extent that the judge, without the need for thorough study or analysis beyond the wording of the rules allegedly violated, observes such violation for being obvious and overt, pursuant to the requirement of clear violation provided in paragraph 2 of Article 152 of the CCA.

The defendant agency has the right to reply to the complaint,[73] present its substantive and procedural arguments and request the collection of evidence.

Subsequently, the court will issue the corresponding writ to collect evidence, which writ is subject to appeal. Once this writ is final, the court begins the collection of evidence. The court always retains jurisdiction to rule on and obtain evidence *ex officio*. Following this, there is an opportunity to submit closing arguments, and finally the administrative court issues its decision. The procedure includes the possibility of requesting a hearing to present the case before the court, which will take place only at the court's discretion.[74]

The final decision by the court must be substantiated, and may award judicial fees based on the parties' procedural behaviour. This judgment is binding both for the complainant and the defendant, and has *res judicata* effect, unless appealed in first-instance cases. Authorities are obliged to

---

[72] The same happened in the proceedings initiated against Decree 1153/96.
[73] It is also possibile to add claims to the complaint.   [74] Article 147, CCA.

comply with the court decision within 30 days from its date of service on them.[75]

Finally, it should be stressed that all complaints with respect to trade remedy determinations have been filed by an attorney or the affected companies located in Colombia.

VIII   Appeal

In actions for annulment against a trade remedy determination, the Council of State has exclusive jurisdiction as the court of sole instance. In such cases, there is no appeal or second instance against its decisions, except that an extraordinary reviewing petition[76] before the full bench is possible if certain strict conditions are met. As explained above, in proceedings for annulment and reinstatement of rights against trade remedy determinations where the court of first instance is the Administrative Tribunal of Cundinamarca, the final court decision may be appealed to the Council of State.[77]

If a case is brought before the administrative judge, his or her decision may be appealed before the Administrative Tribunal of Cundinamarca in accordance with Article 133.1 of the CCA. However, no case on trade remedy determinations has yet been brought before administrative judges, due to the amount at stake.

In the case of appeals submitted to the Council of State, the appeal must be filed directly (and not as a reconsideration petition subsidiary of appeal) before the contentious-administrative tribunal, within three days from the date on which the decision is served.

The processing of this appeal involves: (i) a duly substantiated request, failure of which will cause rejection; (ii) acceptance of the appeal that complies with the requirements set by law; (iii) request for evidence and practice, if requirements set out in Article 214 of the CCA are met; (iv) closing arguments; (v) preparation of their statement by the speaker; and (vi) final decision from the Council of State.

IX   Standard of review

Both actions for nullity and actions for annulment and reinstatement of rights against trade remedy determinations may be based on one or more of the following grounds: (i) issuance by incompetent officials or

---

[75] Article 176, CCA.   [76] Article 185, CCA.   [77] Articles 129 and 181, CCA.

agencies; (ii) irregular issuance; (iii) disregard of the right to a hearing and defence; (iv) false reasoning; (v) misuse of powers; and (vi) violation of the rules on which the act should be based.

The cause of *issuance by incompetent authority* primarily relates to the situation in which the administrative act is issued by an officer without power assigned under the applicable law. It has been argued that: "incompetence is perhaps considered the most serious vice, which scholars and jurisprudence believe cannot be remedied and therefore, it may be declared ex officio once it appears proven in the process".[78] Incompetence has not been a common ground put forward in the judicial proceedings seeking the annulment of trade remedy determinations.

The cause related to *irregular issuance*, refers to "external requirements that should be taken into account at issuance of an act, as there are formalities established by law that are intended to secure to the administered their rights of defence and due process, aspects proper to procedures".[79] This cause was used indirectly in the partial annulment action filed by Comercializadora Internacional SA Invermec with respect to an anti-dumping duty. In the judicial review proceedings pertaining to trade remedy determinations, one of the major arguments has been the alleged "use of the concept of confidentiality in a manner contrary to national law", although this was not formally identified in the decision by the Council of State.

The *lack of the right to assist to a hearing and defence* is a ground frequently raised in judicial review proceedings. It refers to the relevant agency's obligation to respect the rights of the governed while exercising its administrative functions. Thus, in the case of BASF AG et al. against the Incomex resolution which imposed an anti-dumping duty, the complainant alleged a violation of the right to a fair trial in the following terms:

> the complainant asserts that due process includes both the right of defence and the right to be assisted by counsel, which rights were disregarded by Incomex, because even though its attorney raised, in writing, the confidentiality of information, this authority communicated directly with complainant and asked the complainant to change its attorney's statement.[80]

---

[78] Palacio, *Procedural Administrative Law*, p. 218 (in Spanish).   [79] Ibid.
[80] This ground was also invoked in the *Invermec SA Comercializadora Internacional* case.

On this basis, the complainant argued that the contested investigation process did not respect its due process rights and thereby invalidated the entire determination to impose anti-dumping duties.

As to *false reasoning*, this is directed to preventing the possibility of issuing administrative acts with apparent or non-existent motivation. The judicial review will be permitted to confirm whether the factual reasons asserted as grounds are consistent with such act. This cause applies, as opposed to the misuse of power (which assumes that the reasons are real), when "the reasons identified as the source of the decision or the circumstances under which the decision was issued, are made up, unreal or do not exist".[81] Such an argument was presented in the action against Decree 1153 of 1996, which imposed a provisional safeguard measure on *certain textiles and clothing*. In that dispute, the complainants argued that there was a clear disregard by the Government, when issuing the act on the basis of facts other than those provided in Decrees 2657 and 809 of 1994, that clearly determines the factual situation that must be established prior to the issuance of provisional safeguard measures.

The ground related to the *misuse of power* presents an important evidentiary difficulty, since in this case, "the official issuing the act has the necessary power to issue the act, i.e. the act is within the scope of his or her functions, but the act is issued for reasons other than those indicated by the law that attributes such power".[82] This ground was raised in Invermec International Trading's action, where complainants argued: "since there is lack of evidence of injury to the domestic industry or the presence of dumping, there is misuse of power in the imposition of an anti-dumping duty; this meant pursuing a goal from those laid down in Articles 2 and 3 of Decree 991 of 1998".

Finally, the *breach of the rules on which the act should be based* pertains to the objective and content of the act and its compliance with the superior rule. "The violation of the superior rule occurs not only when it is disregarded, but also when it is applied improperly, in which case we are dealing with a rule that applies to other matters and not for the case at issue."[83] This cause is one of the most commonly used in judicial review proceedings concerning trade remedy determinations. One example is the case that challenged Decree 1153 of 1996, which imposed a provisional safeguard measure on the imports of *certain*

---

[81] Palacio, *Procedural Administrative Law*, p. 219 (in Spanish).   [82] Ibid., p. 221.
[83] Ibid., pp. 226–7.

textiles and clothing, where the complainant claimed that the petition for the initiation of the contested investigation did not meet the full requirements of the applicable standard set forth in Decree 809 of 1994. A similar situation occurred in the judicial review proceeding initiated by BASF AG et al., where the complainants presented a careful identification of all constitutional, legal and regulatory provisions that, in their opinion, had been violated by the administrative authority.

X   Remedies

In an action for annulment, the reviewing court may approve, or partially or totally annul the disputed determination.

An action for annulment and reinstatement of rights has two aspects: the request for the annulment of the disputed act and the reinstatement of the complainant's rights that have allegedly been violated. As far as the first aspect is concerned, the court's powers are the same as in annulment proceedings: it may either approve, or partially or totally annul the action. Where the court annuls the action, it may also order the reinstatement of the complainant's rights. To this end, the court may change the disputed act as it deems necessary. For example, it may reduce the rate of an anti-dumping duty from 30 per cent to 20 per cent if it finds the latter to be the legally justified rate. In an action for annulment, this is not possible.[84]

XI   Overall assessment of the effectiveness of judicial review in Colombia

Colombia is a country that applies trade remedy measures in a very conservative manner. Since the first enactment of trade remedy regulations, approximately 40 anti-dumping investigations, and around the same number of safeguard investigations have been conducted. The country is yet to initiate a countervailing duty investigation.

Thus far, there have been very few judicial review proceedings on trade remedy determinations: only four proceedings on anti-dumping investigations and one on safeguard investigations have been initiated. It is important to note that none of these proceedings resulted in a decision in favour of the complainants; judicial reviewers have always endorsed the investigating authority's standpoint. An important characteristic of

---

[84] Article 170, CCA.

these judicial decisions has been that they focused more on procedural than substantive issues.[85]

While this may be seen as an indication that the investigating authority's determinations are based on an adequate ground, it may also be interpreted as showing the need for a mechanism that would enhance the knowledge of judges on trade remedies so that judicial review in this field focuses more on substantive matters.

Another area of concern pertains to the duration of judicial review proceedings and what that implies for the effective administration of justice. On average, judicial review proceedings on trade remedy determinations take two-and-a-half to three years, whereas some have taken four years. Such long periods, taking into account also the fact that judges usually reject requests for the provisional suspension of disputed acts, significantly lessens the effectiveness of judicial review and discourages its use.

XII   Concluding remarks and suggestions for improvement

We consider that the current judicial review system for trade remedy determinations is an adequate mechanism that can control the legality of the Colombian investigating authority's actions. Nonetheless, this system may benefit from certain improvements to make it more effective for those seeking redress from the actions of the investigating authority.

The most important change, in our view, would be the creation of a special section in each of the judicial review instances, to deal exclusively with free trade and other economic issues, such as the implementation of the WTO Agreement and other sub-regional and bilateral free trade agreements and, among others, the application of competition rules. This would allow administrative judges to refine their skills and therefore ensure a more effective administrative justice capable of discussing not only procedural issues, but also the substantive elements of the challenged determinations. Colombia has made significant efforts to train professionals in the administrative judiciary on this matter. Some law schools are now offering undergraduate courses on free trade and competition, giving lawyers adequate business knowledge.

Furthermore, taking into account the impact of trade remedy measures on the flow of free trade, it would be of utmost importance to

---

[85] These court proceedings also witnessed significant discussions concerning the scope of the investigating authority's powers in the conduct of investigations.

establish a special procedure for the judicial review of trade remedy determinations. Among others, such procedure should involve shorter periods and a special rule that would facilitate the decision for temporary suspension of the disputed measures. Such a system would generate efficiencies necessary for procedural justice to be administered properly and effectively.

Finally, we would note that, unfortunately, the changes introduced by Law 1437/2010 do not address any of the concerns identified above.

6

Brazil: the need for enhanced effectiveness

RABIH A. NASSER AND LUCIANA B. COSTA

I Introduction

This chapter addresses the Brazilian legal system concerning the imposition of trade remedies and the review by local courts of determinations made by the investigating authorities.

The creation of the Brazilian trade remedies legal and institutional framework, as we know it today, dates back to 1995. It is a direct consequence of the results reached in the Uruguay Round of Multilateral Trade Negotiations (hereinafter Uruguay Round) regarding anti-dumping, countervailing and safeguard measures.[1] The Uruguay Round Agreements were incorporated into the Brazilian legal system through presidential decree no. 1355, of 30 December 1994, which provided that as of 1 January 1995 the Final Act Embodying the Results of the Uruguay Round would become fully enforceable in Brazil.[2]

Upon their incorporation, the Uruguay Round Agreements acquired the status of ordinary federal law. As a result, there was a need to modify the existing federal legislation in accordance with the provisions

---

[1] Before that, the trade remedies legislation in force was based on the relevant provisions of the General Agreement on Tariffs and Trade (GATT)1947, incorporated into the Brazilian legal system in 1948 through Law 313. In the 1980s, the administration of the imposition of anti-dumping and countervailing measures was deferred to the Customs Policy Commission (*Comissão de Política Aduaneira*, CPA) and CACEX (*Carteira de Comércio Exterior*), which was responsible for the trade policy measures in Brazil.

[2] According to the Brazilian Constitution, the president of the republic (head of the executive branch) has the authority to sign international treaties and agreements (Article 84, VIII), but to become binding and effective in Brazil, these international acts must be approved by Parliament through legislative decrees. The issuance of a legislative decree is followed by the deposit of the ratification instrument with the organ under the auspices of which the agreement or treaty was signed, and by the publication of a presidential decree which renders the treaty or convention enforceable in the country.

contained in the agreements. In other words, it became necessary to adopt additional domestic rules to implement what was agreed upon at the multilateral level. As part of this implementation process, three decrees dealing with trade remedies were issued during 1995. The purpose of enacting these decrees was to create the administrative framework within which the investigating authorities would conduct anti-dumping (Decree 1602, of 23 August 1995), countervailing duty (Decree 1751, of 19 December 1995) and safeguard (Decree 1488, of 10 July 1998) investigations. However, these decrees did not require prior approval by Parliament. In the Brazilian legislative system, the head of the executive branch has the power to "issue decrees and regulations" directed to ensure full performance of the laws enacted by Parliament,[3] provided such additional rules do not violate or contradict the laws that they are meant to implement.

Obviously, the "laws" which Decrees 1602, 1751 and 1488 (hereinafter Brazilian Trade Remedies Decrees) were to implement are the Anti-Dumping Agreement (hereinafter AD Agreement), the Agreement on Subsidies and Countervailing Measures (hereinafter SCM Agreement) and the Agreement on Safeguards (hereinafter SG Agreement). Some amendments have been introduced to the Brazilian Trade Remedies Decrees since 1995, but overall they remain practically unchanged and constitute the main legal basis for trade remedies investigations.[4]

It was also in 1995 that the authority currently in charge of carrying out trade remedies investigations was first created. The Trade Defence Department (*Departamento de Defesa Comercial* – DECOM) is one of the departments of the Foreign Trade Secretariat (*Secretaria de Comércio Exterior* – SECEX), which is part of the Ministry of Development, Industry and Foreign Trade (*Ministério do Desenvolvimento, Indústria e Comércio Exterior* – MDIC).

DECOM is the administrative body responsible for conducting investigations for the imposition of trade remedies. However, its role is limited to determining whether the legal requirements for the imposition of a trade remedy measure are present in each case. To perform the

---

[3] Article 84, IV of the 1988 Brazilian Constitution.

[4] On 29 August 2011 the federal government announced its intention to review and make improvements to Decree 1602 (which provides for the rules applicable to anti-dumping investigations). The main purpose is to speed up the investigation procedure and make it more efficient. SECEX granted interested parties a period of 40 days for the presentation of suggested amendments to the Decree. As a result, a new decree is expected sometime in 2012.

duties assigned to it, DECOM collects the necessary data and information from all interested parties and issues opinions with a technical assessment as to whether (i) an investigation should be initiated; (ii) an investigation should be terminated without a measure; or (iii) a trade remedy measure should be imposed and, if so, at which rate.

The final decisions regarding these three aspects, however, do not fall within the competence of DECOM. Regarding the initiation and termination of an investigation without measures, the secretary of SECEX (to which DECOM is hierarchically linked) is responsible for the decision. On the other hand, the authority concerning decisions on the imposition of trade remedy measures is vested in the Foreign Trade Chamber (*Câmara de Comércio Exterior* – CAMEX), which is the governmental body responsible for trade policy measures in Brazil.

Thus, administrative procedure concerning imposition of trade remedies in Brazil is divided into two phases: the technical phase and the decision making phase. The former is carried out exclusively by SECEX (mainly through DECOM), while the latter includes the participation of other ministries (besides MDIC) which are represented in CAMEX. This two-step approach was instituted in 1995 through Law 9019/1995. Originally, the Brazilian Trade Remedies Decrees provided that decisions regarding the imposition of trade remedy measures were to be taken by the Ministry of Finance and the then Ministry of Industry, Trade and Tourism. The Provisional Measure (*Medida Provisória*)[5] no. 2158–35, enacted on 24 August 2001, shifted this power to CAMEX. Currently, Decree 4732 of 10 June 2003 provides for the organization, and sets forth the powers, of CAMEX.

CAMEX is an inter-ministerial body responsible for the "formulation, adoption, implementation and coordination of activities and policies related to the foreign trade of goods and services, including tourism".[6] Its specific tasks are set forth in Article 2 of Decree 4732, which provides that:

> It is the competence of CAMEX, among other acts necessary for the attainment of the objectives of the foreign trade policy, to:
> (...)

---

[5] A Provisional Measure (*Medida Provisória*) is a legislative act which may be issued by the president of the republic in cases of necessity and/or urgency and comes into force without prior approval by Parliament. However, it is later reviewed, and may be rejected or converted into a law by Parliament.

[6] Article 1 of Decree 4732.

VIII – provide for guidelines and procedures for investigations concerning unfair practices in foreign trade;

(...)

XV – impose anti-dumping and countervailing duties, whether provisional or definitive, and safeguards;

XVI – decide upon the suspension of the enforcement of provisional measures;

XVII – homologate price undertakings;

XVIII – set forth guidelines for the destination of the amounts collected as a result of the imposition of the duties referred to in item XV of this article;

(...)

The need for decisions taken by CAMEX to be consistent with the obligations undertaken by Brazil in the World Trade Organization (hereinafter WTO) is acknowledged in paragraph one of Article 2, which provides that:

> In the implementation of the foreign trade policy, CAMEX must observe:
> I – the international commitments undertaken by the Country, in particular:
> a) In the World Trade Organization – WTO;
> b) In MERCOSUL; and
> c) In the Latin American Association for Integration – ALADI;
> (...)

The main body of CAMEX is the Ministries Council (*Conselho de Ministros*) in which each of seven Ministries of State holds a seat.[7] This plenary body is in charge of taking the final decisions regarding trade remedies. However, the results of the investigations conducted by SECEX are also reviewed by other bodies of CAMEX, namely, the Technical Group on Trade Protection (*Grupo Técnico de Defesa Comercial* – GTDC) and the Executive Committee of Management (*Comitê Executivo de Gestão* – GECEX), before a decision is taken. GTDC is composed of representatives of the seven ministries represented on the Ministries Council and is the body that first reviews the results of the investigation conducted by DECOM, including in particular the recommendation issued. GTDC's assessment in general will be limited to the technical requirements for the imposition of the measure (i.e. dumping, injury and causal link in the case of an anti-dumping investigation).

The next step is to take the matter to GECEX, which has a broader composition. It has 26 members, representing several ministries. Among

---

[7] Ministries of Development, Industry and Foreign Trade; Executive Office of the President of Brazil; Foreign Relations; Economy; Agriculture; Planning; and Agricultural Development.

these members are the vice-ministers of the seven ministries that form the CAMEX Ministries Council. That is usually where the decisions regarding trade remedies will be agreed. In the event that there are disagreements at the GECEX level, however, the matter may be taken still unresolved to the Ministries Council.

While the secretary of SECEX will almost certainly rely on the technical advice provided by DECOM regarding initiation and termination of investigations without measures, the same does not apply to the decisions taken by CAMEX. Although it will always take into consideration the technical assessment carried out by DECOM, CAMEX may decide not to follow entirely its recommendations. For instance, it may decide to impose a duty at a lower rate than was suggested. It may also apply the measure, but order its temporary suspension. The legal provisions that allow CAMEX to deviate from the technical determination reached by SECEX can be found in the Brazilian Trade Remedies Decrees. In that regard, Article 64 of Decree 1602 provides as follows:

> The determinations or decisions, whether provisional or final, related to the investigation, shall be adopted based on the opinion issued by SECEX.
> (. . .)
> §3° – In exceptional circumstances, even with the proof of existence of dumping and the injury caused by it, the authorities referred to in Article 2 [currently, CAMEX Ministries Council] may decide, *for reasons of national interest*, for the suspension of the imposition of the duty or for the non homologation of price undertaking, or, provided sole paragraph of Article 42 is complied with [which provides that the anti-dumping duty cannot be higher than the margin of dumping], for the imposition of a duty in an amount different from what was recommended, in which case the act must contain the reasons which justified the decision. (emphasis added)[8]

In practical terms, this and similar provisions contained in the other Brazilian Trade Remedies Decrees allows for a public interest test to be performed by the Ministries Council of CAMEX. However, there is no specific procedure provided in the current regulation on how the determination concerning public interest should be made. Usually parties will

---

[8] Almost the same provision is found in Article 73, paragraph 3 of Decree 1751, regarding countervailing duties, whereas Decree 1488 provides in Article 10 that the CAMEX Ministries Council may suspend a safeguard measure when circumstances have changed and it is demonstrated that the adjustment efforts undertaken by the domestic industry are insufficient or inadequate.

schedule meetings and file papers with the ministries represented in CAMEX in order to present their views regarding the issue of public interest.[9]

Thus, during the first stage of an investigation carried out by DECOM while there is no possibility for arguments other than those related specifically to the technical requirements for the imposition of a measure to be taken into consideration, such a possibility does exist during the decision-making phase. Parties may argue either for or against the imposition of a measure, based on the effects that it will have on the economy as a whole, including its impact on other industries or consumers.

The choice to transfer the decision on trade remedies to a body composed of members from different areas of federal government had the very intention of enhancing the legitimacy of the decisions and of allowing a broad assessment of the possible consequences of such measures for the country, not only for the domestic industry asking for protection. This two-step approach is applied to all three trade remedies. In all cases, SECEX (through DECOM) heads the investigation, at the end of which it issues a recommendation, and CAMEX is responsible for taking the final decision.

One possible criticism of the system in place is that, once the final hearing is held by SECEX and the interested parties have had the opportunity to present their final arguments regarding the technical elements of the investigation, the steps followed at the CAMEX level are not made public until the final decision is issued. Parties do not have access to the final recommendation of SECEX, and they are not informed of the measures undertaken in GTDC, GECEX and the Ministries Council of CAMEX. Thus, it can be difficult to predict both what the decision may be and the timing of its issuance.

One final introductory remark concerns some measures announced recently to reinforce the Brazilian trade remedies system. As part of the plan entitled "Brasil Maior", which consists of several initiatives aimed at making Brazilian industries more competitive, the following measures were announced:

- increasing the number of DECOM's investigators from 30 to 150;
- shortening the duration of investigations from 15 months to 10 months on average;

[9] As part of the ongoing revision of Decree 1602, one of the aspects that may be contemplated is the inclusion of more detailed rules regarding the public interest test performed by CAMEX.

- extension of anti-dumping and countervailing measures to imports that undermine the effectiveness of trade remedy measures in force (anti-circumvention);
- rejection of import licences in the event of false statements of origin, after investigation;
- establishment or expansion of administrative treatment regarding imports of products subject to compulsory certification and empowerment of customs control of these products.

While the actual implementation and effectiveness of these measures remain to be seen, their announcement demonstrates the importance attached to trade remedies in dealing with the challenges currently faced by Brazilian industry.

The existence of a large consumer market, improving income levels, the reality of a country not affected as severely as others by the ongoing international financial crisis and the appreciation of the local currency (Real) are all factors that make Brazil an attractive destination for exports. This adversely affects some sectors of Brazilian industry, which see in trade remedies a possible way to offset some of the negative impact. With the above-mentioned measures, the government has indicated that it intends to give the trade remedies system the means to properly address this increasing demand.

In light of this overview of the legal and institutional framework of the Brazilian trade remedies system, next we address the judicial review of the determinations made by the Brazilian investigating authorities in the course of trade remedy investigations.

II   Judicial review of trade remedy determinations

1   Legal and institutional framework

The vast majority of the ongoing investigations, as well as of the measures imposed in Brazil, are related to anti-dumping. Countervailing and safeguard measures are quite rare; they account for less than 3 per cent of the 79 measures currently in force, and no investigation concerning these two measures is currently ongoing.[10] This is probably similar to what happens in other countries, and is explained by the greater difficulty in imposing

---

[10] According to the Ministry of Development, Industry and Foreign Trade, as of August 2011 there were 76 anti-dumping measures, one countervailing duty, one safeguard measure and one price undertaking currently in force in Brazil. They concern different kinds of products such as food, construction, medical and chemical supplies. Currently,

such measures. As a consequence, judicial review of trade remedy determinations in Brazil will generally deal with anti-dumping issues.

A second remark is that both the investigating authority (SECEX/DECOM) and the decision-making body (CAMEX) are part of the Brazilian federal (or central) government.[11] Therefore, any judicial challenge to the decisions taken by such administrative bodies will be reviewed by the so-called "federal judiciary", which is composed of:

(i) federal judges acting in each Brazilian state;
(ii) regional federal courts, responsible for appeals concerning decisions taken by federal judges; and
(iii) the Higher Court of Justice (*Superior Tribunal de Justiça* – STJ) in Brasília,[12] which is responsible for the review of the decisions taken by the regional federal courts.

The federal judiciary is responsible for resolving legal disputes in which one of the parties is a body or entity which is part of the Brazilian federal government. That is why any challenges to trade remedy determinations fall within its jurisdiction.

The investigations for the imposition of trade remedy measures are considered "administrative procedures" and, as such, are subject to the principles provided for both in the Brazilian Constitution[13] and in Law 9784 of 29 January 1999. This Law sets forth the rules that apply to administrative procedures within the federal public administration. Besides determining how the administrative procedures must be conducted, it provides for the possibility of appeals being filed to a higher administrative body against any administrative decisions. The administrative review procedure outlined in this Law applies whenever there is no specific appeal procedure regarding an administrative decision provided for by a different law.

---

there are also 45 anti-dumping investigations and two ongoing anti-circumvention investigations. The number of investigations is based on the number of origins being investigated. If a specific investigation comprises imports from three different origins, it is counted as three investigations. Data is available at www.desenvolvimento.gov.br.

[11] As opposed to the governments of the 26 Brazilian states and Federal District and of the 5,565 municipalities.
[12] Tribunal composed of 33 judges, which is responsible for the final decisions concerning the interpretation and enforcement of federal laws (those that apply in the entire Brazilian territory).
[13] Article 37 of the Brazilian Constitution provides for the general principles that must be observed by all governmental bodies, whether at federal, state or municipal levels, when carrying out their duties.

Therefore, decisions taken by CAMEX concerning trade remedies are first subject to administrative review. However, appeals must be directed to the same body in charge of issuing the decisions (Ministries Council), because there is no higher authority at the administrative level when it comes to trade remedies. Technically, this appeal is considered a reconsideration request. While a total reversal of a decision through such an administrative appeal is highly unlikely, there are cases in which a partial reversal may be obtained. Such a partial reversal could pertain to the form of imposition of the challenged measure.[14]

The possibility of judicial review of any administrative act, whether or not the decision has been appealed at the administrative level, is also provided for in the Constitution, Article 5 of which provides that:

> All persons are equal before the law, without any distinction whatsoever, and it is assured for Brazilians and foreigners resident in Brazil the inviolability of the right of life, liberty, equality, security, and property, on the following terms:
> (. . .)
> XXXIV – it is assured to everyone, regardless of the payment of fees: a) the right to petition Public Authorities for defence of rights or against illegal acts or abuse of power;
> (. . .)
> XXXV – the law shall not exclude any violation of or threat to a right from the possibility of being reviewed by the Judiciary; (. . .).

Although judicial review of decisions taken by bodies of the federal executive branch is usually performed first by federal judges, with the possibility of appeal to the other levels of the federal judiciary (regional federal courts and then the Higher Court of Justice),[15] in some cases the Higher Court of Justice has exclusive jurisdiction. This is the case when an interested party files a writ of mandamus against a decision taken by a Ministry of State.[16] This kind of lawsuit can only be used when it is directed against an administrative act that is manifestly illegal, and provided there is no need for fact-finding or producing evidence. Thus,

---

[14] Recently, CAMEX Ministries Council, through Resolution 16, of 17 March 2011, accepted the request by a Brazilian industry to change a specific anti-dumping duty (US$82.77 per ton) to an *ad valorem* duty (10.6 per cent) which originally had been imposed through Resolution 86 of 8 December 2010.

[15] If the decision violates any constitutional provision, an appeal may also be filed with the Supreme Court (*Supremo Tribunal Federal* – STF).

[16] Article 105 of the Constitution provides that the Higher Court of Justice is competent to assess writs of mandamus against acts of ministries of state.

the scope of such judicial procedure is very narrow, as only matters of law may be discussed. Recourse to this mechanism is limited to cases in which the complainant can clearly show that there is an illegality in the decision taken by a Ministry of State which violates an unquestionable right of the complainant.

Otherwise, if the complainant intends to file an ordinary lawsuit that requires fact-finding and the production of evidence, it has to do so at the first level of the federal judiciary. This does not prevent the complainant in either case, from requesting a preliminary injunction to anticipate the effects of the lawsuit while the final decision is pending.

2   Procedure and remedies

The procedure to be followed in order to submit trade remedy determinations to judicial review does not differ materially from that which applies with respect to cases brought against other governmental acts. There are no courts or tribunals specialized in trade remedies, and this is certainly one of the reasons for the misconceptions and errors that can be found in judicial decisions. Trade remedy measures are usually considered an issue of administrative, economic or tax law and are therefore reviewed by the federal judges or groups of judges (within federal courts) responsible for such matters.

Determinations made by CAMEX related to the imposition of any of the three types of trade remedies may be subject to judicial review. They may either be the subject of a writ of mandamus filed directly with the Higher Court of Justice, or they may be challenged through ordinary lawsuits, which may be filed with the first level of the federal judiciary in the state where the complainant is based, or in the state through which the importation of the goods is taking place. Further, decisions on whether or not to initiate an investigation, to impose provisional duties,[17] to accept or reject price undertakings and to terminate the investigation without measures for reasons of public interest, may also be subject to judicial review. It is also possible to question determinations regarding reviews (changed circumstances, sunset reviews, etc.).

In theory, a judicial review proceeding may lead to the confirmation of the legality of the measure or to its partial or total reversal. Courts may

---

[17] When a provisional measure is not imposed during the investigation, there is no formal decision issued denying the imposition of the provisional measure. Thus, there is no administrative act that may be subject to judicial review.

issue injunctions (provisional decisions) suspending the effects of a trade remedy determination when the complainant is able to show the verisimilitude of the legal basis invoked to support his or her request and that an urgent and precautionary decision is necessary to avoid damage. Thus, there have been cases where the importers requested the courts to order the release of imported goods by customs authorities without the collection of anti-dumping duties.

The granting of such injunctions may be, and usually is, conditioned upon the presentation of a guarantee by the complainant, in the amount equivalent to the anti-dumping duty that will not be paid. Many times, judges will require this guarantee to be in cash. The only advantage for the complainant, in this case, will be for him or her to have this cash readily available in case of a decision in his or her favour, instead of having to wait a long time for tax authorities to reimburse the amount.

As to the final decision, courts are not legally prevented from reviewing the merits (or the technical requirements) of the imposition of a trade remedy measure, and may even annul it. However, they are not inclined to do so, because they usually consider that the administrative authorities are better placed to make the technical and complex assessment needed to determine whether a trade remedy measure should be imposed or not. Therefore, judicial decisions affecting the enforcement of an anti-dumping measure will generally be based on procedural aspects of the investigative process that led to the imposition of the measure.

Importers who are trying to avoid the negative impact of an anti-dumping duty on their businesses initiate most judicial review proceedings. In many cases, such importers have not participated in the investigation procedure and were probably surprised by the imposition of the measure. In other instances, they are importers who participated in the investigation but were not satisfied with the outcome.

Other parties, such as exporters, are also entitled to file a judicial review proceeding with respect to the investigating authorities' determinations. However, this is far less common, probably due to the difficulties of pursuing a lawsuit in Brazil over several years. One of the inconveniences for foreign complainants is the obligation to deposit money for the payment of judicial fees in case of an unfavourable result. Another factor is the length of judicial review proceedings conducted by the federal judiciary, particularly where the complainant challenges the substantive aspects of the disputed determination. In our view, these are factors that render judicial review ineffective.

It is also uncommon to see the domestic industry which filed the application for the underlying investigation questioning the investigating authorities' decisions. This is probably due to scepticism regarding the willingness of the courts to examine the technical details that led to the unfavourable decision, namely, the termination of the investigation without measures.

3   Standard of review

In general, federal courts tend to approve the administrative acts concerning the imposition of anti-dumping duties. It is unlikely the courts would be convinced to reverse the conclusions of DECOM/SECEX and CAMEX as to the merits, mainly because the technical matters involved in trade remedy investigations are complex, and the courts consider that the specialized administrative body is better placed to take decisions on such matters. As a consequence, the courts will normally not evaluate the merits of the administrative decision. Instead, they will usually limit their assessment to the procedural aspects of the measure and/or the investigative process. The excerpt below illustrates the pattern that is usually followed by federal courts when reviewing the acts of the federal executive branch:

> As a general rule, the Judiciary should not substitute the Administration and establish the technical criteria to determine the existence of dumping, unless in cases of patent illegality, lack of publicity, immorality or lack of proportionality in the motivation of the administrative procedure.[18]

Furthermore, the decisions are usually based on the provisions of national law, including Decree 1602, without recourse to the text of the AD Agreement. The reasons for this are twofold. First, as the legal discussion is focused mainly on procedural issues, courts see no reason to resort to the AD Agreement, which would be more useful if they were to review the merits of a case. Second, it seems to us that the complainants make little use of the AD Agreement's provisions, either because of lack of familiarity with the agreement and with WTO jurisprudence, or because they find it difficult to convince a judge to look into the technicalities contained in the agreement; they probably consider that this could further complicate the understanding of the case.

As a consequence, WTO jurisprudence on anti-dumping has not played an important role in the interpretation of the Brazilian Trade

---

[18] Appeal no. 1168359, Regional Court of the Third Region, Third Panel, Date of Judgment: 19/06/2008.

Remedies Decrees by the courts. At the administrative level, however, the situation is very different. During the course of the investigations, it has become increasingly common to have the parties invoke both the AD Agreement and WTO jurisprudence to support their arguments either for or against the imposition of trade remedy measures.

4   Legal issues discussed

It may be interesting at this point to address briefly the most common issues and arguments submitted to judicial review in Brazil.

Usually lawsuits (writs of mandamus or ordinary lawsuits) are filed by importers in an effort to avoid the collection of the duty imposed or to suspend its enforcement.[19] They may be based on arguments of a formal nature (such as non-retroactivity of the law or violation of the due process of law) or raise issues on the merits of the trade remedy determination (such as the calculation of the margin of dumping or the existence of material injury or causal link).

We have identified hundreds of lawsuits filed against anti-dumping determinations.[20] Many of them have the same scope; thus, we will briefly assess the most common legal issues brought to the federal courts. These cases should help one understand the current state of judicial review of trade remedy determinations in Brazil.

4.1   Treatment of China as a non-market economy

One of the main arguments used by complainants to defend the un-enforceability of anti-dumping duties is the nullity of the CAMEX

---

[19] We have identified only five cases in the Higher Court of Justice which were filed by foreign exporters to question the legality of anti-dumping duties. These cases were: (i) Writ of Mandamus no. 7.045 – DF, filed by Hercules Incorporated and Hercules International Limited, exporters from the USA; (ii) Writ of Mandamus no. 8.236 – DF, filed by the China Chamber of Commerce for Import & Export of Foodstuffs, Native Produce & Animal Byproducts, a Chinese exporter; (iii) Writ of Mandamus no. 8.913 – DF, filed by Cedar Petrochemicals Inc, exporter from the USA; (iv) Writ of Mandamus no. 15.406 – DF, filed by IL (MCO), exporter from Macao, China; and (v) Writ of Mandamus no. 10.876 – DF, filed by Novo Nordisk A/S, a Danish company. Novo Nordisk A/S also filed a Writ of Mandamus (lawsuit n. 200134000062981 – JFDF).

[20] We have identified and reviewed the available information concerning almost 200 judicial review proceedings – currently ongoing or already completed – which were reviewed by the regional federal courts, the Higher Court of Justice and the Supreme Court. If we were also to consider the judicial review proceedings filed with the first level of the federal judiciary and which were not appealed, the number of lawsuits would be much higher.

determination due to the fact that the calculation of the margin of dumping for Chinese exporters was invalid. This, goes the argument, is because China is a country with a market economy and, therefore, the normal value used should have been based on prices in China, and not those in a third country.

The majority of judges have refused this argument, on the grounds that the Protocol of Accession of China to the WTO (Article 15, subparagraph (a)), concluded in Doha, Qatar, on 10 November 2001, and incorporated into the Brazilian legal system through Decree no. 5.544 of 22 September 2005, allows WTO members, for a maximum period of 15 years from the date of China's accession to the WTO, to continue to use the methodology applicable to countries which are considered non-market economies.

Some complainants argued that the provisions of Article 15 subparagraph (a) were not applicable, since Brazil had recognized China as a market economy in November 2004. In fact, on 12 November 2004, the Brazilian government entered into a Memorandum of Understanding with China concerning cooperation in trade and investment. Pursuant to the terms of this Memorandum, Brazil stated that it recognized the market economy status of China. However, Brazil later clarified that this was a political statement, and that in order for it to have consequences in the field of trade remedy investigations, this decision required to be regulated internally, which has not happened to date.

Therefore, when it comes to trade remedies, the investigating authorities always emphasize that China is considered a non-market economy and invoke the provision of Article 7 of Decree 1.602 which provides:

> When difficulties occur in determining the comparable price in the case of imports from a country that is not market economy, where domestic prices are mostly set by the State, the normal value may be determined based on the price applied or on the constructed value of the like product in a third country market economy, or the price charged by the country in exports to other countries, excluding Brazil, or, where this is not possible, based on any other reasonable price, including the price paid or payable for the like product in the Brazilian market, duly adjusted, if necessary, to include a reasonable profit margin.

The courts have accepted this reasoning, and the conclusion to be drawn is that the methodology used by the investigating authorities conforms to the provisions of China's Protocol of Accession.

It is worth noting that during the investigation procedure it is possible for Chinese exporters to provide information and documents to prove that market conditions prevail in the specific sector under investigation. If it is shown that these conditions exist, the investigating authorities are able to apply the rules that are valid for market economy countries. However, so far there has been no record of acceptance of such an argument presented by Chinese producers subject to investigations in Brazil.

4.2   Violation of due process of law

Another argument frequently put forward by importers is that the anti-dumping duty is not valid because the due process of law has not been respected and the rights of defence were not granted. This is probably the most common procedural argument presented in judicial review proceedings.

The breaches allegedly committed by the investigating authorities or CAMEX range from a lack of assessment of the degree of support for the written application filed by the domestic industry to the obliteration of the interested parties' right to contradict information and/or documents presented by the domestic industry. This argument is also used by some parties who did not participate in the investigation because they were not aware of it, although the initiation of an investigation is made public through the federal government's *Official Gazette*. Once again, most judges do not accept these arguments and confirm the legality of the procedures followed by the authorities, which are now paying particular attention to procedural aspects of investigations, precisely to avoid future challenges on procedural grounds.

As an example of the recourse to this and to the previous argument, we would mention a judicial review proceeding initiated by a Chinese exporter[21] requiring the annulment of a CAMEX determination, which applied an anti-dumping duty on imports of fresh or chilled garlic from China. The exporter claimed, in this case, that China was a market economy country and alleged that its legal rights to due process of law had been violated on the grounds that the initiation of the investigation deviated from the terms provided for in Decree 1602. Both arguments were rejected by the Higher Court of Justice.

4.3   Legal nature of anti-dumping duties

Some of the claims raised in judicial review proceedings take issue with the application to anti-dumping duties of certain concepts and rules which are normally applicable to taxes. One such rule is a precedent of the Federal Supreme Court (*Súmula 323*) to the effect that "the seizure of

---

[21] Writ of Mandamus no. 8236 – DF (2002/0026717–7).

goods as a coercive manner of obtaining payment of taxes is not admissible". Based on this argument, in some judicial review proceedings the importers requested the release of imported goods by customs authorities without collection of anti-dumping duties.

The prevailing jurisprudence has been that an anti-dumping duty is not in the nature of a tax, but of compensation for the injury caused by dumped imports. Nevertheless, there are judges who consider that since the seizure of goods is not permitted to guarantee the payment of taxes, the same should be the case for the collection of anti-dumping duties.

On this basis, many imported goods enter the country while avoiding payment of the anti-dumping duty, with the support of court injunctions. In some cases, the judge requests security (judicial deposit of the amount of the anti-dumping duty) to grant the injunction. Even if the injunction is later cancelled and the amount of the security payment is transferred to the tax authorities, clearance of the goods without the payment of the anti-dumping duty may have caused a negative impact in the market. Thus, even though these injunctions, which are provisional decisions, do not discuss the merits of the CAMEX determination, they may have the effect of temporarily nullifying the intended purpose of eliminating the injury caused to domestic industry.

On the other hand, some judicial decisions have acknowledged that *Súmula 323* was not applicable, as it is intended to prevent arbitrary retention of goods. As the payment of the anti-dumping duty is a legal requisite for customs clearance, the retention of products would not be arbitrary if the importer did not pay the duty. Such decisions rely on the understanding that not every retention of goods is irregular or punitive, especially when it is based on a legal provision and is carried out as a means of enforcement of such a provision.

4.4   Collection of anti-dumping duties at the time of registration of the import declaration

According to Law 9019/1995, the payment of anti-dumping duties is a necessary condition for the importation of the subject products, and the duty is due at the time of registration of the import declaration,[22] the act

---

[22] "Art. 7. The fulfilment of obligations resulting from the application of anti-dumping and countervailing duties, whether they are definitive or temporary, shall be a precondition for entering into the Country of dumped or subsidized products.

§2°. The anti-dumping and countervailing duties are due on the date of registration of the import declaration."

which initiates the importation procedure. This is also the time when all other taxes levied on imports have to be paid.

Despite this rule, several importers have filed judicial review proceedings seeking exemption from anti-dumping duties on goods ordered prior to the imposition of the duties. The argument is that if the commercial transaction had already started at the time of the imposition of the anti-dumping duty, it should not be subject to the duty. The imposition of the duty in such cases would constitute a change in the rules under which the transaction had been concluded. The courts are not accepting this argument. In light of the above-mentioned legal provision, the prevailing opinion is that once the initiation of an investigation is made public, the importers are already aware of the risk of a duty being applied. Therefore, the burden which they may have to face becomes foreseeable for each ongoing import transaction and for those commenced after the initiation of the investigation.

4.5   Suspension of provisional anti-dumping duties

A number of judicial review proceedings targeted decisions by CAMEX denying requests for the suspension of provisional anti-dumping duties and refusing importers' requests to submit a guarantee (deposit or bond) instead of paying the provisional duties. The Higher Court of Justice reasoned that such claims should be rejected on the grounds that it was within the discretion of CAMEX to decide whether or not a provisional duty should be suspended until the end of the investigation, or whether it should be replaced by a guarantee. The Court underlined that CAMEX would make such decisions taking into consideration the likely impact of such suspension or guarantee on the rationale for imposing anti-dumping duties, namely, the elimination of the injury caused by dumped imports.

Accordingly, the Higher Court of Justice usually considers that the administrative decision to deny such requests must prevail, therefore validating the understanding that the suspension or replacement by a guarantee would undermine the purpose of the anti-dumping duty, the elimination of the injury caused by dumped imports. It should also be noted that, as most lawsuits that had been filed in the Higher Court of Justice were writs of mandamus, many challenges against CAMEX determinations not supported by *prima facie* evidence of an illegality were immediately rejected by the Court.

In summary, the review of the caseload in federal courts concerning trade remedy determinations shows that the scope of the assessment made by judges and courts is limited to procedural issues. As regards merit, courts tend to confirm the consistency of the measures with the requirements set forth in the AD Agreement or in the Brazilian Trade Remedies Decrees. They tend to consider that the administrative authority has discretionary power and is better placed to assess whether the technical requirements for the imposition of a measure are fulfilled. In short, courts tend to defer to the decisions taken by CAMEX.

Finally, it is important to mention one case that may have a systemic impact on the judicial review of trade remedy determinations in Brazil. The National Association of Producers of Garlic (hereinafter ANAPA) filed a Breach of Fundamental Precept Lawsuit[23] (ADPF 177) in July 2009 in the Federal Supreme Court, aiming to annul all injunctions and other judicial decisions that suspended the enforcement of the anti-dumping duty on imports of fresh or chilled garlic from China.[24]

According to ANAPA, such decisions were based on four main arguments:

 (i) the dumping margin found for China was not valid because China was a market economy country;
 (ii) there was no proof of injury to the domestic industry caused by the imports from China;
 (iii) the imposition by CAMEX of anti-dumping duties violated the constitutional principle of tax legality set forth in Article 150, I of the Federal Constitution, according to which the government could not impose or increase a tax without issuing a law;
 (iv) the Supreme Court Precedent no. 323 does not allow imported goods to be retained for purposes of tax collection.

---

[23] According to Article 102, § 1° of the Brazilian Constitution, the Supreme Court is responsible for safeguarding the Constitution. Law no. 9882 of 3 December 1999 stipulates that the Breach of Fundamental Precept Lawsuit shall be brought before the Supreme Court, and shall be intended to prevent or remedy a fundamental precept injury resulting from the acts of public authorities. In such lawsuits, the Supreme Court decision is effective against all, and is binding on other governmental bodies.

[24] On 5 December 1994, the investigation regarding the existence of dumping in the fresh or chilled garlic exports from China to Brazil was initiated. The investigation was closed with the imposition of an anti-dumping duty of US$0.40/kg, effective for a period of five years (from 1995 to 2000). On 19 June 2000, ANAPA petitioned requesting a sunset review. The anti-dumping duty was increased from US$0.40/kg to US$0.48/kg, effective for an additional period of five years (from 2001 to 2006). In a new sunset review, initiated on 21 September 2006, the anti-dumping duty was raised again, from US$0.48/kg to US$0.52/kg, effective for a new period of five years (from 2007 to 2012).

ANAPA argued that such decisions were based on false assumptions and that their continuation could irreparably compromise the objective of anti-dumping duties and render them ineffective. In this respect, ANAPA was pursuing a preliminary Supreme Court injunction to suspend all proceedings under way, as well as cancel the effects of all court decisions suspending the imposition of anti-dumping duties on garlic imported from China.

In addition, ANAPA sought a declaration from the Supreme Court of the illegitimacy and unconstitutionality of the judicial decisions which allowed the imports of Chinese garlic without the payment of the anti-dumping duty and, as a consequence, the recognition of the constitutionality of the CAMEX determination, with retroactive and *erga omnes* binding effect. In March 2011, the reporting judge issued an interlocutory decision emphasizing that ANAPA's case aimed to protect national development and the domestic market. A final decision regarding the requests made by ANAPA is still pending.

This is the first time that this subject has reached the Federal Supreme Court. The outcome may have considerable impact on the way federal judges and courts assess challenges to trade remedy determinations. If the Supreme Court suspends the validity of all injunctions against the collection of anti-dumping duties, it will become more difficult than it already is for importers to obtain favourable decisions in judicial review proceedings. Moreover, a decision by the Supreme Court may contribute to a more uniform pattern of decisions by lower courts. Today, it is not uncommon for lawsuits on the same subject, using similar arguments, to conclude with different outcomes, depending on the place where they were filed and on the judge or court in charge of reviewing them.

If the Supreme Court issues a decision in the above-mentioned case, it may constitute a guideline to which courts and judges will turn in future cases. However, it is difficult to predict when a final decision will be made by the Federal Supreme Court in this case.

III   Concluding remarks and suggestions

The judicial review system currently in place in Brazil is far from flawless. While it is positive that the Constitution gives interested parties the right to go to court and to question any decision made by the investigating or decision-making authorities, there are certain factors that lessen the effectiveness of the system. Some of these pertain to the problems faced by the Brazilian judiciary in general, while others are specific to trade remedies.

One important problem is the amount of time it takes for the federal judiciary to reach a final decision. A judicial review proceeding can easily take several years before it concludes, particularly when there is an appeal to the regional courts or the Higher Court of Justice. The important implication of this delay is that the interested parties will not be able accurately to predict the real cost of their commercial transactions until the courts make a final decision.

A second problem worth mentioning is the judges' lack of familiarity with the legal and economic concepts discussed in trade remedy investigations. This is natural, since the judges and courts in charge of reviewing trade remedy determinations are also responsible for the review of a multiplicity of issues related to administrative, tax and economic law. Thus, often they do not have the specialized knowledge needed for a thorough assessment of trade remedy determinations.

The difficulties faced by judges create three main repercussions: first, they reduce the number of cases in which substantive issues are discussed; second, they prevent judges from discussing the merits of a case; third, they result in conceptual errors in court decisions. As a result, the effectiveness of the judicial review system as a whole is lessened significantly.

A third significant problem stems from the fact that the judicial review system is decentralized. Although most of the cases are filed in the states where the main Brazilian ports are located, as mentioned above, judicial review proceedings concerning trade remedies may be filed in virtually any state. As the federal judges are not obliged to follow the jurisprudence of the higher courts, unless there is a precedent that is binding (súmula), it is not uncommon to have different decisions in similar cases, depending on the place where the case is filed. This obviously reduces legal predictability in trade remedies-related cases.

Arguably, however, the aforementioned weaknesses of Brazil's judicial review system have not increased the number of dispute settlement cases brought against the government of Brazil in the WTO. Only a few dispute settlement proceedings have been initiated against Brazil so far, and it was in only one of them that a panel was established and a report issued.[25]

---

[25] First, both Philippines (DS22–*Brazil – Measures Affecting Desiccated Coconut*) and Sri Lanka (DS30–*Brazil – Countervailing Duties on Imports of Desiccated Coconut and Coconut Milk Powder from Sri Lanka*) challenged a countervailing duty imposed by Brazil on 18 August 1995 on the imports of desiccated coconut and coconut milk. In the former, both panel and Appellate Body reports were issued – and ruled in favour of Brazil – while in the latter the panel was not established. There was also a complaint

In our view, there are two factors that explain the low number of WTO cases initiated against Brazil. One is the quality of the work usually carried out by the Brazilian investigating authorities. The second is that the effects of trade remedy measures imposed by Brazil are probably not considered sufficiently relevant to justify the filing of a complaint in the WTO. Thus, we do not consider that this is due to the effectiveness of the judicial review conducted by Brazilian courts.

We consider that certain steps could be taken in order to enhance the effectiveness of the judicial review of trade remedy determinations in Brazil. The first step would be to increase the awareness of the federal judges of trade remedies and the relevant WTO rules. This may be achieved through courses or seminars with the participation of the representatives of the investigating and decision-making authorities, members of the federal judiciary and of the private sector (including academia and practitioners). One specific objective of such activities could be to encourage more frequent recourse to the provisions of WTO agreements in the context of domestic judicial review.

The second measure would be to create specialized sections in federal courts that would hear cases concerning trade remedies. This would certainly create more consistency in judicial decisions and improve their quality.

A third measure would be an effort to harmonize the decisions taken by different courts. The higher courts could play an important role in this regard by setting forth, when they have the opportunity to do so in specific cases, clear and detailed guidelines as to how the rules regarding trade remedies should be interpreted.

Encouraging interested parties' participation in investigations would also be helpful. This would enhance the quality and transparency of the work carried out by the investigating authorities and could reduce the need for recourse to the courts. In that regard, the measures announced

initiated by India on 9 April 2001 (DS229–*Brazil – Anti-dumping Duties on Jute Bags from India*) which did not pass the consultation phase. India requested consultations concerning the determination by the Brazilian government to continue to impose anti-dumping duties on jute bags and bags made of jute yarn from India. Finally, Argentina filed a request for consultations on 26 December 2006, regarding anti-dumping measures on imports of PET resins (DS355–*Brazil – Anti-dumping Measures on Imports of Certain Resins from Argentina*). On 7 June 2007, Argentina requested the establishment of a panel, but it later requested that the panel suspend its work pursuant to Article 12.12 of the Dispute Settlement Understanding. The panel's work was therefore suspended, and on 5 February 2009 the case was terminated.

recently by the government and referred to in section I above, and the revision of Decree 1602, currently underway, are steps in the right direction.

Finally, and perhaps most importantly, continued improvement of the structure of the investigating authorities and the provision of more resources to them would be helpful.

Argentina: a well-structured but unsuccessful judicial review system

MERCEDES DE ARTAZA

I Introduction

1 History of trade remedies in Argentina

Argentina's first national legislation on trade remedies was part of the Argentine Customs Code[1] dated 1981, which governed the conduct of trade remedy investigations. Throughout the years, different national laws incorporated the international obligations assumed by Argentina and regulated the procedural aspects of these investigations.

Act No. 24176 of 1992 incorporated the Tokyo Round Anti-Dumping and Subsidies Codes into the Argentine legal system. The Act also provided that the Customs Code would continue to apply to trade remedy investigations as a supplementary legal source. Decree No. 2121 of 1994 regulated all matters regarding the conduct of anti-dumping and countervailing duty investigations.

Following the establishment of the World Trade Organization (WTO) and enactment of the new agreements, Argentina adopted Act No. 24425 of 1994 (hereinafter Trade Remedies Act), in order to incorporate into its legal system the Agreement on Implementation of Article VI of the General Agreement on Tariffs and Trade 1994 (hereinafter AD Agreement), the Agreement on Subsidies and Countervailing Measures (hereinafter SCM Agreement) and the Agreement on Safeguards (hereinafter SG Agreement) that now rule the substantive aspects of anti-dumping, countervailing duty and safeguard (jointly hereinafter trade remedies) investigations, respectively.

The Safeguards Decree[2] (hereinafter SG Decree) regulated all matters regarding the conduct of safeguard investigations. Likewise, Decree No. 1326[3] repealed the old Decree No. 2121 and laid down the new rules that

---

[1] The Argentine Customs Code was enacted by Act No. 22415 of 1981.
[2] Decree No. 1059 of 1996.
[3] Decree No. 1326 of 1998. Decree 2121 was formally repealed by the AD/CVD Decree; however, in practice Decree No. 1326 replaced Decree No. 2121.

applied to anti-dumping and countervailing duty investigations. In 2008, the latter was replaced by the Anti-Dumping and Countervailing Duties Decree (hereinafter AD/CVD Decree).[4]

The issuance of the new legislation on anti-dumping and counter-vailing duty investigations was aimed at improving and accelerating investigative procedures as, under the political and economic context of the time,[5] trade remedies acquired a fundamental importance in economic policy. Compared with the former regime, the main changes that resulted from the new legislation were as follows.

(1) The creation of Specialized Information Counselling, in charge of help-ing applicants to access the necessary information to proceed with the initiation of an anti-dumping or countervailing duty investigation and to assist them in filling out the forms required for a complaint. Such assistance was made a mandatory stage prior to the filing of a complaint, in order to avoid unnecessary delays in the process leading to the initiation of an anti-dumping or countervailing duty investigation.

In the case of anti-dumping investigations, this counselling also helps applicants to access information regarding normal value through the Economic and Commercial Office of the Ministry of Foreign Affairs, International Trade and Worship.

(2) The reduction of the consideration of anti-dumping and counter-vailing duty investigations from 12 to 10 months, while maintaining the possibility of extending the deadline under Article 5.10 of the AD Agreement and Article 11.11 of the SCM Agreement.

As a result of the foregoing, during 2008 and 2009 Argentina reached the highest level of its initiations of trade remedy investigations, with anti-dumping taking the lead.[6] According to the National Foreign Trade Commission *2010 Annual Reports*, between 1995 and 2010, Argentina

---

[4] Decree No. 1393 of 2008.

[5] Since 2004, the Argentine Government has adopted a protectionist policy focusing on national industry and international competitiveness aimed at reversing the effects – especially on small and medium-sized companies – of years of unfettered trade liberal-ization. To that end, together with the implementation of productive development and export promotion policies, several protective measures against the rise of imports were applied. Trade remedies were no exception.

[6] According to the last annual report of the National Foreign Trade Commission, in 2008 and 2009 35 and 32 anti-dumping investigations, respectively, were initiated. Initiations in 2008 represented a 150 per cent increase compared to 2007, where only 14 investigations had been initiated. Compared with the average number of initiations between 2004 and 2007, the increase was 105 per cent; 20 investigations were initiated in 2010.

initiated 325 anti-dumping investigations, seven safeguard investigations and nine countervailing duty investigations.[7]

Despite the number of cases, only a few were subjected to judicial review by national courts. This may lead to the conclusion that the determinations of the investigating authority in most cases were not challenged by the interested parties. Even though the investigating authority does not publicize the number of administrative claims made in the course of an investigation, and therefore we do not have precise information on this, it would be safe to assume that parties, particularly importers and foreign producers, raise such claims in most investigations.

As we explain below, Argentina's judicial review system for trade remedy determinations is complex and unpredictable, which discourages interested parties from using it.

2   Structure and functioning of Argentina's investigating authority

Argentina's investigating authority is organized as follows.

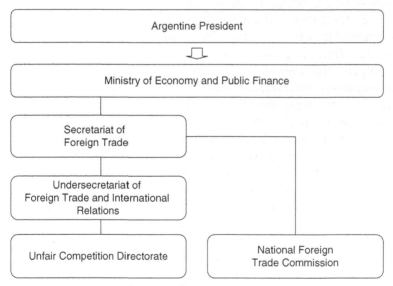

Figure 7.1   Organization of Argentina's investigating authority

---

[7]   The Commission includes sunset reviews in these figures and counts investigations on the basis of the number of exporting countries targeted. Hence, an investigation initiated against two exporting countries would count as two initiations.

The Ministry of Economy and Public Finance (hereinafter Ministry) is the highest authority on trade remedies in Argentina, and its main responsibility is to issue decisions imposing anti-dumping and counter-vailing duties, whether provisional or definitive, as well as safeguard measures. The Secretariat of Foreign Trade (hereinafter Secretariat) and the Undersecretariat for Foreign Trade and International Relations (hereinafter Undersecretariat), are relevant agencies that take part in the decision-making process and recommend future actions to the Ministry on the basis of the analysis and relevant reports of the Unfair Competition Directorate (hereinafter Directorate) and the National Foreign Trade Commission (hereinafter Commission).

Trade remedy investigations in Argentina are conducted on the basis of a bifurcated procedure. Supported by the Undersecretariat, the Directorate is responsible for dumping and subsidy calculations, as well as the assessment of the increase in imports in the case of safeguard investigations. On the other hand, the Commission, a decentralized body under the Secretariat, is responsible for determining the existence of domestic like product, the standing of the applicant, injury to the domestic industry and the causal link.

The Directorate and the Commission are also responsible for the Specialized Information Counselling associated with anti-dumping and countervailing duty investigations. Given that the AD/CVD Decree established this counselling, it is not formally intended for safeguard investigations; however, it would not be wrong to assume that, if it is requested, the same service would be made available to domestic producers seeking the initiation of a safeguard investigation.

The Undersecretariat is responsible for overseeing trade remedy proceedings and providing technical advice to the Secretariat in the course of such proceedings. Based on technical reports from the Directorate and the Commission, the Undersecretariat makes recommendations, among others, with respect to the initiation of an investigation, rejection of an application, termination of an ongoing investigation without measures, and the determination of the scope of the measures to be adopted. After receiving the Undersecretariat's recommendations, the Secretariat makes the decisions on these three issues. The relevant resolutions are also issued by the Secretariat.

As far as the imposition of provisional or definitive measures is concerned, having heard the Undersecretariat's recommendations, the Secretariat makes a recommendation to the Ministry as to the immediate application of such measures. The final decision on the imposition of measures is made by the Ministry. Where it is decided to impose a provisional or definitive measure, the Ministry issues the corresponding resolution. If the Ministry decides not to impose measures, the file will be returned to the Secretariat for it to proceed with the issuance of a resolution for the termination of the investigation without measures.

Where a price undertaking is proposed, the Undersecretariat issues a report to the Secretariat explaining its views on the feasibility of accepting the undertaking, taking into consideration the technical reports from the Directorate and the Commission. The Secretariat will then issue a recommendation to the Ministry, which will make the final decision. If the Ministry decides to accept the undertaking, it will issue a resolution to that effect. However, if the Ministry rejects the undertaking, the file will be returned to the Secretariat for it to notify the interested party which proposed the undertaking. The Undersecretariat's and the Secretariat's recommendations are not binding on the higher authority. Thus, in the case of a disagreement between the higher and lower authority, the final decision will be taken by the former. The same decision-making process also applies to anti-circumvention investigations, sunset reviews and changed circumstances reviews.

All resolutions on the initiation or termination of an investigation, as well as those imposing measures, are published in the *Official Gazette* and sent to the interested parties. Decisions on the acceptance or rejection of an undertaking may be conveyed by a letter addressed to the interested party proposing the undertaking.

II   Previous administrative review of trade remedy determinations

1   Legal framework

The Argentine legal system provides all citizens with access to the judiciary to file their claims. This principle stems fundamentally from Article 18 of the National Constitution, which stipulates that the defence of individuals and rights through judicial review proceedings is uninfringeable. This principle means that everyone, without exception, is entitled to access to a judicial body in order to file a lawsuit, submit evidence, obtain a fair judgment, appeal a judgment deemed unfair or illegitimate before higher courts and request the execution of such a decision once it is final.

In most cases, however, the complainant first has to request an administrative review of the disputed administrative act before proceeding to judicial review.[8] Argentina's Supreme Court has affirmed that this administrative review is aimed at opening a conciliation phase prior to a court review, to give the administration an opportunity to review its decision and modify any errors that it may contain.[9] It also provides an opportunity to ensure conformity of the disputed decision with the legal system. However, it is hard to determine whether administrative review serves this purpose in practice. It simply represents a step that the complainant must observe before seeking redress from a court. In most cases, administrative review results in the approval of the disputed decision by the agency which made it.[10]

When an administrative act in an actual or imminent way affects or may affect a right or a legitimate interest, the affected party can initiate a legal proceeding to challenge either the relevant general administrative

[8] Administrative review is required as a prior condition to filing a judicial review proceeding against an administrative act before the courts. This is specifically mentioned in Article 67 of the AD/CVD Decree, which provides that interested parties may bring a court case against any decision subject to administrative review when the administrative review process is completed. In the *Hisisa* case, in which the complainant requested compensatory damages for loss caused by the delay in the initiation of an anti-dumping investigation, the Supreme Court emphasized that after requesting an administrative review of the preliminary resolution which did not impose provisional anti-dumping duties, Hisisa had not exhausted the administrative or judicial review: therefore neither the legitimacy of the administrative act nor the existence of reparable damage had been determined. As a consequence, none of the aforementioned issues were reviewable at that time. These conclusions were reached on the basis of the Customs Code (applicable at the time to anti-dumping investigations), the Ministry resolutions and the records of the administrative files of the case: Supreme Court (12.08.2008) Lexis N° FC331_1730 - 331:1730. In another case, on the contrary, the Court of Appeals waived this requirement on the ground that the exhaustion of administrative review could turn into a pointless and excessive formal requirement, in violation of the right of defence guaranteed by Article 18 of the National Constitution: Court of Appeals, La Ley 2003-B, 141, AR/JUR/398/2002.

[9] Agustín Gordillo, *Tratado de Derecho Administrativo*, Chapter XV, "Los Entes Reguladores", p. 6, available at www.gordillo.com/tomos_pdf/1/capitulo15.pdf (in Spanish).

[10] Regarding this administrative review requirement, an outstanding Argentine scholar stated: "We believe that facing the truth is unavoidable; the requirement for an administrative review prior to a formal claim is a useless mechanism in all cases, and its certainty is doubtful. Besides, the filing of the claim, especially before the Central Administration where this regime is applied, takes as long as a trial. And we are speaking of years, not months." Gordillo Chapter XII, "El Reclamo Administrativo Previo", p. 16, www.gordillo.com/tomos_pdf/4/capitulo12.pdf (in Spanish).

act, or an act that implements a general administrative act. Challenging a general administrative act has preventative purposes, whereas challenging an act implementing a general administrative act seeks to compensate the effects of an actual violation of a right. The claims put forward in a judicial review proceeding will therefore depend on the nature of the challenged administrative act.

The request for the administrative review of trade remedy determinations must be filed with the Undersecretariat, who then informs the Ministry's Legal Service, which will decide whether the claims put forward are pertinent. If the claims are deemed pertinent, the request will be forwarded to the Directorate and the Commission for the issuance of new technical reports. On the basis of these reports, the Undersecretariat will submit a recommendation to the Secretariat, and the latter to the minister for a final decision. As stated above, administrative review rarely leads to its intended objective of providing for conciliation between the investigating authority and the complainant. This is natural, since the review is conducted by the same agency that is the author of the challenged measure.

In general, initiation of an administrative review does not affect the implementation of the challenged measure. Exceptionally, the investigating authority is authorized to suspend the application of the measure where its implementation is likely to cause damage that would be irreparable or hard to repair, where the measure has a serious defect, where there is an absolute and evident nullity of the measure, or where public interest is involved. To the best of our knowledge, however, this has never been used in the administrative review of a trade remedy measure.

In terms of applicable law, administrative review is conducted pursuant to the Argentine Administrative Procedure Act[11] (hereinafter APL) and, as a supplementary source, pursuant to the rules of the Civil and Commercial Procedural Code (the Procedural Code). It should be noted that the AD/CVD Decree and the SG Decree also contain procedural rules which apply in the administrative review process. In fact, the AD/CVD Decree specifically provides for the supplementary application of the APL, particularly with respect to deadlines. The AD/CVD Decree does not contain a definition of "interested parties", thus, the broad definitions set forth in the AD Agreement and SCM Agreement will

---

[11] Act No. 19549/1972, as regulated by Decree No. 1759/1992.

apply in terms of determining who is entitled to seek administrative review of the investigating authority's determinations. The SG Decree defines interested parties as all individuals and legal entities, public or private, which expressed an interest following the initiation of an investigation. It should be underlined, however, that the complainant who requests the administrative review must have participated in the underlying trade remedy proceeding. This will demonstrate the existence of a lawful interest to seek the administrative review of the relevant measure.

Following the conclusion of the administrative review, the complainant will be entitled to resort to judicial review. It is useful to recall here that administrative review has rarely yielded a positive result for the complainants so far. Thus, in its current status, this could be described merely as a step that must be exhausted before resorting to the judicial review of the contested trade remedy measure.

III   Judicial review of trade remedy determinations

1   Jurisdiction and competent courts

The Argentine justice system is basically composed of the federal judiciary and the provincial judiciary in each of the country's provinces. Federal justice and courts have jurisdiction throughout the country and deal with cases on federal matters referred to them by the National Congress, such as trade marks, competition, maritime law or patent matters. All disputes in which Argentina is a party, and those pertaining to issues addressed in the Constitution or international treaties, come under federal jurisdiction.

There is also provincial or ordinary jurisdiction, which has been vested in provincial courts, and which deals with matters arising under the laws enacted by both national and local congresses. Disputes pertaining to non-federal matters such as torts, contracts, bankruptcy, commercial papers or company law, fall under this general jurisdiction. As far as subject matter jurisdiction is concerned, it should be noted that most courts preside over specific issues (i.e. civil, commercial, criminal, labour, administrative). This applies both to federal and provincial courts.

The Federal Administrative Justice is in charge of overseeing the correct performance of the administration and settling disputes that arise between the administration and private parties. In this context, interested parties may challenge the decisions of the administration by filing a case before a Court of First Instance on Federal Administrative Litigation Matters (hereinafter Court of First Instance), whose decisions may be appealed to the National Court of Appeals on Federal Administrative Litigation Matters (hereinafter Court of Appeals), a court that is divided into tribunals, each having three judges. The final appeal court is the Supreme Court of Justice (hereinafter Supreme Court), which has seven members.[12] Decisions made by the Court of Appeals may be appealed to the Supreme Court.

All of the above is applicable to the judicial review of trade remedies investigations. Thus, in order to challenge an investigating authority's determination, the complainant must file its claim before a Court of First Instance.

2 Types of judicial review proceedings

Administrative acts are judicially challengeable when they affect or may affect a right in an actual or imminent manner. To that end, a complainant may follow: (i) the annulment of the challenged administrative act which, as explained above, can target a general act or a specific act implementing a general act; and/or (ii) the compensation of damage caused by the actions or omissions of the administration. These two objectives may be pursued by initiating one of three types of judicial review proceedings: (i) a general or ordinary lawsuit; (ii) a special appeal when it is expressly provided for in the relevant laws or regulations; and (iii) exceptionally, an *amparo*. Since the trade remedies legislation does not provide for a special appeal, a complainant wishing to challenge a determination of the Argentine investigating authority may either initiate an ordinary lawsuit or an *amparo* proceeding.

---

[12] The Supreme Court exercises general appellate jurisdiction, special appellate jurisdiction, and exclusive and original jurisdiction. General appellate jurisdiction is exercised over matters that have previously been treated by the courts of first and second instance. Such matters are those governed by the National Constitution and federal laws, such as disputes arising under international treaties, or maritime law issues. Special appellate jurisdiction is exercised through what is commonly referred to as "constitutional control", since the Supreme Court has been endowed with the power to control legal rules and administrative acts. The Supreme Court's exclusive and original jurisdiction pertains to matters involving ambassadors, ministers and foreign consuls, and those involving a province.

In terms of the objective pursued, most cases brought against the investigating authority's determinations sought the annulment of the disputed determination. In the exceptional *Hisisa* case, the complainant requested compensatory damages resulting, *inter alia*, from the delay in the initiation of an anti-dumping investigation. The Supreme Court rejected the case on the ground that the four-month delay in the initiation of the investigation was caused by the complainant itself, who had not submitted the information on normal value to the investigating authority.[13] Excluding the above-mentioned case, in most cases, parties have chosen to seek the annulment of the disputed determination by initiating an *amparo* proceeding on the basis of alleged violations of the AD, SCM and SG Agreements.

Section 43 of the National Constitution expressly provides affected parties, the ombudsman, non-governmental organizations (NGOs) and/or consumer groups with the right to file *amparos*, an expedited proceeding that may be followed in disputes involving acts or omissions (committed either by the government or individuals) which actually or potentially infringe, restrict, alter or threaten, in a manifestly arbitrary or illegal way, rights and guarantees recognized by the National Constitution.[14]

Despite being the most frequently used type of judicial review proceeding, *amparo* has not been particularly satisfactory for complainants who challenged the Argentine investigating authority's determinations: there was only one case when *amparo* yielded a positive result for the complainant. This case involved a request addressed to the court to direct the Ministry to refrain from ordering a full or partial extension of a safeguard measure on footwear, which had been imposed in 1997. The complainant argued that the investigating authority was planning to extend the measure in violation of the relevant provisions of the SG Decree. He also argued that the original imposition of the measure was inconsistent with the SG Agreement, because it was not accompanied by a plan for a progressive liberalization. The investigating authority

---

[13] Supreme Court (12.08.2008) Lexis N° FC331, 1730 – 331:1730.

[14] Article 43 of the National Constitution reads: "Every person is entitled to bring a summary *Amparo* action, provided always there is no other judicial proceeding which is more appropriate, against any act or omission of public authorities or individuals, which damages, restricts, distorts or threatens, arbitrarily or illegally, rights and guarantees acknowledged by this Constitution, a treaty or a law. In such case, the judge may declare the unconstitutionality of the rule on which the damaging act or omission is founded."

proceeded with the extension of the measure. The Supreme Court granted the complainant's motion, and declared the safeguard measure as issue null and void, reasoning that it was evident from the investigation file and the grounds presented in the disputed resolution that the conditions set forth in the SG Decree had not been fulfilled. The Supreme Court did not discuss the consistency of the initial imposition of the challenged safeguard measure with the SG Agreement.[15]

One important difference between an *amparo* and an ordinary lawsuit is that the exhaustion of the administrative review process is not required prior to the filing of an *amparo*. This is not surprising, given that *amparo* is an alternative that is available only with respect to administrative acts that are clearly illegal or arbitrary.

IV Procedure

1 General procedure

The applicable procedure is set down and may involve any of the following stages: complaint, answer, defences to the complaint, counter-claim, collection of evidence and final ruling. Parties to judicial review proceedings must be represented by a registered attorney. In cases involving foreign exporters, the court may also ask the foreign exporter to submit what is called an *arraigo* – a sort of guarantee to cover court fees – since foreign exporters typically have neither residence nor property in Argentina.

As soon as a case is filed, the court notifies the National Public Treasury Attorney's Office, seeking its advice, and requests the Public Prosecutor to issue a decision on the fulfilment of the substantive and procedural requirements by the complainant, such as the existence of subject matter and territorial jurisdiction, exhaustion of administrative remedies and the existence of legal standing. If these requirements are not fulfilled, the complaint may be opposed *in limine*. If all requirements have been fulfilled, the administration (the Ministry where the case concerns a trade remedy determination) is notified and given 30 days to respond to the complaint.

The administrative file becomes extremely important in court proceedings, because it contains evidence that is essential for the resolution

---

[15] Supreme Court (21.05.2002) La Ley 2002-C, 864 – DJ2002-2, 392 – RDM2002-3, 161 – *Colección de Análisis Jurisprudencial Elementos de Derecho Administrativo* – Comadira, Julio Rodolfo, 532. – AR/JUR/4074/2002.

of the dispute. Under Argentine law, administrative acts benefit from the presumption of legality. Under the APL, until and unless a court sets them aside, such acts are deemed to be consistent with the legal system and, therefore, valid. In a judicial review proceeding, what a complainant seeks from the court is that this presumption be set aside with respect to the challenged act.

As already mentioned, the judgment by the Court of First Instance may be appealed to the Court of Appeals and then to the Supreme Court. The appeal may be filed by any of the parties within five working days from the notification of the decision of the Court of First Instance. The Court of Appeals makes its decisions by a majority of its three members, each of whom must explain in the decision the legal basis of his/her opinion. The lower court's decision may be approved or reversed for being arbitrary, for contradicting the applicable law, or for the non-observance of the relevant procedural rules.

If there is no further appeal, the decision by the Court of Appeals becomes final. However, decisions of the Court of Appeals may be appealed to the Supreme Court by any of the parties to the case within five working days from the notification of the decision. In this case, the Supreme Court's decision represents the final resolution of the dispute.

2   Applicable law

The matters filed before the courts of the Federal Administrative Justice and the judicial action chosen will determine the law that will govern the judicial review proceeding. In proceedings challenging the investigating authority's determinations, the Trade Remedies Act and the AD/CVD and SG Decrees will apply. Procedural aspects of judicial review proceedings are governed by the procedural code corresponding to the jurisdiction in which the judicial review has been initiated. In *amparo* proceedings, the main governing instrument will be the Amparo Act,[16] whereas the procedural codes will be only supplementary sources.

To the best of our knowledge, the Federal Administrative Justice has never cited WTO case law in its decisions concerning the investigating authority's determinations. In the judicial review proceeding concerning the safeguard measure on footwear, however, the complainants invoked WTO case law. Prior to the filing of this domestic judicial review proceeding, the safeguard measure had been challenged in WTO dispute

---

[16] Act No. 16986.

settlement, and the Dispute Settlement Body (hereinafter DSB) had found the measure to conflict with WTO law, and recommended that Argentina bring it into consistency with its WTO obligations. The complainants based their claims partly on the DSB's findings and recommendations in the domestic judicial review proceeding challenging the same determination.

The investigating authority, which, at the time of the domestic judicial review proceedings, had extended the disputed measure, argued that the WTO's findings had been taken into account in the extension decision. However, it also took the view that WTO decisions were not binding on the parties to the dispute, because the WTO comprises sovereign states and that, therefore, there was no obligation to modify a measure which was found to be WTO inconsistent, but to try to modify it. It also argued that the DSB had found the measure to be inconsistent with Argentina's obligations under the WTO Agreement, but had not recommended the termination of the measure.[17]

It should be noted, contrary to judicial review, that WTO case law has been invoked frequently during trade remedies investigations and administrative reviews, both by the petitioners and the investigating authority.

3 Reviewable determinations

Article 67 of the AD/CVD Decree provides that interested parties may challenge through judicial review any decision subject to administrative review when the administrative review process has been exhausted, as provided in Article 68. Article 68 states that administrative review may be lodged against measures imposing or refusing to impose provisional or definitive anti-dumping or countervailing duties, and against decisions that suspend, refuse, revoke or terminate investigations. Other decisions adopted during the investigation are not subject to appeal.

Thus, under Argentine law, the following determinations made in anti-dumping and countervailing duty investigations are judicially reviewable: (a) imposition of provisional or definitive measures, (b) refusal to impose provisional or definitive measures, (c) refusal to initiate an investigation, (d) termination of an investigation without measures, and (e) acceptance of undertakings (if the underlying investigation is suspended after acceptance of the undertaking).

---

[17] Court of Appeals, Laley 2003–13, 141 AR/JUR/398/2002.

According to Article 68 of the AD/CVD Decree, other determinations made in the context of anti-dumping and countervailing duty investigations would not be reviewable: for instance, decisions to initiate an investigation or to reject a price undertaking. It is difficult to predict what stance courts would take on the reviewability of these determinations, because no such case has been filed as yet.[18] The Argentine AD/CVD Decree does not specify review possibilities with regard to decisions adopted in the context of changed circumstances, new exporters, or sunset reviews and anti-circumvention investigations. In our view, however, the principles explained above should also apply, *mutatis mutandis*, to these proceedings.

Regarding safeguards, Article 32 of the SG Decree stipulates "decisions that are adopted in the context of an investigation or as a consequence of it are not reviewable". This provision gives the impression that no determination related to safeguard investigations is reviewable under Argentine law. However, as explained above, in practice there have been situations where both administrative review and judicial review were sought and granted against safeguard determinations. Thus, the meaning of this provision is not clear. This was discussed by the Court of First Instance in the judicial review proceeding concerning the safeguard measure imposed on footwear, and the court interpreted this provision as meaning that safeguard determinations are exempt from administrative review and, based on that interpretation, exempted the complainant from that requirement. This decision implies that such determinations are subject to judicial review.[19]

This interpretation is in consonance with Article 23 of the APL, which entitles affected parties to resort to judicial review against any definitive administrative act when the act affects, or may affect in an actual or imminent way, individual rights of the complainant, and the administrative remedies have been exhausted. In the *Footwear* case, the Court of First Instance took note of the fact that no administrative remedy was available with respect to safeguard determinations, and concluded that denying the

---

[18] It can be argued that Article 68 of the AD/CVD Decree may be challenged as being unconstitutional, since it conflicts with the international obligation laid down in Article 13 of the AD Agreement and Article 23 of the SCM Agreement, which specifically provide that each member whose national legislation contains provisions on anti-dumping or countervailing measures should provide judicial, arbitral or administrative courts to ensure an independent review of the final determinations taken during anti-dumping and countervailing duty investigations and reviews.

[19] Court of Appeals, La Ley 2003-B, 141 AR/JUR/398/2002.

possibility of judicial review of such determinations would violate the right of defence recognized under Article 18 of the National Constitution.

In most of the judicial review proceedings that we have studied, the cases were aimed at challenging the imposition of definitive anti-dumping or safeguard measures. Only in one case did the complainant, a national producer, take issue with the investigating authority's decision not to impose provisional measures in an anti-dumping investigation. The Court of First Instance ordered the Undersecretariat immediately to take the necessary measures to limit imports of chicken from Brazil by imposing a quota on the imports of the subject product until the effective adoption of anti-dumping duties. According to the court, the measure ordered sought to replace the failure to act on the part of the investigating authority, which had found injury to the national industry in the preliminary phase of the investigation, but which had not imposed provisional measures for reasons of public interest. Basing itself on the findings made by the Commission, the court considered that the complainants had shown the critical situation of the national industry at the time.

The decision was appealed by the investigating authority, alleging that it disregarded the international commitments assumed by Argentina in the field of international trade[20] and that the imposition of anti-dumping duties was an exclusive power of the administration that fell outside the area of the judiciary's responsibility. The Court of Appeals reversed the decision of the Court of First Instance. The decision was then appealed under extraordinary motion by the complainant, and was dismissed, as it was a clear and illegitimate intervention from the judiciary in matters falling under the competence of the Executive.[21]

In another case, the complainant, also a national producer, sought damages caused by the delay in the initiation of the underlying anti-dumping investigation, yet the Supreme Court rejected this claim, pointing out that the investigating authority was not liable for such damages.[22]

4 Standing

Article 67 of the AD/CVD Decree establishes that interested parties may challenge through judicial review any decision subject to administrative

[20] GATT 1994, Treaty of Asunción and Act No. 24425.
[21] Court of Appeals (30.12.1999), LLLitoral 2001, 490 – RDM2000-2, 269 – AR/JUR/680/ 1999.
[22] Supreme Court (12.08.2008), Lexis Nº FC331_1730 – 331:1730.

review. The Decree does not define the term "interested party". In our view, the wide definition provided for in Article 11.6 of the AD Agreement[23] and Article 12.9 of the SCM Agreement[24] should apply. Regarding safeguard investigations, the SG Decree stipulates that all individuals and legal entities, public or private, which expressed an interest following the initiation of an investigation, are considered to be "interested parties". As far as a judicial review is concerned, Argentine law requires the existence of active legal standing, which means that the complainant must be the holder of the substantive right litigated, and a legally protected interest must be affected.[25]

With respect to trade remedy determinations, domestic producers, importers and foreign exporters can initiate a judicial review proceeding when they consider that their individual rights have been affected by the challenged measure. In practice, there have been cases initiated by each of these parties. Trade or business associations are also eligible to initiate a judicial review proceeding provided they represent producers, exporters or importers, and the challenged action has affected all of their members. For example, an association would not be entitled to bring a case with respect to the acceptance of an undertaking by an individual exporter, since that decision affects only that individual exporter. However, If the case concerns the imposition of provisional or definitive anti-dumping duties, the association would be able to bring a case, because such measures would affect all or many of the members of the association. It should be noted, however, that we have not spotted any case initiated by such an association so far.

---

[23] "6.11 For the purposes of this Agreement, 'interested parties' shall include: (i) an exporter or foreign producer or the importer of a product subject to investigation, or a trade or business association a majority of the members of which are producers, exporters or importers of such product; (ii) the government of the exporting member; and (iii) a producer of the like product in the importing member or a trade and business association a majority of the members of which produce the like product in the territory of the importing member. This list shall not preclude members from allowing domestic or foreign parties other than those mentioned above to be included as interested parties."

[24] "12.9 For the purposes of this Agreement, 'interested parties' shall include: (i) an exporter or foreign producer or the importer of a product subject to investigation, or a trade or business association a majority of the members of which are producers, exporters or importers of such product; and (ii) a producer of the like product in the importing member or a trade and business association a majority of the members of which produce the like product in the territory of the importing member. This list shall not preclude members from allowing domestic or foreign parties other than those mentioned above to be included as interested parties."

[25] Court of Appeals (24.10.2008).

Neither the SG Agreement nor the SG Decree contains a provision on the issue of standing in judicial review proceedings against the investigating authority's determinations in safeguard investigations. In our view, standing in cases initiated against safeguard determinations should be decided on the basis of the same rules that determine standing in cases involving anti-dumping and countervailing duty determinations.

5 Procedural rules governing judicial review

5.1 Ordinary lawsuits

By virtue of the principle of *ne ultra petita*, the case brought before the court will be limited to the issues identified during the administrative review procedure. This does not imply a necessary identity between the claim and the challenged action, but it does demand the latter not to exceed the former, pursuant to the reviewing nature of a judicial review, which prevents courts from hearing cases that have not previously been heard by the administration. Ordinary lawsuits allow multiple opportunities for the parties to exercise their right of defence. After the exhaustion of administrative remedies, the APL provides for a deadline of 90 working days for the filing of the case with the Court of First Instance, which is calculated from the date of notification of the definitive decision concluding the administrative review. The definitive decision is either the Ministry's or Secretariat's final resolution, depending on the scope of the challenged decision, as explained above.

Under the APL, in cases of silence on the part of the administration, the judicial review proceeding may be initiated after the challenged act acquires a definitive nature. In such cases, the administration's silence is construed as denial, unless provided for otherwise in a special regulation. Having thus cleared the way for a judicial review proceeding, the interested party is entitled to file a case before the Court of First Instance.

The APL states that an administrative act is null and void when it was issued on the basis of an essential error, or fraud, or on the basis of facts that are non-existent or false, or by moral or physical violence exerted on the agent, or in the case of absolute simulation, or whenever the defendant agency was incompetent to issue the disputed act because of the matter, territory, time or degree, or for violation of the law or the essential and substantive procedures to be met for its enactment or the purpose that inspired its issuance.

Where it is not clear on the face of the disputed act that it suffers from one of the above-mentioned defects, but further investigation by the court shows that indeed it has such a defect, it can still be declared null and void by the court. To this end, parties should allege and demonstrate that the irregularity stems from the violation of the essential requirements imposed by the law for the issuance of a legitimate administrative act. That is to say: (i) the act should have been issued by the competent authority; (ii) it should be based on all the facts and available information and on the applicable law; (iii) its object must be true and physically and legally possible, issued after hearing the interested parties, not affecting acquired rights; (iv) its enactment must have met the essential and substantive procedures under the applicable law; (v) it must be motivated, expressing in concrete terms the reasons that led to its issuance; (vi) it should comply with the objectives of the rules vesting the issuing authority with the relevant power, and should not pursue objectives, public or private, other than those justifying the act, its cause or object.

Once a judgment is obtained in the Court of First Instance, the interested party may challenge the decision through the filing of a motion of appeal aimed at obtaining the amendment or annulment, by a higher court, of a previous judicial resolution that has been deemed questionable or illegitimate. The motion of appeal may also be filed in order to appeal a decision of the Court of Appeals to the Supreme Court. The affected party may also file an extraordinary appeal before the Supreme Court, an exceptional action that serves exclusively constitutional control purposes. This appeal is pertinent against a judicial decision in a case where a constitutional issue has arisen. A constitutional issue may arise in respect of the provisions of the National Constitution, international treaties or federal rules. This type of appeal must be filed with the court which issued the contested judicial decision within 10 working days from the date of notice of issuance of that decision.

In principle, a judicial decision affects only the complainant which filed the case. However, when a general act is challenged, the judgment might affect parties other than the complainant. For example, in a case which challenges the imposition of an anti-dumping duty imposed on imports from a given exporting country, the annulment decision by the court will directly affect all interested parties, including those that did not participate in the judicial review proceeding. However, in the event of an annulment decision in a judicial review proceeding which challenges a specific procedural violation in the treatment of an exporter involved in an anti-dumping investigation, the annulment decision will indirectly affect other exporters with respect to which the authorities committed the same procedural error.

In judicial review proceedings in the form of a collective action, the court decision will affect all parties in the same situation, regardless of whether or not they participated in the court proceedings.

5.2 *Amparo*

As mentioned above, in addition to an ordinary lawsuit, interested parties may also resort to *amparo*.[26] The following requirements must be fulfilled in order to file an *amparo*: (i) there must not be a more appropriate judicial proceeding available;[27] (ii) judicial intervention must not compromise, directly or indirectly, the proper functioning of the national government; and (iii) the alleged arbitrariness or illegality must be manifest, and shall not be subject to proof or debate.[28] Only manifestly illegal or arbitrary behaviour by the investigating authority which causes injury, restriction, alteration, or which threatens the rights and guarantees recognized by the National Constitution, international agreements or national laws may be challenged in an *amparo* proceeding. Its procedure is abbreviated and its defence possibilities limited.

The *amparo* must be filed with the Court of First Instance that has territorial jurisdiction within 15 working days from the date on which the complainant acquired knowledge of the contested administrative act. Only final decisions, decisions to reject the *amparo*, and those which order injunctions or suspension of the effects of the challenged act may be appealed before the Court of Appeals, within 48 hours of the notification of the contested decision by the Court of First Instance.

As stated above, in the area of trade remedies, the *amparo*, together with injunctions requested to obtain the suspension of the disputed measures, is used much more frequently than ordinary lawsuits. It

---

[26] See Article 43 of the Argentine National Constitution, *supra* note 14.

[27] The interpretation of the absence of a more appropriate judicial proceeding should be limited to the judicial sphere, and taking into account the nature of the rights involved. According to scholars: "the viability of *amparo* is not obstructed by the existence of administrative remedies or by the fact that administrative remedies have not been exhausted", German Bidart Campos, *Manual de la Constitución Reformada*, Vol. II, (1998) p. 377.

[28] An *amparo* proceeding may also be filed to challenge, on constitutional grounds, a resolution denying the revision of non-reviewable decisions according to Article 68 of AD/CVD Decree or Article 32 of the SG Decree. In such cases, it would be necessary to prove the violation of the constitutional rights, among others, regarding property, due process and the right to exercise a lawful industry. It should also be noted that this action is not valid in cases where invalidation of the acts requires debate, examination and evidence.

should be noted, however, that *amparo*'s scope is limited to a declaration by the reviewing court that the challenged act or omission of the investigating authority is or is not legitimate. If the court declares the disputed act to be inconsistent with the law, the court may not go further and decide how the investigating authority should have handled the disputed issue. In other words, the court cannot substitute its view for that of the investigating authority; however, it has remand power. Thus, in such a situation, the court will send the file back to the investigating authority for reconsideration in light of the inconsistencies identified in the court decision.

We should also note here that, in some disputes, courts rejected *amparos* on the grounds that there were other more appropriate legal avenues available. For example, in the *Norville* case, the Court of Appeals stressed the exceptional nature of *amparo* and underlined that this exceptional action could be filed only in situations where there is no other suitable procedure, or where the ineffectiveness of standard procedures could cause concrete and serious damage which would only be reparable through an *amparo* proceeding.[29]

In the *Fepasa* case, the Court of Appeals revoked the decision by a Court of First Instance which had adopted a precautionary measure to direct the Undersecretariat immediately to adopt anti-dumping measures, on the grounds that the complainant could have challenged the disputed action through administrative review which he/she did not, and that therefore the complainant should have been deemed to have consented to the challenged action.[30]

5.3 General aspects applicable to both actions

In General under Argentine law, the filing of a judicial review proceeding does not suspend the implementation of the challenged administrative act, unless provided for otherwise in a regulation. This is because of the presumption of legitimacy of those acts that stems from the APL provisions. This principle was expressly laid down in Decree No. 2121, the

---

[29] "It is an exceptional process, viable in the delicate and extreme situations in which, due to the lack of other suitable ways, fundamental rights are compromised, and it requires particular circumstances characterized by the presence of arbitrariness or illegality that, given the ineffectiveness of standard procedures, cause a concrete and serious damage, only reparable under this urgent and expeditious way", Court of Appeals, Sala II (24.11.2009) La Ley AR/JUR/59656/2009.

[30] Court of Appeals (30.12.1999) – available at Litoral 2001, 490 – RDM2000-2, 269 – AR/JUR/680/1999.

first national regulation regarding anti-dumping and countervailing duty investigations.[31]

A complainant may request the court to order the suspension of the challenged administrative act by an injunction as a previous or antici-patory measure, before filing the action. To that end, the interested party should demonstrate the right claimed and the likelihood of risk of irreparable harm that delays would cause.[32] A request for suspension may also be submitted simultaneously with the filing of the case, or after the beginning of the process, for example, when its illegitimacy is assessed during the evidence production stage.

6 Scope of review

An administrative review entails an assessment of the legitimacy, pertinence and convenience of the challenged act. Judicial review, however, is limited to an analysis of legitimacy, namely, the consistency of the challenged act with the applicable law. These general principles also govern the administrative and judicial review of trade remedy determinations.

However, an analysis of the court decisions made thus far clearly reveals the significant degree of deference accorded to the investigating authority's determinations. The courts' analysis has typically been limited to procedural aspects of the determinations rather than substan-tive matters underlying such determinations such as, in the case of an anti-dumping investigation, the validity of the evidence considered for determining normal value, the adjustments made on the normal value, the method chosen for dumping margin calculations, or the factors considered in the determination of injury and casual link. It goes without saying that such an assessment falls short of providing an effective judicial review mechanism. This is due to the Argentine constitutional system, which prevents the judiciary from intervening in matters that fall under the competence of the Executive.[33]

---

[31] Decree No. 2121 was formally repealed by the AD/CVD Decree; however, in practice Decree No. 1326 replaced Decree No. 2121. This provision has not been incorporated into the new legislation.

[32] It should be noted that the only suspension regarding trade remedy determinations was granted by an injunction in the *Fepasa* case, in which the Court of First Instance granted a precautionary measure, which was subsequently set aside by the Court of Appeals.

[33] See Court of Appeals (30.12.1999) Litoral 2001, 490 – RDM2000–2, 269 – AR/JUR/680/ 1999. The Court of Appeals pointed out that the determination of anti-dumping duties was within the competence of the administration and fell outside the scope of judicial

It is interesting to note that the Public Treasury Attorney's Office, the highest-ranking advisory agency of the government whose opinion the reviewing court seeks in the judicial review proceedings initiated against the investigating authority's determinations, expressed the view that the technical and economic determinations made by the investigating authority fell outside its authority. It noted the technical character of the investigating authority's determinations, and pointed out that such determinations had to be judged against the constitutional requirement of fairness.[34]

In our view, the independence that Article 13 of the AD Agreement and Article 23 of the SCM Agreement require for the tribunals conducting judicial review, may only be maintained through review conducted by the courts, not the administration because, as we explained above, administrative review is conducted by the same entity which makes the disputed decision.

V   Remedies

The remedies available to courts in judicial review proceedings are limited. Courts may approve or annul the disputed action totally or partially. Depending on the claims raised, when the court annuls the challenged administrative act (totally or partially), it may also take the necessary measures for the reinstatement of the rights violated. To this end, the court may order the execution of administrative acts to ensure

review, as the judiciary was not empowered to impose anti-dumping measures. The court stated that anti-dumping measures applied by the investigating authority could be questioned before the courts, but only for review purposes. See also, Supreme Court (21.05.2002) 2002-C, 864 - DJ2002-2, 392 - RDM2002-3, 161 - Julio Rodolfo Comadira, *Colección de Análisis Jurisprudencial Elementos de Derecho Administrativo*, 532 - AR/JUR/4074/2002. The Court of Appeals denied that the participation of the Court of First Instance in the case could be considered an intervention in economic policy decisions under the exclusive authority of the administrative branch, since, in its view, judicial review was not meant to substitute an administrative decision, but to control the administration in the execution of its own authorities. The investigating authority filed an extraordinary motion before the Supreme Court on the grounds that the interpretation of federal regulations was in question. The Supreme Court stated that the *thema decidendum* of the review was not the legitimacy of the imposition of a safeguard measure as a matter of economic policy, but the verification of its compliance with the legal conditions laid down in the relevant regulations, confirming the decision of the Court of Appeals. It should be underlined that this is the only case to which we had access in which the Supreme Court found against the investigating authority's determinations.

[34] Public Treasury Attorney's Office Opinion No. 17: (28.01.2004) - Book: 248, p. 68.

the correct exercise of public prerogatives and competence. It may also order reparation for the damage caused by the implementation of the challenged act. The courts cannot modify, reform, substitute or change an administrative act. However, they can order the administrative agency to make the challenged act consistent with the governing rules.

An overall analysis of court decisions in judicial review proceedings on trade remedy determinations clearly shows the courts' tendency to approve the challenged determinations. Such decisions are sometimes based on jurisdictional considerations or non-compliance with the relevant procedural requirements. Irrespective of the grounds identified by the courts, however, the conclusion is always similar.

VI Concluding remarks and suggestions for improvement

Judicial review of trade remedy determinations has not been used frequently in Argentina, although a number of trade remedy investigations have been conducted thus far. There are several reasons, in our view, which explain this situation. The first issue is the time-consuming nature of judicial review. The requirement of the exhaustion of administrative remedies and the uncertain duration of court proceedings make judicial review long and complex. For example, in the *Adidas* case, although the *amparo* was filed in 2000, the final decision after the extraordinary appeal was issued in 2005. As explained above, *amparos* are abbreviated proceedings. Yet, in this particular case, the safeguard measure at issue was terminated by the time the final court decision was issued.

With respect to ordinary lawsuits, the situation is worse. To give an example, in the *Hisisa* case, the disputed anti-dumping duties were applied in August 1991, the judicial review proceeding was filed in August 1993 and the decision of the Supreme Court was issued in August 2008. Therefore, it is clear that the amount of time it takes to obtain a result in judicial review proceedings in Argentina is a factor that could discourage interested parties from using this option. Further, as already mentioned, the courts have never granted requests for the suspension of the effects of the challenged measures during court proceedings. This exacerbates the situation, because by the time the court reaches a decision, either the challenged measure will have been terminated, or will already have done significant damage to the affected economic actors.

In light of this, we consider that it would be desirable to create a specialized administrative review agency to conduct an independent analysis of the investigating authority's determinations which would exhaust the administrative remedies available against the determinations. Additonally, a new judicial review procedure should be created which would conduct an effective assessment of such determinations and which would therefore better protect interested parties' rights. To this end, we propose the following guidelines:

- The proposed administrative review agency should complete its review within six months.
- This review should cover all pertinent legal and technical issues regarding the underlying determination.
- The agency should have the power to order the suspension of the execution of the challenged determination.
- Individuals conducting the review for the agency should possess adequate knowledge of the interpretation and application of the AD, SCM and SG Agreements, including knowledge of the WTO panel and Appellate Body decisions.
- The completion of this administrative review should be deemed to exhaust all administrative remedies available.
- Interested parties should be able to appeal the agency's decisions directly to the Court of Appeals, avoiding the Court of First Instance intervention, in order to shorten the duration of judicial review.
- The agency's decisions, including its interpretations of the relevant legal texts, should be binding on the investigating authority.
- The agency's decisions should be published in the interest of legal certainty.

Although most of our proposals concern administrative reviews, their implementation would undoubtedly have effect on the subsequent judicial review, both by reducing the number of controversies and by producing valuable jurisprudence on trade remedies legislation and practice. Moreover, this might also reduce the number of cases raised against Argentina under the WTO's dispute settlement mechanism.

8

Peru: a sophisticated but underused judicial review system

LUIS ALBERTO LEÓN AND MARÍA ANTONIETA MERINO

I Introduction

Peru is a country which began its economic development in the 1990s. Before this, it had a small and mainly state-protected economy characterized by few producers, low technological capacity, widespread use of subsidies and industrial production with little added value. All of these factors underlined the importance of a complete overhaul of the economy geared towards the establishment and strengthening of the liberalization of the internal market and foreign trade and the promotion of private investments and competition.[1]

Since the 1990s, the Peruvian government has established macroeconomic discipline, strengthened market rules, dismantled the trade protection structure, reintegrated the economy into the world financial markets and put in place an all-encompassing deregulation of the economy. The areas that have been significantly deregulated include investments, adoption of foreign technology, exchange rates, labour regime, financial, insurance and capital markets, foreign trade and the taxation system.[2]

---

[1] From 1990 onward, the Peruvian economy was stabilized to create solid macroeconomic conditions which enabled the economy to overcome the hard test resulting from successive crises in international financial markets in 1998. This base established a redistribution of roles between the government and private agents, leaving productive activity in the hands of the private sector. Thilo Klein, "From Stability to Sustained Development: Peru's Economic Framework in the Nineties", in *The Role of the State in Competition and Intellectual Property in Latin America: Towards an AcademicAudit© of Indecopi*, (Lima, 2000), pp. 28–36.

[2] "The Peruvian government, through an ambitious privatization program, abandoned its former intense business activities and attracted new foreign capital. Through an open policy towards international trade and foreign investment, the freeing of prices and the exchange rate and the creation of a flexible legal and regulatory framework, the government laid the foundations for fostering the development of competitive markets." Ibid.

This liberalization and deregulation of markets has been complemented by the creation of institutions in charge of promoting competition and good business practices. To this end, the National Institute for the Defence of Competition and the Protection of Intellectual Property (hereinafter Indecopi, for its acronym in Spanish)[3] was created. Indecopi's main task is to act as an arbitrator in order to maintain and improve Peru's free market economy, focusing on two critical instruments that undergird it, namely, market competition and intellectual property.[4]

According to Legislative Decree No. 1033,[5] Indecopi is a governmental entity attached to the presidency of the Council of Ministers with technical, economic, administrative and budgetary autonomy. It has an organizational structure that allows it to carry out its functions and to spread a consistent message encouraging the promotion of fair competition in the market. Indecopi has decision-making bodies that act autonomously in the enforcement of legal provisions which regulate the matters under its responsibility, as well as administrative and support units which ensure its functioning as an institution.

Indecopi's functions include the correction of market distortions caused by dumped and subsidized imports.[6] As Peru's investigating authority, Indecopi is authorized to initiate and conduct trade remedy investigations and impose trade remedy measures.

---

[3] Indecopi was created by Decree Law No. 25868, published 24 November 1992.

[4] Beatriz Boza, "The Role of Indecopi in Peru: The First Seven Years", in *The Role of the State in Competition and Intellectual Property in Latin America*, pp. 3–25.

[5] Law on Organization and Functions of Indecopi, published 25 June 2008.

[6] According to Article 2 of Legislative Decree No. 1033, Indecopi has the following functions: (a) to supervise the free private initiative and free establishment of enterprises through the control and suppression of illegal and unreasonable bureaucratic barriers which affect citizens and businesses, as well as to ensure compliance with the rules and principles of administrative simplification; (b) to safeguard free and fair competition, as well as to punish unfair competitive behaviour in order to ensure effective competition in the market; (c) to correct the market distortions caused by dumping and subsidies; (d) to protect the rights of consumers, by making sure that the information provided by suppliers in the market is true, by ensuring the fitness of the goods and services based on the information provided and by preventing discrimination in consumer relations; (e) to supervise the facilitation process by eliminating non-tariff barriers to trade in accordance with relevant legislation; (f) to protect credits through a bankruptcy system that reduces transaction costs and promotes an efficient allocation of resources; (g) to establish policies on standardization, accreditation and metrology; (h) to administer the licensing and protection of intellectual property rights in all its forms, in administrative jurisdiction; and (i) to ensure other rights and guiding principles the supervision of which has been assigned in accordance with current legislation.

II   Overview of trade remedies legislation and practice in Peru

Trade remedies represent a relatively recent phenomenon in Peru. Until 1994, the country had no legislation on these measures. Through Legislative Resolution No. 26407, published in the official gazette, *El Peruano*, on 18 December 1994, the Peruvian Parliament approved the Agreement Establishing the World Trade Organization (hereinafter WTO) and the Multilateral Trade Agreements contained in the Final Act of the Uruguay Round, including the Anti-Dumping Agreement (hereinafter AD Agreement), the Agreement on Subsidies and Countervailing Measures (hereinafter SCM Agreement) and the Agreement on Safeguards (hereinafter SG Agreement).

According to Article 55 of the Peruvian Constitution of 1993, international treaties signed by the government, and which enter into force, become part of Peruvian law.[7] Having been incorporated into the Peruvian legal system, the three WTO agreements on trade remedies have the force of law in Peru, therefore they constitute binding legal texts for Indecopi, as well as for the Peruvian courts in judicial review proceedings initiated against Indecopi's actions.

In order to regulate the AD and SCM Agreements, the Peruvian government approved Supreme Decree No. 006–2003-PCM (hereinafter Anti-Dumping and Countervailing Rules). These rules set out the basic legal framework and principles with regard to the conduct of anti-dumping and countervailing duty investigations initiated against WTO members. In 2009, the Anti-Dumping and Countervailing Rules were amended by Supreme Decree No. 004–2009-PCM and are still in force.[8] Regarding safeguard measures, in 1998 the Peruvian government approved Supreme Decree No. 020–98-ITINCI (hereinafter Safeguard Rules), which contains the legal framework for safeguard investigations and the application of global safeguard measures. The Safeguard Rules were amended by Supreme Decree No. 017–2004-MINCETUR and are still in force.[9]

---

[7] Article 56 of the Peruvian Constitution establishes that treaties which concern human rights, sovereignty, national defence and financial obligations of the state must be approved by Parliament before ratification by the president of the republic. The same applies to treaties which create, modify or suppress taxes, or introduce amendments or repeal of laws.

[8] Published in the official gazette, 20 January 2009. Anti-dumping and countervailing duty investigations initiated against non-WTO members are governed by Supreme Decree No. 133–91-EF.

[9] Published in the official gazette, 8 August 2004.

In addition to the WTO rules, some of the trade agreements signed with other countries also include provisions on trade defence measures, including anti-dumping, countervailing duties and safeguards. To date, Peru has signed trade agreements with the United States, Canada, Singapore, China and the Republic of Korea.[10]

Under the WTO rules that are applicable in Peru, the investigative proceedings concerning trade remedies are anti-dumping and countervailing duty investigations, global safeguards investigations, reviews of measures in force (sunset and changed circumstances reviews) and new shipper reviews. Further, Peruvian legislation provides for two processes related to the collection of anti-dumping and countervailing duties: disputes on the collection of duties[11] and requests for refunds.[12] The first is a procedure that allows importers to challenge duties collected by Customs Administration on the grounds that the imported products fall outside the scope of the product subject to the duties. The second is a procedure that aims at the reimbursement of duties paid in excess of the actual margin of dumping or amount of subsidy.

The Peruvian investigating authorities responsible for trade remedies are Indecopi and the Judicial Power.[13] Inside Indecopi, the investigations are conducted by the Anti-Dumping and Countervailing Measures Commission (hereinafter Commission) and the Defence of Competition Court No. 1. The Commission is the body within Indecopi which conducts the actual investigations and imposes trade remedy measures. It is composed of four members who are elected by Indecopi's Board of Directors for a term of five years, and may be reappointed for a second term. According to Peruvian regulations, members of Commissions are required to have moral reliability and professional skills, as well as five years of experience

---

[10] It is important to mention that Peru is a member of the Andean Community (an integration process in which Bolivia, Colombia, Ecuador and Peru participate), therefore it must comply with the supranational laws issued by the Community. Decisions taken in the Andean context which address the application of trade remedies are Decisions 456 and 457 (which prevent and correct distortions in competition caused by dumping and subsidies on imports from the Andean Community members) and 452 (which regulates the application of safeguard measures on imports from the Andean Community members). The investigations initiated by one member of the Andean Community against another are conducted by the Secretariat.

[11] Anti-Dumping and Countervailing Rules, Article 67.   [12] Ibid., Article 68.

[13] The Ministry of Commerce and Tourism (hereinafter MINCETUR, for its acronym in Spanish) is the national authority responsible for the investigations on bilateral safeguards and the imposition of relevant measures in accordance with the trade agreements.

in the relevant field. Members may come from the public or private sector and work part-time at the Commission. Their autonomy and impartiality are guaranteed by their moral and professional capacity.[14]

As the first administrative instance of Indecopi, the Commission makes the determinations on dumping (or subsidy, as the case may be) and injury. If both findings are affirmative, the Commission issues an order requiring that the Customs Administration collect the anti-dumping or countervailing duties on the imports of the subject product. As mentioned above, the Commission also conducts changed circumstances, sunset and new shipper reviews,[15] as well as proceedings regarding the collection and refund of the duties.

The Commission also conducts global safeguard investigations. However, the decision-making process for safeguard measures differs from anti-dumping and countervail. Decisions to apply provisional or final safeguard measures are adopted by a Multisectoral Committee which consists of the Ministers of Economy and Finance, Commerce and Tourism and the sector to which the domestic like product belongs. It is useful to note that the procedural rules which apply to safeguard investigations also differ from anti-dumping and countervailing duty investigations.[16]

In addition to the Commission, Indecopi also has an Administrative Tribunal (hereinafter Tribunal) of second instance, which is responsible for resolving appeals against decisions issued by the Commission. This Tribunal can confirm, annul or revoke the decisions issued by the Commission. The Tribunal is composed of three administrative courts, each of which has five members. Each of these courts is authorized to establish binding precedents through the determinations that it issues when analysing specific cases, or through interpreting the meaning of the legislation that falls under its jurisdiction.[17] One of these courts, the Defence of Competition Court No. 1[18] (hereinafter Competition Court),

---

[14] Legislative Decree No. 1033, Articles 21, 22 and 26.

[15] It is important to point out that although Peruvian law enables the Commission to conduct these proceedings, there have been no such cases in practice.

[16] Safeguard Rules, Article 16.   [17] Legislative Decree No. 1033, Article 14.

[18] The Defence of Competition Court No. 1 is also responsible on second and final administrative instance, for resolving competition-related matters pertaining to the elimination of bureaucratic barriers, protection of free competition (antitrust), unfair competition control, standardization and non-tariff trade barriers control and bankruptcy proceedings. The other courts are the Defence of Competition Court No. 2 (which resolves disputes related to the protection of consumers' rights) and the Intellectual Property Court.

is responsible for resolving appeals related to the application of anti-dumping and countervailing measures.[19]

Members of the Tribunal are appointed through a Supreme Resolution[20] issued by the executive power. However, such members make their decisions independently on the basis of the relevant technical issues. The decisions issued by the commissions and the Tribunal are not influenced by political agents or the government itself. Since the beginning of Peru's trade remedies system, members of the Commission and the Tribunal have had long-lasting terms of appointment, and changes in the government have not resulted in changes in the staffing of these two important bodies. Members of the Commission and the Tribunal have always been appointed on the basis of their qualifications and professional background. As we explain below, the decisions made by the Competition Court are reviewable by the judiciary.

Although the Tribunal's decisions are binding on the interested parties in the relevant trade remedy proceeding, such decisions have no binding effect under Peruvian law. That said, we should mention that the legal reasoning developed in the Tribunal's decisions may be used in the analysis of future cases decided by the Tribunal of Indecopi, and by the judiciary in reviewing the Tribunal's decisions.

The Commission initiated its first investigation in 1992. Between 1992 and 2010, the Commission received 143 applications for investigations. Most were received in 2001 and 2009 (with 15 and 14 applications, respectively). Of all applications filed between 1992 and 2010, 110 were related to new anti-dumping or countervailing duty investigations, while 33 concerned reviews. Applications for reviews began in 1998 and increased to significant levels after 2007. In fact, between 2007 and 2010, on average the Commission received six review applications per year. Between 1992 and 2010, the Commission initiated 103 investigations and declined to initiate investigations requested in 39 applications. It is important to note that in 2002 and 2009 the Commission initiated 12 and 10 investigations, respectively. Of the total investigations concluded between 1992 and 2010, 57 led to

---

[19]   As mentioned before, safeguard measures are imposed by a Multisectoral Committee. In that sense, Indecopi's Tribunal does not have the power to review those decisions.

[20]   Law issued by the Executive Power, countersigned by the President of the Council of Ministers. The Board of Directors of Indecopi proposes the members of the Tribunal, taking into consideration the opinion of the advisory body of the institution.

the imposition of definitive duties,[21] while 40 ended without measures. In the same period, the Commission imposed 40 provisional duties.

Even though Peru does not have the same experience that other countries have regarding trade remedies, it has, over a relatively short period of time, initiated an important number of investigations in order to ensure fair competition in its domestic market. The initiation decisions are published in the official gazette.[22] The Commission imposes provisional or final anti-dumping or countervailing duties, and the relevant decisions are published in the official gazette. Because anti-dumping and countervailing duty investigations are proceedings which are important for the public, the Commission's determinations are posted on Indecopi's website in the form of press releases. Likewise, all the decisions on the initiation of a proceeding and the imposition of provisional or final decisions are permanently maintained on the website.

As mentioned above, safeguard investigations are procedurally different from anti-dumping and countervailing duty investigations. A safeguard proceeding involves two distinct phases: an investigation phase conducted by the Commission, and a decision-making phase by the Multisectoral Committee. In the first phase, the Commission collects the relevant information and makes the determinations necessary for a decision on the imposition of measures.[23] As part of its work, the Commission issues a technical report at the conclusion of the investigation which details all of the factors analysed during the investigative process, the Commission's proposal to the Multisectoral Committee as to the imposition of a measure and an analysis of the likely effects of that measure.[24] The Safeguard Rules list the factors that should be analysed by the Commission to support its recommendation on whether a measure should be imposed.[25]

In the second phase of the proceeding, the Multisectoral Committee makes a decision on the imposition of a measure. Although the Safeguard Rules stipulate that the Multisectoral Committee's decision will be based on the technical report presented by the Commission, the legislation also

---

[21] In the case of definitive duties, 42 were imposed for the first time in new anti-dumping and countervailing duty investigations, while the remaining 15 arose from review proceedings on existing measures.

[22] Anti-Dumping and Countervailing Rules, Article 33; Safeguard Rules, Article 13.

[23] Ibid., Article 6.

[24] As explained above, the Multisectoral Committee consists of the Ministers of Economy and Finance, Production and of the sector to which the affected domestic industry belongs.

[25] Safeguard Rules, Articles 2 and 23.

clearly provides that in making its decision, the Multisectoral Committee should take into consideration "the country's overall public interest" and "the effects of such measures at the national level and on trade relations with countries which will eventually be affected by such measures".[26]

The Safeguard Rules establish that the Multisectoral Committee must conduct a public hearing if it decides to impose safeguard measures.[27] Regardless of whether the Multisectoral Committee decides to apply the safeguard measure, its decision (contained in a supreme decree) is published in the official gazette. This obligation also applies to the imposition of provisional safeguard measures.

As noted, safeguard measures have an important political aspect, thus their judicial review is not subject to the same procedure as the judicial review of anti-dumping and countervailing measures. Since the decision on whether or not a safeguard measure will be applied is issued by way of a supreme decree, in order to challenge this decision, parties may file a constitutional action called a "popular action".[28] It is important to note that no such case has ever been initiated against a safeguard measure.[29]

We now turn to the judicial review of Indecopi's determinations in anti-dumping and countervailing duty investigations under Peruvian law.

III   Legislative framework for the judicial review of trade remedy determinations in Peru

Although Peruvian trade remedies legislation does not contain any provisions in respect of the judicial review of the investigating authority's determinations, the rules on the organization and functions of

---

[26] Ibid., Article 35.   [27] Ibid., Article 16.

[28] Popular Action is a constitutional process aimed at challenging the legality of legal instruments hierarchically lower than a law (for instance, a supreme decree). Specifically, it aims to ensure that such instruments do not contravene the constitution or other laws. This action must be filed with the competent chamber of the Superior Court of the judiciary, which will specify in its ruling whether the disputed legal instrument contradicts the Constitution or the laws. If the Court finds that this is indeed the case, it will declare the challenged legal instrument unconstitutional or illegal. In such a situation, the disputed legal instrument will lose effect as from the day following the publication of the court decision.

[29] So far, Peru has conducted only two safeguard investigations, one on *Clothing Items* (2003) and one on *Cotton Yarn* (2009). In the first, the government applied provisional safeguard measures through Supreme Decree No. 023–2003-MINCETUR. In the second investigation, through Supreme Decree No.016–2009-MINCETUR, the government decided not to apply any measure. Interested parties did not file a popular action to challenge the decisions made in either of these investigations.

Indecopi (Supreme Decree No. 09–2009-PCM) stipulate that the decisions issued by the Tribunal may be challenged before the judiciary, according to the rules governing judicial administrative review.[30] Therefore, below we describe the legal framework for the judicial review of the actions taken by government agencies that applies equally to trade remedy determinations.

In Peru, the judiciary conducts the judicial review of the actions of government agencies. The Peruvian Constitution stipulates: "administrative decisions can be challenged through an administrative action".[31] Besides the Constitution, the judicial administrative review process is regulated by the 1993 Civil Procedure Code under the title of "challenge of administrative acts or decisions".[32] Further, in 2001, Parliament adopted the Judicial Review Procedure Law (hereinafter Law No. 27584), which sets forth the rules which apply to judicial administrative review proceedings. Law No. 27584 introduced major changes to the previous regulation of this process. According to this Law, the objective of the judicial administrative review process is the judicial control of the decisions issued by the public administration, which must be consistent with the administrative regulations, as well as "material actions" of an agency which are not based on an administrative act.

Before the enactment of Law No. 27584, the judicial review of the decisions issued by government agencies was a restricted process which focused solely on the legality of the disputed decision. However, Law No. 27584 has introduced the system of "full jurisdiction", which allows for much wider judicial review. This system is based on two principles:

(i) *Effective legal control of the actions of the government agencies.* The judiciary conducts this control through judicial administrative review. This process constitutes the legal control of governmental actions and does not involve any element of political control. Further, this mechanism applies to the government's actions taken under the auspices of administrative law; it

---

[30] Supreme Decree No. 09–2009-PCM, Article 34.

[31] Peruvian Constitution, Article 148.

[32] It should be underlined that the judicial review of governmental actions is regulated under a rule governing the civil litigation process, which is of a different nature. Further, the Civil Procedure Code provides, in Article 540, that the objective of the judicial review process is to declare the invalidity or unenforceability of an administrative act. This shows that in many cases the judicial review process was viewed as a mechanism to control the formal aspects of the act, and the work of the reviewing court was seen as being limited to that, and not covering a substantive assessment of the challenged administrative act. In our view, this limited the effectiveness of the judicial protection of the rights of individuals involved in the process.

does not apply to actions governed by other rules. An administrative action within the meaning of Law No. 27584 is an action undertaken in pursuit of the administrative functions of a government agency.

(ii) *Effective protection of the rights and interests of the governed.* By controlling the constitutionality and validity of the government's actions, the judicial administrative review process also serves to protect the administered who may have been injured or threatened with injury by unconstitutional or unlawful administrative actions. Thus, the judiciary's task is not limited to a declaration of the illegality of the disputed action, but also provides the governed with effective protection.

IV   Reviewable determinations

In general, under Peruvian law, the following governmental acts or actions may be challenged before the courts:

(i)   administrative acts and other administrative declarations;
(ii) administrative silence, inertia and any other omission of an agency;
(iii) actions other than those contained in an administrative act;
(iv) administrative acts which violate legal principles or laws;
(v)   acts or omissions of an agency as to the validity, effectiveness, enforcement or interpretation of governmental contracts, except where the law requires that such disputes be resolved through conciliation or arbitration.

The judicial administrative review process may be used against decisions issued by Indecopi, which are final and executable. A final and executable action is one in respect of which there is no step pending in the administrative process before a case may be filed with the competent court.[33] In accordance with this principle, refusal to initiate an investigation and the final determinations made in the context of anti-dumping and countervailing duty investigations, reviews of anti-dumping and countervailing duties and refund proceedings are all reviewable actions.

Decisions such as the imposition of provisional measures, refusal to grant extensions of deadlines for the submission of information, and rejection of a request to see the non-confidential information on the investigation file are not reviewable, because they do not represent final and executable administrative actions. Indeed, according to the Peruvian Administrative Procedure Act (Law No. 27444), administrative actions

---

[33] Legislative Decree No. 1033, Article 18.

such as initiations of investigations and decisions related to confidentiality of the information provided in the investigation cannot be challenged before courts.[34] Further, the Anti-Dumping and Countervailing Rules establish that decisions imposing or rejecting the imposition of provisional anti-dumping or countervailing measures are not appealable.[35] In fact, it is useful to note that the majority of judicial review proceedings initiated so far have concerned decisions imposing or rejecting the imposition of definitive measures[36] and decisions concerning the collection of duties. Below, we provide examples of such cases.

V   Matters raised in judicial review proceedings and standard of review

As already mentioned, the "full jurisdiction" principle embodied in Law No. 27584 provides for the review of the legality of the disputed administrative action, as well as the substantive basis of that action. This principle also applies to the judicial review of the determinations made in the context of anti-dumping and countervailing duty investigations.

In such judicial review proceedings, the complainants usually argue that the disputed decision is inconsistent with the anti-dumping and subsidies legislation on the grounds that it was based on an incorrect application of the law or an erroneous evaluation performed by the investigating authority. In the former situation, the court will review whether the challenged decision was issued in accordance with the WTO agreements and national legislation. In the latter situation, it will review whether the investigating authority conducted a proper analysis. In such cases, it is clear that the court follows the "full jurisdiction" principle. We should also note that there have been cases where the Peruvian courts cited the relevant WTO agreements in developing their legal reasoning in all judicial review proceedings handled so far.

In one case, an association of foreign producers subject to an investigation conducted in Peru, initiated a judicial review proceeding seeking the annulment of Indecopi's decision imposing anti-dumping duties. The claims presented were in relation to aspects of the analysis made

---

[34] Law No. 27444, Article 206.
[35] Anti-Dumping and Countervailing Rules, Article 63.
[36] The Commission has conducted a few countervailing duty investigations thus far. Only one has been challenged before the courts. However, this case was rejected by the court on the grounds of having been filed past the relevant deadline.

by the Tribunal in the second phase of the underlying investigation. The association argued that the Tribunal had acted inconsistently with the AD Agreement by failing to conduct a fair comparison between the normal value and the export price, although evidence had been presented showing the need for an adjustment for differences in taxes. Further, the association argued that the Tribunal had not taken into consideration the differences between the physical characteristics of the product under investigation and the product produced by the domestic producers. In this case, the reviewing court concluded that the association had not proved the existence of the alleged taxes, and that therefore the investigating authority was not required to make adjustments to domestic selling prices under Article 2.4 of the AD Agreement. With respect to the like product analysis, the court concluded that the factors cited by the association were not related to substantive differences in the composition of the two products; rather, they concerned elements, such as consumer perception, which were variable and which did not necessarily change the essential characteristics of such products. The court therefore concluded that the authority's analysis was consistent with the requirements of the legislation, and dismissed the complaint.[37]

In another case, a domestic producer of calcium carbide took to court the investigating authority's refusal to apply an anti-dumping measure. In the underlying investigation, the investigating authority had found that, although there was dumping and injury, the latter was caused by factors other than dumping, such as the domestic industry's lack of competitiveness. The court found there was not sufficient evidence to sustain the causal link between dumping and injury. The judiciary therefore concluded that there was no procedural deficiency in the investigating authority's decision not to impose measures, because the authority had properly applied Article 3.5 of the AD Agreement.[38]

In another case, an importer filed a judicial review proceeding with respect to a final determination issued by Indecopi, which imposed anti-dumping duties on poplin fabrics from China. The importer challenged the investigating authority's like product determination and its treatment of China as a non-market economy. In its ruling, the Superior Court declared the complaint groundless and upheld the like product determination. The Court considered that, as determined by Indecopi during the investigation, fabrics produced by the domestic industry were

---

[37] AP. 2603–2009 of the Supreme Court (Civil Chamber), 24 January 2011.
[38] AP. 405–2000 of the Supreme Court (Civil Chamber), 21 January 2005.

similar to those imported from China in terms of their common physical characteristics, composition, production process, marketing channels and end uses. The Superior Court also approved the authority's treatment of China as a non-market economy, taking into consideration the distortions observed in the Chinese economy during the period of investigation.[39]

In yet another case, an importer of the product (sandals and husks) subject to an anti-dumping duty requested an exemption from it. However, the Supreme Court rejected the case on the grounds that the products imported were like products subject to the disputed duty.[40]

In a different case, an importer challenged Indecopi's decision ordering the payment of anti-dumping duties imposed on tyre imports. The court concluded that the tyres imported by this particular importer were like the tyres subject to anti-dumping duties. It also ruled that if the importer wanted to be exempted from duties, he/she must submit sufficient evidence to demonstrate the differences between the products that he/she imported and those subject to anti-dumping duties, which was not the case in this particular judicial review proceeding.[41]

To sum up, as the cases discussed above demonstrate, in judicial review proceedings on trade remedy determinations, Peruvian courts have analysed whether the investigating authority had issued its decision in accordance with the provisions of the WTO agreements and Peruvian legislation, and whether the aspects of the determinations made in the underlying investigations which were cited by complainants had been evaluated properly. Another important aspect to consider is that the courts limited their review to issues that had been specifically cited by the complainants in the judicial review proceedings.

We should also mention here that the courts have rejected all of the judicial review proceedings initiated in Peru so far. That is, in all such proceedings, the courts found the investigating authority's determinations to be consistent with the WTO agreements and Peruvian legislation.

VI   Parties eligible to bring a case, and defendants

Peruvian law establishes that any person injured or threatened with injury by an administrative action may file a judicial review proceeding. With

---

[39] Decision issued by the Superior Court on 16 September 2009.
[40] AP. 172–2007 of the Supreme Court (Civil Chamber), 7 March 2008.
[41] File No. 1514–03 of the Superior Court, 23 May 2005.

respect to Indecopi's determinations in trade remedy investigations, domestic producers, importers, foreign producers, industrial organizations and governments of the exporting countries may bring a case. In practice, the majority of judicial review proceedings have been initiated by importers and domestic or foreign producers of the subject product.

Just as multiple domestic producers may come together to file a common request for the initiation of an anti-dumping or countervailing duty investigation, a judicial review proceeding with respect to the investigating authority's determinations in such investigations may also be initiated by a group of complainants. Thus, importers of the subject product may bring a collective case to seek the annulment of a decision to impose a trade remedy measure, whereas domestic producers may bring a case regarding the same trade remedy measure to request an increase in the level of the measure.

Although this has not been expressly mentioned in Law No. 27584, the defendant in a judicial review proceeding may only be the entity which issued the disputed action.[42] In a judicial review proceeding involving a trade remedy case, if an importer wishes to challenge a determination made by the Tribunal which approves the Commission's decision to impose an anti-dumping duty, the defendant would not be the Tribunal, but rather, Indecopi. This is because the right to be a defendant is the prerogative of a public entity, not each of the separate offices or organs that it embodies.

VII   Competent courts

Originally, Law No. 27584, as a general rule, had granted the first instance judge specialized in administrative judicial reviews jurisdiction over the judicial administrative review proceedings against administrative actions of

---

[42] Article 13 of Law No. 27584 stipulates that a judicial review proceeding may be initiated against:
    (i) the administrative entity that issued the contested act; (ii) the administrative entity whose silence, inertia or omission is being discussed in the proceeding; (iii) the administrative entity whose act or omission caused damage (the compensation for the damage is discussed in the judicial review process); (iv) the administrative entity and the individual who participated in a trilateral administrative procedure; (v) The particular holder of rights declared by the act whose annulment is being sought, according to Article 11 of the Law; (vi) the administrative entity that issued the disputed act and the person who benefited from that act (second paragraph of Article 11 of the Law); and (vii) legal persons under a private scheme that provides public services or performs administrative functions through concession, delegation or authorization of the state.

government agencies.[43] Later, Parliament adopted Law No. 27709 in 2002, which amended Law No. 27584, and transferred jurisdiction to the Superior Court of Justice.[44] Under this system, the Supreme Court of the Republic was to have the last word as the court of final instance in cases where the judicial review process began in the Superior Court.

In 2009, however, Parliament issued Law No. 29364 and, once again, amended Law No. 27584 with regard to the competent courts in the judicial administrative review proceedings. This amendment reverted to the previous scheme provided for in Law No. 27584, and gave jurisdiction to the first instance judge specialized in administrative judicial reviews.[45] Hence, the decisions issued by the Tribunal of Indecopi are now reviewed by the first instance judge specialized in administrative judicial reviews.

Regarding territorial jurisdiction of administrative courts, Law No. 27584 establishes that the complaint must be filed before the judge where the defendant is domiciled, or where the disputed administrative action was undertaken. As Indecopi is located in Lima, the judge in Lima has territorial jurisdiction in judicial review proceedings initiated against the determinations of Peruvian investigating authorities.

VIII   Procedural steps

Under Law No. 27584, a complainant is required to file a judicial review proceeding within three months[46] from the date of the notification of the disputed determination to the complainant, or the date of publication of Indecopi's decision in the official gazette, as appropriate.[47]

In Peru, all judicial review proceedings are conducted on the basis of written submissions addressed to the competent court. Law No. 27584 states that once the case is accepted, the court must order the defendant to submit the files pertaining to the disputed action to it.[48] Thus, in the case of a proceeding involving a trade remedy determination, the court

---

[43] Law No. 27584, Article 9.   [44] Law No. 27709, single Article.
[45] Law No. 29364, first transitional amendment.   [46] Law No. 27584, Article 17.
[47] Direct notification of the decisions issued by Indecopi is made to parties who participated in the investigation. For such parties, the deadline for initiating a judicial review proceeding is calculated from the notification date of the decision. The parties who did not participate in the investigation, but who may have an interest in it, may initiate a judicial review proceeding within three months from the date of publication of the disputed decision, because these parties do not receive direct notification of it.
[48] Law No. 27584, Article 22.

will ask Indecopi to submit the file pertaining to the underlying investigation. Parties, including foreign companies, have hired Peruvian lawyers to represent them before the courts.[49] The lawyers of Indecopi's Legal Department represent the investigating authority. Legal fees for the initiation of a judicial review proceeding are not very high.

After receiving the complainant's first written submission, the judge will check whether it complies with the admissibility requirements and has been presented in accordance with the law.[50] Specifically, the judge will check: (i) if the provisions of the Civil Procedure Code have been complied with;[51] (ii) if the court has subject matter and territorial jurisdiction over the case; (iii) if the disputed administrative action is one which is final and executable; (iv) if the deadline for the initiation of a judicial review proceeding has been observed; (v) if the necessary administrative review mechanisms have been exhausted; and (vi) if the complainant has capacity to sue.

With respect to the procedure's length, judicial review proceedings may be divided into "urgent proceedings" and "special proceedings". Urgent proceedings do not have a basis in an administrative act, and are related to pension rights. Other disputes, including those related to antidumping and countervailing duty investigations, are handled in the form of special proceedings.

After the preliminary analysis and the submission of Indecopi's first written submission (within 10 days),[52] the judge will issue a ruling declaring the existence of a valid legal proceeding if all of the legal requirements have been met. If any conditions have not been met, there are two options: the judge will either terminate the proceeding because of the irremediable absence of a legal requirement, or he/she will allow the party concerned additional time to correct the defects in his/her submission. After the correction of any defects, the judge will issue a decree, called a "writ of sanitation", declaring the validity of the process. If necessary for the assessment of the case, the judge will set a date for a

---

[49] Article 132 of the Civil Procedure Code provides that documents presented before courts must be approved and signed by attorneys admitted to the bar with a clear indication of his/her name and registration number. According to the Statute of the Lima Bar Association (the largest bar association in Peru), a lawyer with a foreign law degree may be registered as a bar member if that degree undergoes a revalidation process.

[50] Law No. 27584, Articles 20 and 21.

[51] Article 246 of the Civil Procedure Code contains the following requirements: (i) the petition must be complete; (ii) it must fulfil the relevant legal requirements; (iii) it must indicate the type of process pursued.

[52] Law No. 27584, Article 28.

hearing – called an "evidentiary hearing" – in which he/she will review the evidence. After issuing the writ or conducting the hearing, the case file will be forwarded to the prosecuting attorney for a written opinion.[53] With or without the prosecuting attorney's report, the case file will be returned to the judge for him/her to issue judgment. Although the judge is not required to hold a hearing before the judicial decision is issued, a hearing must be held if it is requested by one of the parties.[54] On appeal, the Superior Court has discretion over whether there will be a hearing.[55]

During the judicial review proceeding, the measure challenged remains executable, except where the judge issues precautionary measures ordering its suspension.[56] Although there is a presumption of the legality of the measure subject to a judicial review proceeding, that does not prevent the judge from granting a precautionary measure. After the proceedings begin, the judge, through a reasoned and motivated decision, and with sufficient evidence, may adopt precautionary measures if he/she considers them necessary to ensure the effectiveness of his/her decision. These precautionary measures may be modified or lifted during the course of the proceedings, *ex officio* or at the request of a party, taking into consideration the developments subsequent to the adoption of the measures that could not have been considered at the time of their adoption. Precautionary measures expire when the deadline for their execution expires or when a final decision is reached on the substance of the case. It is important to note, however, that to date the courts have not adopted precautionary measures in any judicial review proceeding initiated against Indecopi in respect of its determinations in anti-dumping or countervailing duty investigations.

Regarding the length of the entire process, Peruvian legislation does not expressly set a deadline for the judge to reach a final decision. On average, it takes a judge one year to issue a decision in proceedings concerning trade remedy determinations.

IX   Appeals

The decisions issued by the first instance judge are appealable to the Superior Court of Justice. Only parties to the dispute may appeal the

---

[53] In disputes involving an action of a government agency, the prosecuting attorney presents an opinion before the judge issues the judgment.

[54] Law No. 27584, Article 28.

[55] Civil Procedure Code, Article 375 (supplemental application).

[56] Law No. 27584, Article 23.

judge's decision. An appeal must be filed within five days from the date of notification of the judge's decision.[57] The Superior Court may approve, reverse or partially approve the judge's decision.

In principle, the Superior Court's decision definitively resolves the dispute. Nevertheless, parties may file what is called a "cassation" before the Supreme Court to challenge the Superior Court's decision in cases involving unquantifiable claims. In the case of quantifiable claims, parties may file a cassation when the disputed amount exceeds 140 "Procedural Reference Units"[58] (hereinafter RPU for its acronym in Spanish), or where such a contested decision comes from a provincial, regional or national authority. By way of exception, in respect of administrative acts issued by district administrative authorities, parties may file a cassation when the amount exceeds 140 RPU. However, this is an exceptional mechanism.[59] It is important to point out that a cassation is not an appeal; it is a mechanism aimed at identifying the correct interpretation of the law and paving the way for the emergence of a consistent body of jurisprudence of the Supreme Court. For instance, in a case regarding the refund of anti-dumping duties, the Constitutional and Social Chamber of the Supreme Court issued "Cassation No. 814–2008", through which it declared the annulment of the Superior Court decision, because it was not sustained in law. For that reason, the Supreme Court ordered the Superior Court to issue a new ruling regarding the decision issued by Indecopi.[60]

The Supreme Court, in its decisions, may establish principles on matters related to judicial administrative review that become binding precedents. However, the lower courts and judges may deviate from such precedents, if justified in the particular circumstances of a case and the reasons for such departure are properly explained. Full texts of all judgments by the Supreme Court of Justice are published in the official gazette and on the website of the judiciary within 60 days from the date of the decision.[61]

Finally, parties to a judicial review proceeding may file an appeal against refusal of a request for leave to appeal or to appeal in cassation.[62] This mechanism effectively guarantees the right to challenge the

---

[57] Law No. 27584, Article 28.

[58] This amount is established every year by the government.

[59] Law No. 27584, Article 35.

[60] Cassation 814–2008 of the Supreme Court (Constitutional and Social Chamber), 17 July 2008.

[61] Law No. 27584, Article 37.   [62] Ibid., Article 35.

decisions issued by the judge or the Superior Court. However, both the appeal and cassation require the existence of certain conditions, which are reviewed by the judge or court that issued the challenged judicial decision; that is, it is the body whose decision will be reviewed which decides whether the request for appeal or cassation fulfils all the requirements established under the law. For that reason, the judge or the court whose decision will be reviewed may arbitrarily deny the request for appeal or cassation. The right to appeal such rejection will allow another court to re-evaluate the request.

X   Enforcement of court decisions

In Peru, the enforcement of court decisions is generally addressed under Article 139 of the Constitution, which establishes the right to effective judicial protection, and which provides that no authority may alter court decisions or delay their execution.

Law No. 27584 grants the Superior Court and judges power to execute their judgments. The Law states that in cases where the complaint was upheld by the court, its decision must establish the type of obligation that the defendant is required to meet and the time frame within which that must be achieved. No one may qualify the content of the court's decision or its rationale, interpret its effects, or restrict its scope. The defendant agency must do what is necessary in order to implement fully the court's decision.

In judicial review proceedings with respect to anti-dumping or countervailing duty investigations, if the court annuls the decision imposing the disputed anti-dumping or countervailing duties, the effect of the court ruling is automatic: the duties are annulled and Indecopi need not take any steps in order to give effect to the decision.

XI   Concluding remarks

Although there have been a few judicial review proceedings with respect to anti-dumping and countervailing duty investigations, it is important to note that in most of these cases, Peruvian judges applied the principle of "full jurisdiction" and reviewed not only the formal aspects of the determinations challenged, but also their substantive aspects.

The decisions issued by Indecopi are reviewed through a judicial process before judges specializing in administrative law. However, these judges do not have legal or technical expertise on trade remedies or possess the technical knowledge of the Indecopi investigators. Importantly, the judges do not follow WTO panel and Appellate Body reports on trade remedies, and therefore do not reflect them in their own judgments. This makes it difficult for judges to conduct an effective review of the investigating authority's determinations. We do not consider that there is a need in Peru to create a specialized judicial court on these matters because, given the small number of cases, this would not be an economically viable option. However, training the judges on trade remedies issues would certainly be very useful.

In the past, Indecopi organized training activities for judges in other competition-related areas. Similar activities can be organized on trade remedies covering both national and WTO aspects of the relevant issues. Indecopi has the necessary capacity to organize and conduct such activities. Such training will allow Peruvian judges to conduct a deeper analysis of Indecopi's determinations and will pave the way for more effective judicial review.

The European Union: an imperfect and time-consuming system

EDWIN VERMULST AND JUHI SUD

I Introduction

1 General

The European Union (hereinafter EU) has exclusive powers in the field of trade remedies. This means that EU trade remedy measures are applied EU-wide and that the now 27 EU member states have given up their national power to apply trade remedies.[1] The EU has adopted three Basic Regulations to implement the WTO Anti-Dumping Agreement (hereinafter ADA), the Agreement on Subsidies and Countervailing Measures (hereinafter ASCM) and the Agreement on Safeguards (hereinafter SA) into EU law. These Basic Regulations in substance are largely copies of their WTO equivalents regarding most of the legal aspects. Presently the responsibility of administering these trade remedy laws is divided among the European Commission (hereinafter Commission), the Council of the EU (hereinafter Council) and the member states. The implementing guidelines used by the Commission to apply these Basic Regulations are not publicly available. As presently in force,[2] these regulations apply to imports from non-EU countries. In other words, they do not apply intra-EU, as the EU is an internal market.

---

[1] However, third countries may apply trade remedies against individual EU member states.

[2] Council Regulation (EC) No. 1225/2009 of 30 November 2009 on protection against dumped imports from countries not members of the European Community, [2009] L343/51; Council Regulation (EC) No. 597/2009 of 11 June 2009 on protection against subsidised imports from countries not members of the European Community, [2009] L188/93; Council Regulation (EC) No. 260/2009 of 26 February 2009 on the common rules for imports, [2009] OJ L84/1; and Council Regulation (EC) No. 625/2009 of 7 July 2009 on the common rules for imports from certain third countries, [2009] OJ L185/1.

The basic anti-dumping/countervailing duty regulations apply to WTO and non-WTO members alike. However, as far as safeguards are concerned, the EU has separate legislation for WTO and non-WTO members and a temporary China-specific safeguard regulation.[3] Thus far, this regulation has not been used as a legal basis for the imposition of measures against China.[4]

2   Decision-making process

As far as the decision-making process is concerned, it should be noted that at the time of writing, significant changes are being discussed. On 7 March 2011, the Commission submitted a proposal to the Council and the European Parliament for a regulation that would significantly change – among others[5] – the decision-making process in EU trade remedy matters. At first sight, the proposal would seem to adapt existing trade remedy procedures to the institutional rules of the Lisbon Treaty and of the February 2011 regulation on the Commission's implementing powers (Comitology Regulation).[6] However, if adopted, the proposal will represent an unprecedented power grab by the Commission at the expense of the EU member states. Basically, the Commission proposes that all decisions with respect to trade remedies be taken by it (and no longer the Council), while at the same time a new procedure has been created to involve the EU member states in the decision-making process. In this regard, it is important to distinguish between anti-dumping (hereinafter AD) and countervailing duty (hereinafter CVD) proceedings[7] on the one hand and safeguards (hereinafter SG) proceedings on the other.

---

[3] Council Regulation (EC) No. 427/2003 of 3 March 2003 on a transitional product-specific safeguard mechanism for imports originating in the People's Republic of China and amending Regulation (EC) No. 519/94 on common rules for imports from certain third countries, [2003] OJ L65/1.

[4] However, in 2003 the EU did initiate a safeguard investigation under the China-specific safeguard regulation concerning imports of citrus fruits together with a multilateral safeguard investigation concerning the same product, [2003] OJ C162/2.

[5] The draft regulation seeks to modify basic acts in the field of the common commercial policy that were not previously subject to the procedures laid down in Council Decision 1999/468/EC of 28 June 1999. It is therefore referred to as the "Trade Omnibus".

[6] Regulation (EU) No. 182/2011 of the European Parliament and of the Council of 16 February 2011 laying down the rules and general principles concerning mechanisms for control by Member States of the Commission's exercise of implementing powers, [2011] OJ L55/13 (hereinafter Comitology Regulation). http://eur-lex.europa.eu/LexUriServ/ LexUriServ.do?uri=OJ:L:2011:055:0013:0018:EN:PDF.

[7] As regards anti-dumping and countervailing duty proceedings, this chapter discusses the decision-making process applicable from September 2012, as the current system is a

As far as AD and CVD are concerned, the Commission will initiate the proceedings, conduct the investigations, impose and extend measures or terminate the investigations. The Anti-Dumping/Anti-Subsidy Committee (hereinafter ADC), consisting of representatives of the EU member states, will deliver its opinion on draft acts with respect to outcome-decisive steps of the proceeding[8] through the *examination* procedure. Voting within the ADC will take place by qualified majority.[9] At the same time, an Appeal Committee has been created which will also vote by qualified majority.

For the adoption of most[10] implementing acts, including definitive measures, the Commission will submit the proposed implementing acts to the vote of the ADC prior to their adoption. Three possible scenarios may exist. First, the ADC may reject a draft implementing act proposed by the Commission if it delivers a negative opinion by qualified majority. However, the chair of the ADC (a representative of the Commission) may then submit an amended version to the ADC within two months, or send the implementing act to the Appeal Committee for further deliberation within one month of the delivery of the negative opinion. Second, if the ADC delivers a *positive opinion*, the Commission will adopt the implementing act. Third, if *no opinion* is delivered and a simple majority of the ADC members oppose the draft implementing act, the Commission will conduct consultations with the member states and, within one month after the ADC meeting, will inform the ADC of the results of those consultations and submit a draft implementing act to

transitional one, which will apply for 18 months only. However, following difficulties, the new system will not enter into effect on 1 September 2012, as scheduled.

[8] These are termination of an AD/CVD investigation; termination of an AD/CVD investigation in the case of acceptance of an undertaking; imposition of provisional and definitive AD/CVD measures; imposition/extension of definitive AD/CVD measures following reviews (new exporter, interim and expiry); amendment of AD measures following re-investigations (only for AD); extension of AD/CVD measures following an anti-circumvention investigation; and extension of the suspension of AD/CVD measures after an initial suspension of nine months.

[9] It may be noted that, as of 1 November 2014, a new definition of the qualified majority will apply as per Article 16(4) Treaty on European Union (hereinafter TEU) and Article 3 of Protocol No. 36.

[10] With regard to the adoption of provisional AD/CVD measures, a special procedure exists. The Commission may adopt such measures after consulting the ADC or, in cases of extreme urgency, after informing the member states. If the ADC delivers a negative opinion (if necessary, after adoption of the provisional measures, but no later than 10 days after notification to the member states of measures taken), the Commission must repeal the provisional measures immediately. Therefore, the ADC can as the Council currently can, overturn a Commission decision to impose provisional AD/CVD measures by qualified majority.

the Appeal Committee. If the Appeal Committee delivers a positive opinion or does not give an opinion, the Commission will adopt the draft implementing act. However, if the Appeal Committee delivers a negative opinion, the Commission will not adopt the draft implementing act. As mentioned above, voting within the Appeal Committee will also take place by qualified majority, but as regards delivery of opinions on draft AD and CVD measures, until 1 September 2012, the Appeal Committee will deliver opinions by a simple majority of its component members.

As far as SGs are concerned, the Commission has the competence to initiate and terminate proceedings and to conduct the investigation. An examination procedure similar to that for AD/CVD measures will be followed when the Commission wishes to impose, revoke or amend SG measures (but not when SG measures are imposed on non-WTO members). However, there are two important differences compared to the examination procedure pertaining to AD/CVD measures. First, with regard to *provisional* measures, there is no obligation to conduct prior consultations with the SG Committee, but the adopted act must be submitted to it within a period of 14 days after adoption. If the SG Committee delivers a negative opinion (with a qualified majority) after adoption of the provisional measures, the Commission will be required to repeal the provisional measures immediately. This entails that, unless there is a qualified majority against the provisional measures in the SG Committee, the measures will remain in force. Second, with regard to *definitive measures*, if there is *no opinion* by the SG Committee, the Commission may not adopt any definitive multilateral SG measures. The chair may then submit an amended version of the implementing act to the SG Committee within two months, or send the implementing act to the Appeal Committee for further deliberation within one month. In the *absence of a positive opinion* by the Appeal Committee, the definitive multilateral SG measure will not be adopted.[11] All votes in the SG Committee and the Appeal Committee are again conducted on the basis of qualified majority.

---

[11] For the imposition of definitive China-specific SG measures, a positive opinion of the SG Committee or the Appeal Committee is not required; absence of an opinion can be sufficient, as the rules of Article 5(4)(a) and Article 6(4) of the Comitology are restricted to "definitive multilateral safeguard measures". China-specific SG measures supposedly are not multilateral, because they apply only to goods originating in China.

As of 1 January 2007, a qualified majority requires 255 out of 345 votes.[12] A blocking minority therefore consists of 91 votes. The 345 votes are divided among the 27 member states as follows:[13]

EU member states' votes in the case of qualified majority voting

Germany, France, Italy, United Kingdom	29
Spain, Poland	27
Romania	14
The Netherlands	13
Belgium, Czech Republic, Greece, Hungary, Portugal	12
Austria, Bulgaria, Sweden	10
Denmark, Ireland, Lithuania, Slovakia, Finland	7
Cyprus, Estonia, Latvia, Luxembourg, Slovenia	4
Malta	3
Total	345

3 Administrative procedure

Within the Commission, Directorate-General Trade (DG Trade) – at the working level, more specifically Trade Directorate H[14] – is the key player in the administration of trade remedies laws. Directorate H is headed by a director who technically reports to the Deputy Director General, but in politically sensitive cases is often also consulted directly by the Director General, the Cabinet and the Trade Commissioner. Directorate H over time has grown to include some 170 officials, including temporary agents and support staff, making it the largest Directorate in DG Trade.

Once the Commission decides that a complaint contains sufficient evidence to initiate an AD/CVD proceeding, at least two[15] teams of case handlers are assigned to the investigation, one for the dumping/subsidy determination and one for the injury and EU interest determination. This bifurcation is intended to enable the Commission to meet the deadlines laid down in the Basic Regulations and to enhance the objectivity of the two

---

[12] In addition, a majority of member states (in some cases, two-thirds) must approve the decision, and any member state may ask for confirmation that the votes cast in favour represent at least 62 per cent of the EU's total population.

[13] Source: http://europa.eu/abc/12lessons/lesson_4/index_en.htm.

[14] See http://ec.europa.eu/trade/whatwedo/whois/index_en.htm.

[15] Exceptionally, three teams of case handlers may be assigned to politically sensitive cases, e.g., the 2008 expiry review investigation involving footwear with leather uppers from China and Vietnam.

determinations. For SG, normally only one team is assigned, but it should be noted that use of the SG instrument is comparatively rare in the EU.

Since 2007, DG Trade has formally established the office of the hearing officer for trade remedy cases.[16] The current hearing officer is an experienced DG Trade official who works independently from the services and reports directly to the Director General of DG Trade. He or she has full access to the confidential case files and is supposed to focus particularly on the observance of the due process rights of all interested parties. The hearing officer does not take binding decisions, but prepares recommendations to the services and a report to the Director General in all cases where he or she intervenes, although these documents are not public.[17]

4 Transparency

In terms of transparency (or, rather, lack thereof), it is very important to note that the EU does not have a system of disclosure of confidential information under administrative protective order. As more EU trade remedy cases are directed against non-market economies (notably China) and the EU tends to employ the analogue country concept to calculate normal value in such cases, this means that interested parties have little opportunity to check dumping (and injury) margin calculation details. The increasing tendency to keep the identities of EU complainants confidential because of alleged retaliation threats further exacerbates the lack of transparency and the opportunities for interested parties, notably exporters and importers, to properly defend themselves in EU trade remedy investigations.

II Judicial review of trade remedy determinations in the European Union

1 Legal framework

The Basic Regulations contain no special provisions with regard to judicial review.[18] Consequently, the general provisions of the Treaty on the Functioning of the European Union (hereinafter TFEU) apply. As a

---

[16] See, for more detail, http://ec.europa.eu/trade/issues/respectrules/ho/index_en.htm.

[17] Since 2010, the hearing officer prepares written reports of official hearings and/or meetings. Following comments from the parties concerned, non-confidential versions of the reports are added to the non-confidential case file.

[18] See on judicial review in EU trade remedy cases: Vermulst, *EU Anti-Dumping Law and Practice* (2010), pp. 203–33; Mueller, Khan and Scharf, *EC and WTO Anti-Dumping*

result, a fundamental question in the EU context is whether, and under which conditions, private parties affected by the outcome of a trade remedy investigation may directly challenge the measure before the European courts,[19] or whether they must attack the customs authorities' decision to collect duty before national courts, which may then request a preliminary ruling from the Court of Justice of the European Union (CJEU, formerly the ECJ) to the extent a question of EU law arises (as will normally be the case for trade remedy measures).

Depending on the nature and the addressee of the administrative act, most interested parties will be able to challenge the legality and validity of the act before the (European) General Court under Article 263(4) TFEU.[20] Judgments of the General Court may subsequently be subject to a right of appeal to the CJEU on points of law only. If the appeal is considered to be unfounded, it will be dismissed. If the appeal is held to be well founded, however, the CJEU will quash the decision of the General Court and may itself give a final judgment on the issue or refer the case back to the General Court. In the event that the CJEU refers the matter back to the General Court, the latter will be bound by the decision of the CJEU on the points of law that were appealed.[21] All European court judgments are available online.[22] Both the General Court and the CJEU are general, as opposed to specialized courts.

For other interested parties, notably importers unrelated to exporters subject to AD/CVD duties, or other types of determinations, various indirect actions exist to obtain judicial review of the concerned EU act. First, by virtue of Article 267 TFEU, the CJEU may, at the request of national courts, give a preliminary ruling on the interpretation or validity of the provisions of the Basic Regulations and the EU institutions' day-to-day implementation of commercial instruments. An interested party may also bring a case before the European courts based on Article 265 TFEU (action for failure to act), Article 268 to Article 340

Law: A Handbook (2nd edn., 2009), pp. 761–84; Lewis, "Standing of Private Plaintiffs to Annul Generally Applicable European Community Measures: If the System is Broken, Where Should it be Fixed?", (2007) Fordham International Law Journal 1496–538; Lenaerts, Arts and Maselis, Procedural Law of the European Union (2006), pp. 203–87.

[19] Per Article 19(1) TEU, the Court of Justice of the European Union shall include the Court of Justice, the General Court and specialized courts. It shall ensure that the law is observed in the interpretation and application of the treaties.

[20] Article 256(1), first sentence, TFEU.

[21] Paragraphs one and two of Article 61 of the Statute of the ECJ.

[22] See http://curia.europa.eu/jurisp/cgi-bin/form.pl?lang=en for all judgments since 17 June 1997, and http://eur-lex.europa.eu/RECH_jurisprudence.do for judgments before that date.

TFEU (the non-contractual liability of the Union) or Article 201 TFEU (action for interim relief).

The Basic Regulations implement their WTO counterparts. To the extent that the Basic Regulations (or Commission interpretation thereof) deviate from the WTO rules, the question arises whether private individuals may invoke the WTO provisions before the EU or national courts. The CJEU has held that the General Agreement on Tariffs and Trade (GATT) binds the EU and has a status superior to secondary, but inferior to primary EU law. However, the CJEU has also consistently held that the GATT as such has no direct effect,[23] essentially because of its loosely worded obligations and many derogations. Nevertheless, in the *Nakajima* judgment,[24] the CJEU held that the EU was bound by the 1979 Anti-Dumping Code as much as by the GATT itself, and must respect its provisions. The CJEU then proceeded to determine whether the EU institutions had respected the provisions of the Code.

It is noted that the ADA goes significantly beyond GATT and the 1979 Anti-Dumping Code, as evidenced by the unconditionality and precision of its wording, as well as its comparatively detailed regulation of procedures and substantive issues. However, the Council Decision approving the Uruguay Round Agreements states explicitly that "by its nature, the Agreement establishing the World Trade Organization, including the Annexes thereto, is not susceptible to being directly invoked in Community or Member States Courts".[25]

Parties frequently invoke WTO Agreements and/or WTO panel/ Appellate Body reports in EU court proceedings concerning trade remedy measures. The EU courts are generally reluctant to rely explicitly on these sources, but it cannot be denied that they are influenced by them. The *Ikea* case,[26] in the aftermath of the AB report in *EC–Bed Linen*,[27] provides a good example. The CJEU, in wording that virtually followed that of the AB, confirmed that model zeroing was illegal as a matter of EU law. On the other hand, the General Court has repeatedly upheld

---

[23] See, e.g., Joined Cases 21–24/72, *International Fruit Company* v. *Productschap* [1972] ECR 1219.

[24] Case C-69/89, *Nakajima All Precision Co.* v. *Council* [1991] ECR 2069.

[25] Council Decision of 22 December 1994 concerning the conclusion on behalf of the European Community, as regards matters within its competence, of the agreements reached in the Uruguay Round multilateral negotiations (1986–1994), [1994] OJ L336/1.

[26] Case C-351/04, *Ikea Wholesale* v. *Commissioners of Customs & Excise* [2007] ECR I-7723.

[27] *European Communities – Anti-dumping duties on imports of cotton-type bed linen from India*, WT/DS141/AB/R of 1 March 2001.

simple zeroing applied by the Commission. The Court has held that the use of simple zeroing is not prohibited by Article 2.4.2 ADA interpreted in light of the *Bed Linen* report, or Article 2(11) Basic AD Regulation.[28]

The General Court has jurisdiction to hear and determine at first instance actions for annulment (Article 263 TFEU), non-contractual liability (Article 268 to Article 340 TFEU) and for failure to act (Article 265 TFEU). The General Court has Rules of Procedure which provide detailed rules as regards the conduct of the proceedings to be followed by parties. This includes, among others, regarding the oral and written procedures (lodging of the pleading, defence, reply and rejoinders, among others),[29] expedited proceedings, stay of the proceedings, time limits and forms of procedures.[30] The General Court has issued Practice Directions to parties. These deal specifically with the manner in which pleadings and other procedural documents relating to the written and oral procedures are to be submitted in actions before the General Court and appeals before the CJEU. These directions explain and complement the Rules of Procedure of the General Court.[31]

There are strict time limits for lodging cases before the General Court. As regards an action for annulment, the time limit for lodging the application is two months from the date of publication of the measure, or of its notification to the applicant.[32] Additionally, Article 102 Rules of Procedure of the General Court provides that where the period of time allowed for commencing proceedings against a measure adopted by an institution runs from the date of publication of that measure, that period shall be calculated from the end of the fourteenth day after publication thereof in the *Official Journal* of the EU and, furthermore, an extension of 10 days is automatically granted on account of distance in each case. Thus, the effective time for filing an action for annulment of an AD/CVD Regulation varies between 84 and 86 days from the date of its publication in the *Official Journal* of the EU. An action for failure to act is admissible only if the EU institution concerned has first been called upon to act and if, within two months of being so called upon, the institution has not defined its position, the action may be brought within a further period of two months.[33] Additionally, the 10-day extension on account of

---

[28] Case T-274/02, *Ritek, Prodisc* v. *Council* [2006] ECR II-4305; Case T-167/07, *Far Eastern New Century Corp.* v. *Council* [2011], nya.
[29] Article 4–Article 63, Rules of Procedure of the General Court.
[30] http://curia.europa.eu/jcms/jcms/Jo2_7040/.   [31] Ibid.   [32] Article 263(6) TFEU.
[33] Article 263 TFEU.

distance will also apply.[34] As regards an action for damages, a claim cannot be brought after five years from the occurrence of the event which gives rise to the claim. However, if, prior to the institution of an action for damages, an application for annulment or failure to act has been made by the applicant, the time period in which to bring the action for damages is the same as that applicable for bringing an action for annulment or failure to act, as the case may be.[35] If the day on which the time to file the action stops running falls on Saturday, Sunday or an official holiday, it is extended until the end of the first working day following. Once the case is lodged and the application is served on the defendant, the latter has two months to file its defence, and may seek an extension of the time period. Thereafter, the President of the Court fixes the time periods for the applicant and the defendant, respectively, to file the reply and rejoinder.

Once the General Court gives its judgment, an appeal may be filed against it before the CJEU, and the appellant may seek to have the decision of the General Court set aside in whole or in part, and may request the same order in whole or in part as sought before the General Court.[36] The CJEU has a Statute and Rules of Procedure. The subject matter of the proceedings before the General Court may not be changed in an appeal. Appeals must be confined to points of law.[37] In order to be admissible, an appeal must be filed within two months of the date of notification of the decision appealed against, and the time period commences when the appellant receives the contested decision. Additionally, the 10-day extension on account of distance is also granted to file an appeal.

During the 2000–10 period, the average duration of a procedure before the General Court was 38 months, or more than three years. Where judgments of the General Court were appealed to the CJEU the average duration of the two-step process was 61 months, or slightly more than five years. A possibility exists to request an expedited court procedure. However, the requirements for this procedure are cumbersome and stringent. In the case of preliminary ruling requests, the average duration of the CJEU procedure from the time of the request until

---

[34] Article 101(1)(b) Rules of Procedure of the General Court. The same rule applies as regards the time limit for filing an action before the CJEU: Article 80(2) Rules of Procedure of the ECJ.

[35] Article 46 Statute of the ECJ.   [36] Article 113 Rules of Procedure of the ECJ.

[37] Paragraph two of Article 256(1) TFEU; Article 58 Statute of the ECJ.

judgment was 19 months. This does not take into account the preceding and following national court proceedings.

2 Procedure

2.1 Article 263 TFEU: action for annulment

Article 263 TFEU provides the legal basis for interested parties to protect themselves against unlawful binding acts resulting from trade remedy proceedings. Thus, any interested party may bring an action for annulment if it can show that it meets the conditions of this article.

There are two important limitations in Article 263(4). First, the administrative determination must constitute an 'act'. The principle is that administrative determinations which produce binding legal effects capable of affecting applicants' interests and bringing about a distinct change in their legal position may be appealed.[38] By contrast, mere preparatory acts or intermediate measures cannot be challenged as such under Article 263 TFEU.[39] In the case of acts adopted by a procedure involving several stages, and particularly where they are the culmination of an internal procedure, in principle it is only those acts which definitively determine the position of the Commission upon the conclusion of that procedure which are open to challenge, and not intermediate measures whose purpose is to prepare for the final decision.

Second, *ratione personae*, the applicant must show that (i) it is either the addressee of the act, or (ii) it is directly and individually affected by the act, or (iii) in the case of a regulatory act, that it is directly concerned and that the act does not entail implementing measures.

2.2 Which acts can be the subject of an action for annulment?

Administrative determinations imposing trade remedy measures are appealable acts. Similarly, Commission decisions to terminate an investigation without imposition of measures may be appealed:

> ... not only regulations imposing definitive anti-dumping duties adopted at the end of anti-dumping proceedings, but also decisions of the Commission or the Council to close anti-dumping proceedings without

---

[38] Case 101/76, *Koninklijke Scholten Honig NV v. Council and Commission* [1977] ECR I-2003.

[39] Case T-134/95, *Dysan Magnetics Ltd and Review Magnetics (Macao) Ltd v. Commission* [1996] ECR II-181.

imposing anti-dumping duties may be the subject of actions before the Community Courts.[40]

In *Eurocoton*, the CJEU held that the Council's rejection of a Commission proposal to impose definitive duties constituted a reviewable act, as it produced binding legal effects and was capable of affecting the appellant's interests.[41]

A decision *not* to open a trade remedy proceeding is appealable as far as the complainant is concerned. The CJEU considered in *Fediol*[42] that the EU trade association Fediol, which had brought a complaint that the Brazilian government was subsidizing its soya bean oil-cake industry, could challenge the Commission's decision not to initiate a CVD investigation. Also noteworthy is the *BEUC* case, wherein the CJEU held that a telefaxed letter by the Commission refusing the EU consumers' association BEUC access to the non-confidential file constituted not merely a communication, but a decision which adversely affected the interests of BEUC and could be the subject of an appeal.[43]

On the other hand, the General Court ruled that the Commission's decision to initiate an AD proceeding is a preparatory act not capable of immediately and irreversibly affecting the applicant's position as it:[44]

> does not automatically entail the imposition of anti-dumping duties; the proceedings may be terminated without measures being imposed ... Undertakings involved in an anti-dumping investigation are in no way compelled to alter their commercial policy as a result of the initiation of the proceedings; nor ... can they be required to cooperate in the investigation.

Similarly, a Commission decision made in the course of an AD investigation to grant or deny market economy/individual treatment to exporting producers in non-market economy countries, or to select a particular analogue country, cannot be challenged as such.[45] The same applies to the Commission's rejection of a proposed undertaking.[46] Only once the definitive duty is imposed may exporting producers challenge the definitive regulation and raise such issues. However, the Commission

---

[40] Case C-76/01 P, *Eurocoton and Others* v. *Council* [2003] ECR I-1091.   [41] Ibid.
[42] Case 191/82, *Fediol* v. *Commission* [1983] ECR 2913.
[43] Case C-170/89, *Bureau Europeén des Unions de Consommateurs (BEUC)* v. *Commission* [1991] ECR I-5709.
[44] Case T-134/95, *Dysan Magnetics Ltd. and Review Magnetics (Macao) Ltd* v. *Commission*.
[45] Ibid.
[46] Case C-156/87, *Gestetner Holdings plc.* v. *Council and Commission* [1990] ECR I-781.

decision to initiate a review investigation may be challenged by an exporter which cooperated and offered an undertaking in the original investigation.[47]

2.3   Who may lodge an application?

Where an EU administrative act is addressed to a specific person, the addressee may lodge an application. However, for administrative acts that are not addressed to a natural or legal person, as will typically be the case for acts imposing trade remedy measures, interested parties will have to show that the measure is of 'direct and individual concern' to them. The CJEU has recognized early on that a single act may, on the one hand, operate as an effective decision in relation to some parties (in which case it is directly appealable) and, on the other, as a generally applicable regulation for others (in which case it is not directly appealable).[48] As the Court held in the *Timex* case:

> The [AD] measures in question are, in fact, legislative in nature and scope, inasmuch as they apply to traders in general; nevertheless, their provisions may be of direct and individual concern to some of those traders.[49]

To satisfy the *direct concern* requirement, the applicant must show that the adverse legal effects felt by him are a direct consequence of the challenged EU measure.[50] This chain of causation is broken if the EU measure leaves the national authorities a certain discretion or margin of appreciation regarding implementation. In the *Ball Bearings* cases,[51] the contention of the EU authorities that the collection of provisional duties was secured by national customs authorities and that, therefore, only the implementing measures adopted by the customs authorities were of direct concern to the exporters, was dismissed by the CJEU on the ground that it disregarded that such collection was "purely automatic and, moreover, in pursuance not of intermediate national rules but of Community rules alone".[52] It is therefore clear that this requirement will usually be considered to be satisfied in trade remedy cases.

---

[47] Case T-45/06, *Reliance Industries* v. *Council and Commission* [2008] ECR II-2399.
[48] Case 264/82, *Timex* v. *Council and Commission* [1985] ECR 849.   [49] Ibid.
[50] Case T-80/97, *Starway* v. *Council* [2000] ECR II-3099.
[51] Case 113/77, *NTN Toyo Bearing Company Ltd. and others* v. *Council* [1979] ECR 1185.
[52] Case 118/77, *Import Standard Office* v. *Council* [1979] ECR 1294.

With regard to *individual concern*, the CJEU in the landmark *Plaumann* case[53] set out the principle that:

> [p]ersons are individually concerned if the measures affect them by reason of certain attributes which are peculiar to them or by reason of circumstances which distinguish them from all other persons, by virtue of which they are identified individually just as in the case of the person addressed.

According to CJEU case law, measures imposing AD/CVD measures[54] are of individual concern to *foreign producers and exporters* able to prove either that they are identified in the measures adopted by the authorities, or were affected by the preliminary investigations.[55] Moreover, exporters and producers who can show the existence of certain attributes which are peculiar to them and which, as regards the measure in question, differentiate them from all other traders, may also be considered as directly and individually concerned.[56]

In cases involving non-market economies, parties may not necessarily be identified in the regulation, among others because of the "one country one duty" rule. The question then arises as to the extent to which they were concerned. In *Gao Yao*,[57] the Court found that a Hong Kong sales office of a Chinese producing company was *not* concerned by the preliminary investigation for two main reasons. First, the company was established in Hong Kong, as regards which the EU did not impose AD duties. Moreover, the company had only acted in the investigation as a transmitter of documents between a Chinese producer and the EU institutions: thus its role was limited to that of a representative of the producer. In *Sinochem Heilongjiang*,[58] on the other hand, the Court found that despite the fact that the Chinese exporting producer of oxalic acid was not identified in the measure, the company had been concerned by the investigation, "even where it

---

[53] Case 25/62, *Plaumann and Co. v. Commission* [1963] ECR 95.

[54] As regards multilateral SG measures, the situation is different, because it is on the basis of a complaint by an EU member state that the case is initiated, and the measures are imposed against imports from all countries.

[55] Cases 239 and 275/82, *Allied, Demufert, Transcontinental Fertilizer, and Kaiser Aluminium* v. *Commission* [1984] ECR 1005 (*Allied I*).

[56] Case C-358/89, *Extramet Industrie* v. *Council* [1991] ECR I-2501.

[57] Case C-75/92, *Gao Yao (Hong-Kong) Hua Fa Industrial Co. Ltd* v. *Council* [1994] ECR I-3141.

[58] Case T-161/94, *Sinochem Heilongjiang* v. *Council* [1996] ECR II-695.

was ultimately decided not to accept the information provided by the applicant on the central points at issue". The General Court held that the company had answered the Commission's questionnaire, submitted written comments, corresponded with the Commission regularly, and its representative travelled to join the hearing. Additionally, the Commission evaluated its comments and arguments. In the Court's view, it was the only Chinese company that participated in the investigation, which constituted a factor differentiating it from all other traders as regards the measure.

As regards *related importers*, the courts have held that they are individually concerned in cases where their resale prices are used by the Commission for constructing the export price.[59] *Unrelated importers*, on the other hand, will generally not be considered as individually concerned by a trade remedy measure, despite the fact that they are the ones who will pay the duties. In *BSC Footwear Supplies*,[60] the General Court held that the contested measure was not of individual concern to the applicants (a group of unrelated footwear importers), because they had failed to prove the existence of exceptional circumstances, the existence of dumping was not established by reference to their resale prices and their position on the market was not substantial. The fact that they had participated in the administrative procedure by providing information was considered insufficient to bring an action for annulment.

However, under certain circumstances, the courts have opened the door for annulment actions by unrelated importers. In *Nashua*[61] and *Gestetner*,[62] for example, the CJEU declared the applications of two original equipment manufacturer importers admissible. In *Extramet*,[63] the CJEU considered the application brought by Extramet, the independent importer of calcium metal from China and the Soviet Union, admissible, because it was both the single most important importer and also an end user of the product. The Court considered that its economic

---

[59] Case 118/77, *ISO* v. *Council* [1979] ECR 1277.

[60] Case T-598/97, *British Shoe Corp. Footwear Supplies Ltd. and others* v. *Council* [2002] ECR II-1155.

[61] Joined Cases C-133 and 150/87, *Nashua* v. *Commission and Council* [1990] ECR I-719.

[62] Case C-156/87, *Gestetner Holdings* v. *Council and Commission*.

[63] Case C-358/89, *Extramet Industrie* v. *Council* [1991] ECR I-2501. See also Case T-2/95, *Industrie des Poudres Sphériques* v *Council*, judgment of 15 October 1998, involving the same company.

activities were largely dependent on imports because of the small number of calcium metal producers and because it had experienced problems in obtaining the product from the main EU producer and complainant, Péchiney, which was also its main competitor in the processing market.

It is noted that the second limb of Article 263(4) TFEU, introduced by the Treaty of Lisbon, provides a third possibility to challenge the validity of binding acts of the Commission. This fills the gap in judicial protection for private parties who want to contest a regulatory act which is of direct concern to them, but at the same time cannot be regarded as being individually concerned by that act within the meaning of the *Plaumann* test. Pre-Lisbon, if there was a regulatory act which did not entail any implementing measures, and was of direct, but not individual concern to private parties, the private parties had no right of action either before the EU courts or before the national courts in order to trigger judicial review through the preliminary ruling procedure. The amendment to the wording of Article 263(4) TFEU may have a major impact in the trade remedies field, particularly as far as unrelated importers are concerned.[64] Although customs duties are collected by the member states' customs authorities, we have seen that the CJEU has traditionally held that such collection is "purely automatic and, moreover, in pursuance not of intermediate national rules but of Community rules alone".[65] The question remains whether the CJEU would consider that the collection of the duties by customs authorities constitutes an *implementing measure*. This issue is likely to be decided in *FESI* v. *Council,* in which the Federation of European Sporting Goods Industry challenged the 2009 Council decision to extend AD measures on leather footwear from China and Vietnam.[66]

As mentioned above, *EU complainants* will typically bring a court case against decisions not to initiate an investigation,[67] or to terminate an investigation without measures. They may also decide to challenge issues

---

[64] Compare Ruessmann and Dacko, "The Lisbon Treaty and EU Trade Defence Instruments: A New Framework for Court Challenges and Decision-making", 3 (2010), *Int'l TLR* 63–8.

[65] Case 118/77, *Import Standard Office* v. *Council* [1979] ECR 1294.

[66] Case T134/10, *FESI* v. *Council*, nya. [67] Case 191/82, *Fediol* v. *Commission*.

such as the level of the duty[68] or the scope or duration[69] of the measure. Such challenges have rarely given rise to admissibility issues.[70]

2.4 Article 267 TFEU: preliminary ruling procedure

If a question of EU law arises before a national court of a member state, that court *may* request the ECJ to give a preliminary ruling.[71] However, a national court *must* make a reference for preliminary ruling if there are no further judicial remedies[72] available under national law against the decision of that national court.[73] This course of action is open notably to *unrelated importers*[74] who want to contest the imposition of trade remedy measures, and supposedly also to other categories of interested parties wishing to challenge an SG measure. They may challenge the collection of the duties by the national customs authorities; as collection is based on an act by EU institutions, a question of EU law would arise.[75]

The procedure has many disadvantages, however. First, the fact that foreign exporters and/or EU producers can invoke Article 263(4) TFEU,

---

[68] Case T-210/95, *EFMA* v. *Council* [1999] ECR II-3291, in which the European Fertilizer Manufacturers' Association claimed that by adopting a 5 per cent profit margin for European producers of ammonium nitrate the Council committed a manifest error of appraisal of the facts of the case.

[69] Case T-232/95, *CECOM* v. *Council* [1998] ECR II-02679, in which the Committee of European Copier Manufacturers brought an action against a regulation extending a definitive AD duty on imports of plain paper photocopiers from Japan for two years on the ground that the Council did not have the power to adopt anti-dumping measures for a period of less than five years.

[70] As an exception, in Case 264/82, *Timex* v. *Council and Commission*, an objection of inadmissibility was raised by the Council and the Commission against the action for partial annulment of the regulation imposing AD measures on mechanical wristwatches from the then USSR, lodged by a complainant EU producer, Timex, on the grounds that it was not directly and individually affected by the contested Regulation. However, the court declared the action admissible on the basis of the part played by Timex in the AD proceeding and its position in the market to which the measure applied.

[71] Article 267(2) TFEU.

[72] Appeal on points of law or cassation proceedings are deemed to be judicial remedies within the meaning of this provision; Lenaerts and Arts and Maselis, *Procedural Law of the European Union*, p. 72.

[73] Article 267(3) TFEU. The obligation does not arise if the legal issue is completely clear ("acte clair" doctrine). Unfortunately this opens a major loophole in the system of judicial review.

[74] The CJEU has held that a *related* party which has the right to request annulment of a Regulation imposing duties under Article 263 TFEU cannot use the preliminary ruling procedure, see Case C-239/99, *Nachi Europe* [2001] ECR I-1197. Compare Case C-188/92, *TWD Textilwerke Deggendorf* v. *Germany* [1994] ECR I-833.

[75] See, e.g., Case C-263/06, *Carboni e derivati* [2008] ECR I-01077.

while importers must rely on Article 267 TFEU, means that procedures in several courts may arise simultaneously. Second, the Article 267 procedure does not lend itself very easily to the review of factual determinations such as trade remedy decisions. Third, the expertise of the national courts in the trade remedy field is generally very limited, which tends to lead to deference. Fourth, the willingness of national courts varies significantly among member states regarding their request for preliminary rulings. Fifth, the procedure is time-consuming, because it typically involves three steps: review by the national court(s), request for a preliminary ruling CJEU judgment, and further review and decision by the national court taking into account the preliminary ruling of the CJEU.

2.5 Article 265 TFEU: failure to act

For the sake of completeness, it is noted that a Commission decision not to open an initial or review investigation may be attacked on the ground that the Commission failed to act. However, in the trade remedies area, such cases have been very rare.[76]

3 Standard of review

The scope of review under paragraph four of Article 263 TFEU is intrinsically limited. Measures can only be annulled on the following grounds:[77]

(1) lack of competence;[78]
(2) infringement of an essential procedural requirement;[79]
(3) infringement of the Treaty or of any rule relating to its application (including implementing legislation and, since *Nakajima*,[80] the ADA);
(4) misuse of powers.[81]

---

[76] See, e.g., Case T-212/95 *Oficemen v. Commission* [1997] ECR II-01161.

[77] Article 263(2) TFEU.

[78] This ground has rarely been invoked in actions concerning trade remedies regulations. See, e.g., Case 229/86, *Brother International Ltd. v. Commission* [1987] ECR 3757.

[79] For instance, the principles of non-discrimination, diligence and sound administration, proportionality, legal certainty and protection of legitimate expectations. Joined Cases T-33 and 34/98, *Petrotub and Republica SA v. Council* [1999] ECR II-3837.

[80] Case C-69/89, *Nakajima All Precision v. Council*.

[81] The invocation of this ground has not been successful thus far in cases concerning AD Regulations: Case C-69/89, *Nakajima All Precision Co. Ltd. v. Council*.

The EU courts have traditionally accorded the EU administering authorities significant discretion in conducting trade remedy investigations and assessing dumping/subsidies, resulting injury and Union interest, on the basis of the perceived complexity of the economic, political and legal situations that they have to examine.[82] The courts have typically refused to reconsider the investigation and taken the position that:

> review by the [European] Courts relates to whether the relevant procedural rules have been complied with, whether the facts on which the disputed conclusion is based have been accurately stated and whether there has been a manifest error of appraisal or a misuse of powers.[83]

However, the very fact that the Commission and Council have a wide power of appraisal in the trade remedies field has led the courts to conclude that respect for the *procedural rights* guaranteed by the EU legal order in administrative procedures is of even more fundamental importance here than in other areas.[84] Thus, the courts have repeatedly annulled regulations where they found that the EU institutions had not observed the rights of defence of interested parties.

In *Timex*, for example, the CJEU annulled the contested regulation because the Commission had not made every effort to provide the complainant with the information relevant to the defence of its interests.[85] In *Allied II*, the CJEU annulled a Council regulation imposing definitive AD duties on the grounds that the Council had not considered whether imposition of duties to the full extent of the dumping margin was necessary to alleviate the injury.[86] In *Al Jubail*,[87] the CJEU held, among others, that the Commission had failed to establish that the lawyers of the applicant had actually received a letter which had been sent by the Commission by normal mail. The CJEU indirectly criticized the whole administrative procedure in stating that "[a]s they stand at present, the EC anti-dumping rules do not provide all the procedural guarantees for the protection of the individual which may exist in national systems".

---

[82] See, e.g., Case T-413/03, *Shandong Reipu Biochemicals* v. *Council* [2006] ECR II-2243.

[83] Case 240/84, *NTN Toyo Bearing and Others* v. *Council.* [1987] ECR 1809.

[84] Case C-269/90, *Technische Universität München* [1991] ECR I-5469.

[85] Case 264/82, *Timex* v. *Council and Commission.*

[86] Case 53/83, *Allied, Transcontinental Fertilizer, Kaiser Aluminium* v. *Council* [1985] ECR 1621.

[87] Case C-49/88, *Al-Jubail Fertilizer Company* v. *Council* [1991] ECR I-3187.

Cases such as *Nölle* and *Extramet II* lie on the border between procedural and substantive review. In *Nölle*,[88] the CJEU found fault with the manner in which the Commission had selected Sri Lanka as the surrogate country for calculating the dumping margin for Chinese producers. Before arriving at this conclusion, the Court double-checked virtually all substantive decisions taken by the Commission. Similarly, in *Extramet II*,[89] the CJEU held that the Commission had insufficiently considered competition arguments raised by the applicant.

Review of the case law indicates that the courts have carefully checked whether the EU institutions have observed the *procedural* requirements of the basic AD Regulation, especially requirements concerning the applicant's rights of defence and verification of facts.[90] On the other hand, the EU courts have displayed a marked reluctance to double-check the *substantive* decisions taken by the institutions, despite a few exceptions.[91]

4   Remedies

Where a regulation imposing AD/CVD measures is annulled as such, any duties paid will be reimbursed by the customs authorities of the member states where the duties were collected. Additionally, the Court will normally order the losing party to pay the full or partial legal expenses of the winning party, if so requested in the application. The Court has discretion in this regard.[92] However, it is also possible that the regulation will be annulled only as far as the applicant is concerned.[93] Such partial annulment benefits only the applicant. This means that other companies which were affected by the same illegal approach will not benefit from the judgment.

The Court may further tailor the scope of the annulment to the specifics of the case. In *Medici Grimm*, for example, the General Court annulled the contested regulation in so far as the Council failed to give retroactive effect to the amendment of the rate of the AD duty imposed

[88] Case C-16/90, *Detlef Nölle v. Hauptzollamt Bremen-Freihafen* [1991] ECR I-5163.

[89] Case C-358/89, *Extramet Industrie SA v. Council* [1991] ECR I-2501.

[90] See, e.g., Case T-48/96, *Acme v. Council* [1999] ECR II-3089.

[91] Compare Rovetta and Senduk, "A Survey of the EU Trade Defence Case Law in Year 2010", 6:(6) (2011) GTCJ 303–12.

[92] Article 87 Rules of Procedure of the General Court; Article 69–Article 75 Rules of Procedure of the ECJ.

[93] See, e.g., Case T-221/05, *Huvis Corp v. Council* [2008] ECR II-124.

on the applicant's imports of leather handbags from its associated Chinese exporter. However, because the action's purpose was not to secure the removal of the provision amending the rate of duty applicable to those imports (from 38 per cent to 0 per cent), but rather, to have the provision limiting the temporal effects of that amendment annulled, the Court considered it appropriate to maintain the contested regulation until the competent institutions had adopted the measures necessary to comply with the judgment.[94]

The Commission may also determine that the annulment affects only certain aspects of the underlying investigation, given that an AD investigation is a multi-step procedure. Thus, annulment of one step does not annul the whole proceeding. In such cases, it may decide to reopen the investigation as far as the applicant is concerned and remedy the aspects considered illegal by the courts, while leaving unchanged the uncontested parts not affected by the judgment.[95]

In *Huvis*,[96] the General Court partially annulled the regulation imposing AD duties regarding Huvis by ruling that the duty drawback in the review investigation had been calculated incorrectly. The Commission therefore recalculated the duty for Huvis. Similarly, in *Foshan*,[97] the CJEU ruled on appeal that Foshan's rights of defence had been adversely affected by the infringement of Article 20(5) of the Basic Regulation. The Commission therefore reopened the investigation as far as Foshan was concerned[98] and later re-imposed the duty.[99]

It is possible that correction of the illegalities does not have an impact on the result, for example, where the court rules that EU institutions insufficiently considered (aspects of) the original determination.[100] In other cases, the impact may be very small. In *Stainless Steel Fasteners*, for example, the AD duty for the applicant, Kundan Industries, decreased

---

[94] Case T-7/99, *Medici Grimm* v. *Council* [2000] ECR II-02671.

[95] Polyester staple fibres from China and Saudi Arabia, amending Regulation (EC) No. 2852/2000 imposing a definitive anti-dumping duty on imports of polyester staple fibres from Korea and terminating the anti-dumping proceeding in respect of such imports originating in Taiwan, [2009] OJ L125/1 (amendment).

[96] Case T-221/05, *Huvis Corp.* v. *Council* (judgment of 8 July 2008) [2008] ECR II-124.

[97] Case C-141/08, *Foshan Shunde Yongjian Housewares & Hardware* v. *Council*, judgment of 1 October 2009 [2009] ECR II-9147.

[98] *Ironing Boards from China* [2009] OJ C308/44 (partial re-opening).

[99] *Ironing Boards from China, manufactured by Foshan Shunde Yongjian Housewares and Hardware Co. Ltd, Foshan* [2010] OJ L242/1 (definitive).

[100] *Certain seamless pipes and tubes of iron or non-alloy steel from Romania* [2004] OJ L40/11 (amendment).

from 47.4 per cent to 45.4 per cent,[101] following the Commission's recalculation to comply with the judgment.[102]

While court proceedings are in progress, the measure remains in force. By virtue of Article 201 TFEU, an interested party may apply for suspension of the operation of the measures or for other forms of *interim relief* pending the Court's judgment in the main action. Thus far, such applications have been made in several trade remedies cases, but have been granted only regarding one AD regulation concerning ball bearings.[103] In *Technointorg*,[104] the CJEU held that the applicant must prove that the damage suffered by it as a result of the measure was special *and* that "the balance of the interests at stake points in its favour in the sense that the grant of the interim measures requested would not cause appreciable injury to the [EU] industry". This standard would appear difficult to satisfy in practice.

Article 268 TFEU in combination with Article 340 allows individuals to take the EU institutions to court for payment of *damage* arising from the actions of those institutions or their servants in the performance of their duties. The standard for the adjudication of damage must be found in the general principles common to the law of the member states. In *Lütticke*,[105] the Court gathered the following conditions from those principles:

(1) the applicant must have suffered damage;
(2) the damage must have been caused by a Union act; *and*
(3) the Union act in question must have been unlawful.

As regards unlawfulness, the CJEU case law indicates that a sufficiently serious breach of a rule of law intended to confer rights on individuals must be demonstrated.[106] On the other hand, it is not necessary for invocation of Article 340 TFEU that the contested act has been declared

---

[101] *Stainless steel fasteners from China, India, Korea, Malaysia, Taiwan, Thailand* [2003] OJ L99/22 (amendment).

[102] Case T-88/98, *Kundan Industries and Tata International* v. *Council* [2002] ECR II-4897.

[103] Case 113/77, *NTN Toyo Bearing Co., Ltd.* v. *Council*, Order of the President of the Court of 14 October 1977; Case 119/77, *Nippon Seiko* v. *Council*, Order of the President of the Court of 20 October 1977.

[104] Case 77/87, *Technointorg* v. *Council* [1987] ECR 1793. See also Article 104(2) Rules of Procedure of the General Court and Case C-6/94 R, *Descom Scales Co. Ltd.* v. *Council* [1994] ECR I-1867.

[105] Case 4/69, *Alfons Lütticke GmbH* v. *Commission* [1971] ECR 325.

[106] See, e.g., Case C-352/98 P, *Bergaderm and Goupil* v. *Commission* [2000] ECR I-5291.

void pursuant to an action based on Article 263(4) TFEU. An action for damages will be considered admissible even if no prior action for annulment under Article 263(4) TFEU has been filed, or a preliminary ruling has been requested.

In *Fresh Marine*, the CJEU held that EU law confers a right to reparation subject to the satisfaction of three cumulative conditions: that the rule of law infringed is intended to confer rights on individuals, the breach is sufficiently serious, and the damage suffered by the injured parties is a direct consequence of the breach of an obligation imposed upon the author of the act.[107] There have been few actions for damages in the trade remedies context, and even fewer where the courts granted them. However, in *Fresh Marine*, the CJEU upheld the General Court's finding that the Commission was partially responsible for the inaccurate monitoring of compliance of the applicant's undertaking and was liable for a portion of the loss of profit suffered by the applicant.

In *Medici Grimm*, the General Court rejected a damages claim brought by a German importer.[108] The Court found that the Council had not infringed Article 1(1) of the Basic Regulations in a manner sufficiently serious to give rise to non-contractual liability on the part of the EU.[109]

III   Concluding remarks and suggestions for improvement

Trade defence measures, particularly AD measures, are frequently challenged before the EU courts. Most of the trade remedy cases brought thus far have been based either on an action for annulment by virtue of Article 263(4) TFEU, or have been the result of the preliminary ruling procedure.

As regards admissibility, the situation is generally satisfactory, with the notable exception of the situation of unrelated importers. It remains to be seen whether the revised wording of Article 263(4) TFEU addresses the predicament of this category of interested parties in trade remedy cases.

Concerning the scope of review, the EU courts thoroughly review the work of the administering authorities as far as observance of *procedural*

---

[107] Case TC-472/00 P, *Commission v. Fresh Marine Company* [2003] ECR I-7541.
[108] Case T-364/03, *Medici Grimm v. Council* [2006] ECR II-79.
[109] Compare Case T-429/04, *Trubowest Handel and Makarov v. Council and Commission* [2008] ECR II-128, upheld in Case C-419/08 P, *Trubowest Handel and Makarov v. Council and Commission*, judgment of 18 March 2010 [2010] ECR I-2259.

rules is concerned. However, the courts' unfortunate endorsement of the administering authorities' view of trade remedy measures as matters of trade *policy* automatically entails a significant margin of discretion which limits judicial review of substantive determinations. This is in marked contrast to the type of in-depth review carried out by WTO panels and the Appellate Body and specialized trade courts, such as the Court of International Trade and the US Court of Appeals for the federal circuit in the United States. It seems clear, therefore, that the establishment of specialized EU trade courts or at least specialized chambers within the existing structure, would improve the substantive review of determinations made by the administering authorities.

Compared to WTO dispute settlement proceedings, EU court proceedings are painfully slow, taking on average more than five years for the two-stage process. This might be another reason to establish specialized trade courts or chambers. On the other hand, the fact that only governments may lodge a WTO dispute settlement proceeding and have the possibility of obtaining reimbursement of duties paid and litigation expenses through EU court proceedings constitute clear advantages of the EU road.

As of the time of writing, EU trade remedy measures have been challenged repeatedly in the GATT and the WTO by countries such as Brazil, China, India, Japan and Norway. Many of these followed unsuccessful pursuit of identical or similar claims by interested parties before the EU courts. Two closely related conclusions can be drawn from this. First of all, third country governments are reluctant to take the EU to the WTO unless their private sector can convince them that there is no other way to obtain fair treatment from the EU authorities. Second, more effective EU judicial review of substantive determinations made by the EU authorities in trade remedy investigations would very likely decrease the number of WTO challenges in this area.

10

Turkey: a judicial review system in need of change

MÜSLÜM YILMAZ*

I Introduction

Until 1980, Turkey followed a rather protectionist trade policy. From 1960 to 1980, a development strategy based on import substitution was followed which provided national industries with a fair amount of protection.[1] During this period, governments used various trade restrictive measures such as customs duties and other charges on imports, quotas, import bans and exchange rate controls.[2] The year 1980 marked a turning point in Turkey's economic policies. Starting with the adoption of the famous economic decisions of 24 January 1980, subsequent governments took a series of economic decisions to open up the Turkish market and to integrate it into world markets. Import substitution was replaced by an export-oriented development policy.[3] In this context, quotas were eliminated in 1981, followed by import bans toward the end of 1983. Tariffs were progressively lowered, and the differences in levels of protection among varying industries were eliminated. The process leading to the creation in 1996 of the customs union with the (then) European Economic Community further deepened the liberalization of trade.[4] Literature shows a correlation between trade liberalization and the use of trade remedies. That is, the first use of trade remedies is

---

* The author thanks Korhan Erçoklu for his most helpful research assistance and Mark Koulen and Murat Göğüş for their valuable comments on earlier drafts.
[1] Cihan Dura, *Turkish Economy*, University of Erciyes Publications No. 19 (Kayseri, 1991), p. 194 (in Turkish).
[2] Hasan Olgun and Sübidey Togan, "Trade Liberalization and the Structure of Protection in Turkey in the 1980s. A Quantitative Analysis" 127(1) (1991) *Review of World Economics* 153.
[3] Dura, *Turkish Economy*, p. 207.
[4] Mustafa Sönmez, *80 Years of the Turkish Economy*, 7 No. 2004–28 (Istanbul, 2004), p. 179 (in Turkish).

usually preceded by a period of trade liberalization.[5] The case of Turkey seems to confirm this proposition. It was subsequent to the liberalization movement of the 1980s that Turkish industries felt the need for a trade remedies mechanism.

Trade remedies have a relatively short history in Turkey. Until 1989, the country had no legislation on these measures. In 1989, Parliament adopted the Law on the Prevention of Unfair Competition in Imports (hereinafter AD/CVD Law) which set out the basic principles with regard to anti-dumping and countervailing duty investigations. This was followed by the adoption, in the same year, of the Decree (hereinafter AD/CVD Decree) and the Regulation on the Prevention of Unfair Competition in Imports (hereinafter AD/CVD Regulation) detailing the provisions of the Law and laying down the legal framework with respect to these two types of investigations.

Following the entry into force of the WTO Agreement in 1995, the AD/CVD Law was amended, and the AD/CVD Decree and Regulation replaced by new texts in 1999, in order to comply with the new obligations contained in the new Anti-Dumping Agreement (hereinafter AD Agreement) and the Agreement on Subsidies and Countervailing Measures (hereinafter SCM Agreement) that emerged from the Uruguay Round. Setting aside two subsequent amendments,[6] the AD/CVD legislation as amended in 1999 is still in force.

As for safeguards, the first initiative for the regulation of this trade remedy instrument came with the 1995 introduction of the Decree on Surveillance and Safeguard Measures in Imports, the Administration of Quotas and Tariff Rate Quotas and the Regulation on Surveillance and Safeguard Measures in Imports.[7] The Decree and Regulation cited were repealed in 2004 and the new Decree on Safeguard Measures in Imports[8] (hereinafter SG Decree) and the new Regulation on Safeguard Measures

---

[5] Prakash Narayanan, "Anti-dumping in India – Present State and Future Prospects" 40 (2006) *Journal of World Trade* 1084–6; Thomas J. Prusa and Li Yue, "Trade Liberalization, Tariff Overhang and Antidumping filings in Developing Countries" (2009), Preliminary Draft, www.gwu.edu/~iiep/assets/docs/prusa_gwu_ad_conference. pdf (last visited 28.06.2011), pp. 5–36.

[6] See OG, 2.5.2002, No. 24743; OG, 31.12.2005, No. 26040 4th *bis*; and OG, 26.1.2006, No. 26061.

[7] For both the Regulation and the Decree, see OG, 1.6.1995, No. *bis* 22300. For subsequent amendments to the Decree and the Regulation, see OG, 1.11.1995, No. 22450.

[8] OG, 29.5.2004, No. 25476.

in Imports[9] (hereinafter SG Regulation) were introduced. The SG legislation enacted in 2004 is still in force.[10]

In addition to the above-described domestic legislation, the WTO's three agreements dealing with trade remedies, namely, the AD Agreement, the SCM Agreement and the Agreement on Safeguards (hereinafter SG Agreement), also have the force of law in the Turkish legal system. Article 90 of the Turkish Constitution provides that duly ratified international treaties gain the force of law under Turkish law.[11] Further, it stipulates that such treaties cannot be challenged on constitutional grounds before the Constitutional Court.[12] As such, the Constitution treats duly approved international treaties more favourably than domestic laws adopted by Parliament. In line with the procedure laid down in Article 90 of the Constitution, the WTO Agreement was approved with effect from 31 December 1994.[13] Therefore, the WTO Agreement, including its three annexed agreements dealing with trade remedies, has the force of law under Turkish law. The legal significance of this is that these three agreements constitute binding legal texts for the Turkish authorities conducting trade remedy investigations. Similarly, Turkish courts must give due consideration to these agreements in judicial review proceedings initiated against the actions of the Turkish investigating authority. As for WTO jurisprudence on trade remedies, it has no binding effect under Turkish law. However, there is no legal provision to stop a court from taking such jurisprudence into account in interpreting the relevant WTO agreement, and even in interpreting the relevant provisions of the Turkish trade remedies legislation.

---

[9] OG, 8.6.2004, No. 25486.

[10] An amendment was made to the SG Decree in 2007 by introducing a paragraph to Article 6 to prevent the circumvention of safeguard measures. See OG, 5.12.2007, No. 26721.

[11] According to this constitutional principle, provisions of a duly ratified treaty which contain clear and concrete obligations, as opposed to principles, have direct effect. Such provisions are to be implemented by government agencies and the courts without need for further domestic legislation. Serap Akipek, "The Question of Harmonization of Turkish Legislation with Duly Ratified International Treaties" 48 (1999) *Journal of Ankara University Faculty of Law* 14 (in Turkish). Treaty provisions that lay down principles would only be implemented through further domestic legislation.

[12] Pursuant to Article 148 of the Constitution, laws passed in Parliament may be challenged before the Constitutional Court on constitutional grounds.

[13] OG, 25.2.1995, No. *bis* 22213.

Turkey initiated its first anti-dumping investigation in 2003, and its first safeguard investigation in 2004. The first and only countervailing duty investigation was initiated in 2008. Despite the relatively short history of its trade remedies legislation and practice, however, Turkey appears high on the list of active users of anti-dumping and safeguard measures. Between 1995 and June 2010, Turkey imposed 142 anti-dumping measures which made it the fifth most active user of this instrument. In the same period, it imposed 12 safeguard measures and became, along with India, the most active user of such measures.

Turkey's investigating authority for the three trade remedies is the Directorate General for Imports of the Ministry of Economy (hereinafter Ministry). One department in this Directorate General deals with anti-dumping and countervailing duty investigations and another with safeguard investigations. Further, there is also a department which deals exclusively with anti-circumvention investigations. The procedural rules that apply to anti-dumping and countervailing duty investigations are different from those that apply to safeguard investigations. The decision-making processes are also different.

In the case of anti-dumping and countervailing duty investigations, the decision to initiate an investigation lies with the Board on the Prevention of Unfair Competition in Imports (hereinafter AD/CVD Board), which consists of representatives of several ministries, the directorates general of the Ministry other than that for imports, other government agencies and business associations.[14] The initiation decision takes the form of a communiqué and is published in the *Official Gazette*.[15]

The imposition of a provisional or final anti-dumping or countervailing duty requires the decision of the AD/CVD Board and the approval of the minister.[16] The acceptance of an undertaking require only a decision by the AD/CVD Board.[17] The decision to impose a provisional or final anti-dumping or countervailing duty and the acceptance of a price undertaking is published in the *Official Gazette* in the form of a communiqué.[18] The decision to initiate a safeguard investigation lies with the Board for the Evaluation of Safeguard Measures in Imports (hereinafter SG Board), which also consists of representatives of several ministries, other government agencies, directorates general of the Ministry other than the Directorate General for Imports and some

---

[14] AD/CVD Law, Article 6.1.   [15] AD/CVD Regulation, Articles 20.5 and 31.
[16] AD/CVD Law, Article 12 for provisional duties, Article 13 for definitive duties.
[17] Ibid., Articles 6.3(d) and 11.1.   [18] AD/CVD Regulation, Article 31.

business associations.[19] The initiation decision takes the form of a communiqué and is published in the *Official Gazette*.[20]

Interestingly, the SG legislation does not specify the decision-making process for the imposition of provisional and definitive safeguard measures. In practice, the type of measure determines the procedure for its adoption. All safeguard measures are first approved by the SG Board. If the measure takes a form other than that of a tariff surcharge, it is published as a communiqué in the *Official Gazette*. If the measure takes the form of increased tariffs, following the decision by the SG Board, a decree is to be obtained from the Council of Ministers, which is also published in the *Official Gazette*. This distinction also applies to the imposition of provisional safeguard measures.

Turkey has a judicial review system for its investigating authority's determinations, and this system has so far been used frequently. Yet, it has also proven to be completely ineffective, since there has not been a single case in which a court found the investigating authority's determination to be illegal. Below, we will first explain different aspects of Turkey's judicial review system, then discuss its effectiveness, and finally explain how, in our view, it may be improved.

The explanations in this chapter are based both on the legislative framework for judicial review and the jurisprudence of the Turkish courts that has emerged from judicial review proceedings that have taken place so far. Since 1992, according to our research, 95 judicial review proceedings have been initiated in connection with the determinations of the investigating authority, of which 77 dealt with anti-dumping investigations, including anti-circumvention proceedings, and 18 with safeguard investigations. In terms of complainants, the vast majority of judicial review proceedings have been initiated by importers; only a few have been initiated by foreign or domestic producers.

II Legislative framework for judicial review

Turkey's trade remedies legislation does not contain any provision with respect to the judicial review of the investigating authority's determinations.

---

[19] SG Decree, Article 4.1.

[20] Article 4.1 of the SG Regulation provides that the initiation decision must be published in the *Official Gazette*, but does not specify the form that the decision should take. In practice, however, all initiation decisions take the form of a communiqué and are published in the *Official Gazette*. See, for instance, the initiation communiqué in the investigation on *Yarns* (2005/8) (OG, 22.11.2005, No. 26001).

These determinations are subject to judicial review in the same way as other actions by government agencies. Thus, in this chapter, we will describe the legal framework for the judicial review of governmental actions in general, which equally applies to trade remedy determinations. With respect to each topic, we will first explain the general rule and then its application in the context of trade remedy determinations.

In Turkey, the administrative judiciary conducts the judicial review of actions by governmental agencies. Regarding the legislation that forms the basis for administrative judicial review, we should first cite Article 125 of the Constitution, which lays down the general principle that "all actions and acts of the administration are subject to judicial review".[21] In addition to the Constitution, there are three laws directly relevant to administrative judicial review in Turkey. The structure and functions of the courts that conduct administrative judicial review are set out in the Law on the Council of State and the Law on the Constitution and Functions of District Administrative Courts, Administrative Courts and Tax Courts. The procedural rules that apply to administrative judicial review proceedings, in turn, are set out in the Administrative Procedure Law No. 2577 (hereinafter Procedure Law).

Two courts participate in the judicial review of trade remedy determinations: the Council of State and, to a lesser extent, administrative courts.[22] As explained below, the judicial review of the most important determinations, such as initiation, imposition of provisional or final measures, acceptance of undertakings and termination of an investigation, is conducted by the Council of State in its capacity as the court of

---

[21] Article 125 introduces a few exceptions to this principle, but these do not affect the judicial review of trade remedy determinations.

[22] The administrative judiciary consists of three levels of courts: courts of first instance, district administrative courts and the Council of State. Courts of first instance are divided into two categories: administrative courts and tax courts. Tax courts are tribunals that deal with cases involving the imposition and collection of taxes and similar fiscal charges, which includes duties imposed as trade remedy measures. Administrative courts have general jurisdiction over the remainder of administrative judicial review cases. District administrative courts review certain decisions made by administrative and tax courts. The Council of State has two important judicial functions. First, it is the last judicial resort in the administrative judicial branch and hears appeals from the decisions by the courts of first instance. Second, it acts as the court of first instance in disputes over administrative actions that are specifically identified in the Law.

first instance. Administrative courts review other less important and less frequent determinations.[23]

In some judicial review proceedings, complainants went beyond the specifics of the relevant trade remedy investigation and asked the courts to annul certain provisions of Turkey's trade remedies legislation. Importantly, in a number of cases, complainants argued that the AD/CVD legislation was unconstitutional, since it allowed the government to impose trade remedies in the form of duties. The main argument presented in these cases was that the imposition of anti-dumping duties was inconsistent with Article 73 of the Constitution, which stipulates that taxes may only be imposed through a law. The courts have consistently rejected this argument.[24] There has been one case where the complainant requested the court to annul certain provisions of the AD/CVD Regulation, but the request was rejected.[25]

Although the WTO Agreement has the force of law under Turkish law, the agreements on trade remedies have not, thus far, been invoked in an important way in judicial review proceedings. This is partly because parties to judicial review proceedings, particularly complainants, do not rely on these agreements in their submissions to the courts and partly because the courts are not familiar with their provisions.

Since court decisions contain only a very short summary of the complainant's arguments, it is difficult to know whether, and if so, to what extent, complainants cite the agreements on trade remedies in presenting their claims. As for the investigating authority, we know that there have been a few cases where it referred to these agreements in its written submissions. Such references, however, were not directed at specific provisions of the agreements; they were merely arguments as to

---

[23] As already explained above in note 22, tax courts deal with cases involving the collection of taxes, including trade remedy measures that take the form of duties. Most trade remedies-related cases brought before tax courts pertained exclusively to the procedural issues that arose in the collection of duties, which we did not include in the body of court decisions analysed in this chapter. That said, there have been a few tax court proceedings which, while mainly concerning the collection of duties, also related to the underlying determination by the investigating authority, such as the decision retroactively to collect provisional duties. Court decisions made in such cases are part of the jurisprudence on which our study is based.

[24] See, for instance, Council of State decision (24.3.2006, 10th Chamber), E. 2003/1286, K. 2006/2060, p. 3; Council of State decision (5.2.2008, 10th Chamber), E. 2005/7337, K. 2008/402, p. 7.

[25] Council of State decision (14.11.2005, 10th Chamber), E. 2002/3455, K. 2005/6714, pp. 4–5.

whether the disputed investigations had been conducted consistently with the relevant agreement.[26] We cannot say, based on these general statements, whether the investigating authority defended its actions on the basis of the agreements on trade remedies.

The courts have occasionally referred to the AD Agreement and some other provisions of the WTO Agreement[27] in developing their legal reasoning. For instance, in one case, the Council of State cited the provisions of different articles of the AD Agreement, along with the relevant provisions of the national legislation, and referred to these two together as the "relevant legislation".[28] The Court subsequently made the same remark with respect to the SG Agreement.[29] These statements, however, constituted *obiter dicta* and were not part of the legal basis of the decisions. There has been no case where a court based its decision on the provisions of the agreements on trade remedies. Nor has there been any case where there was reference to the WTO jurisprudence.

III   Types of judicial review proceedings

Turkish administrative law provides for two types of judicial review proceedings that may be brought against the actions of the government: "annulment proceedings" or "full judicial review proceedings". Through an annulment proceeding, the complainant may request the court to annul the disputed administrative action. A full judicial review proceeding allows the complainant to ask the court to direct the government to pay damages for loss caused by the disputed action. Although full

---

[26] See Council of State decision (19.10.2004, 10th Chamber), E. 2000/4016, K. 2002/4030, p.1; Council of State decision (16.3.2009, 10th Chamber), E. 2006/5348, K. 2009/1884, p. 1.

[27] Interestingly, but not so understandably, in some cases, the Council of State referred to Article XX(d) of the GATT 1994 to imply that the government has the right to impose duties. See, for example, Council of State decision (24.3.2006, 10th Chamber), E. 2003/1286, K. 2006/2060, p. 3; Council of State decision (11.4.2006, 10th Chamber), E. 2003/3186, K. 2006/2338, p. 6. Article XX(d) of the GATT 1994 addresses measures taken by WTO members against deceptive practices, and has no bearing on the imposition of anti-dumping measures. It is difficult to tell why the court relied on this provision, and not, for instance, Article VI of the GATT 1994, which is directly relevant to the issue.

[28] Council of State decision (19.10.2004, 10th Chamber), E. 2000/4016, K. 2002/4030, p. 4. In another case, the Council of State again referred to the AD Agreement, but it noted generally that, in addition to the national legislation, the Agreement also contained provisions that regulated the use of anti-dumping measures. Council of State decision (30.5.2006, 10th Chamber), E. 2004/6370, K. 2006/3663, p. 11.

[29] Council of State decision (27.12.2005, 10th Chamber), E. 2004/3025, K. 2005/8181, p. 4.

judicial review proceedings may also be used against the determinations of the investigating authority, virtually all judicial review proceedings in this field have been annulment proceedings. Consequently, we will focus only on annulment proceedings in this chapter.

The initiation of an annulment proceeding requires the violation of an "interest".[30] This is a lower standard compared to the violation of a "right", and allows a wide range of individuals or entities to initiate an annulment proceeding: it is sufficient to show some link to the disputed administrative action.[31] Where the court annuls a determination by the investigating authority, all interested parties benefit from the decision. For instance, if an importer challenges a final safeguard measure on the grounds that the investigating authority's causality determination was flawed, and the court agrees with the complainant, that determination will be annulled with respect to all importers, not only the complainant. If, however, the scope of the case is limited, only interested parties falling within that scope will benefit from the annulment decision. For instance, if the court annuls an anti-dumping duty with respect to a given exporting country, only importers buying the subject product from that country will benefit from that decision.

IV   Reviewable determinations

As we have already noted, under Article 125 of the constitution, all government actions are subject to judicial review. The only condition is that the action must be final and executable. A final administrative action is one in respect of which the necessary administrative review mechanisms have been exhausted before a case is filed with the competent court. If this is not the case, the court will forward the file to the competent agency for the necessary administrative review.[32] However, this is not relevant to the judicial review of trade remedy determinations, since the investigating authority's determinations are not subject to any administrative review. An executable action is one that directly affects the legal situation of persons. Administrative judicial review cannot be used with respect to actions which do not have such an

---

[30] Procedure Law, Article 2.1(a).
[31] Şeref Gözübüyük, *Administrative Judiciary*, 30th edn (Ankara: Turhan Publications, 2010), p. 167 (in Turkish).
[32] Procedure Law, Article 15.1(e).

effect and which simply restate a legal situation or a fact.[33] For instance, what is said in an investigating authority's internal memorandum cannot be challenged in court, because it is not considered an executable action.

Under this legal standard, determinations made in the context of all trade remedy investigations, reviews and refund proceedings are reviewable. The most important decisions made in an investigation, such as the rejection of a complaint, initiation, imposition of provisional or definitive measures, acceptance or rejection of undertakings and termination of an investigation without measures, are all reviewable actions.

However, judicial review is not limited to these most important determinations made in the course of an investigation. Decisions such as a refusal to initiate an investigation, refusal to grant extensions of deadlines for the submission of information, rejection of a request to see non-confidential information in the investigation file are all reviewable by the courts, because typically these are final and executable administrative actions. The vast majority of judicial review proceedings initiated so far have concerned decisions to impose provisional or definitive measures. However, cases have also been initiated with respect to other types of decisions made by the investigating authority.

In one case, a domestic producer took issue with the investigating authority's decision not to impose measures in an anti-dumping investigation. In the disputed investigation, the authority had found that there was no causal link between dumping and injury and decided not to impose measures. The domestic producer then filed a case, arguing that the authority's determination was not based on an adequate analysis of the circumstances surrounding the domestic market. The Council of State found that the challenged determination conformed to the relevant legal requirements, and dismissed the case.[34] In another case, an importer objected to the distribution of the overall quota imposed as a safeguard measure, and this objection was rejected by the investigating authority. The importer then filed a case and requested the administrative court of Ankara to annul the administrative action in the form of rejection.[35] In yet another case, an importer requested exemption from a provisional anti-dumping duty, and this request

---

[33] Council of State decision (26.4.2005, 7th Chamber), E. 2001/1274, K. 2005/794.
[34] Council of State decision (23.10.2002, 10th Chamber), E. 2000/4016, K. 2002/4030.
[35] See decision of the 2nd Administrative Court of Ankara, 12.5.2006, E. 2004/360, K. 2006/1133.

was rejected by the investigating authority. The importer challenged the rejection by filing a case with the administrative court of Ankara.[36]

Interestingly, in a separate case, a domestic producer took the investigating authority's refusal to initiate an anti-dumping investigation to the court. After receiving the domestic producer's complaint, the investigating authority replied in writing that the complaint lacked the supporting documents required under the legislation. The producer subsequently submitted another complaint which contained certain additional arguments, which the authority also found to be insufficient, and rejected. The administrative court found a procedural deficiency in the investigating authority's rejection, because it came from the head of the relevant department of the Directorate General for Imports, rather than from the Director General.[37]

Under Turkish law, the scope of judicial review is not limited to determinations in the form of a concrete action on the part of the investigating authority; it also covers situations where the authority remains silent vis-à-vis a request made by an interested party. The investigating authority's failure to reply to an interested party's request within 60 days of its receipt of the request is deemed to be rejection. An interested party that does not receive a response to its request may, after 60 days from the submission of the request to the investigating authority, initiate an annulment proceeding against the authority and ask the court to annul the authority's decision to reject the request.[38]

V Parties eligible to bring a case

Any interested party in a trade remedy investigation may initiate a judicial review proceeding. This includes domestic producers, importers, foreign producers and also the governments of exporting countries, consumer organizations and industrial users of the subject product. In practice, the vast majority of judicial review proceedings have been initiated by importers, but there have also been a few cases initiated by foreign producers.[39]

[36] See decision of the 6th Administrative Court of Ankara, 23.11.2005, E. 2004/2991, K. 2005/1677.

[37] Decision of the 16th Administrative Court of Ankara (28.11.2008), E. 2006/671, K. 2008/1466.

[38] Procedure Law, Article 10.

[39] For a case initiated by a foreign producer subject to an anti-dumping duty, see Council of State decision (19.10.2004, 10th Chamber), E.2000/4961, K. 2004/6877. However, it

A judicial review proceeding is usually initiated by a single complainant. Exceptionally, however, multiple complainants may collectively bring a case where the rights or interests of the complainants are common and the factual or legal elements underlying the complaint are the same.[40] A third party may join an ongoing judicial review proceeding. In one case, the domestic industry joined a judicial review proceeding concerning an anti-dumping duty along with the defendant investigating authority, and acted collectively with it.[41]

VI Competent courts

The courts' subject matter jurisdiction is determined on the basis of the administrative action at issue. With respect to affected parties, administrative actions may be divided into "regulatory administrative actions" and "individual administrative actions". Regulatory administrative actions lay down rules of general application, or rules which apply to entities in the same situation, whereas individual administrative actions are those that affect particular parties. Both types of actions may be the subject of an annulment proceeding.

In the context of trade remedy investigations, regulatory and individual administrative actions take different forms. Regulatory administrative actions such as initiation, imposition of provisional or final measures, acceptance of undertakings and termination without measures, take the form of a communiqué or a decree and are published in the *Official Gazette*. Typically, an individual action, such as refusal to include a foreign producer in the sample for dumping determinations, is a written communication issued by the investigating authority.

The form of the administrative action determines which court has subject matter jurisdiction. Subject matter jurisdiction over cases brought against regulatory administrative actions lies exclusively with the Council of State, which reviews these actions in its capacity as the

should also be noted that in another case initiated by an association of foreign producers subject to an anti-dumping duty, the Council of State reasoned that, unlike with the producers themselves, an anti-dumping duty cannot be seen as impairing the interests of an association, and it rejected the case on the grounds that the complainant was not eligible to bring a case: Council of State decision (25.2.2009, 10th Chamber), E. 2008/6920, K. 2009/1337.

[40] Procedure Law, Article 5.2.

[41] See Council of State decision (19.11.2002, 10th Chamber), E. 2000/4015.

court of first instance.[42] The cases are handled by one of the chambers of the Council of State, which consists of one chairperson and four members. Administrative courts have general subject matter jurisdiction over the cases brought with respect to individual administrative actions. As far as territorial jurisdiction of administrative courts is concerned, with the Ministry being located in Ankara, the cases against individual administrative actions of the Turkish investigating authority must be brought before the administrative court of Ankara.[43]

VII Procedural steps

The deadline for filing a case is 60 days.[44] With respect to administrative actions that come into effect upon publication in the *Official Gazette*, the deadline runs from the day following publication.[45] With respect to other administrative actions, it runs from the date of service of the action on the complainant.[46]

Administrative judicial proceedings are conducted on the basis of written submissions. A case must be initiated by way of a written submission addressed to the competent court. Normally the first written submission is filed with the court that has subject matter and territorial jurisdiction over the case. Where this is not possible, however, Procedure Law provides the parties with alternative means of transmitting their submissions to the competent court. The submissions may be sent to the competent court via another administrative or tax court, or – where there is no administrative or tax court – via a legal court, or even a Turkish consulate in a country.[47] Thus, a foreign company wishing to initiate a judicial review proceeding in Turkey has the right to transmit its written submissions to the administrative court through the Turkish consulate in that country. In theory, the whole proceeding may be pursued in this manner, without travelling to the competent court's location. In practice, however, this

---

[42] Article 24 of the Law on the Council of State lists the annulment and full judicial review proceedings to be handled by the Council of State as the court of first instance. Listed therein are decrees by the Council of Ministers and the regulatory administrative actions by the government agencies that are applicable throughout the country.

[43] As a general rule, the administrative court in the area where the agency that took the disputed administrative action is located has territorial jurisdiction over the case (Procedure Law, Article 32.1).

[44] Ibid., Article 7.1.   [45] Ibid., Article 7.4.   [46] Ibid., Article 7.2(a).   [47] Ibid., Article 4.

option is almost never used, since parties, including foreign companies, hire lawyers to represent them before the court. Foreign lawyers are not permitted to appear before national courts, thus complainants must hire Turkish lawyers.[48] The investigating authority is represented by the Ministry's lawyers. Legal fees for filing a case are not very high.

Following receipt of the complainant's first written submission, the court conducts a preliminary analysis[49] to ensure that: (a) it has subject matter and territorial jurisdiction over the case, (b) the necessary administrative review mechanisms have been exhausted,[50] (c) the complainant has capacity to sue, (d) the disputed administrative action is one which is final and executable, (e) the deadline for the initiation of a case has been observed, (f) the defendant agency has been properly defined, and (g) the provisions of Articles 3 and 5 of the Procedure Law have been complied with.[51]

If, at preliminary analysis, the court finds no shortcomings in the complainant's first written submission, it is served on the defendant agency, namely, the investigating authority. It has 30 days from the date of service to submit its first written response to the court. This is followed by a second round of written submissions by the complainant and the investigating authority, each within 30 days from the service of the other party's written submission or response. Normally there are no further written submissions.[52] The investigating authority sends the tribunal a copy of all relevant documentation in the investigation file.[53] This completes the case file.

If the case is handled by the Council of State as the court of first instance, the file goes first to a prosecutor of the Council of State, who prepares a written opinion and sends the file to the relevant Chamber. The chairperson of the Chamber appoints as *rapporteur* one of the

---

[48] See Articles 35.1 and 3 of the Law on Attorneys.   [49] Procedure Law, Article 14.

[50] This requirement is not relevant to the judicial review of trade remedy determinations, because such determinations are not subject to any administrative review.

[51] Article 3 of the Law sets forth the contents of the complainant's first written submission. Article 5 explains when one may initiate a judicial review proceeding against multiple administrative actions and where multiple complainants may initiate a proceeding against the same administrative action.

[52] However, if the second written submission of the investigating authority raises new issues to which, in the court's view, the complainant has to respond, the latter is given sufficient time to respond to such issues: Procedure Law, Article 16.2.

[53] Ibid., Article 16.

members of the Chamber, who prepares a report on the case and presents it to the Chamber. The *rapporteur* may also use the services of an investigating judge. In practice, it is the investigating judges who conduct the preliminary examination and brief the members of the Chamber. After hearing the investigating judge, the Chamber then decides the case.

Administrative courts have one chairperson and two members. If the case is handled by an administrative court, the chairperson of the court appoints as *rapporteur* one of the members, who prepares a report on the case and presents it to the court. The court decides the case. It is not bound by the presentation of the claims and the defence. On its own initiative it can extend the review and request the parties or other relevant entities to submit the evidence it needs. The recipients of the court's order must provide the information requested by the deadline given by the court.[54]

In principle, the court is not required to hold a hearing. However, in annulment proceedings before a court of first instance, it must hold a hearing upon the request of one of the parties.[55] On appeal, the Council of State has discretion over whether there will be a hearing.[56] A court may also decide to hold a hearing on its own initiative.[57]

A judicial review proceeding before a court of first instance must be completed within six months from the completion of the file.[58] In practice, however, this can take longer, depending on the court's work-load and the nature of the case. On average, it takes an administrative court around one year to issue its decision. It takes the Council of State much longer (around two years) to issue a decision in cases where it acts as the court of first instance. An appeal by the Council of State can also take two years or more.

Decisions are made by the majority of all members of the court. Abstention is not permitted. The views of members who disagree with the majority's decision are explained in the decision.[59] Although this is not common, there have been a few cases where a dissenting opinion was recorded.[60]

---

[54] Ibid., Article 20.1.   [55] Ibid., Article 17.1.   [56] Ibid., Article 17.2.
[57] Ibid., Article 17.4.   [58] Ibid., Article 20.5.   [59] Ibid., Article 22.
[60] See, for instance, Council of State decision (26.11.2002, Board of Chambers of Administrative Cases), E. 2003/1144, K. 2006/2150, pp. 5–6; and Council of State decision (28.2.2006, 10th Chamber), E. 2003/3948, K. 2006/1656, p. 9.

VIII   Appeal

The decisions made by administrative courts and by a chamber of the Council of State as the court of first instance are both appealable to the Council of State. Appeals from the decisions of administrative courts are handled by one chamber of the Council of State. Appeals from the decisions of the Council of State as the court of first instance are handled by the Board of Chambers of Administrative Cases of the Council of State. For ease of reference, under this heading, we refer to administrative courts and the relevant chamber of the Council of State which makes a decision as the court of first instance, as the "lower court". Only parties to the dispute may appeal the lower court's decision. In cases involving multiple complainants, each complainant is entitled to appeal.[61] An appeal must be filed within 30 days from the date of service of the lower court's decision.[62]

The Council of State may approve, reverse or partially approve the lower court's decision. If the decision is approved by the Council of State, that becomes the final decision on the dispute. There are three grounds on which the Council of State may reverse a lower court's decision: (a) where it lacks subject matter or territorial jurisdiction, (b) where the decision by the lower court contradicts the law, or (c) where the procedural rules have been disregarded by the lower court.[63]

The Council of State has remand power. Thus, upon reversal, it remands the case to the lower court.[64] Where an appeal from a decision of the Council of State as the court of first instance is concerned, the relevant chamber of the Council of State must modify its initial decision in accordance with the decision by the Board of Chambers of Administrative Cases of the Council of State, and this becomes the final decision which resolves the dispute.

Where an appeal from an administrative court decision is concerned, one more layer is involved. On remand, the administrative court has two options: it may either follow the Council of State's reasoning and correct its initial decision, or insist on its initial decision. Where the administrative court follows the Council of State's reasoning, it modifies its decision in accordance with that reasoning, and this becomes the final decision resolving the dispute. Where the administrative court insists on its initial decision, the latter is reviewed by the Board of Chambers of

---

[61] Gözübüyük, *Administrative Judiciary*, p. 506.   [62] Procedure Law, Article 46.2.
[63] Ibid., Article 49.1.   [64] Ibid., Article 49.3.

Administrative Cases of the Council of State. If the Board agrees with the administrative court's decision, that decision is approved. However, if the Board agrees with the decision by the chamber of the Council of State which reversed the administrative court's decision on appeal, the administrative court must follow that reasoning and modify its initial decision accordingly.[65] This brings the dispute to an end.

In exceptional circumstances, the decision made on appeal by a chamber of the Council of State or by the Board of Chambers of Administrative Cases may be reviewed through what is called a "correction of decision" proceeding. This is a very exceptional mechanism and, to the best of our knowledge, it has been used only once in the context of trade remedies.[66]

IX Standard of review

The standard of review for annulment proceedings is set forth in Article 2 of the Procedure Law. The court will annul an administrative action if it finds that an illegality with respect to the elements of "authority", "form", "reason", "subject matter" or "objective" of the disputed administrative action has impaired an interest of the complainant.

An administrative action is illegal with respect to the element of "authority" if it has not been taken by the agency or by the government official authorized to take such actions. It will be illegal with respect to "form" if it has not been taken in the form prescribed in the law. For instance, the law requires that the initiation of an anti-dumping investigation be published in the *Official Gazette* through a communiqué. If the Ministry initiates an investigation without publishing such a communiqué in the *Official Gazette*, that administrative action (initiation) will be illegal with respect to form. The element of "reason" refers to the motive which prompts the administration to take an administrative action. Each administrative action must have a reason. Sometimes the law prescribes the reason for certain administrative actions. In such situations, the agency taking the administrative action must make sure that the conditions set forth in the law are fulfilled.[67] Trade remedy

---

[65] Ibid., Article 49.4.
[66] This case related to the collection of anti-dumping duties, not the determinations of the investigating authority in the underlying investigation, and was rejected by the relevant chamber of the Council of State. See Council of State decision (6.7.2006, 7th Chamber), E. 2005/4996, K. 2006/2360.
[67] Gözübüyük, *Administrative Judiciary*, p. 223.

investigations fall into this category of administrative actions. The law explains in detail the conditions on the basis of which a trade remedy action may be taken; therefore, any determination made by the investigating authority must explain how the conditions for that particular determination have been met.

The element of "subject matter" refers to the result that the administrative action produces. An administrative action can only produce the result prescribed in law. For instance, the only action that the investigating authority can take with respect to a significant increase in imports which causes serious injury to the domestic industry, is to impose a safeguard measure. If, for example, the authority decides to ban the imports of the subject product to counteract such serious injury, that action will be illegal with respect to its "subject matter".

The final element – "objective" – pertains to the subjective motive behind a particular administrative action. The general objective for all administrative actions is public interest. If it is shown that an action has been taken for any other reason, such as personal interests of the government official in charge, it will be illegal with respect to "objective" and be annulled by the court.

Although Procedure Law provides these five specific grounds for annulment, in practice, complainants do not usually frame their claims on the basis of them, nor do the courts explicitly link their decisions to them. Typically, the complainant argues that the disputed determination is inconsistent with the legislation, that it is vague, or that the investigating authority did not perform a proper analysis. The courts, in turn, in their decisions, discuss whether the disputed determination is illegal on the grounds identified by the complainant. They do not usually go beyond this to explain whether the disputed determination is or is not illegal with respect to the five elements for annulment cited in the Procedure Law. Typically, the courts base their decisions to reject a case on more or less standard language, such as "that the disputed administrative action is not inconsistent with public interest or the legislation"[68] or "that it is not inconsistent with the law".[69]

---

[68] See, for instance, Council of State decision (9.2.2009, 10th Chamber), E. 2006/5523, K. 2009/760, p. 6.

[69] See, for instance, Council of State decision (21.4.1994, 10th Chamber), E. 1992/3878, K. 1994/1778, p. 4.

There have been exceptional cases where the complainant cited one or more of these five elements in its submissions to the court. In such situations, the court did take these specific arguments into account and decided whether the disputed determination was illegal with respect to the elements cited by the complainant.[70]

X   Remedies

Article 138.4 of the Turkish Constitution requires that final court decisions be respected by all government agencies. This principle is reiterated in Article 28.1 of the Procedure Law. Thus, where an administrative court annuls a determination made by the investigating authority, as soon as the court decision is served on it, the latter must take the steps necessary to comply with the decision. The modalities of compliance with an annulment decision depend on the nature of the annulled action. Sometimes the annulment decision is automatic; the administration does not require to take any steps in order to give effect to the court decision. This is usually the case with respect to the annulment of regulatory actions. For instance, when a communiqué initiating an anti-dumping investigation is annulled, the court decision stops the investigation; the investigating authority cannot proceed with it. However, an annulment decision with respect to an individual administrative action usually requires action from the agency. For instance, where a court annuls the investigating authority's decision to base its determinations on facts available with respect to a foreign producer, the authority is required to change its approach and to rely on the information provided by that producer. Where the annulment decision requires action from the investigating authority, compliance must take place within 30 days after service of the court decision on the authority. If the investigating authority does not comply with the decision within this period, the complainant may initiate a new case and seek damages caused by such delay.[71]

The Constitution imposes one very important limitation on the powers of administrative courts. Article 125.4 stipulates that the courts cannot make decisions that would amount to an administrative action, or which would eliminate the administration's discretionary power.[72] Thus, the

---

[70] See, for instance, ibid., pp. 2–3.   [71] Procedure Law, Article 28.3.
[72] This principle is reiterated in Article 2.2 of the Procedure Law.

administrative court's job in an annulment proceeding is to decide whether or not the disputed determination of the investigating authority is illegal. If the court finds that the determination is indeed illegal, the only power that it has is to annul the determination. The court cannot, for instance, explain how, in its view, the determination should have been made. That would violate the principle laid down in Article 125.4 of the Constitution.

In principle, the filing of a case does not stop the execution of the disputed determination. However, in clearly described circumstances, the court may order a stay of execution during the course of court proceedings. For the court to order the stay of execution, the complainant must show that the execution of the disputed action will lead to damage difficult or impossible to repair, and that the action is manifestly illegal.[73] Where the court orders the stay of execution, the disputed determination cannot be executed until the end of the court proceedings. The investigating authority may object to the court's decision on the stay of execution. Upon objection, a higher court specified in the Law will make the final decision.[74] The decision on the stay of execution is made upon the deposit of a guarantee. However, taking into consideration the circumstances, the court may opt not to require a guarantee.[75]

Typically, the first written submission initiating a judicial review proceeding includes a request for a stay of execution. In such cases, the reviewing court first makes a decision on this request on an emergency basis and issues a decision within a couple of months from the receipt of the complainant's first written submission. In most cases, a complainant whose request for a stay of execution is rejected also loses the case on the merits, and vice versa. Thus, the court decision on the request for a stay of execution usually foretells the result on the merits of the case.

It is important to underline that although virtually all cases initiated against trade remedy determinations involved a request for a stay of execution, the courts granted such requests in very few cases. Further, it should be noted that these were cases handled by tax courts, which concerned the collection of anti-dumping duties, not the underlying determination by the investigating authority.[76]

---

[73] See Article 125.5 of the Constitution; Article 27.2 of the Procedure Law.
[74] Ibid., Article 27.6.   [75] Ibid., Article 27.5.
[76] See, for instance, decision of the 6th Tax Court of Istanbul (9.10.1992), E. 1992/1222.

XI   Overall assessment of the effectiveness of judicial review in Turkey

Turkey has a long-standing culture of subjecting governmental actions to judicial review. The administrative judicial review system in its modern sense started in 1927, and has since been functioning relatively well. The different courts functioning within the administrative judiciary have been conducting effective judicial review of governmental actions. Many administrative actions have been annulled by the courts so far. Similarly, the courts have ordered a stay of execution in many cases.

The cases involving trade remedy determinations, however, have yielded significantly different results. The situation with respect to these cases is striking. In close to 100 cases initiated since the early 1990s, the courts have never faulted the investigating authority for its actions. There has not been a single reversal of a determination. Further, the courts almost never ordered a stay of execution in such cases. This stands in sharp contrast with the courts' attitude in the judicial review of other types of administrative actions. What is it that makes the judicial review of trade remedy determinations so different from the judicial review of other governmental actions? An analysis of court decisions in cases involving trade remedies is needed in order to understand the reasons for this difference.

The most evident characteristic of court decisions concerning trade remedy determinations is that they are based on a mechanistic legal analysis. The term "mechanistic" is used in the sense that regardless of the particular claims put forward by the complainants, the courts' legal reasoning is strikingly similar in all cases. Below, we describe the nature and components of a typical court decision involving the review of a decision to impose anti-dumping duties.

A typical court decision usually starts with an explanation as to the statutory authority that the Ministry has with respect to the conduct of anti-dumping investigations and the imposition of anti-dumping measures. In this context, reference is made to the relevant provisions of the AD/CVD Law and the Law establishing the Ministry. There may or may not be a simple reference to Article XX(d) of the GATT 1994 which allows WTO members to take action against deceptive practices. The court then provides a lengthy description of the main provisions of the AD/CVD Law. This starts with a reference to Article 1, which sets out the objective of the Law, and goes on to state provisions which address issues, such as the definitions of technical terms used in the Law, the main substantive conditions for the imposition of a measure, the filing of the complaint and the pre-initiation examination, the powers of the Directorate General for Imports with respect to the initiation and conduct of an investigation, the tasks and powers of the AD/CVD Board and the procedure for the imposition of an anti-dumping duty. On the basis of this brief summary, the court concludes that the Ministry is authorized to issue communiqués in connection with anti-dumping investigations. This summary is usually two pages long.

The court then turns to the AD/CVD Regulation and offers a lengthy summary of its provisions relevant to anti-dumping investigations, including the provisions dealing with the determination of normal value, calculation of costs, determination of export price, fair comparison, determination of injury, and the consequences of failure to cooperate with the investigating authority. This summary, which is usually one page long, is followed by a long paragraph which repeats the main principles governing an anti-dumping investigation.

Next, the court turns to the facts of the investigation at issue. This part always includes a long paragraph identifying the subject product, the complaining domestic producers, exporting countries involved, and date of initiation and termination of the investigation. The court then provides a lengthy summary of the findings reached by the investigating authority in the investigation. This summary, which is usually around one page long, merely restates what is in the disputed communiqué imposing the measure.

Finally, the court reaches its conclusion in the final paragraph of the decision. This paragraph almost invariably concludes that, in light of the foregoing explanations, the communiqué at issue which provides for the imposition of an anti-dumping duty as a result of an investigation initiated and conducted in compliance with the legislation in which the investigating authority found that dumped imports were causing injury to the domestic industry producing the like product in Turkey, is not inconsistent with the legislation.

The most striking characteristic of such court decisions is the significant degree of deference to the investigating authority's determinations. The decisions are limited to noting what the investigating authority did in the disputed investigation and the relevant legal provisions. The court's legal analysis and conclusions take only one paragraph, and, as noted, this concluding paragraph contains no original legal reasoning, but simply states that, given the relevant legal provisions and the facts of the investigation at issue, the court finds no illegality.

It should be stressed that judicial administrative review in Turkey generally has a good reputation in terms of its rigour and effectiveness. In fact, the administrative judiciary has sometimes been criticized for being overly active. The question this begs, then, is, why is it that the courts have taken such a deferential approach in cases involving trade remedy determinations?

The best explanation seems to be the lack of technical knowledge on trade remedies. It should be borne in mind that until very recently no Turkish law school has offered courses on WTO law or Turkish trade remedies law. Thus, the judges who serve in the Council of State and the administrative courts lack formal training on trade remedies. Further, it should be noted that the administrative judiciary deals with all governmental actions. Such actions involve a very wide range of issues, varying from privatization projects to the regulation of universities, and from the promotion of civil servants to municipalities' construction projects and traffic regulation. Trade remedies occupy a very narrow part in the overall responsibilities of the administrative judiciary. Thus, the judges operating in this system are not able to master the fine details of trade remedy investigations which would allow them to conduct a more rigorous review.

XII Concluding remarks and suggestions for improvement

Clearly, the current state of affairs with respect to the judicial review of trade remedy determinations is far from ideal. A judicial review system which does not consider the details of the investigating authority's determinations cannot be seen as effective. Further, such a system may give a wrong impression that the courts are disinclined to find inconsistencies in the determinations of the investigating authority. Another shortcoming is that after 20 years of activity and close to 100 cases handled, there is practically no jurisprudence that may be discerned from court decisions with respect to the conduct of trade remedy investigations. This should therefore change.

In our view, the administrative judiciary is the right place to conduct the judicial review of trade remedy determinations in Turkey. However, the system needs to be modified in a manner that would allow the judges to conduct effective review. We do not necessarily argue that an effective judicial review system is one where the courts frequently find inconsistencies in the investigating authority's determinations. An ideal judicial review system, in our view, is one where the judges have the opportunity to review the details of the determinations, rather than restating what is in the legislation and what was done in the relevant investigation and consistently summarily finding that there is nothing that contradicts the legislation.

Two steps must be taken to make this happen in the Turkish legal system. First, judicial review of trade remedy determinations must be conducted by specialized courts. This is not to say that these courts should deal only with trade remedy cases. These may be courts which review not only trade remedy determinations, but also governmental actions in other fields that are related to international trade, such as customs, standards in international trade, inward and outward processing regimes, free zones, or even foreign investment measures. Second, the government should provide adequate technical training for the judges who work in these specialized courts. The Turkish administration has the capability to provide such training itself. If needed, some sort of international training could also be used as a supplement.

In reforming the system, particular attention should be paid to the fact that the judges and prosecutors who will conduct the judicial review of trade remedy determinations will have to follow international developments pertaining to trade remedies, such as the decisions of WTO panels and the Appellate Body. Following this jurisprudence will pave the way for a more thorough judicial review at national level. Therefore, judges serving in such specialized courts should have the language skills that will allow them to follow the relevant international jurisprudence.

Israel: a comparative study of two models

ARIE REICH AND GILL NADEL

I Introduction

This chapter describes and analyses the various venues that exist at present, and that have existed in the past in Israel for the judicial review of trade remedy determinations. In doing so, it presents two different models of judicial review that have been attempted in Israel and evaluates their respective advantages and disadvantages based on the experience that has been accumulated. It will also discuss other important aspects of judicial review at the national level in connection with the Israeli experience. It shows that the standards of review employed by the various review bodies are a crucial factor in determining the effectiveness of the review. In view of this conclusion, it is surprising that the WTO agreements in the field of trade remedies have failed to address this issue and have left it for the member states to determine the standard of review to be employed by their domestic judicial review tribunals. Given the advantages of such review at the national level over international review by WTO dispute settlement panels, we will also argue in favour of extension of the former to provisional measures and to safeguard measures.

II Israel's trade remedies legislation and practice

The law that currently regulates trade remedies in Israel, the Trade Levies and Protective Measures Law, 1991 (hereinafter the Law),[1] was adopted in its original version in 1991. It may perhaps be seen as paradoxical, but its adoption was part of a general move aimed at the

---

[1] The Trade Levies and Protective Measures Law, 1991–5751, was originally adopted under the name The Trade Levies Law in 1991, and published in *Sefer Chukim* 1337 (2.1.1991), p. 38. It has been amended several times and its new name was introduced through the amendment of 2008 (see *infra* note 22).

liberalization of Israel's foreign trade policy.[2] This move was partly unilateral and partly the result of international obligations that Israel had assumed, mainly in bilateral free trade agreements. Such agreements had been signed with the European Community in 1975 and with the United States in 1985, and the full tariff elimination under both agreements was to come into effect at the beginning of the 1990s. Along with this elimination of most trade barriers against European and US products, Israel had also embarked on a unilateral reduction of trade barriers *vis-à-vis* "third countries", that is, countries with which no free trade agreements had been signed. This reduction took the form of a "tariffication" of non-tariff barriers (that is, translation of such non-tariff barriers to their equivalent tariffs) followed by a gradual reduction of these new tariffs over a few years, generally until they reached the level of 12 per cent for manufactured products and 6 per cent for raw materials. In view of this trade liberalization, it was felt necessary to have in place an effective mechanism for the imposition of various trade remedy measures in order to protect domestic industry from injurious imports. Thus, the Israeli experience also confirms that a correlation exists between trade liberalization and the use of trade remedies.[3]

Today the Law provides for several types of trade measures, but here we will discuss only three: anti-dumping duties, countervailing duties and "protective measures", which are what is known as safeguard measures. We shall describe briefly their nature and the procedures that govern their imposition.

Anti-dumping duties and countervailing measures are trade remedies available to the domestic industry in response to dumped or subsidized imports, respectively, which cause material injury to domestic production. They are administered by a two-stage system comprised of the Commissioner of Trade Levies and the Advisory Committee on Trade Levies.[4] The Commissioner is authorized to decide whether an

---

[2] See explanations to the bill of 1987 (*Hatzaot Chok* 1859): The Special Levies Law Bill, 1987–5748.

[3] See Prakash Narayanan, "Anti-dumping in India – Present State and Future Prospects" 40 (2006) *Journal of World Trade* 1084–6, and Chad P. Bown and Patricia Tovar, "Trade Liberalization, Antidumping, and Safeguards: Evidence from India's Tariff Reform" 96 (1) (September 2011) *Journal of Development Economics* 115–25 for a similar correlation in India, and the contribution of Müslüm Yilmaz in Chapter 10 of this volume, which confirms the same for Turkey.

[4] For a further discussion of this vertical bifurcated system, see Arie Reich, "Institutional and Substantive Reform of the Antidumping and Subsidy Agreements: Lessons from the Israeli Experience" 37 (2003) *Journal of World Trade* 1037.

investigation shall be initiated following the submission of a complaint by the domestic industry,[5] to conduct such investigation and to submit his or her findings on whether dumped or subsidized products are being imported into the country and whether they cause or threaten to cause material injury.[6] The Commissioner, who is a civil servant,[7] also has the authority to decide whether to impose provisional measures,[8] usually in the form of a security by cash deposit or bond guarantee, as well as having the authority whether to accept price undertakings.[9] The Commissioner's findings are submitted to the Advisory Committee.

The Advisory Committee, which is a quasi-judicial tribunal, has 14 members, six of whom are public representatives, including at least two jurists, and another eight who are civil servants (four from the Ministry of Industry, Trade and Labour and four from the Ministry of Finance).[10] The chairperson and deputy chairperson are always public representatives, which means that they are not state employees and are independent from direct government influence in their discretion. They often come from the ranks of academia or free professions and tend to be less inclined to protect the domestic industry. They are therefore somewhat similar in their status to the members of the US International Trade Commission,[11] with the important difference that the jurisdiction of the Israeli committee is not restricted to the finding of injury, but covers all of the elements of the investigation. In practice, the committee sits in panels of a maximum of seven members chosen by the chairman.[12] The committee invites interested parties to submit their comments and objections to the findings of the Commissioner, both in writing and in the course of an oral hearing.[13] However, new evidence or arguments not first presented to the Commissioner cannot then be presented to the committee, unless it finds special reasons to justify an exception.[14] Following deliberation, the committee submits its report to the Minister of Industry, Trade and Labour. The report includes the committee's findings regarding the existence of dumped or subsidized

---

[5] Article 24 of the Trade Levies Law.   [6] Ibid., Articles 32–32.8.
[7] Ibid., Article 5. The Commissioner must have knowledge and expertise in economics and foreign trade.
[8] Ibid., Articles 28–9.   [9] Ibid., Article 32.12.
[10] Ibid., Article 6. The Committee members must have knowledge and expertise in economics or foreign trade.
[11] G.W. Bowman, N. Covelli and D. Gantz, *Trade Remedies in North America* (2010), p. 54.
[12] The Trade Levies Law, Article 6(e).   [13] Ibid., Articles 32.9–32.10.
[14] Ibid., Article 32.9.

imports, as the case may be, regarding the margin of dumping or the rate of subsidization and the existence of material injury to the domestic industry and a causal link between the two. It also makes recommendations on whether an anti-dumping duty or a countervailing duty should be imposed, and if so, its rate, its scope of application and the period during which it should be in force.[15]

If the committee decides to recommend the imposition of an anti-dumping or countervailing duty, it is then for the Minister of Industry, Trade and Labour, together with the Minister of Finance, to decide whether to impose such a duty. In other words, the approval of both ministers is required, or at least the approval of the former (who actually issues the decree imposing the duty) and the lack of opposition of the latter.[16] When considering whether to levy the duty, the minister, who is a politician, is to take into account, *inter alia* ,"the trade relations between Israel and foreign countries" as well as "reasons pertaining to the economy in general". In the Israeli system, therefore, the imposition of an anti-dumping or countervailing duty is "permissive", as recommended, but not required, by the WTO Anti-Dumping Agreement and Subsidies Agreements,[17] i.e. the authorities have discretion whether or not to impose a duty, even where the formal requirements have been met. The possibility of considering "reasons pertaining to the economy in general" is very similar to the requirement under EU law to consider "Community interest" before imposing such a duty.[18] But in addition to this consideration, Israeli law also authorizes the minister to consider the

---

[15] Ibid., Article 32.11.

[16] Ibid., Article 32.18. According to Article 32.18(a) the Minister of Industry, Trade and Labour must forward a copy of the report of the Committee to the Minister of Finance as soon as received. If the minister decides to impose a duty, this decision must be submitted for the approval of the Minister of Finance (Art. 32.18(b)). If the Finance Minister approves, or if he or she does not submit his or her refusal within 15 days, the Minister of Industry, Trade and Labour shall levy the duty within 5 days (Art. 32.18(c)).

[17] See Article 9.1 of the Anti-Dumping Agreement (hereinafter AD Agreement) and Article 19.2 of the Agreement on Subsidies and Countervailing Measures (hereinafter SCM Agreement). Both provisions use the words "it is desirable" (that the imposition be permissive), thus falling short of imposing a "hard-law" obligation. Indeed, in the United States, no such consideration is taken, and imposition is automatic once the formal conditions have been fulfilled (see Bowman et al., *Trade Remedies in North America*, p. 131).

[18] See EU Council Regulation No. 1225/2009 on protection against dumped imports from countries not members of the European Community, OJ L343/51 (22.12.2009), Article 9.4.

trade relations between Israel and foreign countries, i.e. those countries against which the protective duties are contemplated. In our opinion, this is a problematic provision in that it unnecessarily politicizes the process and invites international pressure.[19]

Of the three other types of contingent protection that the Law deals with, the most common is that termed "protective measures". This is also the one which falls under the definition of "safeguard measures" that are imposed under the General Agreement on Tariffs and Trade (GATT) Article XIX and the WTO Agreement on Safeguards (hereinafter SG Agreement), which are discussed in this book. This is quite confusing, since the Hebrew translation of safeguard duty ("*hetel bitchah*") has been maintained for a whole range of different types of import and export levies that are not "safeguard duties" in the internationally accepted meaning of this term. The explanation for this confusion is that until 2008, Israel did not have a special procedure for the imposition of safeguard measures, in the sense of GATT Article XIX and the SG Agreement.[20] Instead, there was a provision in the Law which authorized the Minister of Industry, Trade and Labour to impose a wide range of levies for various purposes, some of which were reminiscent of safeguard duties,[21] but without providing for the due process requirements of the SG Agreement. In 2008,[22] as part of an extensive amendment to the Law, a whole new chapter was added (Chapter B2) in order to provide for the imposition of what is known as "safeguard measures" in accordance with the requirements of the SG Agreement.[23] However, since the term "*hetel bitchah*" was already in use, and since the SG Agreement permits not only levies but also import quotas, the new measures were coined "protective measures" ("*emtzaey haganah*") and the Law was also

---

[19] We are aware of several instances of attempts to exert such political pressure after the completion of the investigation, and of one instance that was successful in preventing a safeguard duty.

[20] For an extensive discussion of Israel's safeguard regime prior to the 2005 amendment, see Gill Nadel, "Safeguard Levies for the Protection of the Local Industry against Competing Imports: An Israeli Legislative Failure in the Face of a Tightening International Regime", in Arie Reich (ed.), *The WTO and Israel: Law, Economics and Politics* (Bar Ilan University Press, 2006) (in Hebrew).

[21] In particular, what was then Article 2(a)(3): "to protect local production against material injury caused or threatening to be caused to it by competing imports".

[22] The Trade Levies Law (Fourth Amendment), 5768–2008, *Sefer Chukim* 2185 (5.11.2008), p. 5.

[23] As explained in the Trade Levies Bill (Protective Measures), 5767–2007, *Hatzaot Chok* 311 (27.6.2007), p. 682.

renamed "The Trade Levies and Protective Measures Law" to take account of the important amendment.[24] In addition, Article 2 of the Law was amended so that the previous authority to impose safeguard levies on all types of products without due process was replaced by the authority to impose "special safeguard measures" on agricultural products, in accordance with the WTO Agreement on Agriculture.[25]

Investigations on whether to impose protective measures (safeguards) are conducted entirely by the Commissioner of Trade Levies, without any involvement of the Advisory Committee. Such investigations are conducted in accordance with the provisions of the SG Agreement, giving all interested parties the opportunity to submit comments and evidence in the course of the proceedings. The Commissioner has the right to provide provisional remedies, usually in the form of a security by cash deposit or bond guarantee, if there is an increase in imports, serious injury to the domestic industry and a causal link between the two.[26] The Commissioner is required to complete the investigation within 215 days from initiation and to submit the findings to the Minister of Industry, Trade and Labour along with recommendations on whether to adopt any protective measure, and if so, what type of measure and for how long.[27] Here, too, as in the case of anti-dumping and countervailing duties, the minister has to take into consideration not only the fulfilment of the legal conditions for imposition of such measures (a significant increase in imports which has caused serious injury to the domestic industry) but also "considerations pertaining to the economy in general" and "trade relations between Israel and foreign countries".[28] If the minister decides to impose a protective measure, this decision must be approved, or at least not actively opposed, by the Minister of Finance, who traditionally has been more liberal in his economic convictions and less prone to support protective measures.[29]

---

[24] Ibid., Article 1 and explanations thereto. However, in the English version submitted by Israel to the WTO, the term was translated as "safeguard measures".

[25] See Article 5 of the WTO Agreement on Agriculture.   [26] Ibid., Article 3.8.

[27] Ibid., Article 3.10.

[28] Ibid., Article 3.13. Our critique of this provision expressed above (see text following note 18) is applicable here, too.

[29] Ministers of Industry, Trade and Labour traditionally consider it their job to protect domestic industry and domestic jobs. Ministers of Finance, in contrast, are responsible for the macro-economic well-being of the State. They are worried about inflation and the consumer price index and how to promote competitiveness of local industry. Therefore, they tend to be less supportive of trade protective measures. The same is true to an even larger degree for the civil servants of these respective ministries.

Israel is not a heavy user of trade remedies, although several investigations have been conducted over the years. Since the Trade Levies Law came into force in 1991 until August 2011, the Commissioner received about 60 requests for the initiation of anti-dumping, countervailing duty or safeguard investigations.[30] Of these, 26 resulted in final duties or price undertakings. In 12 cases, there were provisional duties but no final duties, either because the Advisory Committee gave a negative recommendation, or one of the ministers refused to approve such duties, or because the complaint was withdrawn. In another 17 cases, there was no provisional duty, nor any final duty, for one of the reasons set out above. Six cases are still pending before the authorities, and in some of them provisional duties have been imposed. Most of these are anti-dumping duties and some are "safeguards"[31] or protective measures. No countervailing duty has ever been imposed in Israel.[32]

All decisions to impose trade levies, both provisional and final, can be judicially reviewed, and this is often done. However, the types of judicial and quasi-judicial review mechanisms available and the applicable standards of review underwent a major reform in 2005, as explained below.

III   Legislative framework for judicial review until 2005

The legislative framework for judicial review of trade remedy determinations in Israel was completely overhauled in 2005. We believe that the system that existed before 2005 was more effective than the new one, therefore we want to devote the first part of this chapter to discussing the pre-2005 model and proceed to describe the current model. We will then compare the two models and explain why we believe the previous one was preferable.

---

[30] Based on data collected by the authors from the website of the Trade Levies Unit in the Ministry of Industry, Trade and Labour: www.moital.gov.il/NR/exeres/4271208E-B717-44F0-9413-79C6C2345DBA.htm (last visited 12.9.2011).

[31] The term "safeguards" is in parentheses because, according to Israel's official position, they are not safeguards in the WTO sense of the term, the reason being that these levies did not exceed Israel's bound tariff rates, and therefore do not come within GATT Article XIX.

[32] There have been a few complaints on subsidized imports, but none of them resulted in a countervailing duty. For instance, in 1993 Osem's request to impose such a duty on pasta from Italy was rejected by the Advisory Committee, and a few years later its request for imposition of a countervailing duty on baked goods from Italy was rejected by the Commissioner after a decision by the Chairman of the Advisory Committee.

From 1991 until the 2005 amendment, the Trade Levies Law provided for its own particular arrangements for judicial review of trade remedy determinations. The most important feature of those arrangements was that many of the Commissioner's decisions could be challenged before the chairman of the Advisory Committee.[33] For instance, the decision to impose or not to impose a provisional anti-dumping or countervailing duty and the decision to accept or not to accept a price undertaking could be challenged before the chairman, who was authorized to scrutinize these decisions based on the substantive law of trade remedies. Since the chairman was usually an expert in the field and a lawyer,[34] this scrutiny was very significant and could be made based on both the domestic and international law of trade remedies. The chairman's decision could then be appealed before the District Court, which is the second-highest instance in the Israeli judicial system.[35] However, the chairman did not have any authority in relation to safeguards or any other protective measures aside from anti-dumping and countervailing duties.

The option of challenging the Commissioner's decision on provisional duties, an option that is not required under any of the WTO agreements,[36] was attractive to the parties involved and was therefore used very frequently. The submission of a challenge did not require the payment of any type of administrative fee, and the Chairman was not considered authorized to award legal fees against the losing party. Thus, the only costs confronting a party who wanted to file a challenge were the legal fees of its own lawyers. The procedure was also quite quick to execute. The chairman was required to issue a decision within two

---

[33] Article 49 of the Law, prior to the 2005 amendment, allowed challenge before the chairperson of four types of decisions by the Commissioner: (1) a decision not to initiate an anti-dumping or countervailing duty investigation, because the complaint has not shown a *prima facie* basis; (2) a decision to terminate an investigation because a price undertaking has been accepted; (3) a decision to impose or not to impose a provisional anti-dumping or countervailing duty ("temporary guarantee"); and (4) a decision not to initiate a review of an existing trade levy.

[34] According to Article 6 of the Law, in order to be appointed, the chairperson must be a lawyer who has knowledge and expertise in foreign trade and economics. Since the chairperson is also involved in formulating the findings and recommendations for the final trade remedies in all of the cases that have been investigated by the Commissioner, he or she naturally gains much experience and knowledge in this field, even if they did not have it at the outset.

[35] Article 50 of the Law, prior to the 2005 amendment.

[36] Article 13 of the AD Agreement requires WTO members to maintain judicial review only of final determinations, not of provisional duties and determinations. The same is true in relation to Article 23 of the SCM Agreement.

months, and if no such decision was issued, the Law provided quite a drastic remedy: the challenge was deemed to have been accepted![37]

Even if the chairman rejected a challenge, the challenging party could still sometimes gain indirectly from the process, since the deliberations on a final duty would soon come before the Advisory Committee chaired by the chairman. Often, in the decision on the provisional duty, the chairman would express his opinion on the substance of the case, on issues such as how dumping margins should be calculated or how to relate to questions of material injury or causality in the special circumstances of the case at hand: questions that were bound to come up in both the preliminary and final stages. These pronouncements were likely to direct the Commissioner in the ongoing investigation and in the formulation of his or her final findings. There would usually be no point in disregarding these pronouncements, if the Commissioner wanted his or her recommendations to be adopted by the Committee.[38] This then gave the chairman the opportunity to influence the methodology of the investigation at quite an early stage, before the case reached the Committee for final dispensation.

Decisions to impose *final* trade remedy measures could be appealed before the District Court until 2005.[39] The possibility to appeal final safeguard measures was especially important, given the lack of involvement of the Advisory Committee in these procedures, which otherwise might have served as a balancing factor. The decision of the District Court could be appealed to the Supreme Court.[40] It should be noted that the Law allowed only appeals of decisions to impose trade levies, not of decisions to refrain from imposing such levies.[41] This resulted in a

---

[37] Article 49(c) of the Law, prior to the 2005 amendment. This provision could create unsolvable problems in some cases. For instance, what if both parties had challenged the provisional duty, the importer claiming that it should be revoked and the domestic industry that it should be raised? How could both challenges be deemed to have been accepted if the chairperson failed to decide within the given time limit? In practice, the authors are not aware of any case where the chairman failed to do so.

[38] While, formally, the chairperson has only one vote out of seven on the Committee, he or she has usually been the one who has written the final recommendations and who therefore, and because of his or her position, has the strongest influence on their formulation.

[39] Article 50 of the Law, as it was before the 2005 amendment.

[40] See, for instance, CA 2313/98 *Minister of Industry and Trade* v. *Minkol* (decision by the Supreme Court of 27.2.2000).

[41] Article 50 provided that anyone who "disputes his liability to pay a trade levy" could appeal to the District Court. If the Advisory Committee recommended against imposing

certain asymmetry in the procedural rights of the various parties to the proceedings, where only the importers and foreign producers could appeal the final decision, whereas the complainants, i.e. the domestic producers, did not have the right to appeal a decision not to impose a trade levy or the amount or duration of such levy.[42] This asymmetry was only rectified in the 2005 amendments.

In addition to these two venues of review (a challenge to the chairman and an appeal to the District Court), there was and still remains, a residual original jurisdiction of the High Court of Justice (i.e. the Supreme Court) over any issue that is not addressed by other procedures.[43] Thus, for instance, in a case where the Commissioner refused to extend the time limit for submission of a response by the exporter, the latter petitioned directly to the High Court of Justice.[44] On the other hand, the practice of the Customs Authorities and the Commissioner to demand a renewal of the bank guarantee for each new shipment, imposed in the framework of a decision on provisional duties, was challenged by a motion (not an appeal) to the District Court. The motion was accepted, and the Court struck down this practice, ruling that a guarantee would be valid for six months and could not be renewed once it had expired.[45]

IV   Legislative framework for judicial review since 2005

The Third Amendment of the Trade Levies Law, passed in 2005, revoked both the challenging procedure before the chairperson and the appeal procedure before the District Court.[46] Instead, the amendment added

a trade levy and the Minister of Industry and Trade consequently refrained from imposing one, there is no liability, and the domestic producers would seem to have no right to appeal such a decision. Even if a levy had been imposed and the domestic producers were unhappy with its rate or duration, they still would not have the right to appeal according to the language of the Law, because they were not disputing their liability. It is not clear whether this was an intentional or inadvertent result.

[42] Ibid.

[43] This jurisdiction is based on Article 15(c) of the Basic Law: the Judiciary, which provides that the Supreme Court "shall hear matters in which it deems it necessary to grant relief for the sake of justice and which are not within the jurisdiction of another court".

[44] See HCJ 10246/01 *C & L Limited* v. *Commissioner of Trade Levies*, judgment given on 28.12.2001 (petition was dismissed).

[45] HP 498/96 (Tel-Aviv) *Golmat* v. *Director of Customs and VAT* (judgment of 29.11.1998).

[46] Trade Levies Law (Third Amendment), 5765–2005, *Sefer Chukim* 2012 (7.7.2005), Articles 7 and 8, which repealed Articles 49(a) and 50, respectively, of the Law.

decisions taken by authorities under the Trade Levies Law to the list of decisions that can be reviewed by the administrative courts under the Administrative Courts Law, 5760–2000.[47,48] These courts, which are parallel to the district courts and staffed by district court justices, were established in 2000 in order to lighten the caseload of the High Court of Justice.[49] The matters that these courts can hear are specified in the appendices to the Law, which have gradually been expanded over time. They include administrative actions in matters such as public procurement, municipal taxes, schools and education, business permits, urban planning, immigration, foreign workers' status and many other matters.[50] Where the administrative courts do not have jurisdiction, the residual jurisdiction still lies with the High Court of Justice, i.e. the Supreme Court of Israel.[51] Appeals from decisions of the administrative courts also go to the Supreme Court.[52]

The administrative courts are authorized under the Law to hear three types of cases: Administrative Petitions, Administrative Appeals and Administrative Actions. The latter relates to claims for damages against a governmental agency for alleged violation of administrative law that has caused damage to the claimant, whereas the first two are types of judicial review of actions or inactions of governmental agencies.[53]

---

[47] Ibid., Article 14.

[48] The Administrative Courts Law, 5760–2000, *Sefer Chukim* 1739 (11.6.2000), First Appendix, para. 24: "A decision by an authority under the Trade Levies Law, 1991 . . . except for the decision to legislate regulations".

[49] See Article 1 of the Administrative Courts Law, as well as the explanations to the bill, *Hatzaot Chok* 2821 (13.10.1999).

[50] The First Appendix, which refers to matters where administrative petitions may be filed, includes a very long list of administrative decisions, and we have mentioned only a few of them. The Second Appendix, which refers to matters where administrative appeals may be filed, is also quite long and includes 19 different matters that may be appealed to the Court. The Third Appendix, which refers to matters where administrative actions, i.e. claims for compensation from the government, may be filed, includes only two matters: claims for damages for violation of public tender rules (usually in connection with government procurement); and class actions against a government agency.

[51] See *supra* note 43 and *infra* note 89.

[52] Article 11 of the Administrative Courts Law. Because decisions of the Administrative Courts in relation to trade remedies are challenged through administrative petitions, they can be appealed without leave. Administrative appeals, in contrast, can be appealed only if leave is given by a Supreme Court judge (ibid., Article 12).

[53] Article 5 of the Administrative Courts Law. For more on the matters where these types of actions may be employed, see *supra* note 50.

V   Standards of review: comparison of the two models

As noted above, until 2005 the chairperson of the Advisory Committee was authorized to scrutinize some of the Commissioner's decisions based on the substantive law of trade remedies. The standard of review that would be employed by the chairperson in these challenges was set out in an early decision, which was later quoted and repeated in many subsequent cases:

> The purpose of the challenge is to examine the Commissioner's decision on three levels:
> A. Whether the findings, which originate from the evidence that has been submitted to the Commissioner, reflect the reality or whether he has erred in his findings;
> B. Whether the Commissioner's Decision has correctly applied the law to these findings;
> C. Whether the Commissioner has acted reasonably and fairly, that is whether he has used his discretion in a way that complies with the legislative scheme and the system of balances between the various values embedded in the legislation.[54]

In our opinion, this quote reflects a *de novo* standard of review, where not only the legal foundations of the Commissioner's decision are scrutinized and reviewed anew, but also his or her factual findings, and even the way the Commissioner's discretion in balancing the opposing interests involved in the investigation has been applied. Indeed, several decisions by the chairman have implemented this type of profound review and reached conclusions very different from those of the Commissioner.

A prominent example is the chairman's decision in the matter of the provisional anti-dumping duties imposed on *Imports of Pasta from Italy*.[55] There, the chairman decided to overturn the Commissioner's decision to impose provisional duties, holding that such duties were not

---

[54] *Ion S.A. Coca & Chocolate Manufacturer* v. *Elite Industries Ltd*, Chairman Professor David Glicksberg's decision in a challenge, dated 2.5.1993, quoted in *James Plass Ltd.* v. *Electrochemical Industries (Fruitarome) Ltd.*, para. 12, Chairman Dr Arie Reich's decision in a challenge, dated 16.9.1996. (This and all other quotes from Israeli decisions are the authors' own translation from Hebrew.) In a later decision, the chairman added the words "and international law" to point C, after the words "the legislative scheme", as part of the criteria of review: *In re Hydrogen Peroxide, Degussa AG* v. *Negev Peroxide Ltd*, para. 4, Chairman Dr Arie Reich's decision in a challenge, dated 30.3.2002.

[55] *Vita Quality Foods Ltd. et al.* v. *Nakid Ltd. et al.* (decision of 15.12.1996).

warranted in the case at hand. He did so after having scrutinized the Commissioner's dumping calculation based on the evidence in the file. The scrutiny led to the conclusion that proper adjustments for indirect selling costs had not been made and that the basis for the Commissioner's determination of an export price for many of the Italian exporters was unfounded.[56] A proper calculation, based on the legally correct principles, in the chairman's view, should have led to a finding of no dumping. In doing so, the chairman also rejected the Commissioner's view that one should adopt the European Union (EU)'s approach with regard to indirect selling costs, holding that this approach did not comply with logic or with accepted norms of international and Israeli law.[57] The chairman also disputed the finding of injury and the causal relationship between dumping and injury. His analysis of the evidence led to the conclusion that there was no injury to the domestic industry, not even *prima facie*, and that no causal link had been proven.[58] Having found no proof of dumping or of any injury caused, the inevitable conclusion was that the provisional anti-dumping duties were unjustified and had to be revoked.

The chairman concluded his decision with an important statement about how anti-dumping investigations should be conducted:

> As a rule, the goal of the Trade Levies Law, 5751–1991 is to protect domestic producers from inappropriate and unfair trade practices of foreign producers, which cause material injury to the Israeli industry. The Law should be applied only in accordance with the basic principles of the Israeli legal system, and among them the basic right to freedom of occupation, to equality and to protection of the right to property. The Law should not be used for unjustified protection of monopolies or narrow economic interests at the expense of the general public of consumers.[59]

The domestic producer tried to appeal the decision before the District Court. His main argument was that the chairman was not entitled to conduct this type of *de novo* review and to substitute the Commissioner's discretion with his own.[60] Eventually, the appeal was dropped on the advice of the Court.

---

[56] Ibid., paras. 6–7.   [57] Ibid., para. 6.   [58] Ibid., para. 9.   [59] Ibid., para. 10.
[60] See report in *Globes* newspaper: Hadas Magen, "Osem Appeals to Court on non-imposition of anti-dumping duty on pasta imports from Italy" (17.2.1997), www.globes.co.il/news/article.aspx?did=104646 (last visited 21.12.2011).

There have been several other cases where a *de novo* review was conducted by the chairman and resulted in a change in the provisional anti-dumping duty rates.[61] In many others, such review was conducted and the Commissioner's decision was upheld. There have also been reviews of decisions on price undertakings.[62]

As for the judicial review of *final* duties, this, as was explained above, was conducted by the district courts whenever the importer appealed the duty. By using the term "appeal", the legislature had in fact authorized the court to scrutinize the decisions of the administrative agencies involved in the process leading up to the imposition of the final duty (the Commissioner, the Advisory Committee, the Minister of Industry, Trade and Labour and the Minister of Finance), and in particular their legal foundations. If the court reached the conclusion that the imposition of a duty was based on an incorrect interpretation or implementation of the law, it could overturn the decision to impose the duty, or change its amount or duration. Consistent with its approach in all other appeals, the Court usually refrained from questioning the factual findings of the Commissioner or the Advisory Committee and restricted its judicial review to legal points.

This approach was reflected in the Court's decision in the matter of *Golmat* v. *Minister of Industry, Trade and Labour*:

> This court does not tend to interfere in the discretion of the administrative agency ... In view of that, it is clear that where a proper factual foundation has been established, the court will not readily substitute the discretion of the administrative agency so long as it is not inflicted by a significant flaw ... the appeal court examines in such proceedings a decision of a quasi-judicial body that is an expert in its field. Indeed, in such cases, the court of appeal does not usually interfere with the factual findings but only with the legal conclusions.[63]

Nevertheless, the Court then went on to find that the Advisory Committee and the ministers had erred when they imposed the anti-dumping duty for a period of three years, without having considered the

---

[61] For instance, *In re Pipes from Germany, Combe* v. *Vulcan Casting Houses*, Decision by the chairman given on 28.5.1991; *In re Hydrogen Peroxide; In re Elbow Butt Pipe Fittings, Zibo Yuanfeng Metal Products Co. Inc. et. al.* v. *Carmiel Pipe Fittings Ltd*, Decision by the chairman given on 19.4.2002.

[62] For instance, *Celsa – Cia Espanola de Laminacion, S.A* v. *MAPAM (In re: Building Steel from Spain)* (Decision of 12.8.1996).

[63] VA 740/98 (District Court of Tel-Aviv) *Golmat Ltd.* v. *Minister of Industry, Trade and Labour* (1998), pp. 7–9.

harm that this would cause to consumers and to free competition in the marketplace. The Court considered this both a procedural and substantive error in law. The Court found support for its wide discretion in this regard in Article 50(5) of the Law, which authorized it to approve or revoke the duty, increase it or lower it, "or to rule in any other way which it shall deem fit".[64] Consequently, the Court decided to shorten the duration of the duty considerably, from three years to one year and four months.[65]

The Court took a similar approach when reviewing the decisions of the chairman in challenges of the Commissioner's decisions. In one such case, the Court held:

> This rule [that the Appeals Court should not dispute factual findings of the lower court] is even stronger when we are dealing with an appeal on the decision of the Chairman of the Committee, who himself is an appellate body, who hears a challenge against a professional Commissioner and who in this case had decided to adopt the original factual findings. However, when we are dealing with the conclusion that arises from the facts, the appeal court can interfere and come to a different conclusion ... This is the situation here. Without changing the factual findings of the Commissioner and the Chairman in relation to dumping and price comparison – I wish to disagree with the legal conclusions that one must deduce from these facts, in relation to the provisional remedy of a temporary guarantee.[66]

The Court then went on to limit the scope of the provisional duty, so that it would not apply to products that the domestic industry was not yet producing.

How do these standards of review applied by the chairman and the District Court, respectively, compare to the standard of review employed by the Administrative Court following the 2005 amendment? There can be no doubt that this amendment significantly raised the standard of

[64] See also VA 3820/98 (Tel-Aviv) *Neumann Steel for Building Industries Ltd* v. *Minister of Industry and Trade* (judgment of 17.2.1999), where the Court found support for this position in the special regulations that applied to the appeal.
[65] Ibid., para. 7.
[66] VA 1328/95 (District Court of Tel Aviv) *Golmat Ltd* v. *Ta'amas Ltd*, (1995), para. 5. Another case where the District Court reached the conclusion that the chairman had erred in law by not giving one of the parties the right to respond to a challenge is VA 1231/04 (District Court of Tel Aviv) *Nesher, Israeli Cement Industries Ltd.* v. *Chairman of the Advisory Committee* , a judgment of 5.6.2005.

review, and that this was one of its objectives.[67] One should note in this regard that when this amendment added "decisions in relation to trade remedies" to the First Appendix of the Administrative Courts Law, in effect it classified their review as administrative petitions, not as administrative appeals. This means that the standard of judicial review was changed from an appellate standard to an administrative review standard.[68] No longer is the court expected to re-examine the entire legal reasoning that served as the basis of the decision to impose a provisional or final trade remedy measure. Rather, the Administrative Court now reviews the decision in light of the causes of action that exist under administrative law, such as lack of authority, violation of due process, bad faith, arbitrariness, favouritism, discrimination, unreasonableness and disproportionality. This standard of review (which resembles the US "arbitrary and capricious" standard) is mandated by Article 8 of the Administrative Courts Law, which provides that the administrative courts should rule according to the same causes of action, authorities and remedies applied by the High Court of Justice. It means also that the Court does not substitute the discretion of the administrative agency with its own. Only if the reviewed decision is clearly unreasonable may the Court decide to interfere and overturn it. As was held by the High Court of Justice:

> As is well-known, the rule is that the court will not substitute the discretion vested with the administrative agency with its own discretion, unless the agency has employed its authority unlawfully and not in accordance with the criteria prescribed by public law. Examples of interferences required from the court are when a decision is arbitrary and unreasonable; is found to be in conflict with natural justice; or that the agency acted based on inappropriate considerations or with lack of good faith.[69]

---

[67] The explanations to the bill do not say much about the reasons for the change, only that such change "is needed based on the experience that has been acquired since the passing of the law". However, in personal conversations with the officials in the Ministry of Industry, Trade and Labour who initiated the amendment, they explained that they were frustrated about what they considered to be "excessive interference" with the provisional duty determinations of the Commissioner by the chairman, as well as with the frequent interference of the District Courts with final safeguard duties.

[68] On the difference between those two standards, see AP 191/04 (Tel-Aviv) *Nichsey Sokolov Ltd* v. *Director of Municipal Tax, Herzlia* (Decision of 7.9.2006); AP 1073/10 (Tel-Aviv) *Local Council Shorkot* v. *Appeals Committee* (Decision of 30.12.2001).

[69] HCJ 5294/09 *Sergeant Major Mordechai Tuvi* v. *Chief of Staff* (Judgment of 27.7.2009). (This case had nothing to do with trade remedies.)

Indeed, an examination of decisions of the administrative courts on trade remedies cases since 2005 shows that they are much less willing than before to interfere in the decisions of the authorized agencies in these matters, and that their review is shallower. This is certainly true compared to the chairman's review of the Commissioner's decisions, but also to a certain extent, compared to the district courts' review of final duties within the appellate procedure. While we can find several instances in which the District Court decided to interfere in decisions to impose final trade remedies,[70] interfering in decisions of the administrative courts seem to be much more rare,[71] even though they have taken over both the review function of the district courts and that of the chairperson.[72] Indeed, the general view among the practitioners in this field is that it has become much harder to overturn a decision by the trade remedies authorities, ever since the authority was given to the administrative courts.

[70] For instance, *Golmat* v. *Ta'amas*; *Golmat* v. *Minister of Industry, Trade and Labour*; *Nesher* v. *Chairman* VA 835/93 (Tel-Aviv) *MDK Administration & Trade* v. *State of Israel*, (Judgment of 9.4.1998); VA 793/95 (Jerusalem) *Regent Glida (1995) Ltd et al.* v. *Minister of Industry, Trade and Labour*; VA 1157/97 (Nazareth) *Minkol et al.* v. *Minister of Industry, Trade and Labour* (Judgment of 19.2.1998). In the last three cases, the District Courts revoked completely the safeguard duties that had been imposed because of what they found to be lack of evidence of serious injury. (In *Minkol*, the Supreme Court later overturned the decision and reinstated the duty.)

[71] We can point to only two instances where the Administrative Court has agreed to interfere in trade remedies decisions: one was AP 12957–06-10 (Jerusalem) *Bitum Ltd et al.* v. *Commissioner for Trade Levies* (Judgment of 1.8.2010), where the Administrative Court (Judge Solberg) approved the provisional anti-dumping duty on bituminous membranes from Italy, but revoked it in relation to Greece. The reason was that the Commissioner had had no evidence whatsoever on the normal value of the products in Greece and therefore no basis to find dumping. This, then, was not a case of evaluating the evidence differently from the Commissioner, but one where the Court refused to accept a completely unsubstantiated assumption that the normal value of the product in Greece was identical to the normal value in Italy. Indeed, the Court stressed that such a fundamental flaw in the decision of the Commissioner left the Court no choice but to interfere. The second instance was AP 1715/09 (Jerusalem) *Best Carton Ltd et al.* v. *Commissioner for Trade Levies* (Judgment of 2.9.2009), where the same judge pressed the Commissioner to agree to a shortening of the duration of the provisional duty, again because of some serious deficiencies in the evidence supporting the imposition. This, then, was an agreed settlement, and not a judgment. In most other cases, the Court refused to interfere, seeing these as professional decisions where the Court should defer to the expertise of the investigating authorities.

[72] We are aware of six decisions by the chairman and six by the district courts that interfered in trade remedies actions over a period of 14 years (1991–2005), compared to only two interfering in decisions by the administrative courts over a period of six years (2005–11).

This situation has led to the conclusion among some of the decision-makers that it has become too easy for the Commissioner to impose provisional duties and that more checks and balances are needed in this regard. As a result, a new bill was introduced which proposed a duty of consultation with the chairperson before imposing a provisional anti-dumping or countervailing duty, and with the Director-General of the Ministry of Industry and Trade before imposing a safeguard measure.[73] While this proposal fell short of reviving the challenging procedures before the chairperson, nevertheless it did intend to reinstate him as an important player in the process of imposing a provisional duty, presumably as a restraining factor. However, the final version that passed recently instead imposed the requirement to obtain the approval of the Director-General for all types of provisional duties.[74] Thus, the legislature has decided to opt for an *ex ante* political-economic review of the imposition of such duties instead of reviving the *ex post* quasi-judicial review by the chairperson.[75]

VI   Substantive law of review: national or international?

Before 2005, as noted above, both the chairman and the District Court reviewed trade remedy determinations, and they did so based on Israeli law. The chairman also made extensive use of WTO instruments and jurisprudence when doing so. Indeed, before the amendments of 2005, this practice was very important, because the 1991 Trade Levies Law until then had failed to implement the Uruguay Round Agreements. Thus, there were significant discrepancies between the text of the Law and Israel's commitments under the AD, SCM and SG Agreements. In view of the fact that Israeli law, like English law, does not implement international treaty law unless it has been expressly enacted by the national legislature,[76] this could potentially have posed a serious problem. The problem was overcome by a somewhat creative decision by the chairman in a challenge by James Plass Ltd.,[77] where it was held that the Law must be interpreted in a way that conforms to the WTO agreements. This decision was later adopted by the full Advisory Committee and

---

[73] For a discussion (in Hebrew) of the proposal, see: www.industry.org.il/?CategoryID=1214&ArticleID=5267 (last visited 8.11.2011).

[74] The Law was amended by The Economic Policy for the Years 2011–2012 (Legislative Amendments) Law, Art. 47(4) and (5), *Sefer Hukim* 2271 (6.1.2011).

[75] Of course, the judicial review of the Administrative Court has not been revoked.

[76] HCJ 2717/96 *Wafa Ali et al.* v. *Minister of Defence* PD 50(2)842.   [77] *Supra* note 54.

became standard practice in all investigations, including reliance on relevant rulings by WTO panels and the Appellate Body. In contrast, an examination of judgments of the district courts during this period shows that most of them did not rely explicitly on WTO agreements or jurisprudence, but mostly on the Trade Levies Law and on general principles of Israeli administrative law. Only a few rare judgments can be found which made use of WTO material.[78]

The 2005 amendments to the Law not only changed the procedures for judicial review, but also finally implemented the provisions of the Uruguay Round AD and SCM Agreements.[79] The SG Agreement was implemented in the amendments of 2008.[80] Following those amendments, the need to rely on WTO agreements has become less pressing, since their provisions have already been absorbed into Israeli law. Therefore, and as a result of the new standard of review that restricts interference of the courts considering violations of administrative norms, we have not found any reliance on WTO law by the administrative courts since 2005.

VII   Which decisions can be reviewed?

The Administrative Courts Law authorizes the administrative court to review petitions in relation to any "decision by an agency under the Trade Levies Law ... except for decisions to issue regulations".[81] The Court's authority therefore relates both to provisional and to final duties. It extends also to decisions in relation to safeguard measures, both provisional and final, even though the SG Agreement does not require judicial review of such measures.[82] Decisions that may be reviewed also include decisions to refuse to initiate investigations; decisions to accept or to refuse to accept price undertakings; decisions to extend or to refuse to extend confidentiality to documents or other material submitted to

---

[78] For instance, in VA 679/01 (Haifa) *Mekor Haformaika Ltd* v. *Minister of Industry, Trade and Labour et al.* (Judgment of 20.11.2001), para. F-3, the Court relied on both substantive and procedural obligations under the SG Agreement (Articles 3.1 and 4); also in VA (Jerusalem) 5217/98 *Pillsbury Israel Ltd* v. *Minister of Agriculture et al.* (Judgment of 13.6.1999) we find discussion of the SG and Agriculture Agreements as well as of bilateral trade agreements.

[79] For a discussion of the amendments, see Guy Harpaz, "The New Israeli Anti-Dumping Legislation" 39 (2006) *Israel Law Review* 260.

[80] *Supra* note 23.   [81] Para. 24 of the First Appendix.

[82] Many safeguard measures have been reviewed by the courts, even though the SG Agreement does not require this.

the Commissioner;[83] and decisions to grant or to refuse to grant extensions of time for the submission of responses or evidence in the course of an investigation.

It is an interesting question as to whether the Commissioner's decision to initiate an investigation in relation to any type of trade remedy may be challenged before the court. On one hand the Law refers to "decisions" with no exceptions, and the decision whether to initiate an investigation after the Commissioner has come to the conclusion that the threshold conditions have been met is also an important decision that would seem to be included in that language, the Law expressly using the term "decision" in this regard. This decision also has a significant impact on importers and foreign producers, because it requires them to respond to the complaint and to the long questionnaires that the Commissioner presents to them, to submit an extensive number of documents and often sensitive information to a foreign authority, and to hire legal counsel to represent them in these proceedings. One could therefore argue that they should be entitled to judicial review of such a decision. On the other hand, the initiation of an investigation is only the beginning of a process during which the parties will have many opportunities to make their pleadings and submit their version of the facts and evidence in the case at hand. If it is an anti-dumping or countervailing duty investigation, they will have this opportunity not only before the Commissioner, but also before the Advisory Committee. In this sense, the decision to initiate an investigation is very different from a decision not to do so, because the latter is a final decision for the complainant, which means that the proceedings have come to an end, whereas the former is only the beginning of the process. One would therefore expect the Administrative Court to refuse to hear the petition based on the "alternative remedy" doctrine, i.e. that the petitioner has an alternative remedy with the administrative agency.[84] Indeed, before the 2005 amendment, the Law clearly distinguished between a decision to initiate

---

[83] An example of such a petition is AP 4216-02-11 (Jerusalem) *Society for Quality Recycling* v. *Ministry of Industry, Trade and Labour* (Judgment of 28.2.2011).

[84] See HCJ 7190/05 *Lubel* v. *Government of Israel* (Judgment of 18.1.06); HCJ 7823/10 *Yesh Gvul Movement* v. *Advisory Committee for Appointment to Senior Positions* (Judgment of 18.1.2011); HCJ 81/11 *Nissim* v. *Legal Advisor to Aviation Administration* (Judgment of 1.6.2011). These rulings of the High Court of Justice are "imported" into the administrative courts through Article 8 of the Law.

and a decision not to initiate an investigation, and allowed a challenge only of the latter.[85]

In a recent decision by the Administrative Court in Jerusalem, this approach was also adopted under the 2005 amendment.[86] The Court, which found support for this approach in the commentary on the amendment bill and in the "alternative remedy" principle, ruled that only final or preliminary decisions could be challenged before it. These include decisions not to initiate proceedings or to terminate or suspend them, a decision not to initiate a review of an existing levy, decisions on provisional duties and on price undertakings and, of course, decisions to impose or not to impose a final levy.[87] On the other hand, decisions that merely represent a phase in the continuous investigation and that do not result in an immediate levy, such as the Commissioner's decision to initiate an investigation, the Commissioner's findings submitted to the Advisory Committee, the Committee's findings and recommendation to impose a levy submitted to the minister, cannot be reviewed by the Court. Only once the process reaches a conclusion, such as when the minister decides to impose a levy, can the entire process be challenged and reviewed by the Court. Even a decision not to impose a final levy, whether taken by the Committee (in which case the minister cannot decide to impose one) or by the minister (based on considerations of foreign relations or the best interest of the economy), may be challenged before the Administrative Court,[88] although the chances that the Court will interfere in purely political or economic considerations of the minister are slim.

While the administrative courts have largely replaced the High Court of Justice in any matter relating to trade remedies, one could imagine cases where the High Court could still be seized with such matters if they fall outside the jurisdiction of the former.[89]

---

[85] Article 49 of the Law, which created the right to challenge some of the Commissioner's decisions before the chairperson of the Advisory Committee, referred only to decisions under Article 18(b) (not to initiate an investigation), and not to decisions under Article 18(c) (to initiate an investigation).

[86] AP 15812-07-11 (Jerusalem) *Mazonit I.SRL. Ltd* v. *Commissioner for Trade Levies* (Judgment of 11.9.2011).

[87] Ibid., para. 6.   [88] Ibid., para. 4.

[89] For instance, if the Commissioner fails to make any decision on whether to initiate an investigation, or fails to submit findings in an investigation within the respective time frames prescribed by the Law, the administrative courts would appear not to have jurisdiction, because there is no "decision by an authority under the Trade Levies Law", as required by item 24 of the First Appendix to the Administrative Courts Law. The High Court of Justice would therefore have residual jurisdiction based on Article 15(c) of the Basic Law: The Judiciary.

VIII   Parties eligible to bring a case

The Trade Levies Law contains a definition of "interested parties" that is similar to that found in the WTO agreements.[90] They include: the exporter or foreign producer or the importer of a product subject to investigation; a trade or business association a majority of the members of which are producers, exporters or importers of such product; the government of the exporting member; a producer of the like product in the importing member; or a trade and business association whose majority of members produce a like product in the territory of the importing member. Just as all of these parties have the right to participate in the proceedings under the Law, one could safely assume that they would have the right to petition the Administrative Court if they were harmed by a decision resulting from such proceedings. But what about parties other than "interested parties"?

The High Court of Justice has drastically developed the right of standing over the last few decades so as to allow public petitioners to bring cases before it, in particular when there is a public interest involved.[91] Thus, one could imagine the Administrative Court permitting a representative consumer organization to bring a petition against the imposition of a trade levy that considerably increases the price of an essential product. However, where the parties that are most directly affected by the decision have decided not to challenge it, the Court may use its discretion to deny standing to such a third party.[92]

Even "interested parties" can be denied standing before the Court if they fail to exhaust their remedies before the investigating authorities. For instance, if an exporter decides not to file answers to the questionnaire and not to cooperate with the Commissioner, it will most probably not be permitted to petition the Court against a decision resulting from this investigation.[93]

---

[90] In Article 3b of the Law, we have a definition for the purpose of safeguard investigations, and in Article 4 there is one for the purpose of anti-dumping and countervailing duty investigations. The latter is based on the definitions found in Article 6.11 of the AD Agreement and Article 12.3 of the SCM Agreement.

[91] Especially so when constitutional principles and the rule of law have been at stake. See HCJ 651/03 *Association for Civil Rights in Israel* v. *Chairperson of Election Committee* (Judgment of 23.1.2003).

[92] HCJ 6492/08 *SAL Society Educational Projects* v. *Commander of IDF in the West Bank* (Judgment of 14.1.2010).

[93] See, for instance, HCJ 9074/09 *Gilead Banay* v. *The Inspector of Insurance* (Judgment of 7.2.2010), where this doctrine was applied in a different context.

IX   Procedures and remedies

The rules of procedure that apply today in the administrative courts are similar to those that apply in the High Court of Justice. Article 13(2) of the Administrative Courts Law prescribes this, and the detailed rules are set out in the Administrative Courts (Rules of Procedures) Regulations, 5761–2000.[94] That usually means that taking of evidence will be based solely on affidavits submitted by the parties. However, the Court may permit cross-examination of a witness on his or her affidavit if it is "necessary in order to resolve the petition",[95] and it appears that this is permitted much more often than in the High Court.[96]

An administrative petition should usually be submitted "without delay", and no later than 45 days after the decision being challenged.[97] Thus, in some cases a petition can be refused even if it is filed within the 45-day time frame, if the Court is of the opinion that considering the circumstances in the case at hand, the petition should have been filed earlier.[98] For petitions against provisional duties, the Trade Levies Law provides a shorter time frame of only 15 days.[99]

The Administrative Court can award all the remedies that a regular court can award. For instance, it can issue interim injunctions against the investigating authority[100] to suspend investigation until the petition is resolved,[101] and can do so *ex parte* if it is urgent. It may accept the petition in full or in part, and enter appropriate orders for the relevant authorities,[102] and it can remand the case to the investigating authority with instructions for further action.[103]

---

[94] *Kovetz Takanot* 6070 (7.12.2000) (hereinafter the Regulations).   [95] Ibid., r. 15(a).

[96] For a discussion of this, see Roee Shahar, "The Administrative Petition and Cross-Examination": www.shahar-law.co.il/2011–05–03–09–53–52/131–2011–05–03–15–43–50 (last visited 21.12.2011).

[97] Rule. 3(b) of the Regulations. The 45 days are calculated from the day the decision was published in the *Official Gazette*, or when it was notified to the petitioner, whichever comes first.

[98] Ibid., r. 4.   [99] Article 28(e) of the Law.

[100] R. 9 of the Regulations. See also Article 15(d)(2) of the Basic Law: The Judiciary.

[101] The Court did this in *Mazonit v. Commissioner for Trade Levies.*

[102] For instance, in *Bitum v. Commissioner for Trade Levies* the Court ordered the Commissioner to instruct the customs authorities that the provisional levy should not apply to imports from Greece.

[103] R. 17 of the Regulations.

X Concluding remarks and suggestions for improvement

As we have shown in this chapter, Israel's system of judicial review of trade remedy determinations underwent a major alteration in 2005. It changed from a system that provided broad review of provisional duties by an expert (the chairperson) and of final duties by the district courts, to one that provides a more limited review by the administrative courts. The depth of the review is a function of the standard of review prescribed by the law, whether a *de novo* review, as was practised by the chairman, an appeal review scrutinizing the legal foundations of the decision, as was practised by the district courts, or an administrative judicial review standard, as is now practised by the administrative courts. Naturally, the deeper the review, the higher the chances that it will result in interference in the decision being reviewed. This in turn is likely to result in a higher number of challenges of these decisions, given the potentially greater chances of success.

Indeed, the data that we have on the use of Israel's two review models seems to support this hypothesis. There was definitely more frequent use of the challenge procedure before the chairman, when such a position existed, than with the current use of the administrative courts. Of some 22 anti-dumping and countervailing duty procedures that occurred between the years 1991 and 2001 and concluded with the Commissioner's decision on provisional duties, about 17 were challenged before the chairman.[104] There were also several appeals to the district courts in relation to final measures, in particular in relation to safeguard measures.[105] By contrast, since the 2005 amendment, only about six of some 20 different cases have been challenged before the Administrative Court, and this includes petitions in relation to both provisional and final duties.[106] As we have

---

[104] This information is based on the list of cases and table of proceedings published by the Ministry of Industry, Trade and Labour for these years.

[105] We have found five decisions by the district courts in appeals against safeguard measures, in three of which the Court overturned the Commissioner's decision: *Minkol, supra* note 70; *MDK ibid.; Regent Glida, ibid.; Mekor Haformaika, supra* note 78; *Pillsbury, ibid.*

[106] The petitions were in relation to the following cases: *Bitum* v. *Commissioner for Trade Levies; Best Carton* v. *Commissioner for Trade Levies; Mazonit* v. *Commissioner for Trade Levies;* AP 895/05 (Jerusalem) *DNA Integrated Technologies* v. *Commissioner* (Decision of 15.1.2006); AP 1706/09 (Jerusalem) *MSK Almor* v. *Commissioner* (Decision of 1.10.2009); AP 1490/09 (Jerusalem) *Association of Contractors and Builders in Israel* v. *Commissioner* (withdrawn 31.8.2009).

shown,[107] the rate of success of these challenges has also dropped significantly.

On the other hand, one could argue that a deep review of those decisions of a temporary nature, such as provisional duties, could be too onerous for the system and might cause undue delays in the completion of investigations. That may be the reason why the WTO does not require any review of provisional duties. We are not convinced by this argument. First, it does not seem that the duration of investigations has decreased since the deep review by the chairperson was revoked in 2005. Second, even provisional duties can cause serious injury to importers[108] and to consumers, and they should be subject to review to ensure that they are justified. The chairperson, as an expert in the field, and as a representative of the public, and thus less inclined than the Commissioner to protection of the domestic industry, may curb any excessive use of provisional measures. Indeed, it seems that the Israeli authorities themselves have now reached the conclusion that the absence of a deep review of these duties has caused them to become too prevalent and too extensive.[109] Finally, the involvement of the chairperson in the proceedings from an early stage can help steer them on a proper course to their final determination. We also believe that final duties should be subject at least to a legal appeal, not only a review based on administrative law criteria.

Generally speaking, the administration of trade remedies tends to be tilted in favour of local producers at the expense of consumers and foreigners. That is why an effective judicial review mechanism is important, in order to prevent overly protectionist decisions and ensure a more balanced application of the rules. It is also in line with the general move towards the strengthening of judicial review in the Israeli legal system.[110]

It is interesting to note that the WTO agreements do not prescribe any specific standard of review. Except for requiring "judicial review", they do not provide any clue as to what exactly it is that "the judicial, arbitral or administrative tribunals" should do when they conduct such reviews.

---

[107] See *supra*, text attached to notes 71 and 72.
[108] They may render the imports unprofitable and have a chilling effect on exporters so as to scare them away from this market.
[109] See *supra*, text attached to notes 73–5.
[110] See, e.g., Yoav Dotan, "Legalising the Unlegaliseable: Terrorism, Secret Services and Judicial Review in Israel 1970–2001", in M. Hertogh and S. Halliday (eds), *Judicial Review and Bureaucratic Impact: International and Interdisciplinary Perspectives* (Cambridge University Press, 2004), pp. 193–4.

Would an administrative review based only on the "arbitrary and capricious standard" suffice? Since the WTO agreements fail to give any guidance on this point, one could probably assume that it would suffice, as long as **some** judicial review is conducted. In this, the AD and SCM Agreements fall short of the WTO Agreement on Government Procurement, which provides that challenge procedures should review "alleged breaches of the Agreement",[111] in other words, a legal scrutiny based on the provisions of the agreement. This is also the case with the independent review required by the WTO Agreement on Pre-Shipment Inspection.[112] Another conspicuous omission that should be corrected is the absence of a requirement for judicial review of safeguard measures.

In these respects, Israel's judicial review procedures, even those after 2005, go far beyond its international obligations: judicial review is also available for safeguard measures as well as for provisional duties of any kind. Indeed, we believe that such procedures are crucial for ensuring a balanced system of trade remedies that will not be abused by domestic protectionist interests. With all due respect to the WTO's review system, i.e. the inter-governmental dispute settlement mechanism managed by the Dispute Settlement Body, it cannot provide the type of immediate remedy that the national judicial review system can provide in the field of trade remedies. First of all, its use is not open to exporters and importers, only to governments. In order to benefit from it, an exporter needs to convince its government to take up the case and initiate proceedings. For instance, Israel has never initiated full proceedings within the WTO in any matter, including trade remedies, nor have any such proceedings ever been initiated against Israel (thanks, perhaps, to its effective domestic judicial review procedures). Second, the WTO proceedings are much more expensive, and they are likely to take longer to resolve and to enforce.

Thus, national review procedures are an important contribution to the international system of checks and balances of trade remedies, and the WTO should encourage and strive to improve such procedures among its various members.

---

[111] Article XX:2 of the Agreement on Government Procurement.

[112] Article 4 of this agreement requires WTO members to establish independent review procedures, and provides: "...the object of the review shall be to establish whether, in the course of the inspection in dispute, the parties to the dispute have complied with the provisions of this Agreement" (Art. 4(f)).

12

South Africa: a complicated, unpredictable, long and costly judicial review system

I Introduction

Owing to space considerations, this section will provide only a very brief overview of South Africa's trade remedies legislation and practices and will focus on the current position, rather than on historical perspectives.[1] During the 1970s and 1980s, South Africa was a closed economy. Several countries imposed trade sanctions against it as a result of its apartheid policy, and the South African government responded by imposing high tariffs to protect local industries, thus minimizing the need for anti-dumping and countervailing action. In the process, many industries were founded on the basis of import-replacement. Several of these industries had very small capacities, enough simply to satisfy domestic demand.[2] In 1977, the Minister of Economy and Trade (hereinafter

---

[1] For more detailed discussions on the evolution of South Africa's trade remedies legislation and practices, see Plant, 'The Anti-Dumping Regulations of the South African Tariff' (February) (1931) *Economia* 63–102; Petersen, 'Africa's Dumping Grounds: South Africa's Struggle against Unfair Trade' 14 (1996) *Boston University International Law Journal* 375–406; Brink, *A Theoretical Framework for South African Anti-Dumping Law* (Unpublished LLD thesis, University of Pretoria, 2004), at pp. 19–54, 690–721; Brink, 'Proposed Amendments to the Anti-Dumping Regulations: Are the Amendments in order?' (2006) Tralac Working Paper 21/2006; Brink, 'A Nutshell Guide to Anti-Dumping Action' 71 (2008) *Tydskrif vir Hedendaagse Romeins-Hollandse Reg (Journal for Contemporary Roman Dutch Law)* 255–71; Brink, 'A Nutshell Guide to Countervailing Action' 71 (2008) *Tydskrif vir Hedendaagse Romeins-Hollandse Reg* 255–71; Brink, 'A Nutshell Guide to Safeguard Action' 71 (2008) *Tydskrif vir Hedendaagse Romeins-Hollandse Reg* 540–55; Brink, '*Progress Office Machines v. South African Revenue Services* Case [2007] SCA 118 (RSA)' (2008) *De Jure* 644–8; Brink, 'Proposed Amendments to the Countervailing Regulations: Moving Forward or a Missed Opportunity?' (2009) Tralac Working Paper 2/2009.
[2] See, e.g., Board (1991) *Report No. 3066: Application for Increase in the Duty on Acetamidophenol (sic.)* (15/10/1991).

Minister), withdrew all anti-dumping duties after finding the domestic industry was adequately protected against both normal and unfair trade in the form of the formula duties then in place.[3]

In the early 1990s, South Africa's economy opened up, customs duties decreased significantly following South Africa's Uruguay Round negotiations and imports started to penetrate the market. With the shift towards free movement of goods, the government recognized that domestic companies would require protection against dumped and subsidized imports, especially since foreign producers often also enjoyed significant economy of scale advantages. The Board[4] and Customs Amendment Acts[5] were promulgated, changing the existing anti-dumping dispensation, including the establishment of the Directorate of Dumping Investigations at the Department of Trade and Industry (hereinafter DTI).[6] This Directorate conducts anti-dumping and countervailing duty investigations on behalf of the Board. Prior to this legislation, the Board dealt with dumping on an *ad hoc* basis.

South Africa's trade remedies legislation dates back to 1914.[7] The Board of Trade and Industry, responsible for investigating trade remedy applications, was set up in 1921.[8] The Board has been an independent statutory body since its establishment, consisting only of the Board members, with support staff seconded from the DTI. The first evidence that can be found of the use of any of the trade remedy instruments dates back to 1921.[9] Board Report No. 30[10] was the first ever report that dealt specifically with dumping, even though anti-dumping duties were imposed on other products prior to this report being issued.[11] From the inception of anti-dumping investigations worldwide, South Africa was a prolific actor in this field.[12] Thus, for example, 22 of the 37

---

[3] See Board (1978) *Report No. 1846: Annual Report for 1977* (13/03/1978), at 54.

[4] Board on Tariffs and Trade Amendment Act 1992 (Act 60 of 1992).

[5] Customs and Excise Amendment Act 1992 (Act 61 of 1992).

[6] See Brink, *A Theoretical Framework*, p. 24.   [7] See the discussion below on legislation.

[8] See *Government Gazette Notices 1044* and *1045* of 8 July 1921 and Board (1922), *Report No. 1: General* (27/03/1922), at 2. The permanent Board was set up in terms of the Board on Trade and Industries Act 33 of 1924. The Board consisted of a chairman and a maximum of 3 other members – see Board (1924), *Report No. 41: Dumping Paper* (24/10/1924).

[9] See Board (1924), *Report No. 42: Dumping or Unfair Competition* (18/11/1924) which indicates the imposition of anti-dumping duties on flour and wheat from Australia in 1921.

[10] Board (1923), *Report No. 30: The Dumping of Cement* (28/11/1923).

[11] See Board (1924), *Report No. 42*.

[12] Brink, *Anti-Dumping and Countervailing Investigations in South Africa* (Gosh, Maroelana, 2002), pp. 2–3.

anti-dumping duties imposed worldwide between 1948 and 1958 were imposed by South Africa,[13] while it also conducted more anti-dumping investigations during this period than all other reporting countries combined.[14]

South Africa was not a signatory to either of the Anti-Dumping Codes[15] or to the Subsidies Code, and thus not bound by international agreements regarding the methodology to be followed in protecting the domestic industry against unfair international trade. Relatively few anti-dumping duties were imposed between the withdrawal of the duties in 1978 and the creation of the Directorate for Dumping Investigations in 1992.[16]

The International Trade Administration Commission (hereinafter ITAC, or the Commission) was established in 2003 following the promulgation of the International Trade Administration Act (ITA Act),[17] and is an independent organ of state[18] reporting to and receiving its budget via the DTI. The ITA Act contains very little of a substantive nature. It provides that the Commission is the sole institution responsible for trade remedy investigations;[19] defines dumping,[20] normal value,[21] export price[22] and subsidies;[23] provides for a fair comparison of the normal value and the export price;[24] and for the treatment of confidential information.[25] It further provides that "any person" may request action regarding trade remedies and that the

[13] J. Michael Finger, "The Origins and Evolution", in Finger (ed.), *Antidumping: How it works and who gets Hurt* (Ann Arbor: University of Michigan Press, 1993), pp. 25–26; GATT (1958) *Anti-Dumping and Countervailing Duties*, p.14. In addition, South Africa also applied 7 "special duties".

[14] GATT (1958), at p. 14 indicates that South Africa conducted 211 investigations during this period. All other reporting countries (with the exception of Canada and New Zealand, which could impose anti-dumping duties without decree) conducted a total of 210 anti-dumping investigations during the same period.

[15] The first Anti-Dumping Code 1967 followed the Kennedy Round of GATT multilateral negotiations in 1967 and was signed by 17 parties. See Vermulst, *EC Anti-Dumping Law and Practice* (Sweet & Maxwell, 1996), p. 5. The Anti-Dumping Code 1979 followed the Tokyo Round of negotiations and was signed by 23 parties.

[16] A total of 41 anti-dumping duties were imposed during this period, following a total of 187 investigations. See the Board's *Annual Reports* for the years mentioned. See also Brink, *Anti-Dumping and Countervailing Investigations*, at 3.

[17] The International Trade Administration Act (ITA Act) 71 of 2002.

[18] Section 7(2) of the ITA Act provides that the Commission is independent and subject only to "the Constitution and the law"; Trade Policy Statements and Directives issued by the Minister in terms of s. 5; and any notice issued by the minister in terms of s. 6 (which relates to import and export control and is therefore irrelevant to the current discussion).

[19] Section 16 of the ITA Act. [20] Ibid., s. 1(2). [21] Ibid., s. 32(2)(b).

[22] Ibid., s. 32(2)(a). [23] Ibid., s. 32(2)(c). [24] Ibid., s. 32(3). [25] Ibid., ss. 33–7.

object of the Act is "to foster economic growth and development in order to raise incomes and promote investments".[26]

As a result of the lack of substantive issues addressed in the ITA Act, three sets of Regulations were promulgated, dealing with anti-dumping,[27] subsidies[28] and safeguards,[29] respectively. The Safeguard Regulations have subsequently been amended to make provision for agricultural safeguards.[30] Each of the regulations provide all substantive and procedural issues related to the particular trade remedy, and the regulations are generally WTO consistent, but provide more detail than any of the three relevant WTO agreements.

The Commission is fully responsible for all investigative aspects of all three trade remedies. It can also directly request the Commissioner for the South African Revenue Service to impose provisional measures for a period, and to the extent requested by the Commission. All final determinations are in the form of a recommendation to the Minister of Economy and Trade. If the minister accepts the Commission's negative determination, it will publish the termination notice. However, if the minister accepts an affirmative recommendation, he or she will request the Minister of Finance to impose definitive measures, and the latter will impose such measures for the period and at the level requested by the minister.

The Commission is headed by a full-time Chief Commissioner and Deputy Chief Commissioner, with (at present) six part-time Commissioners selected from the private and public sectors and labour together making up the Commission. The Commission is supported by its own staff and has an operations division and three technical divisions, one of which relates to trade remedies. Within the trade remedies division there are currently two directorates (Trade Remedies I and II) responsible for all aspects of trade remedy investigations, with investigations allocated according to capacity available in the directorates. Both directorates are responsible for

---

[26] Ibid., s. 2.

[27] The Anti-Dumping Regulations (hereinafter ADR), promulgated through *Government Gazette* 25684 of 14 November 2003. See Brink, 'Proposed Amendments to the Anti-Dumping Regulations' regarding proposed amendments to the ADR.

[28] The Countervailing Regulations (hereinafter CVR), promulgated through Notice 356 in *Government Gazette* 2747 of 15 April 2005. See Brink, 'Proposed Amendments to the Countervailing Regulations' regarding proposed amendments to the CUR.

[29] The Safeguard Regulations (hereinafter SGR), promulgated through Notice 1808 in *Government Gazette* 26715 of 27 August 2004.

[30] New Safeguard Regulations (hereinafter NSGR), promulgated through *Government Gazette* 27762 of 8 July 2005. Regarding the WTO-inconsistent nature of the NSGR, see Brink, 'Agricultural Safeguards in South Africa' (2006) Tralac Trade Brief 3/2006.

Table 12. 1. *Decision-making powers in the Commission*

Properly documented application	Senior Manager
Domestic industry verification	Senior Manager
Initiation of an investigation	Commission
Claims to confidentiality	Senior Manager; Commission
All deficiencies	Senior Manager
General extensions	Senior Manager
Extension granted beyond 2 weeks	Commission
Importer verifications	Senior Manager
Foreign verifications	Chief Commissioner
All verification reports	Senior Manager
Preliminary determination	Commission
Approval for oral hearings	Chief Commissioner
Final submission	Commission recommends to the Minister of Trade and Industry
Imposition of duty	Minister of Trade and Industry requests the Minister of Finance to impose duties
Implementation of duties	South African Revenue Service (SARS)
Publication of termination notice	Senior Manager

Source: Senior Manager Trade Remedies I; International Trade Administration Commission.

all aspects of investigations: dumping, subsidized exports or increased imports; injury; causality; and, in the case of safeguards, national interest.

Each directorate has a senior manager, a secretary, a case administrator and either 10 (TR I) or 11 (TR II) investigating officers, making a total of 27 staff. Both senior managers report to the Deputy Chief Commissioner, who, in turn, reports to the Chief Commissioner. At least three Commissioners must be present at any meeting to establish a quorum.[31] The Commission normally meets once a month, but special meetings may be called by the Chief Commissioner in urgent cases.

Notices relating to trade remedies, whether initiation, termination, or imposition of preliminary or definitive measures, are usually published in the general *Government Gazette* which appears on Fridays, except if

---

[31] Section 12(2) of the ITA Act. Note that the language is not clear, as it provides that "[a] majority of the members of the Commission present at a meeting of the Commission forms a quorum".

that is a public holiday, in which case the notice will appear on the last preceding working day. In some urgent cases, e.g. where a provisional measure is about to lapse, a definitive measure may be imposed through notice in a special *Gazette*.

II   Legislative framework for judicial review

South Africa's Constitution[32] provides the highest legal authority, and all legislation must be in conformity with it, failing which the legislation can be challenged before the Constitutional Court. The Constitution guarantees certain rights that are relevant to trade remedies, including access to information[33] and the right to fair administrative action.[34]

The Promotion of Access to Information Act (hereinafter PAIA)[35] was promulgated in 2000 to give effect to the constitutional principle of access to information, while the Promotion of Administrative Justice Act (hereinafter PAJA)[36] was promulgated simultaneously to enshrine the principle of administrative justice.

The ITA Act sets out the basic rules related to trade remedies and specifically provides that:

> A person affected by a determination, recommendation or decision of the Commission . . . may apply to a High court for a review of that determination, recommendation or decision.[37]

The Act further provides for appeals from the High Court to the Supreme Court of Appeal[38] and that ITAC may vary an order if it is found subsequent to a determination that such determination was based on ambiguity, obvious errors or omissions.[39]

All three sets of regulations specifically provide for the judicial review of any determination by the Commission, including "preliminary decisions or the Commission's procedures prior to the finalisation of an investigation"[40] if certain facts can be demonstrated.[41] This is a special

---

[32] Constitution Act 108 of 1996.   [33] Ibid., s. 32.   [34] Ibid., s. 33.
[35] Promotion of Access to Information Act 2 of 2000.
[36] Promotion of Administrative Justice Act 3 of 2000.
[37] Section 46(1) of the ITA Act.   [38] Ibid., s. 47(1).   [39] Ibid., s. 48(a).
[40] ADR 64.1; CVR 64.1; NSGR 22.
[41] It must be shown that the Commission has acted contrary to the provisions of the ITA Act or the regulations; that its action or omission has resulted in serious prejudice to the complaining party; and that such prejudice cannot be undone by the Commission's future final decision. See ADR 64.1; CVR 64.1; NSGR 22.

dispensation, as preliminary or interim decisions are not normally reviewable in South Africa.

There is no differentiation between the judicial review of trade remedy determinations and that of other governmental actions. There is, however, a special customs court (irrelevant to trade remedies) and a Competition Tribunal which reviews determinations of the Competition Commission,[42] but which deals with issues that overlap significantly with those of the Commission. The High Court has jurisdiction over all legal actions in South Africa, although smaller cases may be referred either to the Small Claims Court or the Magistrates Court (depending on the size of the claim). If leave to appeal is granted all High Court decisions may be appealed to the Supreme Court of Appeal. Constitutional issues may also be appealed to the Constitutional Court.

Although the High Court has seats in each of the nine provinces (and two in Gauteng), all reviews of Commission decisions are required to be lodged with the Gauteng Provincial Division in Pretoria, as the Commission is situated in Pretoria. Court Rules determine that all parties must provide an address (not *poste restante* or post office box) within eight km from the High Court, where all documents have to be served on such party,[43] in addition to the serving of the documents on the Registrar of the High Court.[44] In practice, lawyers may often be situated in a different city or province and simply appoint lawyers with offices close to the High Court in Pretoria to receive documents on their behalf.[45]

In each decision the High Court judge has to indicate whether he/she is of the opinion that the case is of interest to other judges or not. If it is of interest, it will be reported in the compilation of High Court decisions, but otherwise the case remains unreported. To date, no trade remedy High Court cases have been reported in the compilations. All Supreme Court of Appeal cases are reported, as are cases before the Constitutional Court. Accordingly, the *Brenco*,[46] *Progress Office Machines*,[47] *SATMC*[48]

---

[42] Section 27(1)(c) of the Competition Act 89 of 1998.

[43] Rule 19(3) of the Uniform Rules of Court.   [44] Ibid., Rule 53(3).

[45] This happened in e.g., *Rhône Poulenc* v. *Chairman of the Board on Tariffs and Trade* (Unreported case 98/6589 (T)); *Algorax* v. *ITAC* (Unreported case 18829/2001 (T)); *African Explosives Limited (AEL)* v. *ITAC* (Unreported case 15027/2006 (T)); *South African Tyre Manufacturers Conference (SATMC)* v. *ITAC* (Unreported case 45302/2007 (T)); *SCAW* v. *ITAC* (Unreported case 48829/2008 (T)).

[46] *Chairman of the Board on Tariffs and Trade* v. *Brenco* 2001 (4) SA 511 (SCA).

[47] *Progress Office Machines* v. *SARS* [2007] SCA 118 (RSA).

[48] *ITAC* v. *SATMC* [2011] ZASCA 137.

and *SCA W*[49] cases are the only ones reported to date, the first three being cases before the Supreme Court of Appeal and the latter a case before the Constitutional Court. Only constitutional issues may be argued before the Constitutional Court, i.e. it is not a final court of appeals in which appeals from the Supreme Court of Appeal may be heard. As will be indicated below, *ITAC* v. *SCA W* considered the constitutional question of the minister's powers in trade remedy investigations.

All judicial reviews are conducted under South Africa's municipal law. At present, the only substantive municipal legislation related to trade remedies are the ITA Act, Chapter VI of the Customs Act, the ADR, CVR and SGR, although constitutional principles regarding access to information and fair administrative procedure may also play a role, both as ensconced in the Constitution and in PAIA and PAJA. However, section 233 of the Constitution provides that in interpreting South African law cognizance must be taken of international law, and South African law must be interpreted in line with such international law, although where there are discrepancies between South African and international law, South African law will take precedence. The WTO Agreement has not been incorporated into South Africa's municipal law and is therefore not binding internally, i.e. while international obligations are incurred, it has not become part of municipal law. Despite this, the High Court has cited the Anti-Dumping and Safeguard Agreements in several judicial reviews (no judicial review has yet taken place of countervailing cases). In addition, in *Progress Office Machines*,[50] the Supreme Court of Appeal held that the Anti-Dumping Agreement was binding on South Africa, and this was followed in *SCA W* v. *ITAC*,[51] even though the WTO agreements "do not form part of South African law and as such are not directly enforceable through South African law".[52]

WTO jurisprudence plays a role in the interpretation of South Africa's trade remedies legislation. In the most recent High Court review of a trade remedies-related matter, both sides (i.e. the applicants and government) referred to WTO jurisprudence in support of their case.[53] Judges will accord some weight to WTO jurisprudence, but will finally still rely on South African legislation.

[49] *International Trade Administration Commission (ITAC)* v. *SCA W South Africa (Pty) Ltd* CCT 59/09 [2010] ZACC 6.
[50] *Progress Office Machines*, para. 6; Schlemmer, 'South Africa and the WTO Ten Years into Democracy' 29 (2004) *SAYIL* 125, at 135.
[51] *SCA W* v. *ITAC*, para. 36.   [52] Schlemmer, 'South Africa and the WTO', at 135.
[53] *SATMC* v. *ITAC*.

III   Types of judicial review proceedings

In essence there are three different types of reviews. Parties may apply for an interdict against the Commission to prevent it from forwarding its recommendation to the minister, but may not obtain an interdict against the Minister, as the Constitutional Court has ruled that the Minister's powers are derived from the Constitution and thus cannot be interrupted.[54] A party may also apply for a Commission or ministerial decision to be set aside. Although the courts have the power to so set aside a finding, in practice they will remand the matter to the Commission for further investigation.[55] A party may also approach the court to claim damages from the Commission and the Minister. To date, only one application for damages has been filed, but the parties decided not to pursue the matter.[56]

IV   Reviewable determinations

All trade remedy decisions may be reviewed by the High Court. As indicated above, the different sets of regulations provide for the review of interim determinations in addition to the review of final determinations. In cases brought by the domestic industry where no definitive measures were imposed, the action is typically brought against the Commission and the Minister, while in cases brought by importers and/or exporters in instances where definitive measures were imposed, the Minister of Finance is also cited as a respondent. In *AEL*,[57] the Commission revoked its decision to initiate an investigation on the basis that the applicant had knowingly submitted false and misleading information. This revocation decision was taken on review to the High Court, which found that the applicant had not submitted false or misleading information. The High Court ordered the Commission to resume the investigation. In *Degussa*,[58] the applicant successfully challenged ITAC's decision to impose a provisional safeguard measure, and the High Court found that there was no basis for the imposition of such measures.

In *SCAW v. ITAC*, the Commission argued that no interdict could be granted against it submitting its recommendation for the termination of

[54] See *ITAC* v. *SCAW*.   [55] See, e.g., *Algorax* v. *ITAC; SATMC* v. *ITAC*.
[56] See *SATMC* v. *ITAC*.   [57] *AEL.* v. *ITAC*.
[58] *Degussa Africa (Pty) Ltd* v. *ITAC* (Unreported case 22264/2007 (T)).

anti-dumping duties to the Minister, as its determination did not constitute a decision that could be reviewed by a court, since the decision
whether anti-dumping duties should be terminated is made by the
Minister.[59] The Court, however, found that the Commission's recommendation "is an important jurisdictional fact for any action the
[Minister] might decide to take",[60] and that the "recommendation is
certainly a decision or step that affects the rights of others and must
therefore be regarded as an administrative action".[61] This confirms that
not only final determinations, but also the procedures prior to the final
determination are reviewable, as provided for in the regulations.[62]

To date, judicial review has taken place of both original investigations
and sunset reviews, but no cases have been lodged regarding new shipper
or changed circumstances reviews. Interdicts were also obtained in at
least two cases, preventing the Commission from forwarding its final
determination to the Minister for finalization. However, most recently
the Constitutional Court in our view incorrectly determined that no
interdict may be granted in such circumstances, as it prevents the
Minister from performing his/her duties under law.[63]

The same procedural rules apply to all cases, regardless of whether
related to trade remedies or not. All cases must be lodged within 180 days
from the date of publication of the determination, while parties must
give the Commission at least 30 days' notice prior to filing any judicial
review proceeding relating to preliminary or final anti-dumping

---

[59] *SCAW* v. *ITAC*, para. 93.   [60] Ibid., para. 94.

[61] Ibid., para. 95, with reference to *Oosthuizen's Transport* v. *MEC, Road Traffic Matters
Mpumalanga* 2008 (2) SA 570 (T); *Grey's Marine Hout Bay* v. *Minister of Public Works*
2005 (6) SA 313 (SCA); *Algorax* v. *ITAC*.

[62] ADR 64.1; CVR 64.1; NSGR 22.

[63] It is submitted that it is not so much the Constitutional Court which made an incorrect
decision, but that the respondents, i.e. the domestic industry, had incorrectly argued
their case. The Constitutional Court held that the Minister had significant powers in
investigations and that the Commission merely made a recommendation to the
Minister, who then had to make a final determination on the basis of the information
before him, and that the Minister had the power to accept or reject a recommendation or
to remand to the Commission for further investigation. It is submitted that this position
is incorrect, as the Minister has no powers in terms of the ITA Act other than to instruct
the Commission to conduct certain investigations, while he or she has the powers in
terms of the Customs and Excise Act 91 of 1964 to request the Minister of Finance to
impose a definitive trade remedy measure. Accordingly, it is submitted that the
Commission has absolute powers in reaching a final decision and, therefore, parties
should be allowed to seek an interdict of its decisions.

determinations.[64] No such requirement exists as regards countervailing duty or safeguard determinations. Cases can take up to four years to be heard by the High Court,[65] while an appeal of the matter can take another year.

Parties to the review before the High Court may appeal any finding of the High Court to the Supreme Court of Appeal, but only if the High Court grants permission for such appeal under Uniform Court Rule 49(1)(b). Such an appeal must then be lodged within 15 days from the date at which the High Court's ruling is made available.

V   Parties eligible to bring a case

Any interested party may lodge a case with the High Court. However, to date, almost all cases have been lodged by the domestic industry, with only one case lodged by an importer[66] and one by an exporter,[67] while the holding company of the importer and the importer combined lodged the only review of a safeguard measure to date.[68] Exporters without domestic presence must provide security for any court-related costs that may be incurred. This applies both to exporters lodging reviews and those who want to oppose reviews lodged by South African parties.

All parties that have an interest in the matter must be included in the review application. This requirement is to ensure that all parties whose rights may be affected by the verdict have the opportunity to be heard. Thus, in the most recent judicial review, the applicants (the domestic producers) had to include all cooperating importers and exporters as respondents and to ensure that all relevant documents were served on each party, including on the exporters in China.

VI   Competent courts

All judicial review cases on trade remedy matters are to be heard by the High Court. As far as territorial jurisdiction of the High Court is concerned, the Commission being located in Pretoria, all reviews have to be instituted in the Gauteng North (i.e. Pretoria) provincial division of the High Court, regardless of where the applicant is domiciled.

---

[64] ADR 64.2.   [65] *SATMC* v. *ITAC*.   [66] *Progress Office Machines* v. *SARS*.
[67] *Ranbaxy* v. *Chairman of the Board on Tariffs and Trade* (Unreported case 659/98 TPD).
[68] *Degussa* v. *ITAC*.

VII   Procedural steps

The deadline for the initiation of a judicial review proceeding is 180 days from either the date that all internal remedies[69] have been exhausted or, where no such remedies exist, the date on which the person concerned became aware of the action and the reasons for it, or might reasonably have been expected to have become aware of the action and the reasons.[70] For cases pertaining to anti-dumping determinations, the Commission must be informed at least 30 days in advance of any impending action,[71] although this requirement may be waived by the High Court where the applicant can prove urgency.[72] No such notification requirement exists in respect of countervailing and safeguards determinations.

Judicial review is conducted on the basis of notice of motion.[73] The notice of motion shall set out the decision or proceedings to be reviewed and shall be supported by an affidavit setting out the grounds, facts and circumstances upon which the applicant relies to have the decision or proceedings set aside or corrected.[74] The notice of motion must be served on the registrar of the High Court in Pretoria and on each party to which it pertains.[75] This is normally done by registered post or physical delivery. In the case of foreign interested parties, this would normally be done by courier. All respondents must indicate whether they will oppose the motion, in which case a cost order may be made against them if the Court rules in favour of the applicant. South Africa follows the British system whereby there is a distinction between the bar (advocates) and the side bar (lawyers or attorneys). Although lawyers

---

[69] Section 48 of the ITA Act provides as follows:

> The Commission may, of its own accord or on application by a person affected by a determination, recommendation or decision of the Commission, vary or rescind that determination, recommendation or decision–
> (a) in which there is ambiguity, or an obvious error or omission, but only to the extent of correcting that ambiguity, error or omission; or
> (b) erroneously sought in the absence of a party affected by it;
> (c) made as a result of a mistake common to all of the parties to the proceedings.

Accordingly, where a party is of the opinion that the Commission's determination was based on ambiguity or an obvious error, it may request the Commission to vary its determination to the extent that the ambiguity or obvious error is addressed without having to turn to a court for judicial review.

[70] Section 7(1) of the Promotion of Administrative Justice Act 3 of 2000.
[71] ADR 64.2.   [72] See *Degussa v. ITAC.*   [73] Rule 6(1) of the Uniform Rules of Court.
[74] Ibid., Rule 53(2).   [75] Ibid., Rule 6(2).

also have standing in the High Court, they will usually only appear in mundane cases, and parties will normally appoint advocates to represent them.[76] Lawyers will do most of the preparatory work, while the advocates will draft the final documents and argue the case before the judges. In complicated cases, parties will often appoint a senior counsel, assisted by one or two juniors. The Commission is always represented by the State Attorney, who will then also appoint advocates from the bar to represent the Commission. Advocates do not have to be members of the Pretoria bar, and it is not uncommon to have advocates from the Johannesburg bar appear before the High Court in Pretoria.

Once the applicant has lodged its review application, it may request discovery in terms of Rule 35(1) of the Uniform Court Rules. Such discovery must be made by the party in possession of the documents within 20 days, or the time stated in any order of a judge, and must specify separately which documents are made available; which documents he/she has a valid objection to produce; and such documents and tape recordings which he/she had but no longer has in his/her possession at the date of the affidavit.[77]

Where any party believes that there are, in addition to the documents or tape recordings disclosed as per above, other documents or tape recordings which may be relevant to any matter in question in the possession of any party thereto, such party may give notice to the latter requiring him/her to make such documents available for inspection.[78] This process can take a long time, especially where the Commission does not furnish the full record, as happened in the *SATMC* case.[79] The full and final record was only received more than a year after the court had instructed the Commission to make the full record available. The applicant will then have the opportunity to scrutinize the documents and may update its founding affidavits.

Once the review application has been lodged, the respondents normally have 15 days in which to indicate whether they will oppose the motion.[80] Any respondent wishing to oppose the matter must serve the necessary affidavits he/she may desire in response to the applicant's

---

[76] Both applicants and respondents have always appointed advocates in all trade remedy judicial reviews to date.

[77] Rule 35(2) of the Uniform Rules of Court.   [78] Ibid., Rule 35(3).

[79] *SATMC v. ITAC.*

[80] Rule 53(5)(a) of the Uniform Rules of Court. The days from 16 December to 15 January (both inclusive) are not counted – see Rule 19(1).

allegations on the registrar and the applicants within 30 days.[81] Where
the founding affidavits were amended following discovery, the respondents will have 30 days from the date of service of the amended founding
affidavits. The High Court may grant extensions in complex cases.[82]

There are no proscriptions regarding the duration of a judicial review
proceeding. South African judicial review proceedings take a long time
and probably fall short of conforming to Article 13 of the Anti-Dumping
Agreement, which requires that judicial review be *prompt*. In the most
recent review, the review application was lodged on 1 October 2007, but
the case was only heard by the High Court on 7 and 8 June 2010.
Judgment was rendered on 18 June 2010, nearly three years after the
case was lodged. Leave to appeal was granted to the Commission on 8
October 2010, and the case was set down for hearing before the Supreme
Court of Appeal from 7 September 2011, effectively four years after the
case was lodged.

Legal fees for judicial review tend to be high by South African
standards, and the costs to the applicants and the Commission each
exceeded US$500,000 in the most recent case, such costs being
lawyers' and advocates' fees. Other than a small stamp duty, there are
no court fees. The Court may give a cost order, whereby the losing party
has to pay the taxed costs of the other party, which means that the
winner can generally recoup between 40 and 50 per cent of its total legal
expenses.

VIII   Appeal

Decisions of the High Court may be appealed either to the full bench of
the High Court, i.e. three judges presiding, or to the Supreme Court of
Appeal.[83] In practice, three of the four trade remedies reviews that have
been appealed, were appealed to the Supreme Court of Appeal,[84] while

---

[81]   Ibid., Rule 53(5)(b).

[82]   In *SATMC* v. *ITAC*, the Commission took more than six months to submit its opposing
affidavits, and this was condoned by the High Court.

[83]   Section 47(1) of the ITA Act provides that "[a]n appeal against a decision of the High
Court in respect of a matter within its jurisdiction in terms of section 46 lies to the
Supreme Court of Appeal, or the Constitutional Court, only with leave to appeal, and
subject to their respective rules." Subsection (4) further provides that: "Section 21 (1A)
to (3)(e) of the Supreme Court Act, 1959 (Act No. 59 of 1959), read with the changes
required by the context, applies to an application to the Supreme Court of Appeal for
leave to appeal under this Act."

[84]   *Chairman BTT* v. *Brenco; Progress Office Machines* v. *SARS; ITAC* v. *SATMC*.

the other case was appealed to the Constitutional Court on a constitutional issue. It is not clear whether any appeals would ever be made to a full bench of the High Court, as it appears that such practice is limited mostly to criminal proceedings.

Only active parties to the dispute, i.e. parties who made representations in the lower court, may appeal the lower court's decision and only issues of law can be appealed. Application for leave to appeal must be filed within 15 days from the date the High Court's verdict was handed down, and the reasons for the verdict have been made available.[85] The application for leave to appeal is normally heard by the judge who presided at the trial.[86] If leave to appeal is granted, the appeal itself must be filed within a further 60 days, unless an extension is granted.[87] The final affidavits must be filed within a further 40 days, failing which the respondent can maintain that the application has lapsed.[88] The Supreme Court of Appeal may approve, reverse or partially approve the lower court's decision. If the lower court's decision is approved by the Supreme Court of Appeal, that becomes the final decision on the dispute.

The question whether an appeal against a decision of the High Court may proceed directly to the Constitutional Court is governed by section 167(6)(b) of the Constitution read in conjunction with Rule 19 of the Uniform Court Rules. The constitutionally prescribed standard is whether it is in the interests of justice for the Constitutional Court to hear an appeal. In *Khumalo*,[89] the Constitutional Court held that it is not a jurisdictional requirement for such an appeal that the matter must involve a "judgment or order" within the meaning of section 20(1) of the Supreme Court Act,[90] but pointed out that it will not often be in the interests of justice for the Constitutional Court to entertain appeals against interlocutory rulings which do not have a final effect on the dispute between the parties.[91] Any application for leave to appeal direct to the Constitutional Court must be lodged with the registrar of the High Court within 15 days of the order against which the appeal is sought.

---

[85] Rule 49(1)(b) of the Uniform Rules of Court.   [86] Ibid., Rule 49(1)(e).

[87] Ibid., Rule 49(6)(a).   [88] Ibid., Rule 49(7)(d).

[89] *Khumalo and Others* v. *Holomisa* [2002] ZACC 12; 2002 (5) SA 401 (CC); 2002 (8) BCLR 771(CC), at para. 8.

[90] Supreme Court Act 59 of 1959.   [91] *Khumalo and Others* v. *Holomisa*, at para. 8.

IX   Standard of review

While judicial review proceedings may be initiated under either the ITA Act[92] or any of the three sets of Regulations,[93] any administrative action, which includes the failure to act,[94] may be challenged under the provisions of PAJA. This includes, *inter alia*, reviews based on unfair procedure, decisions influenced by errors of law or made in violation of law, decisions affected by bias or perceived bias, and where decisions are not rationally connected to the information before the authority. PAJA provides the following grounds for judicial review:

> (2) A court or tribunal has the power to judicially review an administrative action if –
> (*a*) the administrator who took it –
>   (i) was not authorised to do so by the empowering provision;
>   (ii) acted under a delegation of power which was not authorised by the empowering provision; or
>   (iii) was biased or reasonably suspected of bias;
> (*b*) a mandatory and material procedure or condition prescribed by an empowering provision was not complied with;
> (*c*) the action was procedurally unfair;
> (*d*) the action was materially influenced by an error of law;
> (*e*) the action was taken –
>   (i) for a reason not authorised by the empowering provision;
>   (ii) for an ulterior purpose or motive;
>   (iii) because irrelevant considerations were taken into account or relevant considerations were not considered;
>   (iv) because of the unauthorised or unwarranted dictates of another person or body;
>   (v) in bad faith; or
>   (vi) arbitrarily or capriciously;
> (*f*) the action itself –
>   (i) contravenes a law or is not authorised by the empowering provision; or
>   (ii) is not rationally connected to –
>   (aa) the purpose for which it was taken;
>   (bb) the purpose of the empowering provision;
>   (cc) the information before the administrator; or
>   (dd) the reasons given for it by the administrator;

---

[92] Section 46(1) of the ITA Act provides that "[a] person affected by a determination, recommendation or decision of the Commission in terms of section 16 or 17 or this Chapter, may apply to a High Court for a review of that determination, recommendation or decision."

[93] ADR 64.1; CVR 64.1; NSGR 22.   [94] Section 6(2)(g) of PAJA, as quoted in the text.

(g) the action concerned consists of a failure to take a decision;

(h) the exercise of the power or the performance of the function authorised by the empowering provision, in pursuance of which the administrative action was purportedly taken, is so unreasonable that no reasonable person could have so exercised the power or performed the function; or

(i) the action is otherwise unconstitutional or unlawful.[95]

The specific reference that reviews may be brought in cases where the authority's decision is not rationally connected to the facts before it[96] indicates that courts may not only review procedural issues, but may also analyse whether the authority properly considered the facts before it.

In principle, however, courts will not lightly interfere with a decision reached by an authority, but will grant a significant degree of deference to the investigating authority's determinations. The courts have confirmed that the Commission enjoys significant discretion,[97] but this does not mean that a court cannot undertake an analysis of the facts before the Commission to determine whether it has properly applied its mind to the matter before it.[98] Thus, in *Algorax*, the judge, after discussing certain facts in the investigation, held that:

> I find the use of an average dumping margin[99] totally irrational. It had the effect of wiping out or cancelling out evidence of dumping in 16 countries. A positive dumping margin in one country may have a technical explanation, but positive dumping margins in 16 countries point to deliberate dumping as part of a marketing strategy. I cannot understand how one can say that an exporter is, on average, not a dumper. Obviously a producer who can export 93% of his production is not likely to dump most of his exports.[100]

In *SATMC*, the High Court ruled in favour of the applicants, i.e. the domestic industry, after finding that the Commission had failed to consider whether sales in China had been made "under market conditions" and that the determination was separate and distinct from the finding as to whether sales were made in the ordinary course of trade. Its

---

[95] Section 6(2) of PAJA.   [96] Section 6(2)(f)(ii)(cc) of PAJA.

[97] See, e.g., *Association of Electric Cable Manufacturers of South Africa (AECMSA)* v. *ITAC* (Unreported case 33807/2005 (T)), 8 and 14.

[98] See ibid., at 15, where the judge found that "in my mind [the Commission] applied its mind to all the relevant issues at stake and exercised its discretion properly".

[99] Note that this refers to the average margin of dumping for several countries, and not on any of the three bases provided for in the Anti-Dumping Agreement.

[100] *Algorax* v. *ITAC*, at 13.

failure to first determine whether sales were made under market conditions was therefore reviewable.

X Remedies

Essentially there are only two remedies available to an applicant, with a possibility of a third intervention. The first is to obtain an interdict against the Commission, the Minister of Economy and Trade or the Minister of Finance.[101] The second is to have a case remanded by the Court to the Commission for reconsideration, while the third is a claim for damages against the Commission.

Although theoretically the High Court has the power to issue injunctive relief, it will seldom, if ever, use this discretion, as it regards the Commission as a technical expert authority[102] with whose decisions it will seldom interfere. Accordingly, the Commission enjoys a considerable margin of discretion in conducting its investigations. However, the High Court may remand a matter to the Commission, with or without guidelines as to what ought to be done. Thus, in *Algorax*, the High Court specifically indicated that in determining the likelihood of whether dumping would recur if the anti-dumping duties were to be removed, the Commission had to take into consideration only those "countries where there are positive dumping margins and establish, if dumping occurs there, whether it is likely to occur in the SACU".[103] The High Court may also indicate the time frame within which the Commission has to finalize its modified determination. Thus, in *SATMC*, it indicated that the Commission had to give effect to the Court's ruling within a period of four months.

XI Overall assessment of the effectiveness of judicial review in South Africa

Too few trade remedy determinations have been subjected to judicial review for us to be able to assess the effectiveness of judicial review in South Africa. To the best of our knowledge, so far there have been only 10 judicial review

---

[101] Note, however, the Constitutional Court's ruling in *ITAC* v. *SCAW*, where it indicated that no such interdict could be granted. See, on the other hand, the author's comments in this regard in *supra* note 63.

[102] See *Algorax* v. *ITAC*, at 14.

[103] Ibid. The judge, in the next paragraph, also stated that "[t]o negate the *prima facie* evidence of deliberate dumping by applying average dumping is, in my view, an exercise in obfuscation that defies logic".

proceedings[104] (excluding cases filed but not proceeded with), of which one related to the duration of duties and was aimed more at the South African Revenue Service than the Commission.[105] Three cases were appealed to the Supreme Court of Appeal[106] and one to the Constitutional Court.[107] Of the 10 proceedings initiated against it, the Commission lost seven in the High Court. It also lost two of the cases that were finalized by the Supreme Court of Appeal, including one in which it had prevailed at the High Court stage, while it won the *SATMC* case in the Supreme Court of Appeal after having lost in the High Court. The Commission prevailed in the one case brought against it before the Constitutional Court. These statistics confirm that although few cases have been brought, the chances of successfully challenging the Commission are high. On the other hand, the Commission has failed to implement several of the decisions that went against it.[108]

However, this does not mean that the Court's decisions were necessarily correct. We have explained elsewhere that the Supreme Court of Appeal incorrectly ruled in favour of the applicant in the *Progress Office Machines* and the *SATMC* cases, in favour of the Commission in the *SATMC* case, and that the Constitutional Court incorrectly ruled in the Commission's favour in *SCAW*.[109] It is submitted that the incorrect decision rendered by the Constitutional Court is largely owing to the incorrect arguments submitted on behalf of the domestic industry. In *Progress Office Machines*, the Supreme Court of Appeal disregarded clear legislation that specifically provided that a definitive duty would remain in place "for a period of five years from the date of the publication of the Commission's final recommendation" and despite expert testimony being submitted by trade remedy experts in other jurisdictions.[110] In

---

[104] *AECMSA v. ITAC; AEL v. ITEC; Algorax v. ITAC; Brenco v. Chairman of the Board on Tariffs and Trade* (Unreported case 2000 (T)); *Degussa v. ITAC; Progress Office Machines v. SARS; Rhône Poulenc v. Chairman; Ranbaxy v. Chairman; SATMC v. ITAC;* and *SCAW v. ITAC.*

[105] *Progress Office Machines v. SARS.*

[106] *Chairman BTT v. Brenco; Progress Office Machines v. SARS; ITAC v. SATMC.*

[107] *ITAC v. SCAW.*

[108] The decisions in the *Algorax* and *Degussa* cases were never implemented, while the decision in the *AEL* case was incorrectly implemented nearly two years later.

[109] It is submitted that the incorrect decision rendered by the Constitutional Court is largely the result of incorrect arguments submitted on behalf of the domestic industry. See the author's comments in note 63 above.

[110] See Brink *'Progress Office Machines'* 'Duration of Anti-Dumping Duties Shortened following Court Order in South Africa' 3:(6) (2007) *Global Trade and Customs Journal* 217 for a discussion of the Supreme Court of Appeal case in *Progress Office Machines.*

the *SATMC* matter, the Supreme Court of Appeal confused two of the definitions of normal value. It also disregarded information that had been submitted before the Commission, finding that no information in support of the Chinese exporters had been submitted.[111]

There is a significant degree of deference to the Commission's determinations, including its verifications, its evaluation of the facts, its failure to ensure that parties have submitted proper non-confidential submissions, its adjudication of adjustments, and other issues. In addition, judicial review is often too protracted, especially where one of the parties appeals to the Supreme Court of Appeal.

In South Africa, virtually all judicial review proceedings to date have been brought by the domestic industry, which does not have access to the WTO dispute settlement mechanism. Only one case (*Ranbaxy*) was lodged exclusively by an exporter. This case, which centred around the Commission's refusal to grant a specific adjustment requested, was decided (in our view, correctly), in the Commission's favour. The *Degussa* case was lodged jointly by the exporter and the importer, who convinced the High Court that the Commission had incorrectly imposed provisional safeguard measures on the same day the investigation was initiated.[112]

The South African judicial review system takes at least as long as the dispute settlement process at the WTO, and there may be less access to all relevant information. In addition, WTO dispute settlement proceedings are significantly more substantive and properly consider the merits of the case, rather than only the procedures followed. On the other hand, although judicial review in South Africa is relatively expensive, it may still be a more affordable option compared to the costs incurred in WTO dispute settlement proceedings.

Three formal disputes have been initiated against South Africa in the WTO,[113] but none of them progressed to the panel stage. Two disputes

---

[111]   This followed despite the Supreme Court of Appeal itself referring to such information. See Brink (2011a) 'No Need to Investigate China's Market Economy Status in Anti-Dumping Investigations', Tralac Trade Brief (forthcoming).

[112]   This case was heard by the High Court on an urgent basis and was finalized, more quickly than the time taken on average to resolve WTO dispute resolutions.

[113]   WT/DS168/1 South Africa – *Anti-Dumping Duties on Certain Pharmaceutical Products From India* (13/04/1999); WT/DS288/1 South Africa – *Definitive Anti-Dumping Measures on Blanketing from Turkey* (15/04/2003); WT/DS374/1 South Africa – *Anti-Dumping Measures on Uncoated Woodfree Paper* (16/05/2008). See also Brink, 'South Africa's Experience with International Dispute Settlement', in Shaffer and

were resolved during consultations and the third[114] was pursued through review in the High Court.

XII Concluding remarks and suggestions for improvement

In our view, the administrative judiciary is the right place where the judicial review of trade remedy determinations should be conducted in South Africa, but the system needs to be modified to allow judges to conduct effective judicial review. An ideal judicial review system is one where judges have the opportunity substantively to review the details of the determinations, rather than frequently deferring to the authority.

The current state of affairs is far from ideal with respect to the judicial review of trade remedy determinations. There are several reasons for this. First, the courts seldom inquire into the details of the investigating authority's determinations. Second, too much deference is accorded to the investigating authority's determinations. Third, court proceedings are far too long, in part because it takes much time to resolve issues pertaining to counsel's access to confidential information in the investigation file. It would therefore be useful to reform South Africa's system for the judicial review of trade remedy determinations.

With respect to reforming the system, we propose that judicial review of trade remedy determinations be conducted by specialized courts. In our view, there is no need to create a new court for this, since the Competition Tribunal, which is a review body for decisions of the Competition Commission, provides an appropriate forum for the judicial review of trade remedy determinations. Decisions of the Competition Tribunal may be appealed to the Competition Appeal Court. The Competition Tribunal deals with several issues which are similar to trade remedies, and therefore it should not be so difficult to train its officers to enable them to conduct the judicial review of trade remedy determinations. Moving the judicial review of trade remedy determinations to the Competition Tribunal will also have other advantages. Counsel for parties before the Competition Tribunal is given access to the confidential information submitted by opposing parties, and the procedure is significantly faster but much less costly than in the High Court. We acknowledge that this institutional reform would necessitate an increase in the Competition Tribunal's budget because of increased workload, but this would be worth the enhanced efficiency that would be

Meléndez-Ortiz (eds), *Dispute Settlement at the WTO* (Cambridge University Press, 2011), pp. 251–74.

[114] See *Ranbaxy* v. *Chairman BTT*.

obtained. However, the increased budget may be offset against savings incurred in judicial reviews before the High Court.

However, if the High Court continues to conduct the judicial review of trade remedy determinations, in our view, it would be beneficial to the system if the Court changed its practice with respect to judicial economy. Currently, the Court makes excessive use of judicial economy, which undermines applicants' right to have an effective resolution to their dispute. In the recent *SATMC* review, for example, the applicants presented at least 10 claims before the High Court, but the Court ruled on only two of them, without mentioning the other claims at all. Justice would be better served, in our view, if the Court moved away from this practice.

13

Pakistan: an evolving judicial review system

FAIZULLAH KHILJI AND MAZHAR BANGASH[*]

I Introduction

Even though legislation authorizing anti-dumping and countervail action has been on its statute books since 1983,[1] Pakistan's experience with the use of trade defence instruments is a fairly recent one, going back no further than 2002. When viewed from the perspective of domestic judicial review, this experience is nonetheless an eventful one. And it is this very experience that is the subject of the present chapter.

The discussion begins with this introductory section, which explains the background to the promulgation of Pakistan's trade defence laws and the mechanism for the administration of these laws. The next section explores the experience with the domestic judicial review process, describing the Appellate Tribunal constituted for the purpose of adjudicating trade remedy cases, its limited availability and, in the absence of the Tribunal, the interventions by the superior courts in response to petitions by the aggrieved party as a part of the country's normal judicial process.[2] A concluding section draws applicable lessons from the experience with the domestic judicial review process.

[*] The authors are grateful to a number of friends for helpful comments and assistance. Omar Moeen helped authenticate developments at the Commission and Imran Zia and Khizar Hayat made useful suggestions. Saad Shuaib Wyne, Rahmat Kamal and Mahwish Malik carefully read through a number of drafts, filling in the gaps and pointing out errors. Finally, Müslüm Yilmaz's conscientious and meticulous reading of the final version led to improvements in both style and substance. The authors alone are responsible for the views expressed, errors and omissions.
[1] This Pakistan law was the Import of Goods (Anti-Dumping and Countervailing Duties) Ordinance, 1983 (III of 1983), which was repealed in 2000 on the promulgation of Pakistan Anti-Dumping Duties Ordinance 2000; see section 76 of the latter Ordinance. Rules to aid in the implementation of the 1983 Law were never made, and the Law was never used.
[2] For an explanation on "superior courts", see section III.2 below.

II   Background to the promulgation of Pakistan's trade defence laws

Sustained moves over the late 1990s to liberalize trade had exposed the domestic industry to enhanced levels of international competition. A new consciousness for the need and usefulness of applying the WTO trade defence agreements in Pakistan developed as a result.[3] The implementation of these WTO agreements in Pakistan could be expected to provide the affected domestic industry with a well-defined recourse to legal action to defend itself against potentially "unfair" developments in its international trade. The domestic industry recognized the need for these instruments to enable it to function effectively in the new trading environment that was a characteristic of the increasingly globalized world economy. Pakistan's 1983 Anti-Dumping Law, having been promulgated some 11 years before the counterpart WTO Anti-Dumping Agreement (hereinafter AD Agreement) came into existence, naturally could not be expected to reflect the provisions of the AD Agreement, much less be consistent with it. This 1983 law had never been put to use and tested. The 1983 Anti-Dumping and Countervail Law clearly did not meet the needs of the domestic industry in a fast-changing international trade environment.

Pakistan's legal system does not recognize international treaty obligations unless the provisions of any such international treaty are first enacted as law in Pakistan, or incorporated into the existing laws of the country.[4] Even though the Government of Pakistan was a signatory to the Uruguay Round agreements in Marrakesh, thereby making Pakistan a founder member of the WTO, for the WTO trade defence agreements to have legal force in Pakistan it was necessary that laws which mirror the provisions of these agreements be enacted in Pakistan. For this reason, only new domestic legislation could give legal force to the provisions of the WTO trade defence agreements.

---

[3] WTO trade defence agreements in the present context refer to the following three treaties: WTO Agreement on Implementation of Article VI of the General Agreement on Tariffs and Trade 1994, Agreement on Subsidies and Countervailing Measures and Agreement on Safeguards. See World Trade Organization, *The Legal Texts* (Cambridge University Press, 1999).

[4] See *Société Générale de Surveillance SA* v. *Pakistan* (2002) SCMR 1694. Also, Article 175(2) of the Constitution of the Islamic Republic of Pakistan (hereinafter Constitution of Pakistan) specifies that a court has no jurisdiction unless conferred by or under any law or by the Constitution itself.

A three-year trade liberalization programme initiated by the government in 1999, to bring the country's trade regulation and tariffs more closely into line with both a global trade regime that was liberalizing fast, as well as with the requirements of the structural change in Pakistan's economy, also provided an opportunity to develop new domestic legislation that would fully reflect and be consistent with the WTO trade defence agreements. Thus, Pakistan's trade remedy laws, covering anti-dumping, countervailing and safeguards actions, were promulgated between 2000–2, and the respective rules to help implement these laws were made in 2001–3. These instruments provided a trade defence mechanism, consonant with the country's WTO obligations, as part of a larger trade liberalization programme that sharply reduced customs tariffs and also simplified customs and other procedures for international trade.

The new trade defence laws were to be administered by an existing organization, Pakistan's National Tariff Commission (hereinafter Commission). This Commission had been set up in 1990 to consider likely assistance to the domestic industry in order to enhance the latter's competitiveness. The Commission was to achieve its objective chiefly through examining options for limited protection for a specific industry to help the latter achieve competitiveness and viability. Possibilities for protection lay mainly in appropriate adjustments in customs tariffs for a limited period of time to enable the affected industry to establish or re-establish itself. In those cases where the Commission was satisfied that grounds for the provision of such assistance existed, it was to recommend specific measures to the government.

The Commission functioned as an autonomous, quasi-judicial organization under a special law, the National Tariff Commission Act of 1990 (hereinafter NTC Act). The Commission consisted of three members, of which the chairman was to be of a rank not less than a permanent secretary to the federal government. This NTC Act laid out, *inter alia*, the constitution of the Commission, the scope of its work, the due process it was mandated to apply, and its powers.[5] The Commission was specifically granted the powers of a civil court in matters of calling for evidence and enforcing attendance of witnesses. The NTC Act also provides for transparency in its due process in arriving at its findings or recommendations. The Commission's approach to its task was to consider all points of view, invariably by inviting all those having an interest

---

[5] See NTC Act, various sections.

in the matter to a hearing, and also to make submissions in support of thereof.

The Commission's functions under the NTC Act also specifically included advising the government on "measures to counter dumping and other unfair measures adopted in respect of import and sale of foreign goods in Pakistan".[6] Rules that would enable the application and implementation of this provision were never made, much as had been the case with the 1983 Anti-dumping and Countervail Law. An explanation for the dormant nature of these provisions may well lie in the fact that, with the high tariff regimes of the 1980s and early 1990s, the industry did not particularly seem to need recourse to any anti-dumping action, and thus the Commission never had the occasion to proceed under these anti-dumping provisions. In any event, with the coming into force of the WTO-consistent Pakistan Anti-Dumping Duties Ordinance 2000 (hereinafter AD Ordinance 2000), this particular provision became redundant and was repealed.[7]

The standard laid down in the NTC Act, in the context of the Commission's original mandate to enhance competitiveness of Pakistan's industry, and applied by the Commission in making its findings and recommendations in that regard, was a threefold one. It required that the Commission satisfy itself: first, that the product to be protected was a quality product; second, that the protection recommended was needed only for a limited period of time; and third, that the additional cost to the consumer as a result of any protection that was being recommended should not be "excessive". Arguably, the standard could be read as including a public interest element.

Pakistan's new trade defence laws brought about important changes in the Commission's role, adding to its responsibilities the task of administering this set of freshly promulgated legislation.[8] Apart from striving for consistency with the WTO agreements, the new laws changed the character of the Commission from a body that made recommendations to the government to one that was now empowered to decide on trade defence measures

---

[6] See ibid., s. 4(ii).

[7] See AD Ordinance 2000, s. 76. Though the preferred terminology of a law that conforms to WTO agreements is to use the double negative and say that "the law is not inconsistent with WTO agreements", the simpler formulation of "consistent with" is used here instead.

[8] The trade defence laws of Pakistan comprise the following three laws: AD Ordinance 2000, Countervailing Duties Ordinance 2001 (hereinafter CVD Ordinance 2001) and Safeguards Measures Ordinance 2002, as well as rules made in pursuance of these laws.

with finality. Thus the Commission now had the authority to make determinations and to decide on the imposition of anti-dumping and countervailing duties, and whether or not to accept undertakings.[9] In the matter of safeguard actions, however, the Commission's role was to be an advisory one, because any imposition of safeguard measures would likely involve discussions and negotiations with foreign governments, and perhaps for this reason the decisions regarding safeguard measures were left to the government. The due process for trade defence cases was elaborately set out in the new laws, as were the rights of the parties and the schedule for investigations, all closely reflecting the practice contained in or implied by the WTO trade defence agreements.

The trade defence work that built up following the enactment of the new trade defence legislation was in response to the inquiries and applications relating almost entirely to instances of alleged dumping into Pakistan. The first anti-dumping investigation was initiated by the Commission on 26 February 2002, and the provisional determination in this case was made on 22 July 2002. By 23 February 2011, the Commission had initiated 68 investigations and 31 of these had been concluded by way of either final determinations or price undertakings, a few having been terminated without measures.[10] Of the 68 investigations, 67 related to anti-dumping, and the remaining one was a safeguard case where the investigation was terminated without measures.

III   Judicial review of Commission's actions

1   The Appellate Tribunal

Pakistan's anti-dumping law[11] provides for a three-member Appellate Tribunal (hereinafter Tribunal) and largely replicates the provisions of Article 13 of the AD Agreement, albeit with some additions. The

---

[9] Price undertakings in anti-dumping and countervailing duty investigations come from foreign exporters subject to the investigation and involve an increase in the export price. Further, in countervailing duty investigations, the government of the exporting country may make an undertaking to eliminate or limit the subsidy subject to the investigation, or to take other measures concerning its effects.

[10] See www.ntc.gov.pk. The number of investigations is counted by the number of countries included in a particular application. For example, if only one country is mentioned in an application, that counts as one investigation, but if the application mentions three countries it would imply three investigations.

[11] See AD Ordinance 2000, s. 64. Also, CVD Ordinance 2001, s. 62 makes a reference to the Tribunal as defined in the AD Ordinance 2000.

qualifications of the three members are specified in law as, respectively, a judge, retired after serving his/her term on the bench in the Supreme Court of Pakistan, who is also to chair the Tribunal,[12] and two other members, who are to be subject experts. One of the subject experts is required to be a person known for his/her "integrity, expertise and experience in economics with particular reference to international trade related issues", while the other is to be a person known for his/her expertise "in matters related to customs law and practice".[13] It would appear that, keeping in view Pakistan's international treaty obligations relating to trade defence matters, as well as the somewhat technical nature of trade defence work, the legislature had devised a Tribunal that would have a senior judge with an established record supported by recognized subject experts. The law provides for this Tribunal's rulings to be final, and there is to be "no further appeal". Parties may, however, seek "clarification of any of the issues raised by the Appellate Tribunal in its decision", by filing an application within 30 days of the Tribunal's decision.[14] Nonetheless, the fact that there is no further appeal against the Tribunal's rulings would not by itself serve to bar the writ jurisdiction of the superior courts discussed below.[15]

The scope of the Tribunal's work relates to an appeal by any "interested party" against "an affirmative or a negative final determination made by the Commission", and "any final determination pursuant to a review" made by the Commission.[16] The appeal must be filed within 45 days of the final determination made by the Commission. The Tribunal is charged with deciding an appeal "as expeditiously as possible but not later than 90 days from the date of receipt" of that appeal.[17] The opportunity of being heard is to be provided by the Tribunal both to the appellant and to the Commission.[18] The Tribunal has the powers of a civil court, chiefly regarding the examination of such evidence (including an examination of the veracity of evidence) as was used by the Commission in making its determination or has a bearing on the final determination, and in enforcing attendance of witnesses.

In its examination of an appeal, the Tribunal is required to determine "whether the establishment of facts by the Commission was proper and

---

[12] The Supreme Court is the highest judicial body in Pakistan, as is clarified in the discussion below.

[13] See AD Ordinance 2000, s. 64(3).   [14] See ibid., s. 64(11).

[15] See discussion in section III.2 below.   [16] See AD Ordinance 2000.

[17] See ibid., s. 64(5) and (7).   [18] See ibid., s. 64(6).

whether the Commission's evaluation of those facts was unbiased and objective".[19] The standard here appears to track closely the wording of Article 17.6(i) of the AD Agreement. In determining whether the establishment and evaluation of the facts by the Commission was, respectively, proper, unbiased and objective, the Tribunal is required to do so on the basis of the official record maintained by the Commission, or any other documents relied upon by the Commission in reaching the determination under appeal.[20] The Tribunal next has to satisfy itself that "in reaching the impugned determination, the Commission complied with the relevant provisions" of the respective law. These principles, referred to above, arguably constitute the standard of review for the Tribunal.[21]

There appears to be some ambiguity, however, as to whether a party may approach the Tribunal before the Commission has made a final determination. The relevant law in this regard reads:

> Any interested party may refer an appeal to the Appellate Tribunal against – (i) an affirmative or a negative final determination by the Commission; and (ii) any final determination pursuant to a review.[22]

The above provision may arguably be read as stating that the Tribunal may not admit an appeal unless it relates to a final determination that has taken place. On this reading of the law, procedural matters in the course of an investigation, and before the Commission has made a final determination in the case, cannot be subject to an appeal before the Tribunal. Supporting this reading of the law is the argument that interventions in the course of initiation and investigation may very easily lead to delays in the investigation schedule, and the Commission may therefore be put in a situation where it is in violation of the timeline laid down for the initiation, investigation and determination procedures in the law. This is an important consideration, and no doubt in due course the Tribunal may be expected to clarify the matter.

The Tribunal's standard of review, as well as its procedure, has yet to be put to the test.[23] The first Tribunal was appointed for six months, beginning 5 March 2003. The Tribunal was composed of a retired Supreme Court judge, a retired Permanent Secretary who had

---

[19] See ibid., s. 64 (6).   [20] See ibid., s. 64 (6).

[21] Ibid., s. 64(12) reads as follows: "The Appellate Tribunal shall perform its functions under this Ordinance in accordance with such procedures as may be prescribed." The procedures had not been prescribed by August 2011, when this text was finalized.

[22] See ibid., s. 64(2).   [23] See *supra* note 21.

dealt with GATT matters in Geneva for several years, and another serving officer of the rank of Permanent Secretary to the Government, who had long experience of customs administration. Six months was clearly too short a period for the Tribunal to receive an appeal, because the time frame for an investigation runs into almost as many months and, as noted earlier, the Tribunal may only be approached after the Commission has made a final determination. This first Tribunal ceased to exist on 5 September 2003, without having received any applications during its brief life. The chair of the Tribunal felt that he was not in a position to continue, and the Tribunal's life was not extended. It is important to point out that the Tribunal's three members were serving in an honorary capacity, and the matter of their remuneration was to be reconsidered by the government as the work built up.

It is difficult to understand the reasoning behind the government's decision to restrict the life of the first Tribunal to six months, but one might speculate that it was perhaps gauging the volume of the work that the Tribunal would be handling in order to make a more informed decision about the size and permanence of a new institution. Following the end of the first Tribunal, the government made efforts to change the respective provisions of the law to enable one of the existing tribunals, such as that for the settlement of customs-related disputes, to handle any appeals against the actions of the Commission in trade defence matters, but the legislature did not do so.

A second Tribunal was appointed on 17 March 2010. Again a retired Supreme Court judge was appointed as the chair, while the other two members were, respectively, another retired judge of the Supreme Court and a practising lawyer chosen from the legal profession. The appointment of the chair met the qualification prescribed in the law, but the appointment of the other two members seemed to fall short of the requirement laid down, because these two members did not appear to have the *known* expertise in economics and international trade and in customs matters, respectively, that is prescribed in the law. Indeed, this appointment of two members who appear not to meet the criteria for the required expertise, seemed to create the potential for throwing open the composition of the second Tribunal to the possibility of a challenge in the superior courts. The second Tribunal has received its first and only reference to date, which it is in the process of considering.[24]

---

[24] Termination of investigation against alleged dumping of hot rolled coil from Belgium, Japan, Russia, Ukraine and the United States.

Between 5 September 2003, the date when the life of the first Tribunal ended, and the appointment of the second on 17 March 2010, a Tribunal did not exist. This lack caused parties dissatisfied with the Commission's processing of anti-dumping applications to seek remedies from the courts, and this aspect is considered below.

2 The role of the superior courts in trade remedy determinations: review of due process

In the absence of the Tribunal prescribed under the anti-dumping law, parties who were dissatisfied with the procedures adopted and/or decisions reached by the Commission in its handling of their applications, and in undertaking anti-dumping investigations and making determinations, sought relief from the superior courts, invoking the applicable provisions of the Constitution of Pakistan. Superior courts comprise the Supreme Court of Pakistan, being the highest court in the country, and the provincial High Courts, of which there is one in each province, being the next tier of courts. The Supreme Court hears appeals against the decisions of the High Courts and also has review powers regarding its own decisions.

The Constitution of Pakistan empowers the superior courts, that is, the Supreme Court and the High Courts, to restrain such person or persons who are performing functions in connection with "affairs of the Federation, province or a local authority", from acts that the law does not authorize them to do, and to declare any such actions to be without legal effect. Equally, the superior courts may direct a person or persons who are performing functions in connection with "affairs of the Federation, province or a local authority" to carry out such acts as the law required of them where the needful had not been done.[25] In the case of a High Court this is commonly referred to as the *writ jurisdiction* of the superior courts, and petitions seeking redress under this jurisdiction are frequently referred to as *writ petitions*. Ordinarily a writ petition may only be filed after the plaintiff has exhausted all other efficacious remedies available in law.

Actions relating to various laws are taken under this legal principle, and those relating to trade defence matters are discussed below, but there are two points of note. First, in considering the admissibility of a writ petition, the court would importantly take into account whether the petitioner had exhausted all efficacious remedies available, such as with

---

[25] See Articles 184(3) and 199 of the Constitution of Pakistan.

the Appellate Tribunal in cases pertaining to trade defence laws. As the Appellate Tribunal did not exist when the writ petitions were filed, the courts found this aspect to be reasonably addressed. Second, if the court's decision, which would also be binding on the Commission, were to be challenged at the World Trade Organization Dispute Settlement Body (DSB) and the DSB's findings were in conflict with or modified that decision, there is no provision in Pakistan's trade defence laws, or indeed in any Pakistan law, to implement such DSB findings. Clearly, in such an eventuality, Pakistan would require new legislation to implement the findings of the DSB.

It is pertinent to point out here that strict time constraints under the trade defence laws do not in any way bind the superior courts to dispose of a writ petition in adherence to the investigation schedule. The courts may decide the matter immediately, or may take years, but past experience and precedents suggest that generally it takes anything from a minimum of three to a maximum of 36 months to conclude proceedings resulting from a petition. The courts take up a matter when it is brought before them, but proceed with it in accordance with the backlog and quantum of cases pending before the particular court. There have been cases where a stay of proceedings has been granted, *ex parte*, leading to a delay in the conclusion of an investigation by the Commission. Such delay is detrimental to the investigation being conducted by the Commission, and potentially could result in a premature termination of the investigation based on change in market circumstances. Notwithstanding the fact that the Commission may not be at fault, a delay on account of pending court proceedings *prima facie* reflects negatively on the performance of the Commission.[26]

Writ petitions were filed in fair numbers at all stages of the process of an anti-dumping case. The writ petitions discussed here are those which had been filed by the end of 2008, which totalled 59.[27] With regard to the

---

[26] In a couple of instances the questions about the delay in the investigations conducted by the Commission were also raised in the meetings of the WTO Committee on Anti-Dumping Practices. See, for example, 'Minutes of the WTO Anti-Dumping Committee's Regular Meeting held on 26-7 October 2010' WTO document G/ADP/M/39, dated 17 December 2010, paragraphs 67-72.

[27] A systematic record of petitions filed after 2008 is not available, but would need to be compiled from court records. There has been no change in the writ petition process or in the approach of the superior courts in dealing with such petitions. As the purpose here is to use the experience with writ petitions to illustrate the process of judicial review by the superior courts, the explanation and the argument do not suffer by limiting the discussion chiefly to the experience with petitions filed up to 2008.

particular stage of an investigation, 20 of the 59 writ petitions were filed before or on the initiation of the investigation, six between initiation of investigation and preliminary determination, 15 related to preliminary determination, one questioned the imposition of provisional anti-dumping duty on certain goods, and 10 questioned the final determination. Five petitions related to price undertakings. Finally, two related to the initiation of a review.[28]

Eight of the 20 petitions filed before or on the initiation of the investigation raised the issue that the party had been prejudiced because the Commission had not informed it of the receipt of the application. The courts ruled that no prejudice had been caused, as the law provided that the receipt of an application need not be publicized.[29] Therefore the Commission was not required to publicize it, and for these reasons the court dismissed the petitions. In 12 cases, the parties raised the issue that while initiating the investigation the Commission had not disclosed injury. Of these 12 petitions, one was filed before the Federal Tax Ombudsman, pleading that the Tax Ombudsman had jurisdiction because the imposition of a "tax" was involved, the petitioner interpreting the anti-dumping duty as a "tax". After duly examining the case under the Federal Tax Ombudsman Ordinance 2000, the Tax Ombudsman declined jurisdiction. In this regard, it may be noted that the functions of the Federal Tax Ombudsman laid down in the preamble to the respective law are "to diagnose, investigate, redress and rectify any injustice done to a person through maladministration by functionaries administering tax laws",[30] and the Federal Tax Ombudsman's office further narrows down these tasks to the "Disposal of complaints of tax maladministration promptly, justly, fairly, independently investigated, and to rectify any injustice done to a taxpayer by actions of the tax employees of the Federal Board of Revenue (FBR)/Revenue Division, Government of Pakistan."[31] Any duties imposed under the trade defence laws would be trade contingency measures and not a tax, and thus would not fall within the purview of the Federal Tax Ombudsman. In its decision, the Federal Tax

---

[28] It must be said that a writ petition may cover more than one aspect of a determination. Therefore, the classification of writ petitions by the nature of plea and relief sought as is done here can only be approximate. The discussion in this section may be read as illustrative rather than a precise rendering.

[29] See Rule 4 of the Anti-Dumping Duties Rules, 2001. Anti-Dumping Rules were published shortly after the promulgation of the AD Ordinance 2000. See section II above.

[30] See the Preamble to the Federal Tax Ombudsman Ordinance 2000, Ordinance XXXV of 2000.

[31] See "Charter and Functions" at www.fto.gov.pk/aboutfto.php (last visited 8 December 2011).

Ombudsman advised "the Learned Counsel for the complainants to approach the court of law, the NTC itself or the Ministry of Commerce because the complaint is not maintainable before this office".[32] The remaining 11 petitions were filed before the High Courts. These petitions were disposed of with the ruling that no prejudice had been caused, as such disclosure was not required under the law; however, the court's ruling also required of the Commission that it share with the parties the non-confidential version of the application, the Commission's own examination of the accuracy and adequacy of the information concerning dumping and injury to the extent mandated by law.

As noted, six petitions were filed between the initiation of an investigation by the Commission and its reaching a preliminary determination. Three of these petitions sought that the Commission be directed to conduct verification visits and also to determine individual dumping margins for the respective exporters. The court ruled that the law did not require verification visits in every case, and therefore such visits were not mandatory. Separately, the Commission undertook to determine individual dumping margins in all those cases in which the information to enable it to do so had been supplied by the respective exporters. Three petitions pointed out that in situations where the court had granted a stay order, that is to say, had directed the Commission not to pass or issue an adverse order, the Commission had nonetheless carried on with internal examination of the case. The court ruled that the Commission had not violated the court's orders, as it had not taken any step(s) after the court had passed its stay order that could be recognized in law as the making of an adverse order.

In all, 15 petitions filed in the course of preliminary determinations pleaded that the initiation had not met the standards laid down in law because of procedural shortcomings in the determination of domestic industry by the Commission, and also because the evidence used by the Commission was flawed. The court admitted the petitions, but did not stay the Commission proceedings and, as a result, the Commission kept working as per its earlier published investigation schedule. In these cases, the Commission was able to arrive at the final determination in due course. The affected parties then moved to file writ petitions also challenging the final determinations. The court disposed of the petitions against preliminary determination process with the remarks that in view of the fact that the final determinations were now being challenged before the same court, the earlier

---

[32] Findings/Decision of the Federal Tax Ombudsman in Complaint no C-215-K/2007, dated 14 April 2007.

petitions had become redundant. One particular petition challenged the imposition of provisional anti-dumping duties on goods that were lying with customs authorities at the time the Commission made the preliminary determination. The court ruled that this petition's pertinent aspect was two definitions: how to read "entered into commerce" and "consumption". The court followed a principle established through case law pertaining to customs-related matters and restrained the Commission from imposing anti-dumping duties on products already lying with customs. The matter was thereafter challenged before a larger bench of the High Court, and the decision by this bench is still pending.

Of the 10 petitions relating to final determination, in one case of alleged *coram non judice*, the High Court decided in favour of the Commission. The Supreme Court reversed this decision, finding instead that the Commission was not properly constituted in law when it made the determinations. The Supreme Court observed that the Commission was a member short, and also did not have a chairman of a status not less than a Permanent Secretary, as laid down in the law.[33] As a result of this Supreme Court verdict, another four cases before the High Court, where the issue was similar and the decisions were pending, were similarly decided.

In three of the remaining five cases, the initiation was challenged on the grounds that the determination of domestic industry by the Commission was not in accordance with the law, and that the evidence of dumping and injury before the Commission was also flawed. The grounds for petitioning varied between the remaining two of the five petitions. One pointed out that the duty imposed on non-cooperating exporters was equal to the highest duty imposed among the cooperating exporters, and the issue placed before the court in this case was why the non-cooperating exporters were not being treated "less favourably". The court withheld its decision in this case. Finally, in one case, the petition argued that the imported product was "tax-exempt" under a different law, and hence anti-dumping duty could not be applied. The court also withheld its decision in this case. Three petitions also sought the setting up of the Appellate Tribunal as provided for under the anti-dumping law, and the court directed the government to do so immediately. One petitioner claimed that the customs authorities had also fixed an import price for purposes of applying the import tariff, regardless of the invoice value, because the customs authorities suspected under-invoicing by the exporter. The petitioner argued that in such a case the imposition of

---

[33] See explanations in section II above.

anti-dumping duties on the goods which had already been subjected to a fixed import price applied unilaterally by customs authorities, amounted to an instance of "double taxation". The court ruled that the two measures were separately founded in law, and therefore the simultaneous application of fixing an import value as well as an imposition of an anti-dumping duty did not amount to "double taxation".

In the five instances where the Commission had not accepted price undertakings on the grounds that customs authorities were not prepared to monitor such undertakings, writ petitions were filed. The Commission had consulted with the customs authorities, as the price undertakings would have to be monitored by them, but the customs authorities were of the considered view that it was not administratively feasible to do this. The court was petitioned with the plea that the Commission be asked to accept these price undertakings. Furthermore, the parties also pleaded that the customs authorities had not afforded them an opportunity of being heard. The court asked the customs authorities to explain their claimed limitations. The court disposed of the case after hearing the customs authorities, and directed the Commission to resolve the matter appropriately in light of the anti-dumping law, taking into consideration the problems faced by the customs authorities.

In two of the cases, the plaintiff challenged the non-initiation of a review. The Commission explained to the High Court that because its composition had been judged as flawed by the Supreme Court on account of *coram non judice*, it could not initiate the subject review. The court disposed of the petitions in question.

As one can see, the writ petitions chiefly concerned due process, and the courts upheld the procedures, derived from Pakistan's anti-dumping law and the rules made thereunder, that were applied by the Commission. Where the court ordered that Commission proceedings be stayed, the Commission was permitted to carry on with its internal work so long as it did not take any further action under the law. Finally, the court set aside the Commission's actions where it felt that the Commission was not properly constituted in law.

3   Intervention by superior courts in trade remedy determinations: constitution of the Commission

Writ petitions filed on the grounds *coram non judice* were discussed above. A final determination involving the imposition of anti-dumping duties was challenged by an affected importer in the High Court in 2010 in the context of section 5 of the NTC Act, which deals with the number and status of the members of the Commission, and in the context of Section 7 of the NTC Act, which deals with transaction of business by the Commission, authorizing the chairman to delegate work among members. The petitioner argued that the full Commission had not authorized the order, as the full Commission of three members had not signed the initiation, nor the preliminary and final determinations; It had been signed by only two of the three Commission members. The High Court upheld the Commission's point of view that the order of the Commission signed by two of the three members in the case under review was valid in law. The importer proceeded to file an appeal against this order before the Supreme Court. Between the judgment of the High Court and the hearing of the case by the Supreme Court, there occurred a vacancy in the Commission, and it was functioning with only two of its prescribed three members. The Supreme Court, after briefly hearing the appeal, and the Commission not being able to present an appropriate and robust defence on the day (chiefly the authorization for the delegation and distribution of functions among members), ordered that no further action be taken until the Commission was duly constituted with its full membership, and remanded the case back to the Commission. The Supreme Court's decision rendered the Commission inactive until it had been duly constituted. The Commission also faced the problematic situation of how to deal with the case remanded by the Supreme Court's order, keeping in view its functions and the procedures specified in the trade defence laws, as and when it would be duly constituted. Neither the NTC Act nor the trade defence laws provided for the situation of a case being remanded to the Commission by the superior courts.

IV   Conclusions

Even though Pakistan's experience with a WTO-consistent set of trade defence laws spans a short period of a few years, the above account shows that the judicial review of the work of the Commission has nonetheless been quite eventful. The first Tribunal had rather a brief life, its existence limited to six months. As Pakistan's trade defence laws were new and investigations were being initiated, cause for making references to the first Tribunal perhaps did not exist, and by the time a party needed to resort to a Tribunal, the first Tribunal was past its rather short lease of life. Between the date when the first Tribunal ceased to exist and the appointment of the second (i.e. 4 September 2003 and 17 March 2010), the Tribunal prescribed in law did not exist, but there was much in the way of demand for one among the affected parties. All of the final determinations by the Commission, save two, took place in a period when a Tribunal was not in place.[34] Parties which were dissatisfied with the Commission's anti-dumping work sought redress, as needed, through the writ jurisdiction of the superior courts. One might infer that the appointment of the second Tribunal may have been a result of court decisions pursuant to petitions filed before the superior courts by the parties to proceedings before the Commission, some of whom sought, successfully as it turned out, that the court direct the government to constitute the Tribunal required in law.

A point of note is that the larger number of cases that came before the superior courts related to due process in the course of an investigation, before a final determination had been made. Ostensibly, these cases came before the courts because the Tribunal did not exist, but the question may well be asked whether the Tribunal could have admitted such appeals if it had been in place at the time, because, as may be recalled, the law arguably allows an appeal to the Tribunal only after the Commission has made a final determination.[35]

Indeed, if the Tribunal were to interpret the law as permitting it to admit appeals in the course of an investigation without awaiting the Commission's final determination, then it may be prudent for the legislature to amend the law suitably to provide for such intervention.[36] Narrow limits may need to be specified in terms of the time that the Tribunal may take to decide on interventions in the course of an initiation or investigation. Setting such limits helps to preserve the scheduled timeline of an investigation suggested by the underlying law. For the moment and until the law is amended, if the Tribunal were to find such appeals inadmissible, then an aggrieved party may continue the existing practice of approaching the superior courts, and invoking their

---

[34] During the existence of the Tribunal, two final determinations, namely, *Hydrogen Peroxide from Belgium, China, Indonesia, South Korea, Taiwan, Thailand and Turkey* on 6 July 2011, and *Phthalic Anhydride from Brazil, China, Indonesia, South Korea and Taiwan* on 30 September 2010, were made. However, during the Tribunal's existence, one investigation was terminated on 25 February 2011 (*Hot Rolled Coil from Belgium, Japan, Russia, Ukraine and the United States*), and one review was concluded on 30 September 2010 (*PVC Resin (suspension grade) from the Republic of Korea and the Islamic Republic of Iran*).

[35] See AD Ordinance 2000, s. 64(2).

[36] Turkish law appears specifically to include the possibility of a review before a final determination. See Chapter 10 above on the Turkish judicial review system.

writ jurisdiction. The presumed plea in such a writ petition before the court would be that the existing law did not offer a remedy in the course of an investigation (that is, prior to the final determination).

In the absence of the Tribunal, the national judicial system working through the writ jurisdiction of the superior courts did, however, provide relief. In their rulings, the judges by and large upheld the due process applied by the Commission, thus reinforcing the Commission's interpretation of the law and the rules. In a few cases the courts ordered a "stay" in the Commission's proceedings, which is to say that the Commission was directed by the courts not to proceed any further in those cases pending the outcome of the courts' proceedings. A more recent development, noted above, is that some of the Commission's determinations have been remanded back by the superior courts because the constitution of the Commission itself under the NTC Act has come under judicial scrutiny and been found wanting. This issue would appear to be outside the Tribunal's purview, and only the courts are in a position to provide relief under their writ jurisdiction.

It is reasonable to conclude that though a Tribunal was not in place until very recently, and therefore for almost the entire period since the new trade defence laws were enacted, legal processes for the judicial review of the Commission's work were very much available through the well-tested writ jurisdiction of the superior courts. These procedures did provide, *inter alia,* for the review of administrative actions relating to final determinations and reviews of determinations independent of the authorities responsible for the determination or review in question, as intended in Article 13 of the AD Agreement. One might be tempted to argue that easy recourse to superior courts via the writ jurisdiction process may negate the need for a special Tribunal. Should the composition of the Tribunal be challenged before the superior courts as defective in law, this issue could well surface for the government.

There seem to be chiefly two complicating factors with regard to resort to the courts. First, the courts are not bound by the schedule of investigation in considering writ petitions and may take considerably longer to decide than the investigation schedule permits. Second, a mechanism for implementation of DSB findings seems to be lacking, should the matter be disputed at the DSB and should its findings differ from those of the court.

India: a three-tier judicial review system

MADHURENDRA NATH JHA*

I Introduction

India has a long history of common law, with the High Courts established in the former 'presidency' cities of Bombay (now Mumbai), Calcutta (now Kolkata) and Madras (now Chennai) in the first half of the nineteenth century and, thus, a well-established legal system. India has a fairly high litigation rate, an activist, independent judiciary and special constitutional mechanisms in place for the enforcement of fundamental and other rights. The country has a fast-growing economy with a large consumer base and is also a robust user of trade remedy measures, and it is only to be expected that with the passage of time, judicial challenges to trade remedy determinations will arise. There is also an established practice of Indian courts, in some cases, to consider foreign judgments not as binding precedents, but having persuasive value in respect of the correct interpretation of identical provisions or for good practice.

In developing nations, the rise of trade remedy measures has often gone hand in hand with a fundamental policy shift towards trade liberalization. This holds true for India, too. Until the 1990s, India did not have to resort to trade remedy measures because of its inward-oriented economic regime, which relied heavily on conventional measures of protection. Until 1990 imports were highly restricted through a number of tariff and non-tariff measures. However, since 1991, there has been a gradual shift in the policy regime in India, which led to the opening of the economy to foreign competition. Apart from various unilateral

* I have been assisted in compilation and research by Ms Garima Tiwari, Advocate and Ms Purva Juneja, Advocate. I also thank Mr R. Parthasarthi, Advocate and Mr Müslüm Yilmaz, Counsellor of the WTO Rules Division, for their respective comments on the draft chapter.

economic reforms undertaken since 1991, the Indian economy also had to reorient itself to changing multilateral trade disciplines within the GATT/WTO framework.

In this overall context, the legal framework for imposing anti-dumping and countervailing measures in India was put in place in 1982 when sections 9, 9A, 9B and 9C were added to the Customs Tariff Act, 1975. However, the Customs Tariff Rules,[1] which provided detailed provisions for the conduct of anti-dumping and countervailing duty investigations, were not introduced until 1985. Until the early 1990s, however, the need to conduct such investigations did not arise, given the high tariff barriers (100% or more) and the import licence requirement.

After the signing of the legal text resulting from the Uruguay Round Negotiations under the GATT, sections 9, 9A, 9B and 9C of the Customs Tariff Act, 1975 were amended on 1 January 1995 to bring Indian legislation in line with the WTO Agreement on Implementation of Article VI of GATT 1994 (hereinafter AD Agreement) and the WTO Agreement on Subsidies and Countervailing Measures (hereinafter SCM Agreement).[2] The Customs Tariff Rules, 1995 on Anti-Dumping Investigations[3] (hereinafter AD Rules) and the Customs Tariff Rules, 1995 on Countervailing Duty Investigations[4] (hereinafter CVD Rules) were introduced and repealed the earlier Rules. The AD Rules were subsequently amended in July 1999,[5] May 2001,[6] January 2002[7] and November 2003.[8]

As for safeguards, the domestic law to implement the provisions of the WTO Agreement on Safeguards (hereinafter SG Agreement) has been enacted under sections 8B and 8C of the Customs Tariff Act, 1975.

---

[1] *Rules on Identification, Assessment and Collection of Anti-Dumping Duty on Dumped Articles and for Determination of Injury* (for anti-dumping investigations) and *Rules on Identification, Assessment and Collection Of Countervailing Duty on Subsidized Articles and for Determination of Injury* (for countervailing duty investigations).

[2] Article 253 of the Constitution of India empowers Parliament to make any laws for the purpose of implementing international treaties, agreements or conventions.

[3] Official title: "Identification, Assessment and Collection of Anti-Dumping Duty on Dumped Articles and for Determination of Injury".

[4] Official title: "Identification, Assessment And Collection Of Countervailing Duty On Subsidized Articles And For Determination of Injury".

[5] Through Notification No. 44/1999 NT Customs.

[6] Through Notification No. 28/2001 NT Customs.

[7] Through Notification No. 1/2002 NT Customs.

[8] Through Notification No. 101/2003 NT Customs.

The Customs Tariff Rules on Safeguard Investigations, 1997[9] (hereinafter SG Rules) and the Customs Tariff Rules on Specific Safeguard Investigations, 2002[10] (hereinafter Specific SG Rules) govern the procedural aspects. Various amendments[11] have been made from time to time, to bring Indian trade remedies law in line with India's international obligations.

India initiated its first anti-dumping investigation in 1992 against the United States, Japan and Brazil on the imports of *PVC Resin*, and its first safeguard investigation in 1998. It is yet to recommend countervailing duty, having undertaken only one investigation. Despite the relatively short history of its trade remedies legislation and practice, however, India tops the list of active users of anti-dumping measures. It is now by far the most frequent user of anti-dumping globally. It had initiated 637 (based on the WTO's count) anti-dumping investigations between 1995 and 2010, which puts it at the top of the list of users, followed by the United States, with 443 initiations and the European Union, with 420. Most of India's initiations have ended in imposition of duties. It should not be surprising that India has witnessed relatively robust use of its judicial review mechanism.

The Directorate General for Anti-Dumping and Allied Duties (hereinafter DGAD) in the Ministry of Commerce is the administrative investigating authority for anti-dumping and countervailing measures in India. On the other hand, the imposition and collection of duties is undertaken by the Department of Revenue in the Ministry of Finance; safeguard measures with the Directorate General of Safeguards (hereinafter DGSG), a separate authority under the Department of Revenue in the Ministry of Finance. The procedural rules that apply to anti-dumping and countervailing duty investigations are different from those that apply to safeguard investigations. The decision-making processes are also different.

In the case of anti-dumping and countervailing duty investigations, the decision to initiate an investigation lies with the DGAD, appointed under Rule 3 of the AD Rules and CVD Rules, which was on 13 April 1998. The law provides for the appointment of the Designated Authority

---

[9] Official title: "Identification and Assessment of Safeguard Duty".

[10] Official title: "Transitional Products Specific Safeguard Duty".

[11] For instance: Customs Notification No. 44/99 – Cus (NT) dated 15.7.1999; Customs Notification No. 1/2002 – Cus (NT) dated 4.1.2002; Customs Notification No. 101/2003 – Cus (NT) dated 10.11.2003; changes made by the Finance Bill 2001, the Finance Bill 2003 and the Finance Bill 2004.

(hereinafter DA) holding the rank of Joint Secretary to the government of India to head the DGAD.[12] However, in practice the office of the DA has generally been held at the higher rank of Additional Secretary to the government of India. The DGAD comprises officers with background in trade, costing, finance, economics, statistics and law. Officers appointed to the DGAD usually also hold charges under the Directorate General of Foreign Trade, an allied department under the Ministry of Commerce and Industry, or from the Cost Accounts Service under the Ministry of Finance.

The decision to initiate an investigation by the DGAD can either be on receipt of a petition by the domestic industry or on a *suo motu* basis.[13] The initiation decision is published in the *Official Gazette* as a notification and is also posted on the DGAD's website. This is followed by an investigation process as provided for in the respective AD and CVD Rules and ordinarily concludes (unless earlier terminated or suspended) with a recommendation by the DGAD to the Central Government to impose a duty. This recommendation is either accepted or declined by the Central Government's Ministry of Finance. On acceptance, the Ministry of Finance issues a customs notification imposing the duty. This dual process of recommendation by the DGAD and imposition by the Ministry of Finance also applies in the case of provisional duties.

The decision to initiate a safeguard investigation lies with the DGSG and the initiation decision is published in the *Official Gazette* as a notification and also posted on the DGSG's website. This is followed by an investigation by the DGSG that terminates with a finding by it. Unlike at the DGAD, interested parties must separately communicate their intention to respond within a specified time frame before the final date to file questionnaire responses. These provisional or final findings, as the case may be, are then published in the *Official Gazette* and placed before the Board of Safeguards (established by a Cabinet Note and without statutory basis), which is chaired by the Commerce Secretary. In practice, the Safeguards Board takes a second look at the overall public interest and for this reason has not accepted recommendations for safeguard measures (so far in the form of duty

---

[12] Through Customs Notification No. 48/2011 (NT) dated 20/07/2011. Even though this provision exists for appointment of Joint Secretary, this has never happened.
[13] Rule 5 of the AD Rules.

rather than quantitative restrictions) in many cases or has reduced the level of the recommended safeguard measure. On acceptance of the recommendation to impose the duty by the Board of Safeguards, the Ministry of Finance, through a customs notification, ultimately imposes the recommended duty. The SG Rules specify the decision-making process for the imposition of provisional and definitive safeguard measures. The public interest test is provided for and must be applied in safeguard investigations conducted by India, unlike in anti-dumping investigations. In recent years, a number of transitional product-specific safeguard (TP SSG) investigations concerning imports from China have also been initiated in India. However, in the absence of any specific provision for safeguards appeals and of any CVD measures by India, this chapter will largely, though not exclusively, discuss the issue of judicial review of anti-dumping determinations.

As the chapter's title suggests, India has a three-tier judicial review system for its investigating authority's determinations, and this system has so far been used frequently. This has resulted in a variety of pronouncements on various contentious issues and necessary interventions and interference with DGAD/DGSG's findings through judicial supervision and control. Referring to various legal provisions and judicial pronouncements below, we will first discuss different aspects of India's judicial review system, then its effectiveness, and finally explain how it can be improved.

The discussion in this chapter is based on both the statutory basis for judicial review in India arising from trade remedy investigations, and the judicial precedents in this respect by India's courts, and the Central Excise and Service Tax Appellate Tribunal. Comprehensive statistics are difficult, since appeals or petitions dismissed at admission stage prior to issuing of a notice to other parties, or withdrawn prior to such notice, are not usually reported. However, by the end of 2011, it is believed that over 254 appeals had been filed with the Central Excise and Service Tax Appellate Tribunal from anti-dumping findings (and two unsuccessful attempts arising from safeguard investigations), 56 writ petitions in various State High Courts arising from anti-dumping investigations, 25 such writ petitions arising from safeguards or transitional product-specific safeguard investigations, and 25 petitions at the Supreme Court of India. There are also estimated to be 42 appeals currently pending at the Central Excise and Service Tax Appellate Tribunal, 25 writ petitions pending in various High Courts and 20 special leave petitions pending at the Supreme Court.

II   Legislative framework for judicial review

The Customs Tariff Act, 1975, so far as it relates to anti-dumping or countervailing duties, contains a specific provision with respect to the judicial review of the investigating authority's determinations. Such a judicial review is conspicuously absent in the case of safeguard measures. For safeguard measures, the determinations are subject to judicial review, not under any specific provisions, but through writ petitions under the more generic provisions (not limited to cases arising from trade remedies) under the Constitution of India. Interestingly, in the case of anti-dumping duties, it has emerged that these determinations are subject to judicial review by means of a statutory appeal, as provided by section 9C of the Customs Tariff Act, 1975, and the general jurisdiction of Indian courts of all government actions under writ petitions as per the Constitution of India. Thus, this chapter will deal with the legislative framework for judicial review, along with the underlying principles and their application.

The Indian courts have the authority to conduct judicial review of the actions carried out by government agencies. Articles 226 and 32 of the Constitution provide for the general principle that all administrative acts are subject to scrutiny by the courts. Under Article 32 of the Constitution, the Supreme Court of India has power to issue directions, orders or writs, including writs in the nature of *habeas corpus*, *mandamus*, prohibition, *quo warranto* and *certiorari*, as the case may be. Under the more commonly used (in respect of trade remedies matters, at least) Article 226 of the Constitution, the High Courts of states have been conferred with a power wider than the Supreme Court under Article 32 because of the use of the expression "for any purpose" apart from violation of fundamental rights addressed under Part III of the Constitution of India.

The powers under Articles 32 and 226 are supervisory, not appellate in nature. This jurisdiction cannot be coterminous with those of Courts of Appeal, or revision to correct errors of law which do not cause wide injustice, or of facts.[14] Similarly, the exercise of these powers is discretionary in nature. Various judicial pronouncements have settled the principles governing the exercise of these powers, which can no longer be called unguided. It is now established that the power of the court under Articles 32 and 226 is supervisory, a jurisdiction intended to supervise the work of the tribunals and public authorities and officials

---

[14] *Sangram Singh* v. *Election Tribunal*, AIR 1955 SC 425.

and to see that they act within the limits of their respective jurisdiction. In a proceeding under Article 226, the High Court of a state is not concerned with private rights; the only object of such a proceeding is to ensure that the law of the land, i.e. the Constitution, is implicitly obeyed, and that various authorities and tribunals act within the limits of their respective jurisdiction.

In addition to the wide powers available to the Supreme Court and High Courts of states for the purpose of judicial review, the Customs Tariff Act, 1975, in its section 9C, makes provision for appeal to an appellate tribunal, namely, the Central Excise and Service Tax Appellate Tribunal (hereinafter CESTAT) against any final determination by the DA as the forum for appeal against the order of determination or review thereof regarding the existence, degree and effect of any subsidy or dumping in relation to the imports of any merchandise. It should be underlined, however, that this mechanism only applies with respect to final determinations made in anti-dumping and countervailing duty investigations and reviews.

A provision was made in the Finance (No. 2) Act, 1980 for establishing the Customs, Excise and Gold (Control) Appellate Tribunal.[15] Thereafter, with effect from 11 October 1982, CESTAT was constituted as the successor to the earlier CEGAT, under the Ministry of Finance (Department of Revenue) through Notification No. 223/82 – Customs dated 11 October 1982, to provide an independent forum to hear appeals against orders and decisions passed by the Commissioners of Customs and Excise under the Customs Act, 1962, the Central Excise Act, 1944 and the Finance Act 94 relating to Service Tax. CESTAT is headed by its president. There is provision for a senior vice-president and vice-presidents (there are two at present) besides judicial members and technical members. For the purpose of the constitution of benches, the president and vice-presidents are also judicial or technical members, as the case may be. The work of CESTAT has been distributed among various benches, comprising special benches located at New Delhi and at regional locations. All matters relating to anti-dumping and countervailing measures are decided by the anti-dumping bench of CESTAT pursuant to section 9C(5) of the Customs Tariff Act, 1975. CEGAT (now CESTAT) Countervailing Duty and Anti-dumping Duty (Procedure) Rules 1996 provide that the anti-dumping bench shall be situated in New Delhi.

---

[15] CESTAT was previously referred to as "the Customs Excise Gold Appellate Tribunal" (CEGAT).

Thus, judicial review of anti-dumping measures in India rests with CESTAT in a statutory appeal under section 9C of the Customs Tariff Act, 1975 and the High Courts in writ jurisdiction under Article 226 of the Constitution. For safeguard measures, the recommendation of the DGSG in a sense is reviewed by the Board of Safeguards before the imposition of the measure. However, in the absence of a statutory appeal to CESTAT from such measures, parties approach the High Courts of states under writ against them.

It has been India's experience that in certain cases judicial review concluded that the underlying anti-dumping investigation had pervasive flaws going beyond those in respect of the specific exporters seeking such a review. Consequently, the anti-dumping duty against such exporters may have been removed, while those against other exporters who had not sought judicial review remained in place in spite of the flawed underlying investigation.[16]

The WTO Agreement has persuasive force in Indian *fora*, and the provisions of the respective agreements on trade remedies have been invoked in judicial review proceedings. Initially, the rules regarding review determinations in terms of both mid-term and change in circumstances reviews, as well as expiry or sunset reviews in India, were not clear.[17] CESTAT has relied upon and taken guidance from the WTO jurisprudence to interpret India's AD Rules in harmony with the latter in some cases. The main points were that the scope of a mid-term review and of sunset reviews were also broadened to allow for change (increase or reduction) in recommended duty, apart from confirming or removing existing anti-dumping duty. This has helped lend clarity in some cases, although some issues survive, such as the fact that the language of section 9A paragraphs (v) and (vi) of the statute was not addressed.

Consider the case of *Thai Acrylic Fibre Co. Ltd.* v. *Designated Authority*[18] and *BASF South East Asia PTE. Ltd.* v. *Designated Authority*.[19] CESTAT, when posed with a question on whether the DA in a review proceeding can alter the duty levied in a sunset review, relied on *US – Sunset Reviews of Anti-dumping Measures on OCTG from Argentina*, WT/DS268/AB/R dated 29.11.2004; and *US – Sunset Reviews of Anti-dumping Measures on CRCS*

---

[16] http://commerce.nic.in/trade/international_trade_papers_nextDetail.asp?id=125   (last visited 12.1.2012).

[17] These ambiguities have been clarified by amended Rule 23 of the AD Rules and Trade Notice 2/2011, dated 6 June 2011.

[18] 2010 (253) ELT 564 (Tri. – Del.).   [19] 2010 (253) ELT 554 (Tri. – Del.).

Flat Products from Japan, WT/DS244/AB/R dated 15.12.2003, and held in paragraph 17 that "the Government has the power to vary the anti-dumping duty while continuing the same on conclusion of a sunset review under section 9A(5)". However, there is no warrant under section 9A(5) to determine the current dumping margin and limit the anti-dumping duty to such level, as under section 9A(1). If the Government wants to vary the anti-dumping duty under section 9A(5), instead of merely continuing the duty initially imposed under section 9A(1), it must be for a good and sufficient reason, to be indicated in the DA's findings on sunset review, and as concluded in paragraph 19 "the anti-dumping duty shall continue to be levied on such impugned goods at the same rates as applicable during the sunset review". Similarly, in the case of *Kalyani Steels Ltd.* v. *Revenue Secretary, MF*,[20] the High Court of Delhi endeavoured to harmonize the scope of Rule 23 of the AD Rules (pertaining to reviews) with Article 11 of the AD Agreement.

It should be noted that, in general, Indian courts and CESTAT have relied primarily on national legislation and jurisprudence in the national judicial review proceedings.

III   Types of judicial review proceedings

In India, by reason of Articles 32 and 136 of the Constitution, the Supreme Court may exercise the power of judicial review. Similarly, under Articles 226 and 227 of the Constitution, the High Courts of states have the power of judicial review. This power can be utilized for judicially reviewing an enactment passed by the legislature, or a decision of an administrator, an order of a quasi-judicial authority and/or in a given case, a decision of the judiciary. Decisions and actions that do not have adjudicative disposition are not justiciable before a judicial review court.

In recent times, the scope of judicial review has been expanded in several ways. In fact, issues have always been raised with regard to the scope of judicial review, rather than with its existence, particularly in the case of anti-dumping determinations. There is very little in terms of systematic and principled judicial guidance as to when facts ought to be susceptible to judicial scrutiny. The AD Rules provide for both administrative and judicial review of the determination orders.

---

[20]   2008 (224) ELT 47 (Del.).

As already mentioned, the appeals against the decisions of the DA lie, in the first instance, with CESTAT.[21] It reviews final measures and is independent of administrative authorities. This is consistent with Article 13 of the AD Agreement, of constituting independent tribunals for appeal against final determination and reviews. This provision stipulates that each member: "shall maintain judicial ... tribunals ... for the purpose, inter alia, of the prompt review of administrative actions relating to final determinations and reviews of determinations ... Such tribunals ... shall be independent of the authorities responsible for the determination or review in question."

Any second appeal against the orders of CESTAT lies with the Supreme Court of India. However, the High Courts also entertain appeals against the DA's actions in writ jurisdiction under Article 226 of the Constitution of India.

In addition to the judicial review mechanism, it may be observed here that the generic section 25 of the Customs Act, 1962 empowers the Central Government to grant exemption from any duty (including anti-dumping or safeguard duties, since these are provided for under the cognate Customs Tariff Act, 1975) under the Act (and cognate Acts) in the public interest (which is otherwise not provided for in India's anti-dumping provisions). In certain anti-dumping determinations, interested parties (mainly users and importers) have made representations to the Union Finance Ministry against imposition of a recommended anti-dumping measure. In a few rare cases (for instance, *Metcoke* from China), the Ministry of Finance, following such representations, has not levied the measures as recommended (including modifying the applicability of the recommended measure in the case of *Metcoke*). There is no bar to foreign exporters filing such a representation, though as a practical matter it may be more difficult for them to establish a public interest case against recommended anti-dumping duties.

IV   Reviewable determinations

As stated above, section 9C of the Customs Tariff Act, 1975 provides that appeals against the determinations regarding the existence, degree and effect of any subsidy or dumping in relation to the imports of any article shall be brought before CESTAT.

---

[21] For anti-dumping and countervailing measures only. It must be recalled that the safeguards mechanism in India does not contain a provision for appeal.

The notification of the DA publishing the final findings in the Ministry of Finance notification and imposition of measures in any original investigation, decisions from mid-term reviews under Rule 23 of the AD Rules and new shipper's reviews under Rule 22 of the AD Rules, are indisputably appealable. Other determinations, such as refusal by the DA to accept a price undertaking without providing adequate reasons, have been held to be appealable under section 9C of the Customs Tariff Act.[22] Similarly, termination of any investigation by the DGAD under Rule 14 of the AD Rules has also been subject to review before CESTAT.[23]

An anomalous situation persists with respect to the question whether preliminary findings or provisional duties or initiation notification can be appealed. The text of section 9C of the Customs Tariff Act, 1975 does not specifically provide for review of these determinations, as they are provisional in nature and not definitive or executable like final findings or a notification imposing definitive duties. Hence, these have been frequently challenged under writ petitions before the High Courts under their supervisory jurisdiction, and significant jurisprudence on the investigation process vis-à-vis the duties of the DA has emerged from such petitions. Ordinarily, the High Courts have been reluctant to interfere at the preliminary stage.

The power of the High Courts under Article 226 of the Constitution to review the DA's determinations has undergone immense judicial debate in India. Initially, the High Courts viewed interference by the courts to review the findings of the DA in a very restricted and circumspect manner, particularly with respect to challenges to preliminary findings. The courts' initial restraint in entertaining writ petitions against preliminary findings of the DA was evident in the case of *Shrew Kumar Agarwal* v. *Union of India*,[24] whereby the High Court of Calcutta, faced with a challenge to the preliminary findings of the DGAD recommending imposition of provisional duties, declined to interfere, on the grounds that CESTAT is an appropriate forum for appeals against the DA's findings, and the same may not be assumed by the High Court in supervisory jurisdiction. Additionally, the High Court held that, owing to the duality of any anti-dumping investigation involving recommendation by the DGAD and imposition by the Ministry of Finance,

---

[22] *PT Polysindo Eka Parkasa* v. *Designated Authority* 2005 (185) ELT 358 (Tri. – Del.).
[23] *Essar Steel Limited* v. *Union Of India* 2008 (222) ELT 161 (Del.).
[24] 2002 (141) ELT 312 (Cal.).

recommending the imposition of provisional duty cannot *ipso facto* become a ground of appeal unless and until the Central Government accepts the same and gives notification. The rationale that emerged from this judgment was that the High Courts were disinclined to review the DA's determinations, as there existed a special tribunal, i.e. CESTAT, to deal with such appeals, and second, that preliminary findings by the DA could not be appealed, as they were non-executable until a notification imposing the provisional or a final duty had been issued.

The above rationale failed to garner judicial support, as other High Courts, when faced with challenges to preliminary findings as writs, declined to follow it as *stare decisis*. The Rajasthan High Court distinguished its stand in the case of *Rajasthan Textile Mills Association* v. *Director General of Anti-Dumping*[25] and viewed a petition challenging the initiation of an anti-dumping investigation on the ground of a jurisdictional error under Article 226 of the Constitution of India as maintainable for limited review. However, the High Court added the caveat that a writ court entertaining a petition challenging the initiation notification shall not hold a roving inquiry, but will be confined to the existence of evidence provided in the application, i.e. filing of a valid application by the domestic industry and satisfaction of the DA as to the sufficiency of evidence in the application with regard to dumping, material injury and causal link. It also viewed the approach taken in *Shrew Kumar* as correct, in so far as the normal rule is that no interference should be made by a writ court under Article 226 of the Constitution on account of the recommendatory nature of preliminary findings by the DA, and there can be only limited judicial interference if the preliminary finding has been recorded after following the statutory provisions of the AD Rules. The High Court also observed that, while it is at the discretion of the Central Government to impose duties on the basis of a preliminary finding, the same can nevertheless be examined, as the jurisdiction of an administrative authority depends upon a preliminary finding of fact. Thus, the High Court is entitled, in a proceeding of writ of *certiorari*, to determine upon its independent judgment whether or not that finding of fact is correct.

Paradoxically, a contrary stand was adopted by the High Court of Madras in the case of *Sree Karpagambal Mills Ltd.* v. *Director General of Anti-Dumping & Allied Duties*,[26] wherein it was held that the provision of refund of excess duties collected provisionally upon the imposition of

---

[25] 2002 (149) ELT 45 (Raj.).   [26] 2002 (150) ELT 1349 (Mad.).

definitive duties does not warrant interference by courts under writ jurisdiction against preliminary findings, as they are recommendatory only and do not by themselves affect the rights of any party. Accordingly, the court also viewed that interference by courts was likely to render the object of preliminary findings in an appropriate case lost if the proceedings taken under the AD Rules, which are essentially administrative in nature, were allowed to be mired in the judicial controversy at every conceivable stage. Also, as the AD Rules and section 9A of the Customs Tariff Act, 1975 provide for the refund of excess provisional duties paid once definitive duties have been imposed, an importer would not be prejudiced even if ultimately it is found that the imposition of provisional duties was unjustified. The Indian courts have so far not taken cognizance of the potentially longer "trade chilling" impact of initiation of trade remedy investigations and/or of any provisional measures recommended therein.

The opposing views taken by the High Courts were thereinafter settled by the overriding view of the Supreme Court in the case of *Association of Synthetic Fibre Industry* v. *J.K. Industries Ltd.*,[27] wherein the Supreme Court clarified that all steps, including recommendation by the DA and the imposition of anti-dumping duties, in the event of the Central Government forming an opinion to do so on the basis of the recommendation, would be subject to the result of challenges before the High Court, and that the High Court does have the power to grant interim relief at any stage of the proceedings. Thus, in conclusion, the Supreme Court decreed that the decision of the Central Government in the matter of anti-dumping duties is appealable, and also subject to writ jurisdiction on well-settled parameters of constitutional law.

The High Court of Delhi was equally restrained in its view on interference by courts on safeguard measures, and held that writ petitions in such cases ought to be entertained when there is either a complete lack of jurisdiction, or a palpable error so grave that it requires imminent interference by a writ court.[28]

However, the emerging view of courts in cases of challenges to preliminary findings has been that any anti-dumping investigation follows a three-stage process, of which the first is the initiation of the investigation and recording of preliminary findings by the DA on an application made by the domestic industry. This may or may not lead to the imposition of

---

[27] 2006 (199) ELT 196 (S.C.).
[28] *Saint-Gobain Glass India Ltd.* v. *Union of India* 2009 (240) ELT 495 (Del.).

provisional duties. The second stage (post-decisional) involves the DA inviting further comments, objections and response from interested parties and terminating the investigation after duly recording final findings as to dumping, and the resultant injury to the domestic industry. In the third stage, the Central Government imposes definitive duties. While the notification of the DA publishing the final findings is indisputably appealable under section 9C before CESTAT, provisional duties in certain circumstances can also be challenged in a writ petition, but there is no remedy against initiation notifications or preliminary findings. However, this cannot be a ground to repel *in limine* a challenge to initiation notifications or preliminary findings on the ground that there is an effective alternative remedy at a subsequent stage of proceedings.[29]

The petitioners in the case of *Meghani Organics Ltd.* v. *Union of India*[30] had approached the court at the interim stage, when final determination of anti-dumping duty was still pending. The High Court of Ahmadabad, therefore, limited itself to discussing the issue of maintainability of the petitions and held that: "since no appeal lies against the levy of provisional anti-dumping duty this Court is well within its power to entertain this petition since there being no alternative remedy available to the petitioners despite the fact that they are being saddled with the liability of a provisional anti-dumping duty".

An interesting development in Indian anti-dumping jurisprudence as regards the review of determinations has been whether the DA's findings can be reviewed by CESTAT or by courts on grounds of procedural errors, i.e. whether the DA in its capacity as a fact-finding body performs a quasi-legislative function or an executive function. The issue emerged when definitive duties imposed on the imports of *Nylon Tyre Cord Fabrics* from various countries were challenged on the ground that the DA in its investigation as stipulated under Indian law had violated principles of natural justice by denying public hearing to the parties. There had been a change of officer in charge in the course of the investigation, and while the public hearing as desired under AD Rules had been conducted by the predecessor DA, the final findings were issued by the succeeding DA. These findings were challenged on the ground that the DA had violated principles of natural justice by passing orders without providing parties that may be adversely affected by the

[29] *Vuppalamritha Magnetic Components Ltd.* v. *Union of India* 2010 (256) ELT 487.
[30] 2011 (267) ELT 440 (Guj.).

order with an opportunity to be heard. Initially, the High Court of Rajasthan dismissed the writ petition and observed that the findings reached by the DA were not because of any legislative power vested in the DA to adjudicate or decide the dispute. The High Court also asked the parties to approach CESTAT, as it was the appropriate forum for remedy against the imposition of duties. CESTAT also opined that denial of public hearing could not be a ground to quash the imposition of duties on the basis of the following criteria:

(i) An anti-dumping duty has all the characteristics of a tax, as it is imposed under statutory power without the tax-payers' consent, and its payment is enforced by law, therefore, issuance of the notification by the Central Government in the *Official Gazette* under Rule 18 of the AD Rules read in conjunction with section 9A(1) of the Tariff Act imposing an anti-dumping duty upon importation of the subject article in India is purely a legislative function.

(ii) The process of imposing an anti-dumping duty which is legislative in nature does not decide any existing dispute or suit *inter partes*; it only determines whether the imposition of an anti-dumping duty is called for in relation to dumped imports and if so, at what rate, on the basis of the information collected from the exporters, importers and a large number of other interested parties.

(iii) There can never be a suit between the state and its citizens in the matter of exercise of legislative power to impose tax, as there is no "right–duty" relationship between the Central Government imposing an anti-dumping duty under the Tariff Act and the AD Rules, and the exporters or importers who are given an opportunity to submit information under the Rules, and that the principles of natural justice are not applicable to a legislative process for the enactment of law and the persons affected have no right to an opportunity to be heard before the enactment.

(iv) However, if Parliament, in its wisdom, for an impost such as anti-dumping duty, which arises due to and has nexus with the interest of domestic industry, provides a mechanism for taking into consideration the views of those who will be affected and the other interested parties, that will not amount to vesting in them a right to be heard personally, arising as a consequence of the principles of natural justice, against taking legislative action of imposing an anti-dumping duty and fixing its rate for the subject article.

(v) In cases where the investigative procedure leading to the determination of the rates of taxes is undertaken by Parliament, through its agencies, as per its rules of business, there will be absolutely no scope for any judicial tribunal to examine whether any procedural irregularity was committed by not consulting any particular section of the public likely to be adversely affected by such law. This is precisely why legislative enactments generally are not made subject to the principles of natural justice, as doing so may lead to a finding of irregularity of procedure which is prohibited by the constitutional scheme of lawmaking. It is settled law that there is no right to be heard before the making of legislation, whether primary or delegated, unless specifically provided by statute.

The Supreme Court, when deciding on appeal from this decision of CESTAT, held that the scheme of the Customs Tariff Act, 1975 read in conjunction with the AD Rules, leads to the conclusion that the DA exercises quasi-judicial functions and is bound to act judicially. Pursuant to this, upon change of DA during an investigation, through the denial of a fresh public hearing, the successor DA reduces the requirement of public hearing to an empty formality and vitiates the investigation proceeding. On the basis of this, the Supreme Court quashed a notification imposing the anti-dumping duty and remanded the same to the DA. The legality of the Safeguards Board has been an issue in certain High Court writ petitions arising from safeguards cases, as has the issue of the public interest test and the need for a restructuring plan.

V Parties eligible to bring a case

Under section 9C of the Customs Tariff Act 1975, domestic industry and all interested parties on record may file an appeal before CESTAT. In general, interested parties include domestic industries, importers, foreign producers, exporters, government of the exporting country and trade or business associations. In practice, this remedy has so far been used more robustly by domestic industry or importers, rather than other interested parties.

VI Competent courts

CESTAT is the court of first instance for all appeals against the determinations of the DA. Thus, the subject matter jurisdiction of CESTAT has been specified by statutory provision under section 9C of the

Customs Tariff Act, 1975. As regards territorial jurisdiction, it has been stated that the Anti-Dumping Bench shall be situated in New Delhi. Hence, all appeals relating to anti-dumping, and also CVD determinations, must be filed before the New Delhi bench of CESTAT. There is no pecuniary jurisdiction involved in such judicial review proceedings related to trade remedy measures.

The High Courts under writ jurisdiction can be approached under Article 226 of the Constitution, which enables them to have subject matter jurisdiction over all matters relating to executive agencies or quasi-judicial bodies. However, for territorial jurisdiction, the party approaching the court must show that the cause of action or some part of it has arisen within the territorial jurisdiction of the High Court concerned. Similarly, there is no limit on the pecuniary jurisdiction of the High Courts. Since no judicial review is specifically provided for in Indian safeguards legislation, it is the generic power of judicial review of the various High Courts under Article 226 of the Constitution of India that has been resorted to by interested parties seeking judicial review of safeguard measures.

VII   Procedural steps

Section 9C(2) of the Customs Tariff Act, 1975 provides for the deadline for filing an appeal against any order regarding the determination or review regarding the existence, degree and effect of any subsidy or dumping in relation to the imports of any article thereof, to be 90 days. CESTAT may entertain any appeal after the expiry of 90 days, if just cause is shown for such delay. The appeal shall be in the form specified and accompanied by a fee of Rs. 5,000.[31] Any other application for grant of stay or any other purpose shall be accompanied by a fee of Rs. 500.[32]

CESTAT, after giving the parties to the appeal an opportunity of being heard, may pass such orders thereon as it thinks fit, confirming, modifying or annulling the order appealed against.[33] Such appeal shall be heard by a special bench constituted by the president of CESTAT for hearing such appeals, and such bench shall consist of the president and no fewer

---

[31] Section 9C(1A) of the Customs Tariff Act, 1975.
[32] Section 9C(1B) of the Customs Tariff Act, 1975.
[33] Section 9C(3) of the Customs Tariff Act, 1975.

than two members, and shall include one judicial and one technical member.[34]

It is required that the appeal must identify the DA, the domestic industry[35] on whose application the order was passed, and all other interested parties[36] (exporters, importers and trade associations) who submitted representations to the DA during the course of investigation, as respondents, unless the person required to be impleaded as respondent is himself the appellant. Similarly, after a copy of the appeal has been served, the respondents may file a reply within one month, and on receipt thereof, the appellant may file a rejoinder within one month or within such time as may be specified by CESTAT.[37] The appeal shall be defended by the DA through a department representative who has been authorized on behalf of the Central Government to plead and appear on behalf of the DA.

CESTAT shall, where it is possible to do so, hear and decide every appeal within a period of three years from the date on which such appeal is filed.[38] However, appeals at CESTAT in recent years have often taken longer to be decided.[39] It has not been unknown for a few appeals to take longer to adjudicate than the lifetime of the original measure (five years). In certain ways, this could be seen to frustrate the provision of an appeal mechanism.

VIII   Appeal

A second appeal can also be heard by the Supreme Court against any order by CESTAT relating, among other things, to the determination of any question having a relation to the rate of customs duties or to the value of goods for purposes of assessment under section 130E of the Customs Act, 1962. Therefore, CESTAT's orders made in judicial review proceedings on anti-dumping investigations or reviews may be appealed to the Supreme Court of India, since anti-dumping duties are on a par with customs duties within the meaning of section 130E of the Customs Act, 1962.

---

[34] Section 9C(5) of the Customs Tariff Act, 1975.
[35] Rule 2(b) of the AD and CVD Rules.   [36] Rule 2(c) of the AD and CVD Rules.
[37] Rule 15A of the Customs, Excise And Gold (Control) Appellate Tribunal (Procedure) Rules, 1982.
[38] Section 129(2A) of the Customs Act, 1962.
[39] The time frame for concluding anti-dumping investigations by the DA is one year from the date of initiation and is extendable by a further six months in special circumstances.

Similarly, an appeal in the form of a petition from any order by a High Court can be heard by the Supreme Court under Article 136 of the Constitution of India as a special leave petition.

IX Standard of review

It is now well accepted in the field of administrative law that an administrative action is subject to control by judicial review under three grounds, namely, illegality, irrationality ("rule of reason" test) and procedural impropriety.[40] *Illegality* as a ground of judicial review connotes that the decision-maker must correctly understand the law that regulates the decision-making power and must give effect to it. It is always a justiciable matter whether the decision-maker appreciated all relevant facts, applied the correct law and acted within its jurisdiction. *Irrationality* as a ground for judicial review deals with the question whether any sensible person, who had applied his or her mind to the question to be decided, could have arrived at the same conclusion.[41] Lastly, if a decision is in violation of principles of natural justice and contrary to procedural fairness, such decision suffers from *procedural impropriety*, which is the third ground for judicial review.

It is well settled that when making a decision, an administrator evaluates facts and applies the law to the facts. The decision-maker's choice and the finding recorded by such authority shall be treated as final unless it is perverse or irrational. Further, the courts in India have held that after appreciation of the facts, there is a second view possible as per the courts' consideration. Still, the courts cannot interfere with the decision on the ground that the conclusion reached by the decision-maker is not correct "in the eyes of the court". Even if there are two possible views, the decision-maker's finding on facts is treated as conclusive.

It has been observed that the orders of CESTAT are subject to judicial review only if they involve a substantive question of law or a dispute regarding the valuation or classification of goods regarding duty rates. In other words, only the decisions involving questions of fact are final in themselves, as there exists no provision in the law or any statute for any appeal against such decisions.

---

[40] *Tata Cellular* v. *Union of India*, 1994 SCC (6) 651.
[41] This came to be called "*Wednesbury* unreasonableness" following the doctrine developed in *Associated Picture Houses* v. *Wednesbury Corporation* (1947) 2 All ER 640.

It has also been observed many times that when a decision of CESTAT involves a question of fact, there is a tendency to file an appeal in the jurisdictional High Court by manipulating such a question of fact to appear to be a question of law. This results in a long drawn-out judicial battle, because all orders of High Courts are appealable to the Supreme Court, and if such distorted questions of fact as were presented as questions of law have not been admitted by the High Court, its order is further appealed in the Supreme Court of India.

The standard of review before CESTAT can relate to questions of fact or law, or to a mixed question of fact and law. An appeal before CESTAT does not amount to a *de novo* review. However, if there appears to be a clearly patent error on the face of it, CESTAT may operate as a fact-finding authority. It also examines the confidential information submitted by the DA in camera, including the disclosure statements and calculation methods adopted to modify the orders wherever found necessary. This review process is quite elaborate and exhaustive and considers more substantial issues involving determinations and effects of dumping and injury. CESTAT makes its own decision and even sets applicable duty rates.

At present, CESTAT usually adjudicates anti-dumping appeals only on the basis of relatively narrow technical issues, rather than the broader approach it adopts in other cases, and in contrast to the High Courts and the Supreme Court which have sometimes taken a broader view on both procedural and substantive issues.[42]

X   Remedies

Section 129B of the Customs Act, 1962 provides for the remedial powers available to CESTAT. It has the power to remand a matter for fresh determination[43] and also to provide injunctive relief. However, it has rarely granted stay of the definitive duty in force during the pendency of the trade remedies appeal, while it has more often granted such partial, whole or conditional injunctive relief in the nature of stay of pre-deposit of duty or penalty in other customs, excise or service tax appeals. As mentioned above, CESTAT may confirm, modify or annul the

---

[42] Proposals Regarding the Anti-Dumping Agreement Preparations for the 1999 Ministerial Conference available at http://commerce.nic.in/wtoaug2.htm (last visited 12.1.2012).

[43] *BASF South East Asia PTE* Ltd. v. *Designated Authority* 2010 (253) ELT 554 (Tri. – Del.).

challenged order. It can also refer the case back to the authority which made the determination. Orders can be made for fresh adjudication after taking additional evidence, if necessary.

The execution (levy of anti-dumping or countervailing duty) of a determination subject to adjudication is not subject to any injunction *pendente lite* merely because an appeal is instituted, but upon application, the courts may grant such an injunction in whole or in part, or subject to conditions, depending on the facts and circumstances of the case.

However, though the High Courts do not have specific jurisdiction over the proceedings under Indian anti-dumping law, they entertain appeals against the DA's actions under their writ jurisdiction at any stage of the investigation. This mechanism sometimes prolongs the investigation process beyond the 18 months (including extensions) provided for in the Indian AD Rules as well as the AD Agreement. Injunction of the investigation is possible, though uncommon, under the High Courts' writ jurisdiction as it includes writs, orders or directions or any other appropriate remedy.

XI   Overall assessment of the effectiveness of judicial review in India

Though judicial review of administrative actions has been almost a regular feature in the Indian system, it seems that the judicial review of trade remedy determinations has not yet attained its intended pace.

More often than not, the courts approve the determinations of the investigating authorities. There are provisions through which injunctions on measures may be granted, but this has rarely been done. Rather, a stay is usually not granted (particularly by CESTAT) where there is a definitive duty pending appeal. This contradicts the courts' decisions made in the judicial review of other types of administrative actions such as disciplinary issues, service matters or even tax matters.

In 1995–2008, appeals were filed in 68 of 188 (by India's product-specific count, which is different from WTO's product- and country-based count, which would be 390) final anti-dumping measures by various interested parties before CESTAT, and of these, final rulings were made in 49 cases. It is remarkable to note that 31 of these cases ended in favour of the DA, while 13 led to the modification, and five to complete annulment of the challenged decisions. During the period, 44 writ petitions were filed before the various High Courts. Two of these were transferred to the Supreme Court. During the same period there were 19 petitions in the Supreme Court. This period is interesting, because there was a decline in the number of fresh investigations in line with the global trend; even then, the number of appeals or writ petitions remained high.[44]

Indian practice reveals that not only has India complied with its obligations under the AD Agreement, but that it has also gone beyond what is required by maintaining a system of double judicial review, first before CESTAT and then before the Supreme Court of India, with separate judicial review possible by the various High Courts. As already noted, the AD Agreement is not directly applicable in India, but Indian courts do sometimes refer to it, along with the WTO panel and Appellate Body reports, to help interpret the domestic laws.

Though very few law schools offer specialized courses on trade remedies and no professional training as such is provided in this specific area of law in India, it is commendable that the Indian judiciary has been able to study and interpret various aspects of trade law to suit Indian conditions. It is to be submitted here that through judicial interpretations, the courts in India have tightened the otherwise "manageable" standards prescribed under the law in respect of each of these limbs. The Supreme Court has interpreted the rules regarding the determination of dumping on the basis of facts available in the case of *Designated Authority* v. *M/s Haldor Topsoe*.[45] Taking guidance from the observations made by the Supreme Court, in subsequent judicial pronouncements, CESTAT has tried to ensure that even while taking recourse to the "best judgment option", objectivity in evaluating the facts available is not compromised to skew the dumping margins (though this is difficult to enforce without more detailed discipline laid down). Even with regard to the "injury analysis", and "causal link", the judicial authorities have enunciated certain standards.[46]

Thus, various pronouncements made by judicial authorities, vested with appellate jurisdiction in dealing with various contentious aspects of anti-dumping law, making necessary interventions/interferences with the orders passed by the DA and insisting upon objective standards, have done much to mitigate some of the well-known anomalies of anti-dumping practices in India. The partial success achieved by the Indian courts in somewhat containing the abusive application of anti-dumping

---

[44] DGAD Report 2005, http://commerce.nic.in/traderemedies/pdf_ar04_05/ch1.pdf (last visited 12.1.2012).
[45] CA No. 487/2000.   [46] Appeal No. C/384/2000-A.

measures can be attributed to the largely independent nature of its judicial authorities, in particular its immunity from the pressures of domestic lobbies. Domestic industries have been the most robust pursuers of judicial remedies, followed by importers, and common non-participation (despite notice being issued to them) in such judicial reviews by other concerned interested parties has been reflected in the decisions by the court concerned or CESTAT. For instance, greater participation by exporters and users would help to better sensitize the judiciary to the complexity of the issues.

The Indian judicial review mechanism appears to be reasonably effective, in the sense that there are a number of options and increasingly robust use of the same.

XII   Concluding remarks and suggestions for improvement

CESTAT over the years has fine-tuned its examination of the DA's findings. Whereas once it appeared that CESTAT was disposed towards maintaining the DA's recommendations and the levy of anti-dumping duties by the Ministry of Finance, emerging trends have shown that it now sometimes enters into a relatively more objective examination of the DA's findings. However, unlike other revenue matters appealed before CESTAT, there still remains a reluctance to provide *ad interim* injunctive relief *pendente lite* in such appeals.

A multiplicity of *fora* and options has not always led to decisions that are strongly supported by practitioners, due both to institutional inadequacy and non-participation in appeals by a number of concerned interested parties, despite their receiving notice of the same. This sometimes manifests itself in anomalies in findings that cannot be re-examined entirely by CESTAT as an appellate body. Greater clarity, consistency and transparency in Indian provisions, practices and findings would improve the situation. However, it is commendable that the tradition of the "rule of law" in India has also contributed to imparting a degree of transparency and high analytical standards to anti-dumping practices, as compared, unfortunately, to the practices in many other jurisdictions.[47]

As already highlighted, India does not have a separate statute in respect of trade remedies specifically, and recourse is through the rules

---

[47] Sachin Datta, "Bringing Objectivity to Anti-Dumping Investigations – The Indian Model", www.algindia.com/publication/article600.pdf (last visited 12.1.2012).

made under the Customs Tariff Act of 1975. The rules do not cover all aspects of anti-dumping actions in fair detail, compared to the rules and regulations in other major jurisdictions: for instance, there are no manuals. However, through the use of trade notices it may also be possible for practices to be publicized in a transparent manner. This would assist the judiciary in judicial reviews. The rules in some jurisdictions are fairly exhaustive and provide adequate details and guidelines, including methods of calculating various elements in an anti-dumping investigation in different circumstances. Indian AD Rules, for example, lack comparable clarity and transparency and details, and there are a few gaps in the provisions. The rules appear to have been framed as a response to the AD Agreement in 1994, without much prior experience of anti-dumping investigations. The situation is similar in respect of other trade remedy provisions.

In addition, India should build a suitable institutional and administrative system for handling the growing number of complaints and to conduct the kind of analysis that is required. The most suitable institutional framework for India could be the creation of a separate Directorate General of Trade Remedies (hereinafter DGTR), covering all trade remedy actions and also any determination of quantitative restrictions, and free of the administrative control of the Ministry of Commerce and Industry (or any other ministry), for conducting all investigations, and to defend all trade remedy actions by other countries.

Similarly, CESTAT members and High Court and Supreme Court justices may be familiarized with the disciplines of trade remedial investigations and certain inherent complexities. In the case of CESTAT, a strict time frame of one year or so may be stipulated within which an appeal must be adjudicated. These steps would lead to improvements.

It has been suggested at times that Indian authorities have initiated anti-dumping cases represented by one producer only. This issue could perhaps also be addressed by having two distinct wings in the proposed DGTR, one of which could carry out injury analysis of the domestic industry independently. The other wing would carrry out the dumping margin analysis independently. This way, two independent wings would deal with the basic analysis under the same authority and the DA would then take a final view based on the analysis. This would bring more transparency and clarity to the process. Both wings should be comprised of experts in their respective fields. In case in future India considers measures in the form of quantitative restrictions instead of duties, any authority formed for such a determination could also be included as a separate third wing within a DGTR, and not separately. The officers deputed to such a DGTR should not simultaneously be assigned any other duties for which they would be under the administrative control of any ministry.

It has also been suggested that freeing CESTAT from the administrative control of the Ministry of Finance (under which it currently operates) would be the fulfilment of the independent review mechanism envisaged under Article 13 of the AD Agreement. Even better would be if there were a tribunal focusing solely on trade remedies appeals, or at least a well-defined time frame for deciding such appeals and clear process in respect of the review of facts, provisional measures and for injunctive relief and the extent to which it would consider the relevant WTO agreement or the Appellate Body's pronouncements. At times, CESTAT is non-functional for want of appointment of its president. It is headed by a president who, along with two other members, sits in judgment on DGAD appeals. It is noteworthy that for the last two years, the appellate function has been curtailed due to the absence of the president. The Ministry of Finance should take pre-emptive action to ensure availability and continuity of this appellate tribunal.

It should be mentioned here that in light of India's well-established legal system and fairly high litigation rate, the legal fees and costs of Indian appeals are high, and this sometimes discourages foreign exporters from challenging Indian trade remedy determinations in national . *fora* and exporters–users over time would benefit by making more robust use of the appeal mechanisms, or at least contest robustly the appeals filed by domestic industries. Having said that, it may be observed here that the existing mechanisms for judicial review in India remain possibly more cost-effective and sometimes less time-consuming than the WTO's dispute settlement mechanism. However, it is not clear that its overall efficacy over the WTO dispute settlement in qualitative terms can be considered to be established.[48]

In conclusion, India has a well-established legal system that, among others, for reasons of unfamiliarity, was slow to review fully trade remedy measures and findings. However, this has begun to change in recent years and there is an increasing trend towards more rigorous exercise of the judicial review power in India.

---

[48] Law Commission of India, *Sixty-Second Report on Review of Functions of Central Administrative Tribunal; Customs Excise and Gold Tribunal and Income Tax Appellate Tribunal* (1998).

15

China: an untested theoretical possibility?

HENRY GAO

I Introduction

Compared to most other WTO members, China is a latecomer to the trade remedies game. However, such a slow start does not prevent trade remedies from rapidly becoming one of the most favourite weapons wielded by the trade policy establishment in China. As of March 2011, China had launched a total of 189 anti-dumping investigations and four countervailing duty investigations,[1] making it one of the most frequent users of trade remedy measures, especially anti-dumping measures.

While China has made great strides in learning and adopting most of the intricacies of this new craft of trade policy, there is one weak spot in its trade remedy apparatus: judicial review of trade remedy determinations. Under both the WTO trade remedies agreements and the Accession Protocol of China, China is obliged to establish a judicial review mechanism for trade remedy determinations. However, even though formal rules have been established after China's accession to the WTO, there are still many problems and ambiguities within the existing framework. Worse still, as no case has been launched under the judicial review mechanism so far, there is little clue as to how the system will operate in practice. As China is home to one of the world's largest markets, it is crucial that exporting firms have a proper understanding of the judicial review system in China, which is also the objective of this chapter.

The chapter begins with an overview of the regulatory and institutional framework for trade remedy measures, followed by a critical

---

[1] Bureau of Fair Trade, *Maoyi Jiuji Dongtai (Updates on Trade Remedies)*, Volume 1, available at http://gpj.mofcom.gov.cn/aarticle/d/ci/201105/20110507566737.html?34292 17503=4255115554 (last visited 22 September 2011).

analysis of the procedural aspects of judicial review. We will not only address shortcomings in the existing system, but also offer suggestions on how the system can be improved.

II   The regulatory and institutional framework for trade remedy measures

While the enactment of the Anti-Dumping and Countervailing Duty Regulations in 1997 by the Ministry of Foreign Trade and Economic Cooperation (hereinafter the MOFTEC) is commonly regarded as the first trade remedies regulation in China, this is not the first time trade remedy measures appeared in Chinese laws. In 1994, when the first ever Foreign Trade Law (hereinafter FTL)[2] was promulgated, it already included three provisions on trade remedy measures.[3] The emergence of trade remedy regulations in China in the mid-1990s is not by coincidence, but propelled by both internal and external reasons.

First, since 1993, China has been the world's top target of trade remedy measures, and especially of anti-dumping measures. Many of the Chinese companies involved in the cases were assisted by industry associations such as the China Chamber of Commerce of Metals Minerals & Chemicals Importers & Exporters which are affiliated with the MOFTEC. These cases taught the MOFTEC the usefulness of trade remedy measures, and inspired it to follow the same approach. Second, the early 1990s also witnessed foreign companies' growing interest in the Chinese market. As domestic firms started to feel competitive pressure, they turned to the MOFTEC for help. Naturally, trade remedies became the policy tools of choice.

As the 1994 FTL provisions on trade remedy measures were rather sketchy, the MOFTEC issued the Anti-Dumping and Countervailing Duty Regulations in 1997 to provide practical guidance. In the same year, China launched its first anti-dumping investigation on *Newspaper Print from Korea, Canada and the United States*. Fourteen years later, China has built an impressive regulatory framework on trade remedies, which includes the following laws and regulations.

---

[2] Foreign Trade Law, promulgated by the Seventh Session of the Standing Committee of the Eighth National People's Congress of China on 12 May 1994.

[3] Articles 29, 30, 31. Articles 30 and 31 are essentially provisions on anti-dumping and countervailing measures without explicitly naming them. Article 29 is the provision on safeguard measures.

(1) Laws including the Foreign Trade Law, which was first promulgated in 1994 and revised in 2004;
(2) Regulations, including:
    (a) The Anti-Dumping Regulation (hereinafter ADR);
    (b) The Countervailing Duty Regulation (hereinafter CDR);
    (c) The Safeguards Regulation (hereinafter SR);
(3) Administrative Rules, including 12 specific rules on various issues in anti-dumping procedures such as the initiation, public hearing and interim review, four rules on countervailing duty measures, three rules on safeguards measures and one rule on the administrative review of trade remedy measures.

Until 2003, the responsibility for trade remedies was divided between the MOFTEC and the State Economic and Trade Commission (hereinafter SETC); the former is responsible for the determination of dumping or subsidy, the latter for injury determinations. In March 2003, as part of the restructuring of the central government ministries, both functions were merged into the newly created Ministry of Commerce (hereinafter the MOFCOM), which was established to replace the MOFTEC and SETC. Nonetheless, within the MOFCOM, the two functions are still assigned to two different bureaux: the Bureau of Fair Trade, which is in charge of the determinations on dumping, subsidy and increase in imports (in the case of safeguard investigations); and the Bureau of Industry Injury Investigation, which is in charge of the injury determinations in these cases. Most of the decisions regarding the initiation of the investigation, imposition of provisional and final measures, acceptance or rejection of price undertakings and termination of investigations are taken by the Bureau of Fair Trade with assistance from the Bureau of Industry Injury Investigation.

III   The legal framework for judicial review of trade remedy determinations

Under the WTO Agreements, members are required to provide judicial review mechanisms for trade remedy measures.[4] For China, establishing an independent judicial review mechanism is a major challenge for two reasons. First, under the Constitution, there are no formal checks and balances

---

[4] See, e.g., GATT Article X.3.b, Article 13 of the Anti-dumping Agreement and Article 23 of the Agreement on Subsidies and Countervailing Measures.

between the judiciary and the legislature. Instead, according to both Articles 67 and 128, the courts shall be supervised by the corresponding levels of the People's Congress, which in turn is controlled by the China Communist Party. Second, in practice most courts are unwilling or unable to review administrative decisions, as the finance of the court is controlled by the corresponding levels of government. Thus, during China's WTO accession negotiations, several WTO members raised this concern and demanded that China accept an explicit obligation to institute the appropriate judicial review mechanism for the implementation of trade laws and regulations. The resulting provision is section 2(D) of the Accession Protocol, in which China agreed to establish independent tribunals to review trade-related administrative actions.

Upon China's accession to the WTO, the State Council issued the ADR and the CDR, and they each include a provision on judicial review.[5] However, these two provisions state only that judicial review shall be conducted by the People's Court, and do not provide any details on how such a review is to be conducted. To provide guidance on the operation of judicial review, the Supreme People's Court issued three judicial interpretations in 2002: Rules on Several Issues Concerning the Review of International Trade Administrative Cases (hereinafter ITA JI); Rules on Certain Issues Concerning Application of Law in Hearings of Anti-Dumping Administrative Cases (hereinafter AD JI); and Rules on Certain Issues Concerning Application of Law in Hearings of Countervailing Duty Administrative Cases (hereinafter CVD JI). While these rules provide helpful guidance on many procedural issues in the judicial review of trade remedy determinations, they have left many questions unanswered, as we will discuss below.

IV   Procedural issues in judicial review

1   Reviewable determinations

Under the Administrative Litigation Law (hereinafter ALL) of China,[6] administrative acts are divided into two categories. The first is abstract administrative acts, which include administrative regulations, rules and decisions that are applicable to society in general.[7] The

---

[5] See Article 53 of the ADR and Article 52 of the CDR.
[6] Adopted by the Second Session of the Seventh National People's Congress on 4 April 1989.
[7] ALL, Article 12.

second regards specific administrative acts, which are implementations of laws and regulations by the administrative organs which affect the rights and obligations of individuals or firms.[8] The former is not reviewable by court, while the latter is mostly reviewable, unless the law explicitly states that the authority for final decision rests with the administrative organ.[9]

This approach is followed by the judicial review mechanism for trade remedy measures. Under Article 53 of the ADR and Article 52 of the CDR, only the following decisions are reviewable: first, final determinations on the existence of dumping or subsidy, the amount of subsidy or margin of dumping, injury and the extent of injury; second, decisions on whether or not to impose definitive anti-dumping or countervailing duties; third, decisions on whether or not to apply anti-dumping or countervailing duties on a retroactive basis, to grant refunds, and to impose anti-dumping duties on imports from new shippers; and fourth, decisions on interim or sunset review of anti-dumping and countervailing duties and price undertakings. These categories are confirmed in the judicial interpretations on anti-dumping and countervailing measures.

As the scope of judicial review is delineated by positive enumeration, one can conclude that other types of decisions not explicitly mentioned in the regulations and judicial interpretations are not reviewable. These include, among others, the decisions on whether or not to accept an application or to initiate an investigation, to impose provisional measures, to accept or reject an undertaking, or to terminate an investigation without a definitive measure on the grounds of public interest or other reasons.

At the same time, one may argue that some of these decisions could be reviewable according to Article 11.5 of the ALL, which states that administrative litigation can be brought in cases where "an application is filed to request the administrative agency to perform its statutory duty to protect personal or property rights but the agency has either refused to perform or failed to respond to the request". It could be argued that the rejection of an application and decision to terminate an investigation are cases of refusal to perform such statutory duties.[10] The author finds such views rather problematic. In performing their statutory duties, the

---

[8] Ibid., Article 11.   [9] Ibid.

[10] Chen Lianggang, "On Several Fundamental Issues in Judicial Review of Anti-Dumping Measures" 3(2003) *Journal of Legal Application* 46.

administrative agencies usually have wide discretion: they may decide to act in one case, and not to act in another. Thus, the rejection of an application after careful consideration is, by itself, a way of performing the statutory duties. Thus, such cases should not be reviewable in court. Of course, if the investigating authority simply ignores the application and fails to provide any response within 60 days, this is clearly "failure to respond", and thus should be reviewable.

It might be argued that the judicial review obligation under section 2(D) of China's Accession Protocol is very broad, as it covers "the opportunity for appeal, without penalty, by individuals or enterprises affected by *any administrative action* subject to review" (emphasis added). Thus, the rejection of an application falls under "any administrative action" and should be reviewable. In the view of the author, such a reading is incorrect. The passage quoted above refers only to *who* may bring a review rather than *what* may be reviewed. Instead, to determine the scope of administrative actions subject to review, one must consult the first paragraph of the same section, which states that:

> China shall establish, or designate, and maintain tribunals, contact points and procedures for the prompt review of all administrative actions relating to the implementation of laws, regulations, judicial decisions and administrative rulings of general application *referred to* in Article X:1 of the GATT 1994, Article VI of the GATS and the relevant provisions of the TRIPS Agreement (emphasis added).

In other words, only those administrative actions which are referred to under the relevant provisions of the GATT, GATS and TRIPS are included in the scope of reviewable actions. As the rejection of an application is not included in the Anti-Dumping Agreement (hereinafter AD Agreement), it is in turn not included in the GATT and therefore shall not be covered by the reviewable scope.

While the scope of reviewable determinations in China is narrower than some other WTO members, this is entirely consistent with the obligations under the AD Agreement and Agreement on Subsidies and Countervailing Measures (hereinafter SCM Agreement), which only requires members to provide a review mechanism on "administrative actions relating to final determinations and reviews of determinations".[11]

---

[11] AD Agreement Article 13, SCM Agreement Article 23.

2   Parties eligible to bring a case

Neither the ADR nor the CDR explicitly states the categories of persons who may bring a judicial review case. Instead, this can only be found in the two judicial interpretations. According to Article 2 of the AD JI, cases may only be brought by "interested parties", such as individuals or organizations that have a legal interest in the administrative actions on anti-dumping. For clarification, the same article also specifies that "interested parties" include those who file a written application for an anti-dumping investigation, exporters, importers and all other natural or juridical persons or other organizations which have legal interest.

It is worth noting that the list does not explicitly mention the government of the exporter. Some commentators have interpreted this to mean that the government is not eligible to bring a case.[12] The author does not agree with this interpretation. The government of the exporting member has been explicitly included among "interested parties" in both Article 6.11 of the AD Agreement and Article 19 of the ADR. If the Supreme Court really wished to exclude the governments from the scope, it would specifically have stated this in the judicial interpretation.

The definition of "interested parties" under Article 2 of the CVD JI uses language identical to the AD JI. However, the definition of "interested parties" under the CDR is slightly different from the ADR. Article 19 of the ADR states that "the MOFCOM shall notify the decision to initiate an investigation to the applicant, known exporters and importers, government of the exporting Member, and other interested organizations or individuals (hereinafter referred to as interested parties)". In contrast, Article 19 of the CDR states that "the MOFCOM shall notify the decision to initiate an investigation to the applicant, known exporters and importers and other interested organizations or individuals (hereinafter referred to as "interested parties") and the government of the exporting Member". Thus, it seems that the definition of "interested parties" under the CDR does not include the government of the exporting member.

Another potentially problematic issue is the eligibility of foreign persons to initiate a judicial review proceeding. According to Article 10 of the ITA JI, when participating in administrative litigation on international trade cases, foreign parties shall enjoy the same rights and

---

[12] Chen Yuxiang, "Research on the Administrative Litigation Process Regarding Anti-dumping in China" 22(1)(2004) *Tribune of Political Science and Law* 181.

obligations as Chinese parties, except in cases where Article 71.2 of the ALL applies. According to this provision, if a foreign court restricts the rights of Chinese parties in administrative litigation, the Chinese courts shall apply the same restrictions on foreign parties on a reciprocal basis. Some scholars argue that the application of the reciprocity principle could lead to problems.[13] For example, as the United States Court of International Trade does not allow interested parties that have not participated in an anti-dumping investigation to bring a case, courts in China could also prohibit US firms that have not participated in the investigation from bringing a case.[14] However, if the same Chinese court grants European firms standing in the same case, as there is no such restriction in European courts, this could result in discrimination against US firms in violation of the most favoured nation principle.[15]

3   Defendants and third parties

According to Article 25 of the ALL, the administrative agency that takes the specific administrative action shall be the respondent in a judicial review proceeding brought with respect to that action. This general rule is confirmed by Article 3 of the Judicial Interpretation on AD, which states that "the respondent in an administrative litigation on anti-dumping shall be the relevant agency under the State Council that takes the specific administrative action". As mentioned earlier, the power for trade remedy measures used to be divided between the MOFTEC and the SETC before the restructuring of the central government in 2003. At that time, the MOFTEC would be the respondent in cases on determinations on dumping and dumping margins, the SETC the respondent in injury determinations. As power has been consolidated into the new MOFCOM since 2003, the latter is now the respondent in most cases. The only instances where the MOFCOM would not be the respondent are cases where the complainant challenges the decision on the imposition or the review of anti-dumping duties or the actual collection of such duties, of which the Tariff Commission and the Customs Administration respectively are in charge.

On the other hand, even in cases where the decision is made by another administrative agency, the MOFCOM is still very likely to get

---

[13] Sun Wen, "A Study on the Judicial Review of Anti-Dumping Cases in Foreign Trade" (unpublished manuscript), on file with author.
[14] Ibid.   [15] Ibid.

involved. For example, according to Article 38 of the ADR, the Tariff Commission shall make its decision on whether or not to impose anti-dumping duties pursuant to the MOFCOM's recommendations. Unlike its counterparts in other countries, the Tariff Commission is not a technical agency staffed by technocrats. Instead, it is a senior political coordinating mechanism among different ministries. Headed by the Minister of Finance, it has 11 commissioners who are all vice-ministers of various relevant ministries.[16] Thus, it is highly unlikely that the Tariff Commission would refuse to follow the MOFCOM's recommendations. In such a case, even though the Tariff Commission is named as the respondent, it is the MOFCOM rather than the Tariff Commission which will have detailed knowledge on evidence, information and reasons for the decision. In order to have a proper review, the MOFCOM will have to participate in the litigation in some capacity. That is why Article 4 of the Judicial Interpretation on AD states: "other relevant agencies under the State Council which have legal interest in the administrative action under review may participate in the case as third parties". Unfortunately, this provision still leaves many important questions unanswered. For example, shall third parties be added pursuant to the request of the complainant, respondent or the potential third party itself, or by the order of the court? Is the matter part of the rights of the complainant or respondent, or of the power of the court? If an administrative agency is unwilling to participate as a third party, may the court force the agency to appear in court? No answer can be found in the ALL either, as it simply notes in Article 27 that the other interested parties "may request to join the case as third parties, or participate in the case pursuant to the notice of the court". The Judicial Interpretation by the Supreme Court on Implementing the ALL[17] also fails to provide clear guidance on the issue. It would be helpful to have this important issue clarified in the future.

4 Competent courts

In fulfilling the obligation to maintain a judicial review mechanism, Article 13 of the AD Agreement gives WTO members a choice between

---

[16] General Office of the State Council, *Notice on the Main Functions and Adjustment of the Personnel of the Tariff Commission of the State Council*, Guobanfa (2003) No. 33, 26 April 2003.

[17] Supreme People's Court, *Judicial Interpretation on the Implementation of the PRC Administrative Litigation Law*, Fashi (2000) No. 8, 8 March 2000.

judicial, arbitral and administrative tribunals. During the drafting of the ADR, there were several suggestions on the review mechanism. Some suggested creating an independent review body, but this proposal was rejected, because trade remedy measures involve highly specialized and technical work, and it is unrealistic to expect another separate administrative agency to have the same level of technical expertise.[18] Another suggestion was to grant the power of judicial review to a court. As to which court would be responsible for the judicial review, there were again two proposals. The first was to create a specialized court modelled after the US Court of International Trade to deal with all international trade administrative cases such as anti-dumping and countervailing duty measures.[19] This proposal was rejected, as people did not expect that there would be many cases involving international trade administrative measures and creating a specialized court just for that purpose would have been a waste of resources.[20] In the end, it was agreed that international trade cases should be handled by the ordinary courts, for two reasons. First, compared to administrative agencies, courts are generally viewed to be much more impartial and objective.[21] Second, without domestic judicial review mechanism, foreign firms and governments would be forced to resort to the WTO dispute settlement mechanism whenever they had a complaint against an administrative decision.[22] Thus, the preference was to provide a domestic judicial review mechanism to deal with such complaints first.[23]

This new arrangement was later confirmed in the ITA JI, which states in Article 2 that international trade cases shall be tried by the court. In most courts in China, there are three functional divisions: the Criminal Division, which handles criminal trials; the Civil Division, which handles civil cases; and the Administrative Litigation Division, which deals with administrative litigation cases. As international trade cases involve the administrative actions of government agencies, they should be handled by the Administrative Litigation Division.[24]

Another issue involves which level of the court shall hear international trade cases. There are four level of courts in China: the lowest level is the Basic Court, which is usually established at the county level for rural

---

[18] Kong Xiangjun, "A Comparative Study on the Judicial Review Systems of Anti-dumping Cases" (2003) *National Judges College Law Journal* (Issue 202–3) 7.
[19] Chen Yuxiang, "On Several Fundamental Issues", at 179–80.
[20] Kong Xiangjun, "A Comparative Study", at 7.   [21] Ibid.   [22] Ibid.   [23] Ibid.
[24] Article 2.

areas, or district level for urban areas; next is the Intermediate Court, which is usually established in large cities that cover several counties or districts; then there is the High Court, which is the highest court for a province and typically sits in each province's capital; and the highest for the whole country is the Supreme Court, which is the final court of appeal for any case and sits in Beijing. As international trade administrative cases are usually quite complicated and technical, most Basic Court judges will not be equipped to handle them. Thus, according to Article 5 of the ITA JI, the Intermediate Court with jurisdiction over a case has original jurisdiction.

Given that the complainant and respondent in an administrative litigation might be based in different places, an important question emerges: which Intermediate Court shall have geographical jurisdiction? Article 17 of the ALL resolves this problem by stating that the principle of *actor sequitur forum rei* shall be followed; i.e. the court where the administrative agency making the administrative decision is based shall have jurisdiction. Trade remedy measures can only be taken by the MOFCOM, the Tariff Commission and the Customs Administration, all of which are central government ministries based in Beijing. Thus, the Intermediate Court of Beijing has jurisdiction. Due to its importance as the national capital, Beijing Municipality is granted provincial level status. Within Beijing Municipality, there is one provincial level High Court and two Intermediate Courts: the No. 1 Intermediate Court which governs the counties and districts in the western part of the Municipality, and the No. 2 Intermediate Court which governs the eastern part.[25] During the drafting of the ITA JI, there were different opinions as to which court would have original jurisdiction in trade remedies cases.[26] Both the MOFTEC and SETC suggested that the High Court of Beijing should have original jurisdiction, while some scholars and judges argued that the Intermediate Courts have sufficient competency to handle such cases and should be granted original jurisdiction.[27] In the end, even though the AD JI includes language specifically addressing the issue, the problem remains unresolved, as it simply states that both the High Court and Intermediate Court designated by the High Court could have

---

[25] The only exception to the division is Fengtai District which, although physically located in the western part, is governed by No. 2 Intermediate Court.

[26] Kong Xiangjun, "Trial of International Trade Administrative Litigation Cases Concerning WTO Rules" (2002) *National Judges College Law Journal* (Issue 198) 11.

[27] Ibid.

original jurisdiction.[28] Assuming original jurisdiction is granted to the Intermediate Court, another related question arises: which Intermediate Court shall have jurisdiction? This issue was resolved by the High Court of Beijing in 2002, which stated in a Judicial Interpretation that jurisdiction for cases involving anti-dumping, countervailing duty and trade approval shall "temporarily be granted to the No. 2 Intermediate Court".[29] Presumably, this is because the MOFCOM is located in Dongcheng District, which actually falls within the eastern part and thus within the jurisdiction of the No. 2 Intermediate Court.

5 Standard of review, burden of proof, evidentiary rules and applicable law

During the drafting of the ADR, there were discussions on whether the review should be limited to issues of law or should include issues of facts as well.[30] An earlier draft suggested that "judicial review shall be limited to issues of application of law and procedure". However, this language was deleted from the final version and there was no reference to the standard of review. This led to considerable confusion and some commentators, including the former Office of Anti-Dumping and Countervailing Duty at SETC, interpreted this to mean that only review of legal issues is allowed.[31] However, according to Article 54 of the ALL, courts can review both the legal and factual aspects of an administrative action. As the ADR does not contain any rule to the contrary, the general rule under the ALL should apply. This is confirmed by the AD JI, which notes that the court may review the legality of both the legal and factual bases for the administrative action.[32]

5.1   Review of facts

Because trade remedy determinations are highly complicated and technical decisions, one major concern by the administrative authorities was whether the courts could conduct a proper factual examination.[33] As the

---

[28] Article 5.

[29] High Court of Beijing Municipality, *Notice on the Issuance of the Implementation of the Reply by the Supreme People's Court on the Jurisdictions on Patent and Trademark Cases After the Revision of the Patent Law and Trademark Law and the Jurisdictions on International Trade Administrative Litigation Cases*, Jinggaofafa (2002) 195, 20 May 2002.

[30] Kong Xiangjun, "A Comparative Study", 12.   [31] Ibid.   [32] Article 6.

[33] Kong Xiangjun, "A Comparative Study", 13.

ALL does not provide detailed rules in this regard, the Supreme Court made a special effort to address the issue by including three articles in the two judicial interpretations.[34] These articles elaborate the rules with respect to both the burden of proof and evidentiary requirements.

First, the primary burden of proof, i.e. the burden of proving that the administrative action under review is justified, lies with the respondent, who shall produce both the factual and legal bases in reaching the administrative decision. Moreover, such evidence shall be based on the record of the investigation. This is apparently designed to prevent the investigating agency from making a decision first and then conjuring up evidence on a *post facto* basis. It also creates an incentive for the investigating authorities to keep proper records during the investigation process. Only facts that were filed on the record during the investigation can be used to justify the administrative action.

Also, since judicial review will be based on an examination of the record, the court will not conduct a *de novo* review. In other words, the court will not "get its hands dirty" by trying to determine whether a particular fact is true or not, but instead will focus on two questions: first, whether the investigating authority has followed proper evidentiary rules, such as whether the form of evidence fulfils the legal requirements, and whether the authority has followed the proper rules and procedures in collecting, examining and verifying the evidence;[35] second, assuming the evidence is true, whether or not it supports the determinations made by the investigating authorities.

The complainant bears the burden of proving its own assertions. For example, if the complainant argues that the investigating authority has made the wrong determination by finding dumping while the export price is actually higher than the normal value, it would have to prove that this is the case. To prevent unscrupulous firms from deliberately withholding information during the investigation in the hope of unravelling the whole final determinations by producing such evidence later in court, the JIs also explicitly affirm the "best information available" rule. Apparently modelled after Article 6.8 of the AD Agreement and Article 12.7 of the SCM Agreement, this rule has two meanings: first, according to Article 9, if during the investigation, the interested party (presumably the complainant) refuses to provide information without any proper reason, fails to provide information truthfully, or otherwise significantly impedes the investigation, the investigating authority will

---

[34] Articles 7–9 of the JIs.   [35] Kong Xiangjun, "A Comparative Study", 13.

makes its decision on the basis of the facts available, such decision may be regarded as supported by sufficient evidence: second, in the same scenario as above, even if the complainant later produces the information during the judicial review, the court will not admit it.

If the court finds the evidence submitted by the complainant admissible, it will then proceed to examine the relevancy, legitimacy and authenticity of the evidence. If the evidence satisfies these requirements, the court will use it as the basis for its decision.

5.2   Review of law

In contrast with the detailed rules on the standard of review for factual issues, the JIs do not provide much guidance on the standard applicable with regard to the review of the legal reasoning. According to Article 54 of the ALL and Article 10 of the JIs, the court may revise or repeal the administrative action if the investigating authority fails correctly to apply the laws or regulations. Annulment of the administrative action may be ordered by the court if it has one of the following defects: lack of substantial evidence; incorrect application of the law; violation of due process; *ultra vires*; or abuse of administrative power. This seems to suggest that the court may conduct a *de novo* review. On the other hand, because the same provisions also provide that the court may remand the case to the investigating authority for a new determination, this seems to suggest that the court does not wish to interfere too much in the substantive decision made by the authority. In other words, if there are several reasonable approaches in applying the law and the investigating authority adopts one such approach, the court will not repeal the measure even if it might reach a different conclusion. Given the considerable confusion, it would be very helpful if the Supreme Court were to further clarify the standard of review on legal issues in its future decisions or interpretations.

5.3   Applicable law

In conducting its legal analysis, the court applies the laws or regulations on anti-dumping and countervailing duties. In addition, the court may consult the relevant administrative rules made by the relevant government agencies, such as the detailed rules on the conduct of investigations. These administrative rules are used simply as guidance for the court, and it is not required to follow them. However, given the highly specialized nature of trade remedy investigations, the court is very likely to treat such administrative rules with great deference, and to follow them.

One tricky question is whether the WTO AD Agreement and SCM Agreement can be directly applied in the judicial review. As I have discussed elsewhere, this is an issue unsettled in both theory and practice.[36] Justice Li Guoguang, a Deputy President of the Supreme People's Court, takes the view that the WTO Agreements cannot be directly applied in China.[37] In my opinion, such view is problematic, as Paragraph 75 of the Working Party Report explicitly recognizes the rights of individuals and entities to invoke China's commitments under the WTO Agreements and the Draft Protocol, and denying them such rights would probably violate China's accession commitments.

Interestingly, even though Justice Li insisted that the rules prohibit direct application of the WTO Agreements, he also recognized that, when the provisions of the relevant domestic laws and regulations could be subject to two or more reasonable interpretations, and one interpretation is consistent with the provisions of an international treaty that China has concluded or acceded to, such interpretation shall be adopted.[38] However, this only solves part of the problem, in instances when there is a reasonable interpretation of the law or regulation that is consistent with the WTO Agreements. Obviously, when all reasonable interpretations available are inconsistent with the WTO Agreements, then the WTO Agreements will not be applied, leading to a violation of China's WTO obligations.

Given the conservative approach China adopts on the direct application of the AD Agreement and SCM Agreement, it is also very unlikely that, in their judgments, the Chinese courts will refer to the WTO jurisprudence as embodied in the panel and Appellate Body reports.

6 Procedural rules

The JIs contain no special provision on the litigation procedure. Therefore, the general procedure under the ALL applies. Normally, a

---

[36] Henry Gao, "China's Participation in the WTO: A Lawyer's Perspective", in *Singapore Year Book of International Law* (2007), pp. 58–9.

[37] Tian Ji and Lin Zi, "Judicial Review on Administrative Cases on International Trade: Chinese Courts Will Start to Accept Administrative Cases Brought by Foreigners", *People's Daily (Overseas Edition)* (7 September 2002), at 3.

[38] Ibid. See also Rule 9.

judicial review proceeding is initiated when the complainant files a complaint with the court. Some laws might require the exhaustion of administrative remedies before the commencement of judicial review. In such cases, the court will reject any complaint that was filed without first going through the administrative reconsideration process.[39] Under the ADR and CDR, the complainant may choose either to apply for administrative reconsideration first or seek judicial review directly without administrative reconsideration.[40] Thus, the administrative reconsideration process is not a prerequisite and the court cannot reject a case for failing to apply for reconsideration first.

However, if the complainant does indeed choose to apply for administrative reconsideration first, then the court will not accept a complaint until after a final decision has been reached in the reconsideration.[41] In such a case, the complainant may bring a case within 15 days of receiving the decision of reconsideration.[42] If the complainant chose to file a case in the court without first seeking reconsideration, the case shall be filed "within three months of knowing of the administrative action".[43] It is unclear how the date of "knowing of the administrative action" is defined. Normally, the determinations of the investigating authority are published in the *China Foreign Trade and Economic Cooperation Gazette* and will take effect the day after the publication date. Thus, it could be understood to be either the publication date or the effective date. Clarification of this point would be helpful.

Upon receiving the complaint, the court will first conduct a preliminary review to determine if it has been properly filed, against the following criteria: first, whether the complainant is someone who has been harmed by the specific administrative action at issue; second, whether the respondent has been properly identified; third, whether the complaint includes a specific claim and factual basis; and fourth, whether the administrative action is reviewable by court and falls under the proper jurisdiction of the court receiving the complaint.[44] The court will then make a ruling on whether to accept or reject the case within seven days of receiving the complaint.[45] If the complaint is defective and the court orders such defects to be rectified, the seven-day period will only commence from the date when the court receives the properly modified complaint.[46]

---

[39] Article 37, ALL.   [40] Article 53, ADR.   [41] JI on ALL, Article 34.
[42] ALL, Article 38.   [43] Ibid., 39.   [44] Ibid., 41.   [45] Ibid., 42.   [46] ALL JI, Article 32.

Once the court decides to accept a case, it serves a copy of the complaint on the respondent within five days.[47] The respondent must submit its record of administrative action and written defence to the court within 10 days of receiving the complaint. The court then serves a copy of the defence on the complainant within five days. To prevent the respondent from delaying the process by deliberately refusing to submit a written defence, the law also explicitly states that the litigation process shall continue even if the respondent fails to provide a defence.

As mentioned earlier, administrative litigations are handled by the Administrative Litigation Division. For each case, the division will appoint a panel that usually consists of three members, who can either all be professional judges, or a combination of at least one judge and two people's assessors.[48] The people's assessor system is a unique feature of the legal system in China, and there are several important differences when compared to the jury systems in other countries. First, while the jury may only decide factual questions, the people's assessors can decide both factual and legal questions.[49] Second, while jurors are selected from all eligible voters in a region, the people's assessors are not chosen on an *ad hoc* basis in every case. Instead, they are selected from a list of names maintained by the court. Anyone who wishes to serve as an assessor may either apply to the court directly or ask his/her firm or grassroots organization to recommend him/her to the court.[50] The court then selects the most suitable candidates and forwards their names to the Standing Committee of the local People's Congress for official appointment. The term of service of the people's assessors is five years. For each case, the assessors are selected by the court randomly. A third difference is, while jurors may be removed by either party for a wide variety of reasons, the people's assessors cannot be removed unless they are recused for conflict of interest reasons. Fourth, while jurors play only a very limited role during the trial, the people's assessors are much more powerful. Indeed, they have the same powers as judges, except that they may not serve as the presiding judge in a panel.[51] If the panel members disagree on a decision, the assessors have the same voting rights as the judge.[52]

---

[47] ALL, Article 43.   [48] Ibid., 46.

[49] Decision of the Standing Committee of the National People's Congress on the Improvement of the People's Assessor System, adopted by the Eleventh Session of the Standing Committee of the Tenth National People's Congress, 8 August 2004, at Article 11.

[50] Article 8.   [51] Ibid., Article 1.   [52] Article 11.

As the remuneration for people's assessors is meagre, and conducting trials is time-consuming, most people's assessors tend to be retirees who do not need to work and have plenty of free time. Most of them would have little legal knowledge before their appointment, and the training they receive from the court is not nearly enough to make them legal experts. Indeed, those who are lawyers or who work for the legislative, judicial or law enforcement agencies are explicitly prohibited from serving as people's assessors.[53] According to the Supreme Court, the court may appoint assessors with relevant skills in cases requiring specialized knowledge in a field.[54] However, as trade remedy measures are so technical, it is highly unlikely that assessors with such knowledge will be found. Moreover, even if a person has such knowledge, he or she probably would not be interested in serving as a people's assessor due to the high opportunity cost. In the author's view, given the highly specialized nature of trade remedy judicial review cases, they should probably be tried by an all-judge panel rather than one with people's assessors. As mentioned earlier, according to the AD JI, the court will rely only on the record of the investigation as the basis for reviewing the legality of the disputed administrative action. At the same time, the ALL explicitly grants the court the power to request information from the parties, including the administrative agencies, firms or individuals.[55] The question is, if the court collects information that was not in the original record, may it use such information as the basis for the review? Also, according to the ALL, any evidence is only admissible after being properly verified by the court as authentic.[56] As trade remedy determinations involve so many fact-intensive technical pieces of evidence, it would be naïve to assume that the court would have the time and expertise to examine all of that evidence. In the author's view, it would be helpful to clarify that, in the judicial review of trade remedy measures, the courts need not request additional information or verify the authenticity of the information provided by the respondents.

Once the panel is formed, the court will determine a date for an oral hearing which, in principle, shall be open to the public. While the ALL does not specify whether or not the hearing is mandatory, it seems that a hearing is *de facto* mandatory, as the law guarantees the right of parties to

---

[53] Article 5.
[54] Supreme People's Court, *Rules on the Participation of Trials by People's Assessors*, *Fashi* (2010) No. 2, 12 January 2010, Article 5.
[55] Article 34.   [56] Article 31.

oral arguments,[57] which can only be made in a hearing. However, for trade remedy cases, if, indeed, the trial is based primarily on the record of the investigation, a hearing does not seem to be necessary or even useful. Indeed, as stated above, if the court could not request further information from the respondent, it would be very difficult, if not impossible, for the parties to conduct any cross-examination or oral argument, which are the main purposes of a hearing.[58] In this regard, China might wish to borrow from the experience of the US or EU judicial review systems and make hearings optional rather than mandatory for trade remedy cases.

In general, the court is required to issue judgment within three months of accepting the complaint.[59] The court may not employ mediation in administrative litigation,[60] probably due to concerns that mediation might pressure the complainant into dropping legitimate claims, or make administrative agencies forgo their administrative responsibilities simply in order to be rid of lawsuits. However, the parties could choose to settle the case on their own initiative. For example, if the respondent withdraws or revises the administrative action, the complainant might withdraw the complaint. But this also must be approved by the court, and can only be done before the court issues a judgment or ruling.[61]

By definition, trade remedy measures are taken against foreign parties. Thus, the judicial review will also involve foreign parties. To safeguard the litigation rights of foreign parties, the AD JI also states that the court may apply the special rules on foreign-related civil procedures in these cases.[62] Contained in Articles 235–67 of the Code of Civil Procedure, these special rules deal with issues such as jurisdiction, service and filing deadlines, freezing of assets and judicial assistance. However, because most of the rules are only applicable to cases where the foreign party is defendant, they are not of much relevance to the judicial review of trade remedy determinations, where only domestic parties may be respondents.

7 Appeal, remand, petition, re-trial, removal and protest

If the parties are dissatisfied with the judgment of the trial court, they may appeal to the higher court.[63] The right of appeal is not limited to the complainant or respondent, and even third parties may appeal a lower court's judgment.[64] A party has 15 days upon receiving the written

---

[57] Article 9.   [58] Sun Wen, "A Study on the Judicial Review of Anti-dumping Cases".
[59] Article 57.   [60] Article 50.   [61] Article 51.   [62] Article 11.   [63] Article 58.
[64] JI, Article 24.

judgment to file an appeal.[65] In the case of a foreign party with no domicile in China, the period is extended to 30 days.[66]

The appeal shall be filed with the original trial court, which shall serve a copy of it on the other parties within five days of receiving the appeal. The other parties then have 10 days to file a defence, which shall be served by the trial court on the appellant within five days. The trial court will then forward the appeal, defence and all the record and evidence in the case to the appellate court.

Like the trial court, the appellate court has the power to review both the factual and legal aspects of the administrative action, as well as the lower court judgment. If the parties have disputes regarding the facts as determined by the trial court, or if the appellate court is of the view that the trial court failed to make clear factual findings, it will hold an oral hearing.[67] If the facts are clear, the appellate court may also try the case without an oral hearing.[68]

In principle, the appellate court should issue its judgment within two months of receiving the appeal.[69] The court may affirm the original judgment if the original findings of facts were clear and the law was applied correctly.[70] If the original fact-finding was clear, but the application of the law was wrong, the appellate court may modify the judgment. If the original fact-finding was unclear, or the evidence insufficient, or if there were procedural errors in the original trial which may have affected the original judgment, the appellate court may either vacate the original judgment and remand the case back to the original court, or make findings of fact itself and render a judgment. If the case is remanded, the parties may appeal the new judgment.

Normally the judgment of the appellate court is the final judgment and shall become effective upon issuance. However, the finality of the judgment is constrained by several judgment supervision schemes, and may not be as absolute as in most other countries. The first is the petition mechanism, which enables a party to petition the original court or the higher court if the party believes that there are mistakes in the judgment, even after it comes into effect.[71] Of course, to prevent litigants from abusing the scheme, the enforcement of the judgment will not be suspended simply because a petition has been launched. The second

---

[65] Article 59.
[66] Law of Civil Procedure, promulgated by the Fourth Session of the Seventh National People's Congress on 9 April 1991, revised 28 October 2007, Article 247.
[67] JI, Article 67.   [68] ALL, Article 59.   [69] Article 60.   [70] Article 61.   [71] Article 62.

judgment supervision scheme is the retrial mechanism, which can be invoked in two ways: first, if the president of a court discovers legal errors in a judgment issued by the same court, he/she can ask the Trial Committee of the court to decide whether to have a re-trial; second, when a higher court discovers legal errors in the judgment of the lower court, the higher court can order the lower court to hold a re-trial.[72] The third such scheme is the removal mechanism, which enables a higher court to have the case removed to it for a new trial if legal errors are discovered in the lower court judgment.[73] The fourth is the protest mechanism, which gives the People's Procurators' Office the power to protest a legally erroneous judgment of the court at the lower level. The lower court must form a panel to re-try the case upon receiving the protest.[74] Given the special nature of trade remedies administrative cases, it is unclear how these judgment supervision mechanisms could apply in such cases. It would be helpful for the Supreme Court to spell out their application explicitly.

8   Remedies

Article 54 of the ALL lists the types of judgments and remedies a court may order, and these are largely copied into the JIs. If the administrative action is supported by strong evidence, proper application of the law and due process, the court shall affirm the administrative action. On the other hand, the court may order annulment of the administrative action as mentioned above. Where appropriate, the court may specify whether annulment applies to the entire administrative decision or only to part thereof. In addition, the court may also order the investigating authority to make new determinations in trade remedies cases.[75] To prevent the investigating authority from circumventing the court decision in making the new decision, the ALL also states explicitly that the administrative agency may not reach a decision that is essentially the same as the original decision using the same facts and reasons.

Interestingly, two remedies which were included in the ALL were not incorporated into the JIs. First, if the administrative agency refuses to perform a statutory duty or delays performance, the court may order performance within a specific time. Would this be applicable to cases where the MOFCOM refuses to initiate an investigation? As we explained above, the rejection of an application after careful consideration, is of itself a

---

[72] Article 63.   [73] Article 63.   [74] Article 64.   [75] Article 9.

way of performing the statutory duties and thus should not be subject to judicial review. Of course, if the investigating authority simply ignores the application and fails to provide any response within 60 days, this is clearly "failure to respond" and becomes reviewable. In the latter case, the court should have the power to order performance within a specific time period. The second remedy is one where an administrative penalty is obviously unfair and the court may order it to be revised. From their appearance, anti-dumping or countervailing duties bear many similarities to the fines imposed by administrative agencies for violating certain regulations. However, according to an official statement by Justice Li Guoguang, anti-dumping and countervailing duties are special tariffs, and the administrative decision imposing such tariffs are not to be regarded as an administrative penalty.[76] Thus, it shall not be subject to the provision on administrative penalties. In practice, if the anti-dumping and countervailing duties are wrongfully calculated, the court may order the investigating authorities to recalculate them.

Normally the administrative action under challenge continues to apply during the review proceedings. However, the court may order its suspension in three exceptional cases: first, where suspension is deemed necessary by the respondent; second, where the complainant requests suspension, and the court considers the continuing application of the administrative action would cause irreparable damage, while the suspension will not harm the public interest; third, where suspension is required by the specific laws or regulations.

V Concluding thoughts

To summarize the analysis above, China has built a judicial review mechanism which satisfies the minimum requirements of the WTO. However, the existing mechanism merely provides a skeletal framework, and many important detailed rules, especially those on procedural matters, are left undefined. This appears to provide the courts with wide discretion. Depending on the choices made by the courts in practice, the judicial review mechanism may be used either to conduct broad scrutiny of trade remedy determinations, or only a superficial review which

---

[76] Speech by Justice Li Guoguang at the press conference on the Issuance of Rules on Several Issues Concerning the Review of International Trade Administrative Cases and Rules on Certain Issues Concerning Application of Law in Hearings of Countervailing Duty Administrative Cases, 3 December 2002.

simply rubber-stamps the decisions by the investigating authorities. Unfortunately, as there have been no judicial review cases so far, it is impossible to predict how the courts will exercise power.[77] On the one hand, one may argue that, given the tendency of the Chinese courts to rule in favour of the administrative agencies in administrative litigation cases, they may also restrict the judicial review power and give great deference to the determinations of the investigating authorities. On the other hand, as trade remedy judicial review cases involve mostly foreign parties, it is also conceivable that the Chinese government will ask the courts to apply a stricter standard on investigating authorities in trade remedy cases to create an impression of fairness and competency, in the hope of avoiding criticisms of violation of its accession obligation to provide proper judicial review mechanism.

Given the widespread dissatisfaction with the Chinese trade remedy system (especially the anti-dumping regime) by both insiders and out-siders,[78] it is rather surprising that firms are reluctant to bring judicial review cases. In the author's view, the scarcity of judicial review in trade remedy cases might be explained by the following factors.

First, firms do not trust the Chinese courts. The distrust is twofold: as trade remedy measures are highly technical, firms doubt whether the courts have sufficient expertise to deal with such complicated issues; as the relationship between the government and the court is very close in China, firms are worried that the courts might not be fully independent. Second, even if the courts are independent and competent enough to rule in favour of the firms, these firms fear possible retaliation by the Chinese government in future dealings, even if they do win a case. Third, unlike some other commercial disputes where domestic litigation provides the only available remedy, in trade remedy cases foreign firms have another avenue to justice: the WTO dispute settlement mechanism. This is a more attractive option for many foreign firms, as they have their own government as their ally in WTO litigation. That is why foreign firms

---

[77] The only case in which judicial review was explored as an option was when one exporter tried to challenge the decision of the MOFCOM to impose final anti-dumping duties in the *Cold-rolled Steel* case in 2003. Unfortunately, there is no public information available on this case, as no formal lawsuit was brought in the end. See Wu Xiaochen, *Anti-dumping Law and Practice of China* (Kluwer, 2009), p. 287.

[78] See, e.g., Patrick Norton, "China's Anti-dumping Regime, Progress and Problems", in Henry Gao and Don Lewis (eds), *China's Participation in the WTO* (Cameron May, London, 2005), pp. 131–41; W. M. Choi and Henry Gao, "Procedural Issues in the Anti-Dumping Regulations of China: A Critical Review under the WTO Rules" 5(3) (November 2006) *Chinese Journal of International Law* 663–82.

almost always choose WTO litigation when they have a problem with a trade remedy measure imposed by China. The earliest example is the *Kraft Linerboard* case in 2006, in which the United States threatened to sue in the WTO and China hastily removed the anti-dumping measures.[79] Up to mid-2011, the United States and the European Union have brought three cases against China's trade remedy measures in the WTO.

Thus, in the author's view, the main problem facing China is not with the judicial review mechanism of trade remedy cases itself, but, rather, with the general condition of the judicial system. Unless the country is willing to revamp substantially the judicial review system to make it more independent and professional, judicial review of trade remedy measures will continue to be only an untested theoretical possibility.

---

[79] For a detailed discussion of the case, see Henry Gao, "Taming the Dragon: China's Experience in the WTO Dispute Settlement System", 34(4) (2007) *Legal Issues of Economic Integration* 384–8.

Korea: increasing attention and new challenges

JAEMIN LEE

I Introduction

Under the World Trade Organization (WTO) rules, members are required to put in place a reliable judicial review system for the review of the determinations made by their trade remedy investigating authorities.[1] Trade remedy measures refer to anti-dumping measures, countervailing and safeguard measures. The imposition of these measures is subject to international rules embodied in the Agreement on Implementation of Article VI of the General Agreement on Tariffs and Trade 1994 (hereinafter AD Agreement), the Agreement on Subsidies and Countervailing Measures (hereinafter SCM Agreement) and the Agreement on Safeguards (hereinafter SG Agreement), respectively. According to these Agreements, trade remedy measures may only be imposed on the basis of determinations made in the course of investigations to be conducted by the investigating authority (hereinafter IA) of the importing WTO member. As such, the success of a member's trade remedy system is very dependent on the capacity and effectiveness of its IA.[2] What is often overlooked, however, is that the success of a trade remedy system also depends heavily on the effectiveness of the judicial review system of the member in question.

Judicial review plays an important role in the administration of the WTO's agreements on trade remedies. It is one of the key

---

[1] See Article 13 of the AD Agreement and Article 23 of the SCM Agreement. Although the SG Agreement does not contain a specific provision on judicial review, as explained in various chapters of this book, the judicial review systems of WTO members usually also apply to safeguard determinations.

[2] See Jaemin Lee, "Comment and Advice for Trade Remedy Legislations and Policies: Based on Korea's Experience" in *WTO Accession Strategies for Azerbaijan*, Ministry of Strategy and Finance and Korea Development Institute Working Paper (September 2008), at p. 139.

features designed to ensure the fairness and integrity of the investigative process. In addition to the WTO's dispute settlement mechanism which allows affected members to challenge trade remedy measures at multilateral levels, domestic judicial review is an important legal tool which ensures that such measures are imposed as a result of investigations conducted in accordance with the relevant procedural and substantive rules.

This chapter discusses the basic features and current status of judicial review of trade remedy determinations under Korean law. The Republic of Korea's (hereinafter Korea) use of trade remedies pertains mainly to anti-dumping, and a number of judicial review cases have been brought before Korean courts in connection with the determinations made by Korean authorities in anti-dumping investigations. Korea has applied safeguard measures sporadically, none of which have been the subject of judicial review. It is yet to initiate a countervailing duty investigation. Therefore, our explanations in this chapter will focus on the judicial review of anti-dumping determinations made by the Korean authorities. In what follows, we will first explain basic features of anti-dumping investigations, followed by the legal basis under Korean law of judicial review of anti-dumping determinations, the judicial organs responsible for judicial review, and the applicable law in such review.

Unlike judicial review systems of some WTO members, such as the United States and the European Union, little is known by outsiders about judicial review in Korea, the twelfth-largest trading member of the WTO. The lack of research and published information with respect to Korea's judicial review system often leads to questions being raised and inquiries made in various fora. Against this backdrop, in this chapter we will attempt to fill this important gap by providing an overview of judicial review of trade remedy determinations in Korea, with particular emphasis on anti-dumping.

II   Korea's use of trade remedies

Korea's trade remedies investigating authority is the Korea Trade Commission (hereinafter KTC), which is part of the Ministry of Knowledge Economy. As mentioned above, Korea so far has mainly focused on anti-dumping. Recently, however, the KTC has increasingly paid attention to countervailing duty and safeguard investigations as well.

1 Legal basis for trade remedies

Korea has enacted various statutes and enforcement decrees following accession to the WTO in 1995: (i) Act on the Investigation of Unfair International Trade Practices and Remedy for Injury to the Domestic Industry, (ii) its enforcement decree, (iii) Foreign Trade Act, (iv) its enforcement decree, (v) Customs Act and (vi) its enforcement decree.[3]

Over the years, Korea has also made several modifications to these legal instruments to reflect the changes in WTO jurisprudence and to ensure that its national trade remedies law complies with the requirements of the WTO agreements. What is not clear, though, is the status of the WTO agreements within the national legal framework. For instance, what legal status has the AD Agreement within the domestic legal hierarchy, and which norm should come first in the course of judicial review, when there is conflict between the AD Agreement (or panel or Appellate Body jurisprudence interpreting the Agreement) and Korean law? On the surface, the answer is relatively simple, because Korea treats the WTO agreements in their entirety as part of Korean law. But when it comes to a specific question or issue, the jurisprudence is still developing. At least, the clear trend emerging from recent cases is that the court is willing to apply the WTO agreements directly, if such application is warranted. This issue is further discussed below. In any event, the process of amending the national trade remedies law is still ongoing, particularly due to the continuing negotiations on free trade agreements (hereinafter FTAs) with other countries, which sometimes require substantive changes to trade remedies law, within the bounds of the WTO agreements.

On the basis of this legal framework, Korea has been trying to conduct its trade remedy investigations in a WTO-consistent fashion. The KTC has gained considerable practical experience over the past 21 years, partly on the basis of trial and error. Korea is still in the process of evaluating its law and practices on a regular basis to make them more compliant with the WTO rules. This task has been further complicated as a result of the surge in the number of FTAs that Korea has concluded since 2004. Recent disputes with other countries involving trade remedy measures, such as the WTO dispute with Indonesia with respect to anti-dumping duties imposed by Korea on coated sheet papers from

---

[3] The texts of all of these legal instruments are available on the KTC's website (www.ktc.go.kr).

Indonesia, have provided the KTC with further opportunities to fine-tune its investigative procedures.

The increasing difficulty the KTC faces with respect to trade remedies seems to be that the accomplishment of legislative changes takes time. To be more specific, the amendment of statutes and enforcement decrees can be achieved relatively easily, but adjusting the KTC's practice with respect to the trade remedy investigations and measures seems to be more challenging and time-consuming. Development of the WTO juris-prudence and challenges of interested parties, either in the course of investigations or through judicial review, have prompted the KTC to adjust its practice to better defend its determinations.

Recent anti-dumping investigations and ensuing disputes have made the KTC realize that statutory amendments should be accompanied by the adoption of commensurate enforcement decrees, enforcement regu-lations and, more importantly, the adjustment of the KTC's practice. This situation has been mainly prompted by the negotiations of FTAs with major trading partners. Among the issues to which the KTC has paid particular attention is the improvement of procedural due process and transparency.

Continuing efforts to fine-tune the country's trade remedies law and the KTC's practice will likely pave the way for a much better legal framework for the conduct of trade remedy investigations in Korea.

2 Korea's investigating authority

The KTC is in charge of all trade remedy investigations in Korea. It is currently composed of a chairperson and eight commissioners, includ-ing one serving on a full-time basis. Commissioners are appointed by the president upon the recommendation of the Minister of Knowledge Economy.[4] The chairperson and commissioners serve overlapping terms of three years each, and may be reappointed. The KTC is sup-ported in its administrative work by the Office of Investigation, which consists of four divisions, namely the Trade Remedy Policy Division, the Injury Investigation Division, the Dumping Investigation Division and the Unfair Trade Investigation Division. The structure of these Divisions can be illustrated as follows:[5]

---

[4] Previously, Ministry of Commerce, Industry and Energy.
[5] See Jaemin Lee, "Comment and Advice for Trade Remedy Legislations and Policies", at p. 152.

Figure 16.1 The structure of the Korea Trade Commission

Each division of the KTC is responsible for the following activities:

Division	Responsibilities
Trade Remedy Policy Division	– Establishing basic policy on the operation of trade remedies – Conducting research of the relevant laws and institutional issues – Public relations – Administrative tasks, such as reception of the application for trade remedy investigations
Injury Investigation Division	– Conducting injury determinations
Dumping Investigation Division	– Conducting dumping or subsidy determinations
Unfair Trade Investigation Division	– Conducting investigation of serious injury in safeguard investigations

As shown in the above table, the Dumping Investigation Division is in charge of both anti-dumping and countervailing duty investigations. As mentioned above, Korea has not yet initiated any countervailing duty investigations. However, given the increasing disputes involving governmental subsidies with other countries, it would not be surprising if the KTC initiates its first countervailing duty investigation in the near future.[6] The Injury Investigation Division is in charge of injury

---

[6] See ibid., at p. 153.

determinations in the context of anti-dumping and countervailing duty investigations, but the two divisions proceed with their investigations separately and do not exchange views. The Unfair Trade Investigation Division is in charge of safeguard investigations.

Over the years, the KTC has been successful in retaining a wide range of professionals (lawyers, accountants, entrepreneurs, academics, as well as government officials) to carry out its tasks as an investigation authority. The advent of the new environment as a result of the FTAs requires the KTC to be more active in dealing with the increased penetration of the Korean market by dumped and subsidized imports. To this end, it should be expected that the KTC will be given more resources in the near future.

3   Current status of trade remedy measures

As of April 2011, Korea had initiated 118 anti-dumping investigations and imposed 68 definitive anti-dumping duties.[7] Although the investigations started as early as 1987, when the KTC was first established, most of the investigations (105 out of 118) were initiated following the entry into force of the AD Agreement in 1995.[8] On average, five to 10 anti-dumping investigations per year are conducted by the KTC.

On the other hand, the KTC has initiated 33 safeguard investigations, 22 of which have led to the imposition of measures. Unlike anti-dumping investigations, the majority of the safeguard investigations (25 of the 33) were conducted before 1995.[9] Thus, the absence of countervailing duty investigations by the KTC stands out, given the level of activity with respect to anti-dumping and safeguard investigations.

III   Increasing attention to judicial review in Korea

Like other WTO members that use trade remedies, Korea has had a judicial review system in place for trade remedy measures as required under the WTO Agreement since it joined the WTO in 1995. It should be underlined, however, that judicial review of trade remedy measures has not received the attention that it deserved from stakeholders such as the

---

[7] See the Trade Remedy Statistics (April 2011), available on the KTC website.
[8] See ibid.   [9] See ibid.

domestic industries, or from academia. Trade remedy measures have long been seen as technical issues within the competence of the IA, and not amenable to judicial review. In our view, however, this is not the only reason which explains the low level of use of judicial review in Korea. The main reason judicial review has not been used frequently is because Korea has never been one of the very active users of trade remedies. The level of Korea's activity in the field of trade remedies stands out when compared with its share of international trade. Whereas Korea is the second most frequent target of anti-dumping investigations globally, it is only the eleventh most frequent user of such measures. This is mainly because it has been an export-oriented country, and more interested in the anti-dumping investigations initiated against it and pursuing judicial review in foreign jurisdictions. Consequently, inbound trade remedy investigations and judicial review in Korea have been relatively slow in coming and few in number.

This traditional atmosphere, however, is fast changing, with the advent of increasing foreign penetration into the Korean market as a result of the growth of domestic demand, and continuing market opening in all sectors (mainly due to the surge of Korea's FTAs and WTO commitments). Thus, from 2005, judicial review has received attention from Korean and foreign producers. Since 2005, five judicial review cases have been handled by Korean courts, including one which made it to the Supreme Court, and currently there are at least two cases pending. This new trend indicates that judicial review will become an important issue for Korea in the aftermath of the Doha negotiations and the conclusion of FTAs.

In response to the likely further surge in imports in the near future, Korea is likely to strengthen the KTC's infrastructure and start initiating more trade remedy investigations. Consequently, more judicial review cases should also be expected in the future in Korea.

IV   Legal framework for the judicial review of trade remedy determinations

It should be noted at the outset that the judicial review of trade remedy determinations in Korea is conducted by the Administrative Court, pursuant to the general procedures for the judicial review of the actions of government agencies. In this section, we explain different aspects of the judicial review conducted by the Administrative Court.

1   The court

Article 103 of the Korean Constitution guarantees the independence of the judiciary.[10] It stipulates that judges should follow the Constitution, laws and regulations, and their conscience, to render judgment in a particular case.[11] The judiciary is vested with general jurisdiction over all legal matters except in some carefully carved out exceptions, namely, constitutional issues over which the Constitutional Court has exclusive jurisdiction, and in disciplinary measures against law-makers which are handled by the National Assembly.[12]

It is the Court Organization Act which provides for details of the creation and administration of the various Korean courts. According to the Act, the judiciary is composed of six different categories of courts: the Supreme Court, High Court, District Court, Patent Court, Family Court and Administrative Court. The Korean judicial system is based on a three-level adjudication system, composed of trials by district courts, appellate review by the High Courts and final appellate review by the Supreme Court.[13] District Courts, High Courts and the Supreme Court are courts with general jurisdiction. The other three courts, however, are specialized courts with limited jurisdiction: the Patent Court has jurisdiction over patent disputes, while the Family Court has jurisdiction over familial issues. The Administrative Court has jurisdiction over disputes arising from the actions of governmental agencies. The Patent Court is positioned on the same level as the High Courts, while the Family Court and the Administrative Court are on the same footing as the District Courts.[14]

---

[10] See the website of the Supreme Court of Korea: http://eng.scourt.go.kr/eng/judiciary/history.jspz07 (last visited 8 December 2011).

[11] See the website of Supreme Court of Korea: http://eng.scourt.go.kr/eng/judiciary/introduction.jsp#01 (last visited 8 December 2011).

[12] Korea also has a special court hearing constitutional issues arising from the judiciary, executive and legislative branches. Established in 1987, this Constitutional Court handles constitutional issues such as the constitutionality of a law, impeachment, dissolution of a political party, constitutional petitions filed by individuals, and jurisdictional conflicts among governmental agencies. All nine justices of the Constitutional Court are appointed by the president: three are nominated by the president himself, three by the National Assembly, and three by the Chief Justice of the Supreme Court. Thus, the Chief Justice of the Supreme Court also takes part in forming the benches of the Constitutional Court. For more information, see the website of the Supreme Court of Korea: http://eng.scourt.go.kr/eng/judiciary/introduction.jsp#01 (last visited 8 December 2011).

[13] See the website of the Supreme Court of Korea: http://eng.scourt.go.kr/eng/judiciary/introduction.jsp#05 (last visited 8 December 2011).

[14] See the website of the Supreme Court of Korea: http://eng.scourt.go.kr/eng/judiciary/introduction.jsp#01 (last visited 8 December 2011).

The judicial review of the KTC's determinations is conducted by the Administrative Court. As noted, it is a special court which has jurisdiction over the actions of the administrative agencies of the Korean government. Thus, trade remedy determinations, which constitute administrative actions undertaken by the KTC, a governmental agency, also fall under its jurisdiction.

The Administrative Court was established on 1 March 1998. It is located in Seoul, and is composed of approximately 50 judges. As the Administrative Court is located only in Seoul, the respective District Court performs the function of the Administrative Court in each province until a separate Administrative Court is established in that respective region in the future.[15] In the past, the exhaustion of administrative remedies was a prerequisite for initiating a judicial review proceeding with the courts, but since the establishment of the Administrative Court, a judicial review proceeding may be initiated without first resorting to administrative remedies, unless otherwise provided by law.[16] The Administrative Court does not have a chamber or section specializing in trade remedies issues.

In principle, there are many commonalities between administrative and civil judicial proceedings with respect to the procedures that are followed. A significant difference between the two, however, is that a judge in the Administrative Court may intervene, *ex officio*, in the proceedings more actively than a judge presiding over a civil proceeding, as the former is likely to involve a public interest aspect. Thus, in administrative judicial proceedings, the court may examine evidence *ex officio* and consider facts not averred by the parties, although the responsibility for the burden of proof still lies with the parties.[17]

The focus of review by the Administrative Court is to determine whether the disputed administrative action can be considered reasonable. If the action is found to be reasonable, it will be upheld, even if the court might have a different opinion. In other words, the judge does not conduct a *de novo* review, but determines whether the agency action at issue is reasonable under the specific circumstances. This principle applies where the relevant statute provides the agency in charge with

---

[15] See the website of the Supreme Court of Korea: http://eng.scourt.go.kr/eng/judiciary/court_spc.jsp#03 (last visited 8 December 2011).

[16] See ibid.

[17] See Introductory Book of the Supreme Court of Korea, 2009, p. 59: http://eng.scourt.go.kr/eng/supreme/introduction.jsp (last visited 8 December 2011).

discretion in respect of the disputed action, or where the statute is silent regarding certain details. However, where the statute provides precise requirements with respect to the disputed action, the agency must follow such requirements. In such a case, the judge will overturn any administrative action which disregards statutory requirements. Decisions by the Administrative Court may be appealed to the High Court, then to the Supreme Court.

With respect to the format of the trial, in general, all hearings and rendering of judgments should be open to the public unless there exist compelling reasons to do otherwise. Such compelling reasons may include concerns over maintaining national security, public order or public morals. If the court finds the concerns legitimate, it may order the hearing to be closed to the public. In any event, even in those instances, rendering of judgments should be open to the public.

2   The judges

The judges of the Korean courts are career judges who are appointed by the government when they graduate from the Judicial Research and Training Institute.[18] They are then rotated among various judicial positions at all levels of the judiciary.

Such being the case, the judges working in the Administrative Court and hearing cases involving trade remedy determinations usually do not have expertise in trade disputes or disputes of international character. This is in contrast to the court systems of some WTO members, where judges with specific experience in trade issues are appointed to hear disputes involving trade remedy determinations. As at the time of writing this chapter, a plan to cultivate or recruit judges with special expertise in the trade issues has not yet been identified in Korea. However, the situation may well change in the near future, as demand for judicial review of trade remedy determinations is likely to increase.

---

[18] The Court Organization Act sets forth the required qualifications for judges. They are appointed from among those who have passed the National Judicial Examination and completed the two-year training programme at the Judicial Research and Training Institute. The Chief Justice and justices of the Supreme Court are appointed from among those who are judges, public prosecutors or practising attorneys. The candidate must be more than 40 years of age, with judicial experience of 15 years or longer. For more information, see the website of the Supreme Court of Korea: http://eng.scourt.go. kr/eng/judiciary/judges.jsp (last visited 8 December 2011).

3 Standing: parties eligible to bring a case

Probably as with any other country, in Korea any legal entity or individual adversely affected by a decision of the administrative agency has standing to bring a case before the Administrative Court. In principle, only a person who has a direct and concrete legal interest arising from the prospective revocation of the disputed administrative disposition may bring a case before the court. In other words, if the interest to be vindicated is either indirect or abstract, such legal action is not permitted.[19]

At the same time, the Administrative Litigation Act currently in force in Korea provides that for an agency action to be eligible for judicial review, it should be characterized as an "administrative disposition".[20] An administrative disposition is an administrative action that disposes of the rights of private entities in a way that infringes upon the said rights. Therefore, the judicial review of an administrative disposition is a proceeding initiated for the purpose of annulment or modification of the administrative disposition concerned on the grounds of the illegality of such disposition, because it has resulted in the breach of the right of the private entity.

The same rule also applies to an anti-dumping determination, which is an agency determination. First, the KTC is a government agency subject to the Administrative Litigation Act.[21] With respect to the requirement that a person should hold direct interest in the prospective case, in the context of the anti-dumping investigation, parties who satisfy the threshold are foreign exporters, importers and domestic corporations. Thus, so far the plaintiffs in judicial review of anti-dumping determinations in Korea have been domestic industries or foreign exporters. Likewise, a final anti-dumping determination of the KTC is deemed to be an administrative disposition in nature, because the determination renders a disposition that directly affects the property interest of the parties involved. These are the legal underpinnings that enable the domestic judicial review of anti-dumping determinations in Korea.

---

[19] See Introductory Book of the Supreme Court of Korea, 2009, p. 59: http://eng.scourt.go.kr/eng/supreme/introduction.jsp (last visited 8 December 2011).

[20] See ibid., available at http://eng.scourt.go.kr/eng/supreme/introduction.jsp (last visited 8 December 2011).

[21] The government agencies defined in the Administrative Litigation Act are those which can issue specific administrative dispositions under the public law. See Article 2, paragraph 2 of the Administrative Litigation Act. Thus, the KTC falls within such a category.

In the judicial review proceedings so far, domestic industries and foreign exporters have participated as direct parties and not as intervenors. One would not be surprised if, sooner or later, participation of interested parties as intervenors increases. At the same time, foreign governments have not been directly involved in any of the judicial review proceedings in Korea so far, which is not surprising, given the fact that interested parties in anti-dumping investigations are corporations rather than governments. Here also, the situation may change once the KTC starts to conduct countervailing duty investigations.

In general, a judicial review proceeding may be instituted without first resorting to an appeal procedure arranged and administered by the administrative agency which made the original agency determination. However, there are instances where exhaustion of administrative appeal proceedings is a prerequisite to filing an action with the court. Examples include challenges concerning tax authorities' imposition of a tax, or police agencies' suspension or revocation of drivers' licences.[22] The exhaustion of administrative appeal proceedings does not apply to anti-dumping determinations.

In Korea, there have been controversies concerning judicial review of various determinations rendered by the KTC. In fact, the KTC issues a wide range of determinations, such as refusal to initiate an investigation, imposition of anti-dumping duties, and decisions to initiate an investigation or a review, and the like. There is no question that the decision to impose an anti-dumping duty is subject to judicial review as an agency disposition action. What is not entirely clear yet is whether a decision not to initiate an anti-dumping investigation should be deemed to constitute an agency disposition action eligible for judicial review. A similar question also arises regarding the KTC's decision on initiation of a review. Although there is no direct case in point yet, a recent case involving the KTC's non-initiation of an unfair trade practice investigation (relating to infringement of copyrights) describes an interesting development in this respect.

In 2007, the Seoul Administrative Court affirmed that the KTC's decision not to initiate an unfair trade practice investigation does have agency disposition nature and thus is eligible for judicial review.[23] This is

---

[22] See Introductory Book of the Supreme Court of Korea, 2009, p. 59: http://eng.scourt.go. kr/eng/supreme/introduction.jsp (last visited 8 December 2011).

[23] See Revocation of Non-Initiation of Unfair Trade Investigation, 2007 Guhab 825 (14 August 2007).

a significant departure from the previous position of the court that such non-initiation lacks a dispositive nature and thus is excluded from judicial review.[24] Article 5(1) of the Act on Unfair Trade Action Investigation and Industrial Damage Remedy stipulates that anyone who recognizes the existence of unfair trade action may file a petition with the KTC to request an investigation.[25] Thus, the initial filing of the petition is the first step which leads to a chain of actions, including full investigation and imposition of a measure.[26] The court basically reasoned that if the petition for the initiation of an investigation is denied, then the next step obviously does not take place, which means that an interested party is left without any remedy.[27] If the interested party believes that he/she is entitled to the full investigation and a remedy following, such non-initiation would be tantamount to usurping his/her otherwise legitimate right.[28] Thus, the court held that even though the non-initiation decision is made by the KTC based on its expertise in highly complex areas, exercising immense discretion, such a decision also bears a dispositive nature *vis-à-vis* the interested party.[29] It then continued its review and determined that the said non-initiation constituted violation of the law by the KTC.[30]

This court decision bears implications for a similar decision of the KTC not to initiate an anti-dumping investigation. A similar logic can also be applied to a negative determination as a result of an anti-dumping investigation. Although perhaps in many countries it is obvious that non-initiation of an investigation, or negative determination by the investigating authority are also subject to judicial review, this has caused a certain level of controversy in Korea because of the concept of "agency dispositive action" in the administrative law, as discussed above.

On the other hand, in 2009, the Seoul Administrative Court took a slightly different approach when it reviewed the KTC's decision to commence a review.[31] The court stated that the KTC's decision did not have the nature of an administrative disposition, and held that it was not

---

[24] See Revocation of Non-Initiation of Unfair Trade Investigation, 2004 Guhab 557 (Seoul Administrative Court, 17 December 2004).

[25] Article 5 of the Unfair Trade Action Investigation and Industrial Damage Remedy is the provision that authorizes the KTC to investigate various unfair trade practices, including alleged infringements of intellectual property rights and rules of origin.

[26] See Revocation of Non-Initiation of Unfair Trade Investigation, 2007 Guhab 825 (14 August 2007), at 1.

[27] See ibid., at 3.   [28] Ibid.   [29] Ibid., at 4.   [30] Ibid., at 5.

[31] See Revocation of Decision of the Korea Trade Commission regarding Periodic Reviews, 2007 Guhab 16875 (23 July 2009).

subject to judicial review.[32] The court reasoned that the decision to commence a review is a preparatory step for future anti-dumping proceedings, and did not definitely establish or affect the rights and obligations of interested parties.[33] Although framed differently, this decision seems to be in line with the requirement that there be a measure for there to be a WTO challenge or a judicial review proceeding.[34] In this case, the measure to be challenged would be the final outcome of the review, not its initiation.

Another issue to note is that the actual imposition of the anti-dumping duties is conducted by the Ministry of Strategy and Finance (hereinafter MOSF). MOSF is the ministry with responsibility for all of Korea's financial issues and economic policies. As anti-dumping duties are extra duties imposed by the Korean government, this imposition falls under the jurisdiction of MOSF, even if the investigation itself is conducted by the KTC. In fact, the KTC, as the investigating authority of Korea, carries out its investigation in close consultation and cooperation with MOSF. For instance, if it decides to initiate an anti-dumping investigation, the KTC should notify MOSF within two months of receipt of the petition.[35] Likewise, when a final affirmative determination is reached by the KTC, the agency should also inform MOSF of the decision, and it is MOSF which imposes the anti-dumping duties. In practice, MOSF adopts a new regulation which orders the Korean Customs Service to impose the extra duties.[36] This bifurcated approach sometimes raises a question as to which of the two decisions (KTC's final affirmative determination v. MOSF imposition regulation) should be eligible for judicial review. The general position of the Korean courts is that there is no question regarding MOSF regulation as an agency action eligible for judicial review, but that it is not entirely clear with respect to the KTC's determination. Again, the point is that the KTC's determination is a preparatory step for the ultimate imposition of duties.[37]

This issue is mostly moot in the WTO litigation, because many countries list both final affirmative determination and the anti-dumping duty order in their requests for the establishment of panels. But in the context of judicial review in Korea, this issue has not been clearly

---

[32] See ibid., at 5.   [33] Ibid., at 7.   [34] Ibid.

[35] See paragraphs 1 and 3 of Article 60 of the Enforcement Decree of the Customs Act.

[36] See Article 25 of the Customs Act and Article 27 of the Enforcement Decree of the Customs Act.

[37] See 2008 Guhab 43805 (Seoul Administrative Court, 10 March 2009).

settled yet.[38] Hopefully, as more cases are reviewed and precedents accumulated, the discrepancy between judicial review proceedings in Korea and the WTO litigation may be addressed.

4 Standard of review

In principle, the judge hearing a judicial review case of agency determination is likely to defer to the expertise of the agency in charge. Thus, in borderline cases where the judge may have a different opinion to the administrative agency, more likely than not the judge would still uphold the judgment so long as the decision is supported by substantial evidence on the record. Therefore, unless the plaintiff can show that the agency determination is not thereby supported, that the agency has abused its discretion, or that the determination is otherwise unreasonable or against the law, the court will probably render judgment for the defendant agency. Thus, all things being equal, it is more likely that the court will find for the agency. However, this recognition of and deference for agency discretion does not rise to the level of a prohibition of *de novo* review.[39] Thus, it is still possible that a judge in a particular case may disagree with the KTC's determination and reverse it. This is in contrast with the practice of some countries, where a reviewing judge is prohibited from conducting a *de novo* review in particular cases.[40]

5 Applicable law in judicial review proceedings

The applicable law in judicial review proceedings is quite complex. This complexity stems mainly from the fact that Korea maintains the so-called monist system regarding the incorporation of international law into domestic law. Article 6, paragraph 1 of the Korean Constitution reads:

> Article 6 [Treaties, Foreigners]
> (1) Treaties duly concluded and promulgated under the Constitution and the generally recognized rules of international law shall have the same effect as the domestic laws of the Republic of Korea.

---

[38] See Seoul Administrative Court, Judgment No. 2007 Guhab 825 (14 August 2007).
[39] See 2008 Guhab 43805 (Seoul Administrative Court, 10 March 2009).
[40] For instance, the US Court of International Trade is prohibited from conducting a *de novo* review. See *Am. Spring Wire Corp.* v. *United States*, 8 CIT 20, 22, 590 F. Supp. 1273, 1276 (1984).

This provision has been interpreted as a pronouncement of the adoption of the monist system by Korea. As such, all international treaties and agreements, upon conclusion or accession by Korea, are automatically incorporated into the domestic legal system and become binding. These treaties and agreements have the same status as Korean statutes, namely, below the Constitution. In fact, this is quite a convenient provision, because it allows the government to carry out the enactment of implementing legislation each time. Of course, despite the monist approach, sometimes it is necessary to adopt implementing legislation, such as when the treaty requires adoption thereof or contains provisions contrary to existing Korean law.

It should also be noted that the issue of a self-executing or non-self-executing treaty is distinct from the issue of monist or dualist system. Even if an international agreement is incorporated into Korean law based on Article 6 of the Constitution, if the law is considered to be non-self-executing, the judge will have difficulty in applying the agreement in a given case in the absence of implementing legislation, as will the judge when the agreement itself states that private rights are not accorded by it. Korean courts have been quite meticulous regarding these points.[41]

This basically means that international agreements, such as the WTO agreements, become part of Korean law that the judge will apply in reviewing a case before him/her. In a judicial review proceeding, the reviewing judge will apply WTO agreements, FTAs (if any) and the Korean municipal law in making a decision. In the case of conflict among these legal instruments, a special law will prevail over a general one, and a new law over an old one.

5.1   WTO agreements

Despite Article 6 of the Constitution and monism, the GATT and the WTO agreements have not received that much attention as applicable law in judicial review proceedings. This stems mainly from the fact that judicial review of trade remedy determinations is a recent phenomenon in Korea. As an export-oriented economy with a relatively small domestic market, for Koreans, judicial review used to refer to the review conducted by foreign courts against Korean exporters in those countries. However, this traditional trend, is slowly changing. In one recent case,

---

[41] See the Compatibility of Ordinance of Jeollabukdo province with GATT 1994, 2004 Do 2432, Decisions of the Korean Supreme Court (14 September 2005).

the judge directly applied the GATT to render a judgment involving the imposition of anti-dumping duties.

The Seoul Administrative Court, in its judgment of December 2007,[42] held that the KTC's anti-dumping determination was appropriate as it was consistent with the Customs Act, Enforcement Decree of the Customs Act and the WTO's AD Agreement. Thus, the court explicitly referred to the AD Agreement for the disposition of the judicial review of an anti-dumping determination. The court also took the same position in October 2009 regarding another judicial review of an anti-dumping determination by the KTC.[43] However, the Korean Supreme Court, in its January 2009 decision, indicated that the WTO agreements may not directly apply to judicial review by the Korean courts.[44] It is not entirely clear whether the court's opinion should be read as negating the applicability of the WTO agreements to domestic judicial review in their entirety, or whether the decision is simply the reflection of the facts and issues of that case. In any event, if the decision is regarded as negating the applicability of the WTO agreements in judicial review, it seems contrary to its position in another recent case where the court did recognize the GATT as applicable law. In a case where a local government brought an action against the local congress when the latter enacted an ordinance which arguably was in violation of the WTO agreements, the Supreme Court applied the GATT 1994 as applicable law.[45]

The Korean Constitutional Court also took a similar position. In a case where a person was charged by the Korean Customs Service with a criminal violation of the Customs Regulation, which had been enacted as a result of the Marrakesh Agreement, and where the defendant argued that the punishment was unconstitutional because of the principle of *mulla poena sine lege* of the Korean Constitution, the Court rejected this argument, holding that because the Marrakesh Agreement constituted part of Korean law, the punishment at issue was punishment by law.[46]

In any event, it is still not entirely clear whether Korean courts accept the notion that the WTO agreements provide private entities with the right to present their claims in a Korean court. The situation is still

[42] Seoul Administrative Court, Case No. 2006 Guhab 29782.
[43] Seoul Administrative Court, Case No. 2008 Guha 40363.
[44] Supreme Court of Korea, Case No. 2008 Du 17936 (30 January 2009).
[45] See the Compatibility of Ordinance of Jeollabukdo province with GATT 1994, 2004 Do 2432, Decisions of the Korean Supreme Court (14 September 2005).
[46] Korean Constitutional Court, Case No. 97 Hunba 65 (26 November 1998).

unclear. The fact that the Seoul Administrative Court, which is the court of first instance responsible for the judicial review of the KTC's determinations, tends continuously to find the WTO agreements to be applicable law seems to be a barometer indicating the general direction taken by the Korean judiciary in this regard. As the number of disputes of an international nature increases, the judiciary becomes more receptive and amenable to international treaties, including the WTO agreements. In a few instances where it has encountered disputes involving international elements, the Korean Supreme Court has also applied the relevant international treaties, including WTO agreements, as directly applicable legal norms in Korea. As discussed above, this is the reflection of Korea's monist approach in incorporating international law into its national legal system. With respect to the WTO agreements in particular, however, what is still not clear is whether the agreements, in their entirety, should be considered to provide standing to individuals, foreign or domestic, or whether only some of the agreements or provisions thereof should be construed in that way. That is, it is not entirely clear whether the WTO agreements are of a self-executing character under Korean law. As more cases are filed in the future, we may expect further clarification on this particular issue.

5.2.   FTAs

What makes the situation more complex for the future is the introduction of FTAs with many countries. All of the FTAs have provisions on trade remedy measures. Although most include trade remedy provisions which are similar to those of the AD Agreement, different FTAs do have different provisions regulating trade remedy measures. Thus, an anti-dumping measure could constitute a violation of a particular FTA, while it is consistent with another, or with the WTO's AD Agreement.

As the FTA is also an international agreement that is automatically incorporated into the Korean domestic judicial system through the application of Article 6 of the Constitution, a reviewing court will have to apply the FTA in addition to, or in lieu of, the AD Agreement or municipal law.

5.3.   Municipal law

The judge applies municipal law in the judicial review of anti-dumping determinations. Municipal law includes statutes, enforcement decrees and regulations on trade remedy investigations conducted by the KTC. Specifically, these are the Customs Act, Enforcement Decree of the

Customs Act, Act on Unfair Trade Practice Investigation and Remedy for Industrial Injury, and the Enforcement Decree of the Act. These statutes and regulations provide the procedures to be applied in an anti-dumping investigation.

Specific details of the anti-dumping investigations can be found in Articles 51 to 56 of the Customs Act and Articles 58 to 71 of the Enforcement Decree of the Customs Act. These provisions mainly follow the comparable provisions of the WTO AD Agreement, but there are some issues still absent in the municipal law. An example is the absence of a detailed provision requiring the existence of causation between dumped imports and material injury. Ideally, in these instances, the court may resort to the WTO agreements to make a decision in judicial review proceedings. In fact, this is the very reason why many countries adopt the monist system to the extent the international agreement provides the right of private claims.

5.4 WTO precedents

The precedents of the international courts are not accorded binding force, nor do the Korean courts treat them as sources of legally binding obligations. Thus, the jurisprudence of WTO panels and the Appellate Body, in and of itself, is not treated by a reviewing judge as a source of legal norms.

Nonetheless, to the extent the jurisprudence explains how a particular provision of the WTO Agreement should be interpreted, it may be referred to by the reviewing judge of the Korean court as a guideline for the proper interpretation of the Agreement. It may be argued, therefore, that the WTO jurisprudence (decisions of the panel and the Appellate Body) will have a *de facto* precedential value in the judicial review proceedings in Korea. It would not be surprising if the attorneys representing interested parties presented their arguments based on recent Appellate Body decisions in Korean courts.

An interesting question would arise if a Korean court ruled in favour of an anti-dumping measure for the domestic industry in judicial review, but Korea subsequently received an adverse ruling from the panel or the Appellate Body and faced an implementing obligation to bring the aggrieved measure into compliance with the AD Agreement or the GATT 1994. In this case, there would be two conflicting decisions, one from the Korean court and one from the WTO. Of course, Korea should fulfil its implementation obligation to avoid retaliation. Domestically, however, industry may argue that the decision by the Korean court should control because the WTO rulings do not carry direct binding force *vis-à-vis* Korean courts. This situation arises because Korea has not put in place the legal framework to implement adverse rulings of the WTO, as the United States did in section 129 of the Uruguay Round Agreements Act. As more cases are reviewed by the Korean courts and Korea faces adverse rulings from time to time, legislative amendments will soon follow.

6   Enforcement of court decisions

Enforcement of the court decisions in the judicial review of administrative actions is usually prompt. If the judge finds for the complainant, he/ she will direct the KTC to revoke the trade remedy determination or will remand the case back to the KTC for further proceedings, as the case may be. In the case of revocation, if duties have been paid, they will be returned to the importer with applicable interest. In the case of a remand, the KTC will re-investigate the issue for a new determination. If the judgment is not enforced as stipulated in the court decision, the KTC will be further punished for contempt of the court.

V   Overall assessment and future tasks

1   Overall assessment of judicial review in Korea

For some time, foreign exporters used to believe, whether correctly or incorrectly, that an appeal of a trade remedy determination is not effective or recommendable in the context of the Korean judicial system. The perception was that the judge would probably find for the government agency over a foreign exporter. One of the ways to dispel such perception in the long run would be to establish a special court specifically charged with handling customs and trade issues, given the required expertise in dealing with these issues.[47]

More standardized and objective proceedings at the KTC and the judicial review process would provide an effective mechanism through

---

[47] For example, in the United States there is a special federal court, called the United States Court of International Trade, that deals specifically with customs and trade issues. The judges and clerks of this court are experts on those issues. In terms of the difference in the workload and the issues presented, the current situation in Korea is not comparable to that of the United States, but from the longer-term perspective, Korea might have to move in the same direction.

which not only foreign exporters but also Korean petitioners, who believe that an underlying trade remedy determination is not what it should be, could attempt to correct or modify the trade remedy determination. This will further enhance the notion of the rule of law and protect the integrity of trade remedy determinations rendered by the KTC. Recognition is also growing that a well-organized appeal and judicial review process will be able to shield Korea from WTO challenges.

It is increasingly the case that foreign respondents (and governments) bring legal action against the Korean government in the Korean courts, arguing that a particular trade remedy measure is inconsistent with the WTO agreements and Korean law. This trend is causing the KTC more carefully to review and evaluate data in the course of investigations.

As Korea automatically incorporates the WTO agreements as domestic law through its monist system, the reviewing court may also refer to the WTO agreements as a source of applicable law in addition to Korean statutes and regulations. This is now creating another challenge as to what law a court should apply when there is a discrepancy between the WTO agreements and the applicable Korean statutes, and when the WTO (by way of the Appellate Body) pronounces rules with which Korea does not necessarily agree. The addition of new trade remedy norms through FTAs has further complicated the situation. These issues have not been raised in the past, but due to increasing judicial review challenges by foreign respondents and governments, Korean courts will have to address them directly now.

2 Remaining tasks for the future

Article 13 of the AD Agreement contains the requirement that each WTO member must offer an independent and meaningful administrative and judicial review process with respect to final anti-dumping measures. The provision thus states that:

> Each Member ... shall maintain *judicial* ... or *administrative* tribunals or procedures for the purpose ... of the prompt review of administrative actions relating to final determinations ... Such tribunals or procedures shall be *independent* of the authorities responsible for the determination ... (emphasis added).

In this regard, the relevant Korean law/regulation does provide for an administrative appeal and judicial review for a final anti-dumping determination.[48] In reality, however, such appeal mechanism seems to be relatively under-utilized compared to other administrative actions.[49] There may be various reasons for such under-utilization, one being the aggrieved foreign exporters' perception, correctly or incorrectly, that an appeal is not effective or recommendable in the context of Korean anti-dumping investigations. Such perception is also closely related to the fact that the anti-dumping investigations and determination involve a high level of complexity not matched in other administrative action. Thus, regular judges may have a tendency to find for the investigating authority, all things being equal. Such being the case, in the long run Korea might consider establishing a special court specifically charged with handling customs and trade issues, given the required expertise in dealing with these issues. An example can be found in the Court of International Trade, which is a specialized federal district court that has jurisdiction over determinations by the United States Department of Commerce and United States International Trade Commission in trade remedy cases.

A more standardized and objective judicial review process would provide an effective mechanism through which not only foreign exporters but also Korean petitioners, who believe that the underlying anti-dumping determination is erroneous legally or factually, may request correction or modification of an anti-dumping determination. This will further enhance the notion of rule of law and protect the integrity of any anti-dumping determination rendered by Korea. A well-organized appeal and review process will also shield Korea from WTO challenges.

It is increasingly the case that foreign respondents and governments are bringing legal actions against the Korean government in the Korean courts, arguing that a particular anti-dumping or countervailing measure is inconsistent with the WTO agreements and Korean law. This trend is causing the KTC more carefully to review and evaluate data in the course of investigations.[50]

---

[48] See Articles 119 and 120 of the Tariff Act.
[49] See generally Korean Trade Commission, *Statistical Compilation of the Trade Remedy Measures* (January 2005).
[50] See Jaemin Lee, "Comment and Advice for Trade Remedy Legislations and Policies", at p. 155.

VI Conclusion

Although judicial review of trade remedy determinations has been provided for in Korean statutes for a long time, it is a relatively new phenomenon that interested parties are starting to consider this forum as a way to remedy agency determinations alleged to be erroneous. Recent anti-dumping investigations and determinations of the KTC have presented opportunities to test the judicial review mechanism in Korea. Recent judicial review has also presented more structural issues relating to the hierarchy of the WTO agreements within the Korean legal system and how they should be applied by Korean courts to specific cases. As more and more cases are reviewed by the Korean courts, the relevant statutes and decrees will be revised or amended accordingly, and the relevant jurisprudence further elaborated and fine-tuned.[51]

As the number of anti-dumping investigations by Korea has increased recently, various issues have emerged with respect to the investigations conducted by the KTC. These issues are sometimes resolved at the agency level in the course of the investigation, but they sometimes lead to WTO litigation or domestic judicial review. Both the WTO dispute settlement and domestic court proceedings have provided opportunities to compare the KTC's practices in a more objective manner and to improve such practices. In this regard, the judicial review system also plays an important role in preserving the rule of law in the trade remedy sector.

---

[51] The Korean judiciary has been exploring various reform measures to keep up with the changing environment in society. For instance, on 28 October 2003, the Judicial Reform Committee was set up inside the Korean Supreme Court with experts participating from various sectors of the society. As a result of the discussions, at the end of December 2004 the Committee produced specific reform proposals on the following issues, which are being implemented by decrees: (i) *judge appointment system*: to institute a system of appointing judges from attorneys with substantial practical work experience, in order to meet the public request to be tried by experienced judges who possess a broad understanding of the society; (ii) *legal education and qualification of lawyers*: to establish an efficient system for legal education with specialization and international competitiveness, and set up a new qualification system for lawyers; (iii) *public participation in the judicial process*: to study methods in which the public may participate in the trial process, such as the jury system or the lay judge system; and (iv) *legal services and the criminal procedure system*: to create an efficient and fair legal system which can be easily accessed by the public, and research methods which can better protect the rights of the accused and the victim during criminal proceedings. See Supreme Court of Korea website: http://eng.scourt.go.kr/eng/judiciary/judicial_reform.jsp#05 (last visited 8 December 2011).

In any event, judicial review of anti-dumping determinations by Korean courts should be further improved to ensure that the interests of foreign exporters and their importers are adequately protected. As much as Korean exporters have suffered from sometimes dubious trade remedy determinations by foreign investigating authorities, foreign exporters who similarly may have suffered from investigations initiated by Korea should be given full access to an effective tool for review of the KTC's determinations. Obviously, judicial review is the most effective mechanism to achieve this objective. Korea is also fast learning this fact through recent experience.

Indonesia: a judicial review system in dire need of restructuring

ERRY BUNDJAMIN*

I Introduction

The Government of Indonesia ratified the Agreement Establishing the World Trade Organization (WTO) through Law Number 7 of 1994 dated 2 November 1994 on the Ratification of the Agreement Establishing the World Trade Organization (hereinafter Law 7/1994). This ratification made the WTO Agreement part of Indonesian law, thus the obligations set forth in this agreement are to be observed by the Indonesian Government.

For the implementation of laws on trade remedies authorized under WTO law, the government of Indonesia promulgated Law No. 10 of 1995 concerning Customs Law (hereinafter Law No. 10/1995) which contained in its Chapter IV the basic provisions on anti-dumping and countervailing duties. Chapter IV of Law No. 10/1995 therefore constitutes the legal basis for Indonesian anti-dumping and countervailing duty legislation. Law No. 10/1995 was subsequently amended by Law No. 17/2006 Concerning Amendment to Law No. 10/1995 Concerning Customs (hereinafter Law No. 17/2006). Law No. 17/2006 includes safeguard measures in Part 3, and retaliation measures[1] in Part 4 of Chapter IV. It also clarifies that the rates of anti-dumping, countervailing and safeguard measures and retaliation measures are to be determined by the Minister of Finance.[2]

---

* The author would like to thank Darpan Alamsah Pandjaitan, Adhindra Kurnianto Anggoro and Renaldo Pramanta for their kind assistance in collating relevant materials for this chapter.
[1] Article 23C(2) provides that retaliation measures are directed to countries that discriminate against Indonesia.
[2] See Article 23D(2) of Law No. 17/2006.

Subsequently, Government Regulation No. 34 of 1996 on Anti-Dumping and Countervailing Duties (hereinafter PP34/1996) concerning anti-dumping and countervailing measures was also promulgated for the implementation of Law No. 10/1995. Indonesia's investigating authority for anti-dumping and countervailing duty investigations is the Komite Anti-Dumping Indonesia (hereinafter KADI) which was established through Decree No. 136/MPP/KEP/6/1996 (hereinafter Decree 136/1996). Decree No. 261/MPP/KEP/9/1996 on the Rules and Procedures for the Filing of Anti-Dumping and Countervailing Duty Applications (hereinafter Decree 261/1996), issued by the Minister of Industry and Trade, contains the procedural rules on the filing of complaints seeking the initiation of anti-dumping and countervailing duty investigations. KADI is an agency currently attached to the Ministry of Trade[3] and is responsible for the conduct of anti-dumping and countervailing duty investigations. Decree 261/1996 was subsequently amended by Decree of the Minister of Industry and Trade No. 216/MPP/KEP/7/2001 (hereinafter Decree 216/2001).

PP34/1996 contains substantive provisions that govern the conduct of anti-dumping and countervailing duty investigations in Indonesia. Most of the provisions set forth in PP34/1996 were adopted from the WTO Anti-Dumping Agreement (hereinafter AD Agreement) and the Agreement on Subsidies and Countervailing Measures (hereinafter SCM Agreement), although PP34/1996 does not adopt all provisions set forth in these two agreements.

The members of KADI and its investigators are government officials from various government institutions, including the Ministry of Industry, the Ministry of Trade, the Ministry of Finance, and Customs, as well as directors-general representing various industries. A substantial change in KADI's structure took place in October 2000. The Decree of the Minister of Industry and Trade No. 427/MPP/KEP/10/2000 on the Indonesian Anti-Dumping Committee (hereinafter Decree 427/2000) issued on 19 October 2000, which superseded Decree 430/1999, reformulated KADI's organizational structure. Articles 7 and 10 of Decree 427/2000 stipulate that the chairperson of KADI, together with the vice-chairperson and the members, will be appointed by the Minister of Industry and Trade. The Minister of Industry and Trade and the

---

[3] Through Presidential Decree No. 187/2004 dated 20 October 2004, the Ministry of Industry and Trade has been separated into the Ministry of Industry and the Ministry of Trade. In this new system, KADI and KPPI are attached to the Ministry of Trade.

Minister of Finance since then have ceased to act as the chairman and vice-chairman, respectively, of KADI. A senior official from the Ministry of Industry and Trade normally chairs KADI, while its vice-chairman is normally a senior official from the Ministry of Finance. Both ministers' current positions are as advisers to KADI. KADI is in charge of conducting investigations and issuing final recommendations; the final decision, based on its recommendations, rests with the Minister of Industry and Trade and the Minister of Finance.

KADI's current structure frequently causes delays in the decision-making process and leads to situations where investigations are completed past the 18-month deadline provided for in the AD Agreement. While KADI has consistently concluded its investigations in less than 18 months, in a number of cases, the date of the decision by the Minister of Finance went beyond 18 months.[4]

Safeguard investigations were initially governed by Presidential Decree No. 84 of 2002 on the Actions to Safeguard the Domestic Industry From the Results of a Surge in Imports (hereinafter Presidential Decree No. 84/2002). Different than in the case of anti-dumping and countervailing duty investigations, the agency responsible for conducting safeguard investigations is the Indonesian Trade Safeguard Committee (hereinafter KPPI). KPPI's authority is to investigate and issue a recommendation to the Minister of Trade on whether or not safeguard measures should be applied. If the Minister of Trade approves the recommendation to impose a safeguard measure, he or she will implement the measure. Thus, the Minister of Finance will issue a decree for the implementation of the safeguard measure in the form of a tariff[5] as approved by the Minister of Trade.

As a result of the efforts by the Government of Indonesia to improve the trade remedies system and to make it more efficient, a new regulation has been adopted recently. The three trade remedies are now together governed by Government Regulation No. 34 of 2011 dated 4 July 2011 on Anti-Dumping, Countervailing, and Safeguard Measures (hereinafter Government Regulation No. 34/2011). Government Regulation No. 34/2011 supersedes Government Regulation No. 34/1996 and Presidential Decree No. 84/2002. However, provisions set forth in the

---

[4] For example, the *Carbon Black* and *Wheat Flour* cases.

[5] Based on Article 21.2 of Presedential Decree No. 84/2002 , if the measure takes the form of a quota, the decree imposing the measure is to be issued by the Minister of Industry and Trade.

implementing decrees of the revoked regulations, such as Decree 216/
2001, remain applicable, provided they are not inconsistent with
Government Regulation No. 34/2011.[6] It should also be underlined
that the establishment of KADI and KPPI, which was based on the
revoked regulations, is still effective under Government Regulation No.
34/2011.

Clearly, Government Regulation No. 34/2011 attempts to incorporate
more provisions of the WTO AD Agreement, SCM Agreement and the
Agreement on Safeguards (hereinafter SG Agreement). Yet it does not
cover a number of substantive provisions: for example, in the case of the
AD Agreement, the provisions of its Article 2[7] have not been incorporated. In the absence of such provisions reflected in the domestic legislation, KADI, in its practice, cites the corresponding articles in the AD
Agreement.

According to our records, KADI has thus far initiated approximately
38 anti-dumping investigations. In the case of safeguards, we note that as
of 2011, KPPI has initiated at least 23 safeguard investigations, including
those on imports of textile products. It is interesting to note, however,
that KADI has never initiated a countervailing duty investigation. While
there is no clear reason for this, it may perhaps be explained by the
complexity of subsidy calculations and the lack of adequate written
procedures for the conduct of such investigations under Decree 216/
2001, including procedures for the consultations. Apart from these, there
is no clear reason why KADI is reluctant to initiate countervailing duty
investigations.

II   Legal framework for the judicial review of trade
remedy determinations

Prior to the promulgation of Government Regulation No. 34/2011,
Article 35 of Government Regulation No. 34/1996 established the basis
for filing objections against anti-dumping and countervailing measures.
Article 35 provided as follows:

---

[6] This raises an important legal issue. Since Government Regulation No. 34/1996 has been
revoked, it is not clear legally how its implementing decrees, such as Decree No. 216/
2001, can continue to apply. If raised in a future judicial review proceeding, the Supreme
Court may clarify this particular issue.
[7] Article 2 of the AD Agreement contains provisions governing the calculation of dumping
margins.

> Objections to anti-dumping or countervailing measures can be filed to the appeal institution contemplated in Article 97 of Law No. 10 of 1995 concerning Customs.

Under this provision, exporters or importers who had an objection to a decision by the Minister of Finance to impose anti-dumping or counter-vailing duties could file an appeal with the dispute settlement body provided under the Customs Law, namely, the Taxation Dispute Settlement Body (hereinafter BPSP), the name of which was subse-quently changed to Tax Court under Law No. 14 of 2002 concerning the Tax Court (hereinafter Law No. 14/2002).

However, the Tax Court could only deal with disputes relating to decrees issued at the Director General level or below, which would concern, for example, the collection of anti-dumping or countervailing duties. According to Law No. 14/2002, the Tax Court could not examine decrees issued by the Minister of Finance, since it is under the supervision of that minister. Thus, in practice, this framework did not provide exporters and importers with a proper judicial review mechanism with respect to the determinations lead-ing to the imposition of anti-dumping or countervailing duties.

In the absence of such local legal remedy to challenge the decrees of the Minister of Finance imposing anti-dumping or countervailing duties, in practice there were and still are two alternatives by which affected parties may file their objection: an appeal to the Indonesian State Administrative Court and/or initiating a judicial review proceeding with the Indonesian Supreme Court.[8]

However, unlike Article 35 of Government Regulation No. 34/1996 above, Article 99 of Government Regulation No. 34/2011 provides for objection to the imposition of trade remedy measures as follows:

(1) Objections against the imposition of anti-dumping, countervailing, and safeguard measures may only be filed with the Dispute Settlement Body of the World Trade Organization.
(2) Objections against the implementation of anti-dumping, counter-vailing, and safeguard measures during importation shall be filed based on the prevailing laws and regulations.

The above provision clearly states that objections against the imposition of anti-dumping, countervailing and safeguard measures may not be filed with an Indonesian domestic court, but exclusively with the Dispute

---

[8] See Section III below for explanations on judicial review by the State Administrative Court.

Settlement Body of the WTO. However, objections against the implementation of anti-dumping, countervailing and safeguard measures with respect to importation may be filed with the competent court, based on the prevailing laws and regulations.

Article 99 of Government Regulation No. 34/2011 distinguishes between "imposition" and "implementation" of anti-dumping, countervailing and safeguard measures. The term "imposition" in our view refers to the imposition of such measures by the Minister of Finance Decree, while the term "implementation" relates to the rules and procedures governing the collection of duties under decrees of the Director General of Customs and Excise. Therefore this Article does not provide for the judicial review of determinations made by the Indonesian investigating authorities in a trade remedy investigation, the results of which are approved via the decrees issued by the Minister of Finance.

In our view, the new provision is based on an incorrect interpretation of Article 13 of the AD Agreement and Article 23 of the SCM Agreement. The government seems to have interpreted these provisions to mean that judicial review of the investigating authorities' determinations may only be reviewed through WTO dispute settlement. The consequence of this provision is that the interested parties, including the affected individual foreign producers or exporters, users and importers, do not have the opportunity to ask an independent tribunal in Indonesia to review the determinations made by the Indonesian investigating authorities.

We recall that Article 13 of the AD Agreement[9] provides as follows:

> Each member whose national legislation contains provisions on anti-dumping measures shall maintain judicial, arbitral or administrative tribunals or procedures for the purpose, inter alia, of the prompt review of administrative actions relating to final determinations and reviews of determinations within the meaning of Article 11. Such tribunals or procedures shall be independent of the authorities responsible for the determination or review in question.

Clearly, Article 13 requires WTO members to have a judicial review system that provides for the review by an independent body of the determinations made by investigating authorities in a given investigation or review. Judicial review by an independent body of the investigating authority's determinations seems to be the central element of the obligations set forth in Article 13. Hence, Indonesian law potentially

---

[9] Article 23 of the SCM Agreement reflects the same provision, although it contains additional elements with respect to the parties eligible to resort to judicial review.

conflicts with its obligation, since it does not allow for the judicial review of the investigating authority's determinations by Indonesian courts. By the same token, it also conflicts with Article 23 of the SCM Agreement, which contains the same obligation.

Giving importers the right to challenge issues pertaining to the collection of anti-dumping and countervailing duties does not eliminate this inconsistency with WTO law. Therefore, Article 99(1) of Government Regulation No. 34/2011 needs to be amended to allow interested parties in a trade remedy investigation or review to challenge the determinations made by the Indonesian investigating authorities before the courts.

That said, we do not consider that the current text of Article 99(1) of Government Regulation No. 34/2011 prevents interested parties from initiating judicial review proceedings at the State Administrative Court or the Supreme Court to challenge the determinations made by Indonesian investigating authorities in trade remedy investigations or reviews. There are two reasons for this. First, by virtue of Law No. 7/1994, the AD Agreement has become an integral part of Indonesian law. Second, the WTO dispute settlement mechanism is only available to governments which are members of the WTO. Interested parties involved in trade remedy proceedings are private entities, and therefore cannot use WTO dispute settlement. In this sense, the provision of Article 99(1) of Government Regulation No. 34/2011, which states that the objection to the imposition of anti-dumping, countervailing and safeguard measures may only be filed with the WTO's Dispute Settlement Body, does not make much sense. In our view, as long as the legal standing requirement for filing objections with the State Administrative Court or the Supreme Court is met, interested parties may bring judicial review cases before these two courts.

The right to challenge issues pertaining to the collection of duties is granted to importers only. Importers may file their objections on these issues with the Tax Court. An importer may, for instance, challenge the amount of the duty collected. It should be noted, however, that prior to filing its objection with the Tax Court, the importer must first file an administrative appeal with the customs office.[10] Only if the

---

[10] Article 93(1) of the Customs Law reads: "Objections against the decision of the Director General of Customs and Excise concerning tariffs and/or customs valuation for the purpose of calculation of duty can be filed in writing with the Director General of Customs and Excise within 60 days from the implementation date along with the deposit of a guarantee in the amount of the invoice payable."

administrative appeal does not yield a satisfactory result may the importer apply to the Tax Court.

III   Types of judicial review proceedings

As explained above, despite the limitation under Article 99(1) of Government Regulation No. 34/2011, under Indonesian law, judicial review of trade remedy determinations may be conducted by two different courts: the State Administrative Court or the Supreme Court. Objections pertaining to the duties collected by customs are handled by Tax Courts, but these proceedings do not concern the determinations made by the investigating authorities in the underlying investigations. In this section, therefore, we will focus on judicial review by the State Administrative Court and the Supreme Court where such determinations are reviewed.

We note at the outset that, although two different courts deal with the judicial review of trade remedy determinations, in practice complainants have always chosen the State Administrative Court; no judicial review proceeding has ever been initiated at the Supreme Court. The main reason for this is that foreigners cannot file a judicial review request with the Supreme Court; this process is available to Indonesian nationals only. Further, the Indonesian importers and users of products subject to anti-dumping measures are more familiar with the State Administrative Court proceedings compared to Supreme Court proceedings. It should also be stressed that unlike the Supreme Court, the State Administrative Court may order the suspension of the decree imposing the disputed duty.

In terms of subject matter, all judicial review proceedings initiated to date have pertained to anti-dumping investigations; no request has been filed in connection with safeguard measures imposed by the Minister of Finance. While there is no specific reason that explains this situation, it is generally known that safeguard measures are not triggered by unfair trade practices and that the procedure applied in safeguard investigations is different from anti-dumping investigations, in that cooperating interested parties in safeguard investigations are less likely to face unfair treatment by the investigating authorities. Therefore, the jurisprudence that we cite in our explanations in this chapter pertains to judicial review proceedings filed with the State Administrative Court on anti-dumping measures.

Below, we explain the procedural rules that govern judicial review proceedings at the State Administrative Court and the Supreme Court.[11]

1 Judicial review by the State Administrative Court

1.1 Reviewable determinations[12]

The State Administrative Court entertains disputes relating to state administrative decisions. Article 1(3) of the State Administrative Court Law defines[13] "state administrative decision" as a written determination issued by an agency or state administrative officer, which contains an administrative action that is *concrete, individual and final* and which affects an individual or a legal entity.

Elucidation of Article 1(3) provides definitions of the three characteristics that a state administrative decision must possess. A *concrete* determination is one the object of which exists, is specific, or can be measured. An *individual* determination is one addressed to a particular person or entity and not to the public in general. For example, a determination in respect of factory X in China is individual, because it concerns a particular party in a particular territory. A *final* determination is one that is definitive and, unchallenged, has legal effect. When these three

---

[11] It should be noted that only Indonesian importers were eligible to file an objection with the Director General of Customs and Excise and to file an appeal with the Tax Court with respect to the implementation of trade remedy measures. It should also be recalled that this was related to the implementing regulation of the collection of duties imposed by the Minister of Finance. These proceedings normally dealt with issues such as the incorrect calculation of the collectable duty by the customs authorities. They would not touch upon the substance of the decree by the Minister of Finance imposing trade remedy measures based on the investigation conducted by the investigating authorities. Given this fact, in this chapter we do not present an analysis of possible remedies against the implementing decrees issued by the Director General of Customs and Excise.

[12] It should be noted that KADI or KPPI, the Indonesian investigating authorities, are not defendants in the State Administrative Court proceedings, since they issue only a recommendation that is not enforceable per se. The defendant in these proceedings is the Minister of Finance. The investigating authorities will attend the court's hearings in order to present their testimonies. In at least two separate State Administrative Court proceedings on wheat flour involving Chinese and United Arab Emirates wheat flour producers, we observed that the panel of judges also examined the final disclosures issued by KADI.

[13] The State Administrative Court Law here refers to Law No. 5 of 1986 on State Administrative Court; Law No. 9 of 2004 on Amendment to State Administrative Court and Law No. 51 of 2009 on Second Amendment of Law No. 5 of 1986 on State Administrative Court.

requirements are present, a particular determination may be characterized as a state administrative decision and be the subject of a judicial
review proceeding at the State Administrative Court.

Applying these criteria to the decrees by the Minister of Finance
imposing anti-dumping duties, it appears at first sight as if such decrees
are not individual determinations and therefore do not constitute state
administrative decisions, because duties apply to all importers importing
the subject product. The implication of this is that such decrees would
not fall under the jurisdiction of the State Administrative Court.
However, in the *Tin Plate* case, the State Administrative Court admitted
an objection raised by the importers. Unfortunately, since the court's
decision does not contain a detailed reasoning on this particular issue,
we do not know the grounds on which it was based. The decision was
appealed to the Higher State Administrative Court, and the latter upheld
it. That decision was also appealed to the Supreme Court, which reversed
the Higher State Administrative Court on the grounds, *inter alia*, that
since the contested decree applied to the public, the legal requirement on
the individual characteristic of state administrative decisions had not
been fulfilled. This is the only case where importers filed an objection
with the State Administrative Court with respect to a decree of the
Minister of Finance imposing anti-dumping duties.

The foreign producers involved in two different anti-dumping investigations on imports of *Wheat Flour* initiated judicial review proceedings
at the State Administrative Court against the decrees of the Minister of
Finance imposing anti-dumping duties. In our view, as far as foreign
producers are concerned, the individual characteristic of decrees imposing anti-dumping duties is easier to demonstrate because, in principle,
duties for each producer reflect individual calculations made for each
foreign producer on the basis of its own costs and sales data. That is why
the duty rate is different for each producer, and this is clearly indicated in
the decree imposing the duty. This shows that the decrees are addressed
to individual foreign producers and not to the public in general. Indeed,
the State Administrative Court came to this conclusion in two different
judicial review proceedings on *Wheat Flour*, one involving two Chinese
and the other two United Arab Emirates producers.[14] We understand
that in this case the Supreme Court also reversed the decision of the State
Administrative Court, which had been upheld by the Higher State

---

[14] In these three cases, as the issues of the challenged actions were "concrete" and "final",
they were not discussed.

Administrative Court. However, it is not clear whether the Supreme Court's decision was based, once again, on the notion that the disputed decree was not of an individual character.

1.2 Standard of review

The standard of review in judicial review proceedings before the State Administrative Court is laid down in Article 53 of the State Administrative Court Law. This article reads:

1. Persons or civil legal entities that feel their interests are impaired by a state administrative decision can file a written objection with the competent court requesting that the disputed state administrative decision be declared null and void, with or without compensation and/or rehabilitation.
2. The reasons that can support a claim mentioned in paragraph 1 are:
   (a) the state administrative decision is against the prevailing laws and regulations;
   (b) the state administrative decision is against general principles of good governance.

Based on the above provisions, the individual person or legal entity must demonstrate the existence of undermining of its interest by the issuance of the state administrative decision because it is against the prevailing laws and general principles of good governance. In the *Wheat Flour* case involving United Arab Emirates producers, the State Administrative Court stated that the imposition of anti-dumping duties at a rate of 14.85 per cent had allowed the complaining foreign producers to bring a case as set forth under Article 53(1) of the State Administrative Court Law. The court pronounced the same reasoning in another *Wheat Flour* case involving Chinese wheat flour producers, stating that the imposition of anti-dumping duties at a rate of 9.5 per cent had caused the producers to discontinue their exports to Indonesia.

In both cases, the court also considered that the issuance by the Minister of Finance of the decree imposing anti-dumping duties after the 18-month time limit following the initiation of the underlying investigation was inconsistent with Article 11 of Government Regulation No. 34/1996. Further, the court also reasoned that KADI's failure to provide sufficient disclosure with respect to the calculation of dumping margins for the foreign producers concerned had led to doubts concerning the rates of the resulting duties.

In our view, in this case, the State Administrative Court hinted that it could review the consistency of KADI's determinations with the prevailing laws and with the principle of good governance, and whether any inconsistency in this regard impaired the rights of the complainants.

1.3   Rigour of judicial review by the State Administrative Court

Looking at the decisions made by the State Administrative Court in the few judicial review proceedings initiated with respect to KADI's anti-dumping investigations, one clearly sees that the court has consistently avoided discussing substantive issues such as dumping margin calculations, although such issues were raised by the complainants. Instead, it usually focused on procedural and administrative issues, and to some extent, some limited injury indicators. In our view, this is because the judges sitting in these proceedings did not have the in-depth knowledge that would have allowed them to conduct a more rigorous review.

It should be noted that in the two *Wheat Flour* cases involving foreign producers from the United Arab Emirates and China, respectively, the State Administrative Court, in its decisions, referred to the complainants' claims of violation of Article 5.10 of the AD Agreement, since the relevant decrees had been issued more than 18 months from the initiation of the underlying anti-dumping investigations. The court accepted these arguments on the grounds that the setting of deadlines aimed to ensure legal certainty in the investigative proceedings. Therefore, final determinations made beyond the 18-month deadline were not consistent with Government Regulation No. 34/1996.

However, as noted in its legal consideration with respect to the substance of the case, the court did not directly refer to the AD Agreement, and, instead, cited the relevant parts of the Indonesian anti-dumping law. In the *Wheat Flour* case involving the Chinese wheat flour producer, the court was of the opinion that the information submitted by petitioners with respect to market share, wages, employment and cash flows did not show injury. This decision is important, since Government Regulation No. 34/1996 does not incorporate Article 3.4 of the AD Agreement,[15] and yet the court referred to this article in its decision.

---

[15] Article 3.4 of the AD Agreement reads: "The examination of the impact of the dumped imports on the domestic industry concerned shall include an evaluation of all relevant economic factors and indices having a bearing on the state of the industry, including actual and potential decline in sales, profits, output, market share, productivity, return on investments, or utilization of capacity; factors affecting domestic prices; the magnitude of the margin of dumping; actual and potential negative effects on cash flow, inventories, employment, wages, growth, ability to raise capital or investments. This

In the same case, the court also considered that the lack of disclosure of the calculation methodology for the dumping margin calculated for the complainant company had cast doubts over the accuracy of calculations. The court also considered that the issuance of the decree of the Minister of Finance more than 18 months from the initiation of the investigation was inconsistent with Article 11 of Government Regulation No. 34/1996, which reflected the text of Article 5.10 of the AD Agreement.[16]

1.4   Appeal

Decisions by the State Administrative Court may be appealed to the Higher State Administrative Court, which, in turn, may be appealed to the Supreme Court by means of cassation. The appeal to the Higher Court and cassation at the Supreme Court may be based on procedural and substantive reasons. Unlike in the court of first instance, there are normally no hearings in the appeal proceedings at the Higher Administrative Court and the Supreme Court. Another stage of appeal is by means of review, in a case where affected parties still wish to challenge the decision of the Supreme Court at cassation phase. The review can also be filed with the Supreme Court. The grounds for the review process are the discovery of new evidence (*novum*) or incorrect application of the law by the Supreme Court. The review request is also to be filed with the Supreme Court, but it does not prevent the enforcement of the decision made at cassation level.[17] There are usually no hearings in the review proceeding.

While the State Administrative Court and the Higher State Administrative Court are normally required to make their decisions within six months from the date of filing of the case, there is no such

list is not exhaustive, nor can one or several of these factors necessarily give decisive guidance."

[16] Article 5.10 of the AD Agreement reads: "Investigations shall, except in special circumstances, be concluded within one year, and in no case more than 18 months, after their initiation." It seems that under Articles 8, 9, 10 of Government Regulation No. 34/2011, in Indonesian anti-dumping practice the 18-month deadline for the completion of an investigation only applies to the investigation conducted by KADI, not the decision made by the Minister of Finance or the approval by the Minister of Trade. This, in our view, is inconsistent with Article 5.10 of the AD Agreement, because the conclusion of an investigation should also include the final determination, which in the Indonesian system, refers to the decree issued by the Minister of Finance.

[17] The State Administrative Court Law provides that the decision issued by the government institution or government officers will no longer be applicable 60 days after the legally binding decision is issued by the State Administrative Court, should no revocation be made to the decision issued by the government institution or government officials.

specific deadline for the cassation and review proceedings. This is due to the Supreme Court's huge workload, which delays the issuance of decisions. Sometimes the contested decree from the Minister of Finance expires before the completion of judicial review proceedings. Because of delays in the judicial review process, interested parties show little interest in using it.

When the State Administrative Court or the Higher State Administrative Court files no appeals with respect to a decision, it becomes final.[18] The decision made by the Supreme Court on appeal automatically becomes final, even if a review process is initiated against such a decision on the basis of a finding of new evidence or alleged incorrect application of the law by the Supreme Court.

1.5   Injunction by the State Administrative Court

At the request of the complainant, the State Administrative Court can issue injunctions to order the suspension of the implementation of a state administrative decision during the court proceedings.[19] Normally injunctions are requested in emergency situations. It should be noted, however, that, in practice, suspension is sometimes not effective, since it is not directly applicable. To give effect to suspension, the relevant agency must issue a new decree, which sometimes they may not do. Unfortunately, there is no strict sanction for failure to obey court orders.

---

[18] Article 123 of the State Administrative Court Law provides: (1) written request for appeal made and signed by the plaintiff or its proxy must be filed with the State Administrative Court which decided the case within 14 days after such decision has been legally notified to the plaintiff; and (2) the request for appeal should be filed along with the down payment of the case fee, the total amount of which will be estimated by the registrar.

[19] Article 67 of the State Administrative Court Law reads:

   (1) Objection does not suspend or hinder the implementation of the state administrative decision and the state administrative action being challenged.
   (2) The plaintiff may request the suspension of the implementation of the state administrative decision, until a legally binding decision is issued.
   (3) The request mentioned in paragraph (2) can be submitted in a petition which can be decided prior to the substance of the case.
   (4) The request for suspension as mentioned in paragraph (2):
       (a) Can be granted provided there is an emergency situation which may harm the plaintiff's interest should such state administrative decision be executed.
       (b) Cannot be granted if the public interest within the context of general development requires the execution of such state administrative decision.

Injunctive reliefs were requested from the court in the *Tin Plate* and *Wheat Flour* cases, and were granted. However, neither of these injunctions were enforced, since the Minister of Finance did not issue the decrees which would have made such enforcement possible.

2   Judicial review by the Supreme Court

As an alternative to judicial review by the State Administrative Court, Indonesian nationals may request judicial review by the Supreme Court of the decrees of the Minister of Finance imposing anti-dumping duties. This type of judicial review may be requested where there are inconsistencies between the decisions or regulations issued by the government of Indonesia and prevailing laws and/or regulations that have precedence. These include state administrative decisions related to the imposition of trade remedy measures. The requirements that the disputed state administrative decision be "concrete", "individual" and "final" do not apply in judicial review proceedings before the Supreme Court. The decision of the Supreme Court in a judicial review proceeding is final and binding, and such decision will be automatically enforceable 90 days from the date of service on the defendant agency.

In the case of state administrative decisions related to trade remedy measures, only importers or Indonesian legal entities may file a judicial review request with the Supreme Court (because they are Indonesian nationals). Judicial review by the Supreme Court is a useful option for importers because, as explained above, the proceedings before the State Administrative Court require that the determination challenged be of an "individual" nature, which is often difficult to demonstrate in the case of trade remedies measures.

IV   Concluding remarks and suggestions for improvement

It is quite clear from the foregoing that the judicial review by the State Administrative Court of the decrees of the Minister of Finance imposing trade remedy measures has thus far been ineffective. There is also no guarantee that judicial review in the Supreme Court can provide importers with effective remedies. Further, the Supreme Court option has not yet been tested. There is therefore an urgent need to improve the system in a way that would provide legal certainty to interested parties. Article 13 of the AD Agreement and Article 23 of the SCM Agreement lay the foundation for the enforcement of individual rights in the field of trade remedies. Therefore, it is the Indonesian government's obligation to make available a judicial review system of the kind described in the two treaty provisions cited. The current judicial review system in Indonesia, however, is far from meeting these requirements.

In our view, several concrete steps may be taken in order to improve the Indonesian judicial review system. First, the existence of two types of judicial review proceedings, one by the State Administrative Court and the other by the Supreme Court, seems to be complementary, in the sense that the former ensures the observance of the rights of foreign producers, while the latter can deal with appeals brought by Indonesian nationals whenever the element of "individual" appears to be difficult to fulfil. However, introducing a system with a single court that would handle appeals from both foreigners and Indonesian nationals would be ideal. In the new system, the State Administrative Court should hear appeals from both foreign producers and Indonesian producers and importers. To this end, a clear definition of "individual" should be provided to cover the rights of interested parties, including the affected importers and users. As for judicial review by the Supreme Court, it seems difficult to allow foreign producers to use this type of review since, as explained above, this is a mechanism designed to ensure that various legal instruments, such as regulations, decrees and laws that make up the Indonesian legal system, follow a certain order of hierarchy.

Our understanding is that the Indonesian government is currently discussing a draft law called the Indonesia Trade Act. In our view, this provides a valuable opportunity in terms of identifying the court that will handle cases related to trade remedies, and such opportunity should not be missed. Such identification will provide more transparency, in terms of interested parties knowing where to go and how to challenge the determinations of the Indonesian investigating authorities.

Second, Article 99(1) of Government Regulation No. 34/2011 should be repealed, and it should be made clear in the regulation that interested parties in a trade remedy investigation or review may bring a case for the judicial review of the determinations made by the Indonesian investigating authorities in such investigations or reviews.

Third, as indicated above, the State Administrative Law, the Customs Law and Government Regulation 34/2001 should be amended in order to clarify that the determinations of the investigating authorities are of an *individual* nature *vis-à-vis* importers, foreign producers and Indonesian producers, and that all of these interested parties may bring a case for court review of such determinations. Although, as explained above, even the current text of Government Regulation No. 34/2011 does not prevent importers from bringing a case before the State Administrative Court, we think making a textual change such as we suggest here would clarify the situation and provide greater predictability for interested parties.

Fourth, the judges participating in the judicial review of trade remedy determinations must be given the necessary training that would enable them to review the substance of the investigating authorities' determinations. This would certainly pave the way for a more meaningful judicial review.

18

Australia: judicial review with merits review

STEPHEN GAGELER

I Introduction

The Australian legal system draws a sharp distinction in theory[1] and in practice between the judicial review of administrative action and the merits review of administrative action. Judicial review, the province of the courts, is to some extent constitutionally entrenched and is concerned exclusively with the legality of administrative action. Merits review, the province of administrative tribunals and agencies, exists only to the extent specifically provided by statute, is itself a form of administrative action and is concerned with the correctness or advisedness of primary administrative action.

The distinction between judicial review and merits review is amplified in the following negative description of the nature and limits of judicial review that has often been repeated in judgments of the High Court of Australia:[2]

> The duty and jurisdiction of the court to review administrative action do not go beyond the declaration and enforcing of the law which determines the limits and governs the exercise of the repository's power. If, in so doing, the court avoids administrative injustice or error, so be it; but the court has no jurisdiction simply to cure administrative injustice or error. The merits of administrative action, to the extent that they can be distinguished from legality, are for the repository of the relevant power and, subject to political control, for the repository alone.

Affirmatively complementing that negative description of judicial review, the High Court has asserted as an aspect of the rule of law inherent in the Australian constitutional structure the imperative that:[3]

---

[1] S. Gageler, "The Legitimate Scope of Judicial Review" (2001) 21 *Aust. Bar Rev.* 279.

[2] *Attorney-General (NSW)* v. *Quin* (1990) 170 CLR 1, at 35–6 per Brennan J.

[3] *Corporation of the City of Enfield* v. *Development Assessment Commission* (1999) 199 CLR 135, at 157 [56] per Gaudron J, as quoted in *Re Refugee Review Tribunal; Ex parte Aala* (2000) 204 CLR 82, at 107 [54] per Gaudron and Gummow JJ.

within the limits of their jurisdiction and consistent with their obligation to act judicially, [Australian] courts should provide whatever remedies are available and appropriate to ensure that those possessed of ... administrative powers exercise them only in accordance with the laws which govern their exercise.

Consistently with that overall conception of the nature and scope of judicial review in Australia, the High Court has explained its own constitutionally conferred and constitutionally entrenched original jurisdiction to grant specified relief against an officer of the Commonwealth of Australia,[4] as "a means of assuring to all people affected that officers of the Commonwealth obey the law and neither exceed nor neglect any jurisdiction which the law confers on them".[5] An excess or neglect of jurisdiction on the part of an officer of the Commonwealth is labelled "jurisdictional error". Jurisdictional error can always be redressed by the High Court itself granting appropriate relief in proceedings brought within its original jurisdiction.[6]

That original jurisdiction constitutionally conferred on the High Court is supplemented by jurisdiction conferred by two statutes of the Commonwealth Parliament on the Federal Court of Australia, which was itself created by a statute in 1976,[7] and from which an appeal lies, by special leave, to the High Court.[8] One is s. 39B of the Judiciary Act 1903 (Cth), which confers equivalent jurisdiction to grant specified relief against an officer of the Commonwealth for jurisdictional error.[9] The other is the Administrative Decisions (Judicial Review) Act 1977 (Cth), which makes general, although not universal, provision for the judicial review on specified legal grounds of decisions

---

[4] Section 75(v) of the Constitution of the Commonwealth of Australia provides that the High Court shall have original jurisdiction in all matters "in which a writ of mandamus or prohibition or an injunction is sought against an officer of the Commonwealth".

[5] *Plaintiff S157/2002* v. *Commonwealth* (2003) 211 CLR 476, at 513–14 [104].

[6] *Plaintiff S157/2002* v. *Commonwealth*. (2003) 211 CLR 476.

[7] Federal Court of Australia Act 1976 (Cth).

[8] Section 73(ii) of the Constitution of the Commonwealth of Australia and s. 33 of the Federal Court of Australia Act 1976 (Cth).

[9] Section 39B(1) provides that, subject to immaterial exceptions, "the original jurisdiction of the Federal Court of Australia includes jurisdiction with respect to any matter in which a writ of mandamus or prohibition or an injunction is sought against an officer or officers of the Commonwealth". In addition, s. 39B(1A)(c) includes within the original jurisdiction of the Federal Court any matter "arising under any laws made by the Parliament".

of an administrative character made under other statutes of the Commonwealth Parliament.[10]

Those general statutory conferrals of jurisdiction on the Federal Court to engage in judicial review have coexisted, since their inception in the last quarter of the twentieth century, with specific statutes of the Commonwealth Parliament conferring jurisdiction on administrative tribunals and agencies to review the merits of specified administrative action. The pattern of those statutes is to empower tribunals and agencies to reconsider the correctness or advisedness of primary administrative decisions and, generally but not universally, to substitute their own decision where they consider it to be preferable.[11] Indeed, the policy to which the Commonwealth Parliament has generally adhered since the 1970s has been to provide for some form of merits review of administrative action except where the benefits of that course have been seen to be outweighed by detriments such as cost and delay.[12]

It is within the context of these two coexisting forms of review that primary administrative decisions to take anti-dumping or countervailing measures are supervised. The specific provisions of Part XVB of the Customs Act 1901 (Cth) and the Customs Tariff (Anti-Dumping) Act 1975 (Cth), which together constitute a statutory scheme for the administrative taking of anti-dumping and countervailing measures in Australia, were enacted and have evolved within that general legal and policy framework. Safeguards, which are potentially capable of taking a variety of forms, are capable of being made the subject of separate statutory procedures under the Productivity Commission Act 1998 (Cth).[13] As no safeguards have yet been implemented in Australia, the potential for their judicial review is not explored in this chapter.

In relation to the taking of anti-dumping and countervailing measures in Australia, each of the various forms of administrative action for which Part XVB of the Customs Act 1901 (Cth) and the Customs Tariff

---

[10] The Administrative Decisions (Judicial Review) Act 1977 (Cth) is expressed to apply to "a decision of an administrative character made, proposed to be made, or required to be made (whether in the exercise of a discretion or not ...)" under an Act of the Commonwealth Parliament other than a decision included within a class of decisions set out in the Schedule to that Act (s. 3).

[11] See, for example, Administrative Appeals Tribunal Act 1975 (Cth), s. 43(1).

[12] Commonwealth of Australia, Administrative Review Council, *What Decisions Should Be Subject to Merit Review* (1979).

[13] Commonwealth of Australia Gazette, *Establishment of General Procedures for Inquiries by the Productivity Commission into Whether Safeguard Action is Warranted under the Agreement Establishing the World Trade Organization*, No. S 297, 25 June 1998.

(Anti-Dumping) Act 1975 (Cth) provide is subject to judicial review in the original jurisdiction of the High Court and in the Federal Court. Most, but not all, of those forms of administrative action are also subject to merits review by an officer of the Commonwealth, designated the Trade Measures Review Officer (hereinafter TMRO), who is required to consider afresh the correctness or advisedness of the original administrative action and whose own administrative actions are then equally subject to judicial review in the original jurisdiction of the High Court and in the Federal Court.

It is the coexistence of ubiquitous judicial review with specific and targeted merits review that is a distinctive feature of the Australian statutory scheme.

II Statutory scheme

While statutes providing for the taking of anti-dumping measures have existed in Australia continuously since 1906,[14] and statutes providing for the imposition of countervailing measures have existed continuously since 1957,[15] the current statutory scheme has its origins in Australia's response in the mid-1970s to the Kennedy Round of Multilateral Trade Negotiations (1964–7).[16] Since then, the statutory scheme has been significantly revised both in light of the Tokyo Round of Multilateral Trade Negotiations (1973–9)[17] and the Uruguay Round of Multilateral Trade Negotiations (1986–4)[18] and in light of numerous domestic reviews that have inquired into and reported on its functioning. The

---

[14] Provision for such measures commenced with the Australian Industries Preservation Act 1906 (Cth), now repealed.

[15] Customs Tariff (Industries Preservation) Act 1957 (Cth), amending the Customs Tariff (Industries Preservation) Act 1921 (Cth).

[16] The legislative scheme was originally contained wholly within the Customs Tariff (Anti-Dumping) Act 1975 (Cth). The machinery provisions were moved to Part XVB of the Customs Act 1901 (Cth) by operation of the Customs Tariff (Anti-Dumping) Amendment Act 1989 (Cth) and the Customs Legislation (Anti-Dumping) Act 1989 (Cth). There is a succinct legislative history in ICI Australia Operations Pty Ltd v. Fraser (1992) 34 FCR 564, at 568–71 and a fuller account in R. Whitwell, The Application of Anti-Dumping and Countervailing Measures By Australia (Central Queensland University Press, 1997). These domestic measures reflect Australia's international rights and obligations in this area commencing most notably, of course, with membership of the General Agreement on Tariffs and Trade (GATT), which was replaced by membership of the World Trade Organization on 1 January 1995.

[17] Customs Amendment Act 1981 (Cth).

[18] Customs Legislation (World Trade Organization Amendments) Act 1994 (Cth).

most significant of those inquiries and reports, all of which led to some alteration of the statutory scheme, were in 1986,[19] 1996,[20] 2009[21] and 2011.[22] The most recent amendments to the statutory scheme, responsive to the 2009 and 2011 inquiries and reports, occurred as recently as late 2011.[23]

Under the statutory scheme, any decision to take or revoke anti-dumping or countervailing measures is required to be made by the responsible Commonwealth minister (currently the Minister for Home Affairs). Primary responsibility for administration of the statutory scheme, including conducting investigations and reporting to the minister, is formally vested in the Chief Executive Officer (hereinafter CEO) of the Australian Customs and Border Protection Service (hereinafter Customs) and in practice is exercised through a specialized branch of Customs now known as the International Trade Remedies Branch (hereinafter ITRB).

The anti-dumping and countervailing measures that can be taken by the minister are limited to the publication of a "dumping duty notice" or a "countervailing duty notice", or to the acceptance of an undertaking from an exporter on conditions that make it unnecessary to publish such a notice.[24] The effect of publication of a dumping duty notice or countervailing duty notice where that occurs is to create a statutory liability to pay dumping duty or countervailing duty on the importation into Australia of goods to which the notice extends and, pending assessment of that duty, to pay interim duty.[25]

---

[19] F. H. Gruen, *Review of the Customs Tariff (Anti-Dumping) Act 1975: Report*, (Department of Industry, Technology and Commerce, Canberra, 1986); resulting in the Customs Tariff (Anti-Dumping) Amendment Act 1988 (Cth) and the Customs (Anti-Dumping) Amendment Act 1988 (Cth).

[20] L. Willett, *Review of Australia's Anti-Dumping and Countervailing Administration* (Australian Government Publishing Service, Canberra, 1996); resulting in the Customs Legislation (Anti-Dumping Amendments) Act 1998 (Cth).

[21] Productivity Commission, *Australia's Anti-Dumping and Countervailing System, Productivity Commission Inquiry Report No. 48* (2009).

[22] Senate Economics Legislation Committee, *Customs Amendment (Anti-Dumping) Bill 2011*, Canberra, (2011).

[23] Customs Amendment (Anti-Dumping Improvements) Act 2011 (Cth) and Customs Amendment (Anti-Dumping Measures) Act 2011 (Cth).

[24] Sections 269TG and 269TJ of the Customs Act 1901 (Cth).

[25] Dumping duty and countervailing duty, as well as interim duty, are special duties of Customs imposed under ss. 8 and 10 of the Customs Tariff (Anti-Dumping) Act 1975 (Cth) where a dumping duty notice or a countervailing duty notice is in force under ss. 269TG and 269TJ of the Customs Act 1901 (Cth).

The statutory power of the minister to publish a dumping duty notice or a countervailing duty notice is cast in terms of a discretion that is enlivened "where the Minister is satisfied" as to existence of preconditions for the publication of the notice.[26] To enliven the discretion to publish a dumping duty notice, the preconditions of which the minister must be satisfied include that the amount of the "export price" of goods exported to Australia is less than the "normal value" of those goods.[27] To enliven the corresponding discretion to publish a countervailing duty notice, the preconditions of which the minister must be satisfied include that a "countervailable subsidy" has been received in respect of goods exported to Australia.[28] In either case, the minister must also be satisfied that, "because of that ... material injury to an Australian industry producing like goods has been or is being caused or is threatened or the establishment of an Australian industry producing like goods has been or may be materially hindered".[29] The expressions "export price",[30] "normal value",[31] "countervailable subsidy",[32] "material injury to an Australian industry"[33] and "like goods"[34] are each elaborately defined in terms that reflect Australia's international obligations under the Agreement on implementation of Article VI of the General Agreement on Tariffs and Trade 1994 (hereinafter Anti-Dumping Agreement) and the Agreement on Subsidies and Countervailing Measures without directly incorporating those international obligations into the statutory scheme.

The power of the minister to accept an undertaking is cast in terms of a power to defer the decision to publish or not to publish a dumping duty notice or a countervailing duty notice covering an exporter, for so long as the minister considers appropriate, if the exporter offers and the minister accepts, an undertaking (which may be subject to conditions) that the exporter will so conduct future trade to Australia as to avoid causing or threatening material injury to an Australian industry producing like goods or materially hindering the establishment of an Australian industry.[35]

While the minister is empowered to take anti-dumping measures on his/her own initiative,[36] the standard process by which the minister may

---

[26] Section 269TG(1) and (2) (in relation to dumping duty notices) and s. 269TJ(1) and (2) (in relation to countervailing duty notices).
[27] Section 269TG(1)(a) and (2)(a).　　[28] Section 269TJ(1)(a) and (2)(a).
[29] Section 269TG(1)(b) and (2)(b) and s. 269TJ(1)(b) and (2)(b).　　[30] Section 269TAB.
[31] Section 269TAC.　　[32] Section 269TAAC.　　[33] Section 269TAE.
[34] Section 269T(1).　　[35] Section 269TG(4) and s. 269TJ(3) and (3A).
[36] Section 269TAG.

come potentially to consider the publication of a dumping duty notice or a countervailing duty notice begins with the making of a written application in an approved form to Customs by a person who believes that there are, or may be, reasonable grounds for that publication and who has the support of a sufficient part of the Australian industry.[37] The making of such an application triggers a three-stage statutory process of screening, investigation and recommendation by the CEO. The incidents of each stage of that process are closely circumscribed by statute and are required by statute to occur within a specified time frame designed ordinarily to result in the minister making a decision as to whether or not to publish a dumping duty notice or countervailing duty notice within 205 days of the making of the application.

The first stage – screening – is required always to occur within 20 days of the making of application. The CEO is required to examine the application and to reject it if not "satisfied", having regard to its contents and to any other information that the CEO considers relevant, that the application complies with the formal requirements for an application and that "there appear to be reasonable grounds" for the publication of a dumping duty notice or a countervailing duty notice.[38]

The second stage – investigation – is required to commence immediately if the CEO decides not to reject an application at the screening stage. The investigation is initiated by the CEO giving public notice of that decision indicating, amongst other things, the basis on which dumping or countervailable subsidization is alleged to have occurred and inviting interested parties to lodge with the CEO, within a specified period of not more than 40 days after the date of the initiation of the investigation, submissions concerning the publication of the notice sought in the application.[39] There is no provision within the statutory scheme for a public hearing. In practice, the investigation is conducted by the ITRB sending questionnaires to all known importers and exporters, inviting responses within the period of 40 days after the date of the initiation of the investigation, as well as seeking to gather and verify information from importers, exporters and participants in the Australian industry by conducting verification visits and other forms of consultation. The submissions, together with the application and all other information given to the ITRB to be taken into account by the CEO, must be in writing and at least a non-confidential summary of

---

[37] Section 269TB.   [38] Section 269TC(1).   [39] Section 269TC(4).

them must be placed on a public record that is available for inspection at the request of any interested party.[40]

The CEO has a duty to terminate an investigation if he or she becomes "satisfied" in the course of the investigation: that there has been no dumping or subsidization or that the dumping margin or subsidization level is negligible; that the volume dumped or subsidized imports is negligible; or that any injury is negligible.[41] Detailed statutory criteria give content to the concept of "negligibility" in each of those contexts.

The CEO also has discretion to make a preliminary affirmative determination that is enlivened if the CEO becomes "satisfied" in the course of an investigation at any time not earlier than 60 days after the date of initiation that "there appears to be sufficient grounds" for the publication of a dumping duty notice or a countervailing duty notice or that "it appears that there will be sufficient grounds" for the publication of such a notice.[42] If the CEO makes a preliminary affirmative determination, he or she must give public notice of that determination.[43] Customs may then, at the time of making that determination or at any later time during the investigation, exercise a further statutory discretion to require and take securities in respect of interim duty that may become payable if the officer of Customs taking the securities is "satisfied" that it is "necessary to do so to prevent material injury to the Australian industry occurring while the investigation continues".[44]

Within 110 days after the date of the initiation of the investigation, or such longer period as the minister may allow, the CEO is required to place on the public record a statement of the essential facts on which he or she proposes to base a recommendation to the minister in relation to the application giving rise to the investigation. In formulating the statement of essential facts, the CEO is obliged to have regard to the application and to any relevant submissions received by Customs within 40 days after the initiation of the investigation and may have regard to any other matters that he or she considers relevant.[45] Interested parties are invited to lodge submissions in response to the statement of essential facts within 20 days of the statement being placed on the public record.[46]

---

[40] Section 269ZJ. "Interested party", in this context, is defined at length in s. 269T(1).
[41] Section 269TDA.   [42] Section 269TD(1).   [43] Section 269TD(4).
[44] The discretionary taking of securities occurs pursuant to s. 42 of the Customs Act 1901 (Cth).
[45] Section 269TDAA.   [46] Section 269TC(4)(f).

The final stage, the making of a report to the minister, is required to occur within 155 days after the date of initiation of the investigation.[47] The CEO is required to recommend in that report whether any dumping duty notice or countervailing duty notice should be published and the extent of any duties payable because of that notice and to recommend, in particular, whether the minister ought be satisfied as to the matters in respect of which the minister is required to be satisfied before such a notice can be published.[48] In deciding on the recommendations to be made to the minister in the report, the CEO is obliged to have regard to the application, to any submission to which he or she has already had regard for the purpose of formulating the statement of essential facts, to the statement of essential facts itself and any submission made in response to it within 20 days of its being placed on the public record.[49] The report is also required to include a statement of the CEO's reasons for any recommendation that sets out the material findings of fact on which the recommendation is based and provides particulars of the evidence relied on to support those findings.[50]

The minister has a duty to decide whether or not to publish a dumping duty notice or a countervailing duty notice within 30 days after receiving the report of the CEO or, if the minister considers that there are special circumstances that prevent the decision being made within that period, within such longer period as the minister considers appropriate.[51] Whether the decision of the minister is to publish or not to publish a dumping duty notice or a countervailing duty notice, he or she is obliged to give public notice of the decision setting out the particulars thereof.[52] The minister is also required to set out, in a separate report to which the notice refers, the reasons for the decision, including all material findings of fact or law on which the decision was based.[53]

III   Merits review

Since 1998,[54] the TMRO has been given the function of conducting an independent merits review, at the instigation of an "interested

---

[47] Section 269TEA(1) and s. 269TC(4)(bf)(i). If the period of 110 days for the placing of a statement of essential facts on the public record is extended, the period of 155 days for the making of a report to the minister is correspondingly automatically extended by s. 269TC(bf)(ii).

[48] Section 269TEA(1)(c) and (d).   [49] Section 269TEA(3).   [50] Section 269TEA(5).

[51] Section 269TLA.   [52] Sections 269TG, 269TJ and 269ZI.   [53] Section 269ZI(2)(b).

[54] Customs Legislation (Anti-dumping Amendments) Act 1998 (Cth).

party",[55] of decisions of the minister to publish or not to publish dumping duty notices or countervailing duty notices, as well as certain decisions made by the CEO including a decision to reject an application for the making of an anti-dumping duty notice or a countervailing duty notice at the screening stage or to terminate an investigation. There is no provision for merits review of a decision of the minister to accept or reject an undertaking or of a decision of Customs to impose securities.

The current merits review function of the TMRO replaced that of an earlier statutory body, the Anti-Dumping Authority, which existed for 10 years from 1988.[56] The function has been fine-tuned by amendment as recently as 2011.[57] The TMRO is an administrative officer of the Commonwealth who by statute is given a measure of independence from both Customs and the minister. The TMRO cannot be an officer of Customs[58] and, although appointed by the minister,[59] holds office for a fixed term[60] during which he or she may only be removed for specified cause.[61] The minister is obliged to ensure that sufficient resources (including personnel) are made available to enable the effective performance of the functions of the TMRO.[62]

The incidents of the review process conducted by the TMRO are closely circumscribed by statute and are required by statute to occur within a specified time frame. Unlike the form of merits review previously conducted by the Anti-Dumping Authority, which often involved the gathering of further evidence, the form of merits review conducted by the TMRO is in each case essentially a review, on the papers, of the appropriateness of the findings that formed the basis of the decision under review.

In the case of a decision of the minister to publish or not to publish a dumping duty notice or a countervailing duty notice, an application for review must be made within 30 days after the public notice of the decision[63] and must particularize the ground or grounds that, in the applicant's view, would warrant the reinvestigation of a finding or findings that form the basis of the decision the subject of the application.[64] The TMRO must

---

[55] The expression "interested party", in this context, is defined in s. 269ZX to include relevant importers, exporters and participants in the relevant Australian industry.

[56] Anti-Dumping Authority Act 1988 (Cth), repealed by the Customs Legislation (Anti-Dumping Amendments) Act 1998 (Cth).

[57] Customs Amendment (Anti-Dumping Improvements) Act 2011 (Cth).

[58] Section 269ZL(3).   [59] Section 269ZL(1).

[60] Section 269ZO(1). The term must not exceed three years; however, the TRMO is eligible for reappointment: s 269ZO(2).

[61] Section 269ZR.   [62] Section 269ZT.   [63] Section 269ZZD and 269ZI.

[64] Section 269ZZE.

reject an application if he or she is satisfied that the applicant has failed to provide sufficient particulars to establish reasonable grounds to warrant the reinvestigation of the finding or findings specified in the application,[65] but must otherwise conduct a review after giving public notice inviting interested parties to lodge submissions within 30 days.[66] The outcome of the review, in the form of a report by the TMRO to the minister, must occur not more than 60 days after that notification, or such longer period as the minister may allow because of special circumstances.[67] In conducting the review of the minister's decision, the TMRO is confined to considering the information to which the CEO had regard or was required to have regard when making the findings set out in the CEO's report to the minister, and to conclusions based on that information contained in the application or in submissions received from interested parties within the 30-day period.[68] The TMRO has no power to substitute his or her own finding for a finding of the minister under review, or even to substitute his or her own finding for a finding set out in the CEO's report to the minister.[69] Rather, the TMRO is limited to two options. If the TMRO forms the view that the finding or findings specified in the application should be affirmed, his or her report to the minister must recommend that the minister affirm his or her original decision. If the TMRO is unable to form the view that such a finding should be affirmed, the TMRO's report to the minister must recommend that he or she direct the CEO to reinvestigate the finding.[70] In either event, the minister has 30 days from the receipt of the report either to affirm his or her earlier decision or to accept any recommendation of the TMRO to require the CEO to reinvestigate a finding or findings and to direct the CEO in writing to that effect.[71] Receipt by the minister of a recommendation by the TMRO has been described as "a hinge upon which the statutory regime for reinvestigation turns" in that, absent such a recommendation, there is no power in the minister to reinvestigate and no power on the part of Customs to conduct a reinvestigation.[72] Where the minister acts on a recommendation of the TMRO to direct the CEO to reinvestigate, the reinvestigation must occur within a time frame specified by the minister and results in the CEO giving a further report to the minister, following which he or she must either

---

[65] Section 269ZZG(1) and s. 269ZZF.   [66] Sections 269ZZI and 269ZZJ.
[67] Section 269ZZK(1) and (3).   [68] Section 269ZZK(4) and (6).
[69] For a criticism, see D. Moulis and P. Gay, "The 10 Major Problems With the Anti-Dumping Instrument in Australia" (2005) 39 *Journal of World Trade* 75, at 83.
[70] Section 269ZZK(1) and (2).   [71] Section 269ZZL.
[72] *Kimberly-Clark* v. *Minister for Home Affairs* (2011) 193 FCR 15, at 21 [31].

affirm the original decision or revoke that decision and substitute a new decision.[73] There is no further provision for merits review of a substituted decision.

The merits review function of the TMRO in relation to reviewable decisions made by the CEO is somewhat broader and more streamlined. In each case, the application for review must be made within 30 days after the applicant was notified of the relevant decision of the CEO, and the decision of the TMRO on review must be made within 60 days after receipt of the application by the TMRO, or such longer period as the minister may allow because of special circumstances.[74] In each case, the TMRO is confined to considering information that was before the CEO when he or she made the decision.[75] In each case, the TMRO must make a decision either affirming the decision of the CEO or revoking that decision and substituting a new one.[76] A decision of the TMRO on review has effect as if it were a decision made by the CEO, and takes effect when the TMRO makes the decision.[77] The TMRO maintains a public record, available for inspection at the request of any interested party, containing at least a non-confidential version of each application and submission.[78]

Although merits review conducted by the TMRO only occurs on application, in fact applications for merits review by the TMRO occur in the vast majority of cases. In the five years to 2009, the TMRO reviewed about 80 per cent of the decisions of the minister and about 90 per cent of the decisions of the CEO to terminate investigations. The TMRO recommended that the CEO reinvestigate about 60 per cent of the cases where measures had been imposed, and affirmed about 80 per cent of the decisions to terminate investigations.[79]

IV   Judicial review

Judicial review of a decision of the minister, the CEO or the TMRO, each of whom are officers of the Commonwealth, could theoretically occur on the application of any person whose legal interests were affected by the

[73] Section 269ZZM.
[74] Sections 269ZZS(4), 269ZZT(5), 269ZZU(4) and 269ZUA(6).
[75] Sections 269ZZS(3), 269ZZT(4), 269ZZU(3) and 269ZUA(5).
[76] Sections 269ZZS(1), 269ZZT(1), 269ZZU(1) and 269ZUA(1).   [77] Section 269ZZV.
[78] Section 269ZZX.
[79] Productivity Commission, *Australia's Anti-Dumping and Countervailing System*, *Productivity Commission Inquiry Report No. 48* (2009), at p. 136.

decision in the original jurisdiction of the High Court.[80] However, the concurrent statutory jurisdiction of the Federal Court makes recourse to the original jurisdiction of the High Court unnecessary in practice.[81]

Judicial review of decisions of the minister, the CEO and the TMRO fall within the mainstream of the work of the Federal Court, where they are heard and determined by reference to well-established legal principles of general application and in accordance with the ordinary practice and procedure of that court in judicial review matters. The jurisdiction of the Federal Court is invoked by the filing of an application setting out the grounds on which the application is brought.[82] The maker of the decision that is sought to be reviewed is a necessary party, as are persons whose legal rights are directly affected by the decision. Other persons who have an interest may apply to be made parties[83] or to intervene.[84] The making of the application does not affect the operation of the decision or prevent the taking of action to implement the decision. However, where there is shown to be a seriously arguable case for final relief and where the balance of convenience is shown to favour that course, the Federal Court has power (subject to such conditions as it thinks fit) to order that the decision be stayed or that its implementation be restrained pending the hearing and determination of the application.[85]

The substantially overlapping nature of the twin sources of the Federal Court's jurisdiction in judicial review matters – s. 39B of the Judiciary Act and the Administrative Decisions (Judicial Review) Act – has the result that applications are ordinarily framed to rely on both sources of jurisdiction. There is rarely occasion to distinguish rigidly between them.[86] The precise grounds spelled out in the Administrative Decisions (Judicial Review) Act

---

[80] Applications for judicial review of decisions of ministers to impose anti-dumping duties were not unknown to occur in the original jurisdiction of the High Court before the establishment of the Federal Court: see, for example, *Carmody v. FC Lovelock Pty Ltd* (1970) 123 CLR 1.

[81] Absent special circumstances, an application for judicial review commenced in the original jurisdiction of the High Court could be expected to be remitted to the Federal Court under s. 44 of the Judiciary Act 1903 (Cth).

[82] Part 31 of the Federal Court Rules 2011.

[83] Section 12 of the Administrative Decisions (Judicial Review) Act 1977 (Cth).

[84] Rule 9.12 of the Federal Court Rules 2011.

[85] Section 23 of the Federal Court of Australia Act 1976 (Cth) and s. 15 of the Administrative Decisions (Judicial Review) Act 1977 (Cth).

[86] Decisions to take securities under s. 42 of the Customs Act 1901 (Cth) in respect of duty that may be payable under the Customs Tariff (Anti-Dumping) Act 1975 (Cth) are excluded from the decisions to which the Administrative Decisions (Judicial Review) Act 1977 (Cth) applies by para. (p) of Sch. 1 of that Act.

for the judicial review of a decision of an administrative character made under a Commonwealth statute, with few exceptions, are readily capable of being characterized as species of jurisdictional error which, if established to the satisfaction of the Court, would result in a purported decision made by an officer of the Commonwealth under the same Commonwealth statute being held to be in want or excess of jurisdiction.[87] While there are some subtle and highly technical differences in the precise form of relief available under each source of jurisdiction, in a case where relevant legal error is shown, each can result in: the decision under review being quashed;[88] the decision-maker being ordered to remake the decision or undertake other action required to perform a statutory duty that remains in law unperformed;[89] or the decision-maker being restrained from taking or continuing to take action not authorized by the statute under which the decision-maker is purporting to act.[90] Under both sources of jurisdiction the grant of relief is discretionary[91] and, in a rare case, may be withheld in an application to review where the availability of merits review can be shown to provide the applicant for judicial review with an adequate alternative remedy.[92]

The Federal Court operates on a case management system, which results in each application when made being assigned to an individual judge who will make pre-trial directions appropriate to the particular application and who will ordinarily go on to conduct the trial.[93] The practice and procedure of the Federal Court in relation to the hearing

---

[87] Section 5 of the Administrative Decisions (Judicial Review) Act 1977 (Cth) provides that an application for an "order of review" may be made on one or more of nine specified grounds, two of which are subjected to further detailed specification. As well as the ground "that the person who purported to make the decision did not have jurisdiction to make the decision" (s. 5(1)(c)) they include "that a breach of the rules of natural justice occurred in connection with the making of the decision" (s. 5(1)(a)) and "that the decision involved an error of law" (s. 5(1)(f)).

[88] The effect of certiorari (which may be ordered in an application under s. 39B of the Judiciary Act 1901 (Cth), at least where its grant is ancillary to an order of mandamus or prohibition) or an order under s. 16(1)(a) of the Administrative Decisions (Judicial Review) Act 1977 (Cth).

[89] The effect of mandamus or an order under s. 16(1)(b) or (c) of the Administrative Decisions (Judicial Review) Act 1977 (Cth).

[90] The effect of prohibition or an order under s. 16(1)(d) of the Administrative Decisions (Judicial Review) Act 1977 (Cth).

[91] See, for example, *Schaefer Waste Technology Sdn Bhd* v. *Chief Executive Officer, Australian Customs Service* (2006) 156 FCR 94, at 128 [284]–[285].

[92] See, for example, *Darling Downs Bacon Co-Operative Association Ltd and Pork Council of Australia Limited* v. *the Comptroller-General of Customs* (1994) 50 FCR 435.

[93] The case management system is facilitated by Part VB of the Federal Court of Australia Act 1976 (Cth).

and determination of an application for judicial review can include, at the direction of a judge, pre-trial documentary discovery from any party. The hearing of the application is ordinarily in a trial before an individual judge always sitting in public. It is in the nature of judicial review proceedings that the evidence is largely documentary. But where there is evidence in addition to documentary evidence, that evidence is ordinarily given on affidavit and cross-examination is permitted. Where shown to be necessary, commercial confidentiality of information contained in particular documents discovered during the pre-trial process, or of information contained in particular evidence given at trial, can be maintained by orders restricting publication or circulation.[94] The judgment of the trial judge is ordinarily reserved and given in writing a short time after the trial. At the discretion of the trial judge, litigation costs can be, and ordinarily are, awarded in favour of a successful party.[95] Any unsuccessful party has a right to appeal from the judgment of the trial judge to the Full Court of the Federal Court, which ordinarily comprises three judges. The Full Court conducts the appeal as a rehearing and, where it finds error in the judgment of the trial judge, sets aside that judgment and ordinarily substitutes its own.[96] Further appeal to the High Court is only from a judgment of the Full Court and can only be brought by special leave of the High Court.[97]

The processes of the Federal Court are designed to facilitate the just resolution of disputes according to law "as quickly, inexpensively and efficiently as possible".[98] While no time frames are legislatively prescribed, the Federal Court has a benchmark of 85 per cent of all cases being completed with 18 months of commencement.[99] Most judicial review cases are completed within a much shorter period. Applications for special leave to appeal to the High Court in trade measures matters are extremely rare and none has ever been granted.

---

[94] The source of power to make such confidentiality orders lies in ss. 23 and 50 of the Federal Court of Australia Act 1976 (Cth). Limited confidentiality orders have often been made in proceedings for the judicial review of trade measures decisions in accordance with principles discussed in *Kanthal Australia Pty Ltd* v. *Minister for Industry, Technology and Commerce* (1987) 14 FCR 90.

[95] The source of power to order costs is s. 43 of the Federal Court of Australia Act 1976 (Cth).

[96] Sections 24 and 25 of the Federal Court of Australia Act 1976 (Cth).

[97] Section 33 of the Federal Court of Australia Act 1976 (Cth).

[98] Section 37M(1)(b) of the Federal Court of Australia Act 1976 (Cth).

[99] *Federal Court of Australia Annual Report 2010–2011*, p. 135. The benchmark excludes native title cases.

Since its establishment, the Federal Court has in fact heard and determined close to 150 applications for judicial review of decisions of the Minister, the CEO and the TMRO (or the earlier Anti-Dumping Authority) in relation to trade measures, each of which has resulted in a judgment of a single judge and many of which have also resulted in appeals to and judgments of the Full Court.

The nature of the Australian conception of judicial review, focusing as it does on the precise statutory limits of the administrative jurisdiction statutorily conferred on the decision-maker whose decision is sought to be impugned, necessitates in every case that very close attention be paid to the precise incidents of the relevant statutory scheme as expressed or implied in the language and structure of the statutory scheme or as implied by reference to general principles of statutory interpretation. What are treated in many legal systems as free-standing generally applicable principles of administrative law, tend to be treated in Australia as incidents of the relevant statutory scheme produced by implication through the application of general principles of statutory interpretation, unless those general principles are specifically excluded.

In this respect, it is of considerable significance to the practical scope of judicial review of any exercise of the statutory power of the minister to publish a dumping duty notice or a countervailing duty notice, that the power is cast as a discretion to publish such notices that arises where the minister is "satisfied" as to the existence of specified preconditions in terms of the existence of dumping or countervailable subsidization, as the case may be, and causation of material injury to an Australian industry. For similar reasons, it is of particular significance to the practical scope of judicial review of any decision of the CEO to reject an application, to make a preliminary affirmative determination, or to terminate an investigation, the statutory power is in each case cast as a duty or discretion that arises where the CEO is "satisfied" as to existence of specified preconditions.

In accordance with general principles of statutory interpretation, a requirement for "satisfaction" of that nature is interpreted as having the effect of importing by implication jurisdictional preconditions that must be fulfilled for the relevant discretion or duty to be enlivened and without which any purported exercise of power by the minister or CEO would be affected by jurisdictional error and for that reason be legally ineffective. Not only must the decision-maker in fact form a subjective state of satisfaction answering the statutory description as to the existence of the specified preconditions, but also the subjective state of satisfaction actually formed by the decision-maker must be a state of satisfaction that has certain objectively discernible characteristics.[100] First, the subjective state of satisfaction must be formed on a correct understanding of the statute under which the power is conferred. The decision-maker falls into jurisdictional error if he/she misunderstands the statute in a way that causes the decision-maker: to ask the wrong question; to take into account as part of his or her reasoning process considerations that are irrelevant under the statute; or to fail to take into account as part of his or her reasoning process considerations that are required by the statute to be taken into account. Second, the subjective state of satisfaction must be formed reasonably on the material before the decision-maker.

The second of those characteristics, the requirement for the decision-maker to act reasonably on the available material, provides some scope for the judicial review of findings of fact, but that scope is extremely limited. Australian courts have not gone so far as to require an administrative decision to be supported by substantial evidence.[101] Rather, Australian theory and practice accords with the observation that, apart from a rare case of the evidence being "all one way", "where the criterion with which the [decision-maker] is required to be satisfied turns upon factual matters upon which reasonable minds could reasonably differ, it will be very difficult to show that no reasonable decision maker could have arrived at the decision in question".[102] Whether, and if so, to what extent the requirement for reasonableness in this context extends to require logicality in reasoning actually adopted to make an available finding of fact is a controversial topic that has not finally been resolved.[103]

It is the first of the two characteristics, the requirement for the decision-maker to act on a correct understanding of the statute, that provides in principle, and has provided in practice, the most fertile ground for the judicial review of trade measures decisions in Australia. While most cases have turned on narrow and highly technical issues of

[100] *Corporation of the City of Enfield* v. *Development Assessment Commission* (2000) 199 CLR 135, at 150 [34].

[101] *CA Ford Pty Ltd* v. *Comptroller-General of Customs* (1993) 46 FCR 443, at 445–6.

[102] *Schaefer Waste Technology Sdn Bhd* v. *Chief Executive Officer, Australian Customs Service* (2006) 156 FCR 94, at 122–3 [221] quoting *Minister for Immigration and Multicultural Affairs* v. *Eshetu* (1999) 197 CLR 611, at 654 [137].

[103] The traditional view was that mere illogicality did not constitute jurisdictional error: e.g. *Mullins Wheels Pty Ltd* v. *Minister for Customs and Consumer Affairs* (2000) 97 FCR 284, at 296–7 [41]. But see now, e.g., *Re Minister for Immigration and Multicultural Affairs; Ex parte Applicant S20/2002* (2003) 198 59.

statutory construction peculiar to the statutory scheme at a point in time and often overtaken by amendment, there has nevertheless been an accumulation over the years of a considerable and enduring body of case law in the Federal Court examining the meaning of statutory expressions and concepts deriving from Australia's international obligations under the Anti-Dumping Agreement and the Agreement on Subsidies and Countervailing Measures. There is, for example, a body of Australian case law directed to the nature of the causal connection that must exist between dumping or subsidization and any actual or threatened injury to a domestic industry,[104] as well as to the meaning and application of statutory expressions such as "export",[105] "price",[106] and "subsidy".[107] The development of case law has been informed by further principles of statutory interpretation that require Australia's domestic legislation to be interpreted in a case of ambiguity in conformity with its international obligations[108] and that require decisions of foreign courts on the meaning of cognate terms in foreign statutes designed to implement those same treaty obligations ordinarily to be followed in the interests of comity.[109]

The concomitant requirement that the decision-maker take into account as part of his/her reasoning process considerations that are required by the statute to be taken into account has also provided fertile ground for the judicial review of trade measures decisions. However, the Federal Court has repeatedly drawn back from imposing a duty to inquire, emphasizing instead that "[d]ecision making is a function of the real world" that "it is no part of the duty of the decision maker to make the applicant's case", that "[a] decision maker is not bound to investigate each avenue that may be suggested to him by a party interested" and that "[u]ltimately, a decision maker must do the best on the

---

[104] *ICI Operations Pty Ltd v. Fraser* (1992) 34 FCR 564; *Minister of Small Business, Construction and Customs, Anti-Dumping Authority, Comptroller-General of Customs v. La Doria Di Diodata Ferraiolli SPA* [1994] FCA 904; *Schaefer Waste Technology Sdn Bhd v. Chief Executive Officer, Australian Customs Service*, at 115 [147]–[148].

[105] See, for example, *Companhia Votorantum de Celulose e Papel v. Anti-Dumping Authority* (1996) 71 FCR 80.

[106] See, for example, *Nordland Papier AG v. Anti-Dumping Authority* (1999) 93 FCR 454.

[107] *Rocklea Spinning Mills Pty Ltd v. Anti-Dumping Authority* (1995) 56 FCR 406.

[108] See, for example, *Atlas Air Australia Pty Ltd v. Anti-Dumping Authority* (1995) 26 FCR 456; *Pilkington (Australia) Ltd v. Minister for Justice and Customs* (2002) 127 FCR 92, at 100 [26].

[109] See, for example, *Rocklea Spinning Mills Pty Ltd v. Anti-Dumping Authority*, at 421.

material available after giving interested parties the right to be heard on the question".[110]

In accordance with general principles of statutory interpretation,[111] the legal and practical consequences of any decision by the minister to publish or not to publish a dumping duty notice or a countervailing duty notice or of the CEO or the TMRO on review to reject or not to reject an application, to make or not to make a preliminary affirmative determination, or to terminate or not to terminate an investigation, have the additional consequence, by a process of statutory implication and as a condition of the exercise of power,[112] of importing a requirement for procedural fairness to be afforded to those importers, exporters and participants in the Australian industry whose interests may be affected for procedural fairness.[113] Procedural fairness requires that, except to the extent modified or confined by the specific requirements of the statutory scheme, those entities be given a reasonable opportunity to provide information and make submissions during the process leading to the decision, including by rebutting or qualifying by further information, and commenting by way of further submission, on adverse material from other sources.[114] In practice, the requirements of procedural fairness are normally met in circumstances where there is compliance by the CEO and the TMRO with the specific statutory requirements for public notification and for the maintenance of a public file. In circumstances where the minister does no more than act on the recommendation of the CEO or the TMRO, as the case may be, in deciding to publish or not to publish a dumping duty notice or a countervailing duty notice and those entities have been afforded procedural fairness during the course of the investigation by the CEO or the review by the TMRO, there is no requirement for the minister to give those entities any further opportunity to provide information or make submissions.[115] While once quite

---

[110] *Enichem Anic Srl* v. *Anti-Dumping Authority* (1992) 39 FCR 458, at 469; *Orica Ltd & Ors* v. *Anti-Dumping Authority & Anor* [1998] FCA 629; *Vredelco Food Industries Pty Limited* v. *Anti-Dumping Authority* [1994] FCA 1501, at [59].

[111] See, for example, *Plaintiff M61/2010E* v. *Commonwealth* (2010) 243CLR 319, at 352–353 [74]–[75].

[112] *Refugee Review Tribunal, Re; Ex parte Aala* (2000) 204 CLR 82.

[113] Procedural fairness is referred to by the alternative name of "natural justice" in s. 5(1)(a) of the Administrative Decisions (Judicial Review) Act 1977 (Cth).

[114] *Commissioner for Australian Capital Territory Revenue* v. *Alphaone Pty Ltd* (1994) 49 FCR 576, at 591–2, quoted for example, in *SZBEL* v. *Minister for Immigration and Multicultural and Indigenous Affairs* (2006) 228 CLR 152, at 161–2 [29].

[115] *Hyster Australia Pty Ltd* v. *Anti-Dumping Authority* (1993) 40 FCR 364, at 379.

frequent, challenges to trade measures decisions on procedural fairness grounds are now relatively rare.[116]

V   Conclusion

Judicial review in Australia, while narrowly focused on the legality of administrative action and highly technical in its application, has been found generally to produce systemic benefits by promoting the accountability of administrative decision-making as well as consistency and certainty in the administration of statutes.[117] It was observed at an early stage in the evolution of the current statutory scheme for the administrative taking of anti-dumping and countervailing measures that "judicial review has operated to raise the decision-making standards and procedures" in the same way as it has operated in relation to other statutory schemes in Australia.[118] That is undoubtedly still the Australian experience. Yet judicial review is not concerned, other than by those consequential effects, with ensuring the substantive correctness or advisedness of administrative action that is lawful.

That narrow focus of judicial review has nevertheless been tempered in Australia through the widespread availability of a range of specific mechanisms for the administrative review of the merits of primary administrative decisions. The current system of administrative review of trade measures decisions by the TMRO is one of those mechanisms. It is not the first and is unlikely to be the last. It is the product of numerous reviews and reforms undertaken to increase the efficiency and effectiveness of the system while complying with Australia's international obligations. That process of review and reform can confidently be expected to continue.

---

[116] They are not unknown to be successful: see, for example, *Thai Pineapple Canning Industry Corporation Ltd* v. *Minister for Justice and Customs* (2008) 104 ALD 481.

[117] Administrative Review Council, *The Scope of Judicial Review Report No. 47* (2006), at p. 31.

[118] H. Steele, "The Australian Antidumping System", in J. Jackson and E Vermulst, *Antidumping Law and Practice* (1990), at p. 238.

Countries with insufficient judicial review activity

JAPAN: A SYSTEM YET TO BE TESTED

OSAMU UMEJIMA

I Introduction

Japan sets forth its trade remedy rules in the Customs Tariff Law.[1] The first countervailing duty rules were enacted in 1906,[2] and are now in Article 7 thereof. Anti-dumping rules are in Article 8,[3] and general safeguard rules in Article 9.[4] These statutory rules are supplemented by Cabinet orders[5] and guidelines.[6] Quantitative import restriction as a safeguard measure is set forth in the Import Trade Control Order,[7] the ministerial notice[8] and the guidelines.[9]

Japan's investigating authority is established on an *ad hoc* basis upon consultation among the Minister of Finance, the Minister of Economy, Trade and Industry and the minister having the jurisdiction over the product under consideration, when an application for a trade remedy investigation is duly filed, or these ministers have found that the

---

[1] Act No. 54 of 15 April 1910, as amended.
[2] Originally enacted in the former Customs Tariff Law, Act No. 19 of 31 March 1906.
[3] Enacted in July 1920, as amended.   [4] Enacted in March 1961, as amended.
[5] Cabinet Order Relating to Countervailing Duty (Cabinet Order No. 415, December 1994, as amended), Cabinet Order Relating to Anti-Dumping Duty (Cabinet Order No. 416, December 1994, as amended), and Cabinet Order Relating to Safeguard Duty, Etc. (Cabinet Order No. 417, December 1994, as amended).
[6] The Guidelines for Procedures Relating to Countervailing Duties; the Guidelines for Procedures Relating to Anti-Dumping Duties; the Guidelines for Procedures Relating to Safeguard Duties, etc.
[7] Cabinet Order No. 414 of 29 December 1949, as amended.
[8] Notice of the Ministry of International Trade and Industry, No. 715, 28 December 2004, as amended.
[9] The Guidelines for Procedures Relating to Emergency Measures in case of Increase of Imports, Import Caution Item 7, No. 54, 4 August 2005, as amended.

investigation should be initiated. The investigating authority is in charge of all aspects of the trade remedy investigation.

Except for the quantitative import restrictions as a safeguard measure,[10] the authority's final determination, which must refer the determination to the Council on Customs, Tariff, Foreign Exchange and other Transactions (Kanzei Gaikoku Kawase-tou Shingikai) will be presented to the Minister of Finance. Upon the Council's review, the Minister of Finance will present to the Cabinet the draft trade remedy measure in the form of a Cabinet order. A specific trade remedy measure is effective upon the Cabinet's resolution of the order.

Although Japan's trade remedy legislation has a long history, these rules have never been actively used. So far, Japan has imposed four anti-dumping measures,[11] one countervailing measure,[12] and one provisional safeguard measure in its entire trade remedy enforcement history.[13]

Under Japanese law, trade remedy measures are subject to judicial review. However, no complaints for judicial review have ever been filed, and so no judicial review proceedings have ever been initiated. As explained below, since judicial review has never been used in Japan, certain issues on judicial review remain uncertain.

II Legal framework

In Japan, procedural rules for the judicial review of administrative actions, including administrative actions related to trade remedy measures, are set forth in the Administrative Case Litigation Act (hereinafter the Act),[14] separately from the laws guiding civil and criminal proceedings.

Article 9 of the Act provides that a person "who has legal interest to seek the revocation" of an "administrative disposition" may file a complaint with a court. The Act does not however, define an "administrative disposition", i.e., administrative actions which may be brought to the

---

[10] The import quantitative restriction will be set forth by the order of the Ministry of Economy, Trade and Industry. See Article 3.1 of Import Trade Control Order (Cabinet Order No. 414 of 19 December 1949, as amended).

[11] *Ferro-Silicon Manganese from China* (1993–8); *Cotton Yarn # 20 from Pakistan* (1995–9); *Polyether Staple Fiber from South Korea and Taiwan* (2002 to present); *Electrolytic Manganese Dioxide from South Africa, Australia, China and Spain* (2008 to present).

[12] *Dynamic Random Access Memories from South Korea* (2006–9).

[13] *Welsh Onions, Shiitake Mushrooms and Tatami-Omote* (2001). No definitive safeguard measure was imposed.

[14] Act No. 139 of 16 May 1962, as amended.

court. Nor does it set forth any further rules on a person "who has legal interest to seek the revocation", i.e., standing to be a complainant in a judicial review proceeding. We address these two issues below.

1 "Administrative disposition"

As discussed earlier, under Japanese law, an anti-dumping, countervailing or safeguard measure is promulgated and effectuated by an *ad hoc* administrative order for the specific measure, based on the findings in the investigating authority's final determination.[15] Once the administrative order comes into effect, Japan Customs impose and collect duties or other measures on individual imports of the specific goods as set forth in the provisions of the administrative order.

Article 3.2 of the Act describes one form of "administrative disposition" as an "original administrative disposition and any other act constituting the exercise of public authority by an administrative agency". In light of this provision, there is no doubt that an action by Japan Customs to impose the duty or other measure on a specific import transaction at the time of its entry into Japan constitutes an "administrative disposition", and therefore, is challengeable in court. Such importer may challenge the legitimacy of the administrative order in the judicial proceeding because the legality of the administrative disposition to impose the duty or other measure on the specific import depends entirely on the legitimacy of the administrative order.

It is unclear, however, whether or not the administrative order imposing a specific trade remedy measure is a challengeable "administrative disposition" as such. In general, administrative orders are considered as general and abstract rules creating the legal authority, not a specific administrative "disposition" or the exercise of the authority. A court, however, may find an administrative order concerning a specific trade remedy measure challengeable as such, because it mandates Japan Customs to impose the specific measure on specific goods, and thus directly affects the rights of private persons.[16] Since there has been no judicial review proceeding with respect to a trade remedy determination

---

[15] See Articles 7.1, 8.1 and 9.1 of the Customs Tariff Act (Act No. 54 of 15 April 1910, as amended). As discussed earlier, the amount of a quantitative restriction as a safeguard measure will be set forth in an order of the Ministry of Economy, Trade and Industry.

[16] See, e.g., Supreme Court Judgment, 25 December 1979 (Min-Shu Vol. 33 No. 7, p. 753), in which the Supreme Court found that, although a notice to an importer that imports of particular pornographic products were prohibited was an abstract notice, the notice still

in Japan, we do not know which position the courts will take on this particular issue. Having said that, taking into account the recent interpretation by the Supreme Court of Article 3.2 which expanded the scope of an administrative disposition, and Japan's international obligations under the WTO Agreement, there is a good chance that courts will find that an administrative order concerning a specific trade remedy measure is an "administrative disposition".

2 Standing

Article 9 of the Act sets forth that persons, "who have legal interest to seek the revocation of the original administrative disposition", have standing as complainant. It is clear, therefore, that an importer who imported, or attempted to import, the product subject to a trade remedy measure, is eligible to file a complaint for a judicial review proceeding.

The Act also provides that a court may find, on a case-by-case basis, that a person has a legal interest, even though the administrative disposition is not addressed to that person. Article 9.2 of the Act provides that the courts shall decide the standing of such other persons, taking into account "the purposes and objectives of the laws and regulations as well as the content and nature of the interest". This provision would enable a court to find, for example, that exporters or manufacturers in the exporting country or the government of the exporting country have standing. In particular, if a court finds that an administrative order concerning a trade remedy measure is challengeable as such, the court may also find that entities whose imports are affected by that order have standing to initiate a judicial review proceeding. However, this question has not yet been tested in any court in Japan.

III   Procedures

A complaint may be filed with a district court having jurisdiction over the area in which the administrative agency making the administrative disposition in question is located.[17] Judgments of the district court may

constituted an administrative disposition, because it had legal effects on the imports of specific goods. See also Supreme Court Judgment, 17 January 2002 (Min-Shu Vol. 56 No. 1, p. 1), in which the Supreme Court found that the notice by the Governor of Nara Prefecture designating all paths with certain width in the Prefecture as "street" under the Construction Standard Law had legal effects to restrict rights of landowners, and accordingly constituted an administrative disposition under Article 3.2 of the Act.

[17] Article 12 of the Act.

be appealed by the parties to the proceeding. Appeals must be filed with the High Court having jurisdiction over the district court. The judgment of the High Court may be appealed to the Supreme Court.

IV Standard of review

The court will review whether the disputed trade remedy measure violates the laws or regulations, whether the administrative agency abused its discretion, or whether it went beyond its authority under the laws and regulations.

In a judicial review proceeding, the complainant may also consider raising allegations of inconsistency of the measure with the WTO AD Agreement, SCM Agreement or Agreement on Safeguards. Most of the final determinations explicitly state that consistency with specific provisions of these agreements were considered. A complaint may argue that these administrative agencies admit that the WTO agreements apply to domestic trade remedy issues. Further, some lower courts admitted applicability of provisions of the GATT[18] and other international treaties[19] to administrative dispositions, taking into account Article 98.2 of Japan's Constitution.[20]

---

[18] *Nishijin Nekutai Jiken* (*Nishi-jin Necktie* case), Supreme Court Judgment, 9 June 1967 (Shomu-Geppo Vol. 13, p. 1131); Tokyo District Court Judgment, 11 June 1982 (Gyo-Shu Vol. 33 No. 6, p. 1283). In this case, the complaint alleged that a domestic price maintenance system for silk was equivalent to additional customs duty and thus inconsistent with Articles II:4 and XIIV of the GATT. The district court examined the provisions of the GATT, and stated that Article XIX allowed such emergency actions. However, the court also held that Article XIX did not require any remedial actions to domestic persons when its provisions were violated. The Supreme Court did not refer to this GATT issue. In *Kobe Houseki Jiken* (Kobe Jewellery case), Kobe District Court Judgment, 30 May 1961 (Kakyu Saibansho Keiji-Hanrei-Shu Vol. 3, pp. 524–5), the district court stated that Article 98.2 of Japan's Constitution recognized that the treaty superseded the domestic law. Upon reviewing Article VIII:3 of the GATT, however, the court found that the GATT provision did not apply to the particular facts of the case at hand.

[19] See Osaka High Court Judgment, 28 October 1994 (Hanji No. 1513, p. 86), in which Osaka High Court examined the International Covenant on Civil and Political Rights, and stated that ratified and promulgated treaties and international customs laws had effect as domestic law. See also *Kyoto Shimon Ohnatsu Kyohi Kokubo Soshou Kosohin Hanketu* (*High Court Judgment on Kyoto Finger-Printing Refusal National Government Compensation* case), in which Tokyo High Court explicitly stated that the provisions of the International Covenant on Civil and Political Rights superseded the domestic law to the extent that the domestic law conflicted with the Covenant.

[20] It provides that "the treaties concluded by Japan and established laws of nations shall be faithfully observed".

V   Remedies

The court will revoke an administrative disposition wholly or partly to the extent that the disposition violates the laws or regulations (or possibly WTO Agreements, as discussed above); or that the disposition was beyond the authority of the relevant agency under the laws and regulations; or that the agency exercised its discretion abusively.[21] The court's judgment is effective against parties to the judicial review proceeding, as well as third parties.[22] For example, if the court reached the judgment that an individual anti-dumping duty rate for imports from a specific exporting supplier was illegal and thus revoked the duty imposition, this revocation applies not only to imports by the complainant, but also to other imports by all non-participant importers from the same exporting supplier.

Once the judgment revoking the administrative disposition becomes final, the administrative disposition loses its effect as described in the judgment. For example, if the court finds that an individual anti-dumping duty imposition for a specific exporting supplier is unlawful, the duty imposition on imports from the supplier will be invalidated. Any duties previously collected from imports from the supplier will have to be returned to the importer with interest. Anti-dumping duties for imports from other suppliers, however, remain effective.

In addition to the final judgment, the court may also issue a declaration that the administrative disposition is illegal before it issues the final judgment.[23] This interim declaration gives an early warning to the relevant government agency and encourages it to take appropriate remedial steps for the complainant, and to settle the case.

VI   Concluding remarks

Judicial review can be an option for exporters and foreign producers whose products are subject to trade remedy measures in Japan. However, as discussed above, there are some unresolved procedural issues. At the same time, Japanese laws and the WTO agreements provide other alternatives to remedy any errors by the investigating authority in its determination, such as administrative interim reviews, refund proceedings, and WTO dispute settlement. These alternatives may provide a faster

---

[21] Article 30 of the Act.   [22] Article 32 of the Act.   [23] Article 31.2 of the Act.

solution. An aggrieved exporter and foreign producers should choose the best method for them from among those options.

MALAYSIA: STRICTLY OFF THE RECORD

EDMUND SIM

I Introduction

In Malaysia, the Countervailing and Anti-Dumping Act of 1993 and the Countervailing and Anti-Dumping Duties Regulations of 1994 govern anti-dumping and countervailing duty proceedings. Since 1995, Malaysia has initiated 10 anti-dumping cases against foreign exporters. Currently, anti-dumping measures remain on newsprint and polyethylene terephthalate. Malaysia has yet to initiate any countervailing duty investigations. Investigations are conducted by an Investigating Authority, with legal authority vested in the Minister of International Trade and Industry, supported by the Trade Practices Unit (hereinafter TPU) of the Ministry of International Trade and Industry (hereinafter MITI), and are staffed by officials from MITI, the Attorney General's Chambers and Customs. All decisions to initiate an investigation, impose provisional measures, accept or reject undertakings and to terminate an investigation are made by the MITI Minister, based upon the recommendation of the TPU.

The Safeguards Act of 2006 and the Safeguards Regulations of 2007 govern safeguard investigations. To date, Malaysia has initiated one safeguard investigation on hot-rolled carbon steel in coils, which is ongoing. Investigations are also conducted by the MITI and TPU. All decisions are made by the MITI Minister, based upon the recommendation of the TPU.

II Judicial review of trade remedy determinations in Malaysia

Section 34A of the Countervailing and Anti-Dumping Act provides that an interested party may appeal a final determination in an investigation or a review. The Act defines an interested party to include producers, exporters and importers and trade or business associations thereof, foreign governments, domestic producers and associations thereof, and other parties deemed appropriate by MITI. The determination must have been published in the *Government Gazette* before an appeal may be lodged with the High Court. Thus, a final determination would include a determination to impose definitive measures, or a determination to terminate a proceeding, but it would not include a decision to reject initiation of a proceeding (as that would not be published). Nor does a final determination include the initiation of an investigation or the imposition of provisional measures, as that is not "final". The decision to accept price undertakings would not be appealable unless the investigation were continued and resulted in a final determination that would be published. Final determinations in all types of reviews (interim, expiry or changed circumstances) can be appealed.

The appeal is to be lodged with the High Court of Malaysia, which has general jurisdiction on judicial challenges of Malaysian government actions. There are no stipulated differences between judicial review of trade remedy determinations and judicial review of governmental actions in terms of applicable law or court procedure. The court will review whether MITI's decision is illegal (unauthorized by law), unreasonable (arbitrary) or procedurally deficient. High Court decisions may be appealed to the Court of Appeal and then to the Federal Court, the highest court in Malaysia.

There have been two appeals of MITI determinations: (1) the 1999 anti-dumping determination on gypsum board from Thailand, in *Eng Hock Agency Sdn. Bhd. & Thai Gypsum Public Co. Ltd. v. MITI and Government of Malaysia* and (2) the 2001 anti-dumping determination on self-copy paper from Indonesia, in *PT Pabrik Kertas Tjiwi Kimia TBK v. Government of Malaysia*. Compared to other jurisdictions, Malaysia has not conducted many anti-dumping investigations. Accordingly, the potential number of judicial appeals has been limited.

The High Court elected in both cases not to publish its final findings. Malaysian courts can elect not to publish decisions when they are deemed to have insufficient importance. Hence, cases involving highly technical issues frequently are not reported, and this appears to be the case with regard to these cases involving anti-dumping. As such, these cases cannot be cited as legal precedent in Malaysian proceedings, nor do they provide guidance on how the Malaysian courts review decisions made by MITI.

The Safeguards Act of 2006 does not expressly provide for judicial review. The WTO Agreement on Safeguards does not require domestic judicial review.

The relatively undeveloped nature of judicial appeal of anti-dumping cases in Malaysia reflects the relatively infrequent use of anti-dumping and other trade remedies in Malaysia. Fewer anti-dumping investigations mean fewer judicial appeals of anti-dumping decisions. If and when Malaysia begins to become a more active user of trade remedies, there will be more judicial appeals of anti-dumping decisions, and perhaps these previous cases will be deemed to have sufficient value to be published. All of this will encourage greater transparency of the system.

NEW ZEALAND: MANAGING TO AVOID JUDICIAL REVIEW

HUGH McPHAIL

In New Zealand there is no separate review process dedicated to trade remedy actions, and the judicial review of decisions under trade remedies legislation is undertaken through the court system on the same basis as any judicial review of administrative decisions. An alternative approach to seeking review of administrative acts and decisions is available through the Office of the Ombudsman.[24]

I Introduction

1 Trade remedies in New Zealand

1.1 History[25]

Trade remedy legislation has a long history in New Zealand, the earliest anti-dumping legislation being passed in 1905 specifically to protect

---

[24] Under the Ombudsmen Act 1975, an Ombudsman is able to investigate complaints about the administrative acts, decisions, recommendations and omissions of central and local government agencies. Although an Ombudsman cannot investigate complaints against ministers, advice provided to government ministers by government agencies can be investigated. In an investigation, which is at no cost to the complainant, an Ombudsman will seek information from the agency concerned about the subject matter of the complaint and reach a view on whether the agency acted unreasonably or unfairly. Where a complaint is found to be justified, an Ombudsman may recommend that the agency take action to remedy the complaint. Although an Ombudsman has no power to compel an agency to accept a recommendation, most recommendations are accepted.

[25] For a detailed review and discussion of the history of anti-dumping in New Zealand, see Garcia and Baker, *Anti-dumping in New Zealand: A Century of Protection from "Unfair" Trade*, NZ Trade Consortium working paper No. 39, December 2005, available at

domestic and British manufacturers of agricultural implements from American producers. More general legislation providing for duties on dumped or subsidized goods was enacted in 1921, but operated in a climate of protection through high tariffs and quantitative import licensing until the mid-1980s. At that time, economic reforms saw the progressive removal of import licensing and the phased reduction in tariffs. In 1986, New Zealand made the decision to join the GATT Anti-Dumping Code, having joined the GATT Subsidies Code in 1981, and legislation was passed which was designed to conform to the Codes. This was originally Part VA of the Customs Act 1966, but became the Dumping and Countervailing Duties Act 1988 (hereinafter the Act), when responsibility for the administration of anti-dumping was moved from the Customs Service to the newly established Ministry of Commerce (now the Ministry of Economic Development), where it has remained ever since.

In New Zealand, safeguard action is currently subject to the Temporary Safeguard Authorities Act 1987, which provides for a Temporary Safeguard Authority to carry out inquiries into requests for safeguard action. Amendments[26] to this legislation, which is also administered by the Ministry of Economic Development, are currently awaiting a second reading in Parliament. The Bill proposes to remove the role of the Temporary Safeguard Authority and to require investigations to be undertaken on the basis of rules and procedures that closely follow the WTO Safeguards Agreement, and largely parallel the procedures and requirements for anti-dumping and countervailing duty investigations.

1.2   Implementation

In 1994, the Act was amended to take account of the WTO Anti-Dumping and Subsidies and Countervailing Measures Agreements, while the Temporary Safeguard Authorities Act was amended to reflect the WTO Safeguards Agreement. Subsequent amendments have been made to reflect changes arising from bilateral or regional free trade agreements and for other administrative purposes.

1.3   Procedures

Under the Act, the Minister of Commerce makes decisions regarding the termination of investigations, directions relating to provisional

http://nzier.org.nz/publications/anti-dumping-in-new-zealand-a-century-of-protection-from-unfair-trade (last visited 6.12.2011).
[26] Introduced as the Trade (Safeguards) Bill 2008.

measures, the final determination, the acceptance of undertakings and the determination of the rate or amount of duty to be paid. Other decisions, including those on initiation, the establishment of dumping margins, the existence and amount of a subsidy, the examination of material injury, and the management of information and notices, are the responsibility of the Chief Executive of the Ministry of Economic Development and are normally delegated to the official managing the ministry's group charged with administering the Act.

For safeguards, the minister may refer a matter to a Temporary Safeguard Authority, and also make decisions on any recommendations made by an Authority. There have been no safeguard actions taken since 1995.

II   Judicial review

The Act does not include any provisions relating to judicial review. It was considered that existing processes for the review of administrative decisions through the High Court were sufficient to meet the requirements of Article 13 of the WTO Anti-Dumping Agreement and Article 23 of the WTO Subsidies and Countervailing Measures Agreement, and that an additional appeal mechanism specifically involving the review of trade remedy determinations was unnecessary. The Temporary Safeguard Authorities Act 1987 also has no provisions relating to judicial review.

The High Court provides a judicial tribunal for the review of administrative actions, while the Office of the Ombudsmen provides an arbitral or administrative procedure for such review. The High Court is independent of the Chief Executive of the Ministry of Economic Development and of the Minister of Commerce, as is the Office of the Ombudsmen.

1   Legal framework

In New Zealand, judicial review is the review by a judge of the High Court of any exercise of, or any refusal to exercise, public decision-making powers, in order to determine whether that decision or action is unauthorized or invalid. In most cases the decision-making powers derive from statute, but judicial review may also cover public powers that do not have a statutory basis, including decisions under the Crown prerogative.

The courts cannot overrule the statute under which a decision is properly made, since, in New Zealand, Parliament is the supreme law-making body. Rather, in undertaking a judicial review, the High Court will look at the actions of the decision-making body. The judiciary's role in judicial review is to interpret legislation and ensure it is correctly applied.

2   Court structure

The High Court has general jurisdiction and responsibility, under the Judicature Act 1908, for the administration of justice throughout New Zealand. This includes maintaining the consistent application of the rule of law, supervision of other courts and tribunals and the judicial review of administrative power. It has jurisdiction over both criminal and civil matters and deals with cases at first instance or on appeal from the District and other courts and certain tribunals. District Courts deal with minor criminal offences and civil claims.

The High Court comprises the head of the New Zealand judiciary, the Chief Justice, and up to 55 other judges (which includes the judges of the Supreme Court and Court of Appeal). The Court of Appeal is New Zealand's intermediate appellate court with specifically appointed judges, while the Supreme Court is New Zealand's final court of appeal, with the role of maintaining overall coherence in the legal system.

3   Applicable law

The procedures for the judicial review of the exercise or failure to exercise a statutory power are contained in the Judicature Amendment Act 1972. This Act does not attempt to set out the grounds of review. Rather, it merely states that, on application for review, the High Court may grant relief in relation to the exercise, refusal to exercise, or proposed or purported exercise by any person of a statutory power.

4   Legal significance of international obligations

International obligations may be implied as mandatory relevant considerations that the decision-maker should take into account or give rise to a presumption that, where possible, legislation will be interpreted consistently with relevant international obligations. The rulings of various international tribunals, such as the United Nations Human Rights Committee, may also be a relevant consideration for New Zealand courts, but they are not binding.

One of the purposes of the Act is to give effect to New Zealand's international obligations in relation to the WTO and to bilateral agreements. Therefore, these obligations are relevant to the exercise of decision-making under the Act unless a contrary intention appears in the Act. The Act also uses much of the language of the Anti-Dumping and Subsidies and Countervailing Measures Agreements and refers specifically to New Zealand's obligations as a party to the WTO Agreement in relation to negligible import volumes and to the imposition of countervailing duties. It is likely, therefore, that an interested party could seek to invoke the WTO Agreement, but while the courts will give weight to the international obligations, they are not necessarily the paramount consideration in making the decision, and other domestic considerations may also be taken into account. In a recent address, the Chief Justice noted that: "[u]nder domestic law, statute prevails over treaty where there is any inconsistency between the two", and "[a]lthough it has been said that the line between domestic and international law is becoming blurred in New Zealand, it cannot be yet maintained that international law is 'self-executing': founding a direct cause of action in the courts."[27]

5   Procedure

Judicial review is not concerned with the merits of a decision, but with the process by which the decision is made. So long as the processes followed are proper, and unless it is clearly unreasonable, a court will not interfere with the decision. Sometimes it can be difficult to sever completely the decision-making process from the merits of the decision, but it is likely that where there is a degree of complexity and expertise involved, then the factual basis for a decision will not be reviewed.

To establish whether the decision-maker has acted properly and fairly, the courts will look closely at the decision-making process. This overriding concept of fairness to all affected parties is critical. Judicial review is a discretionary remedy, and even where the grounds of review are established and a decision is found to be invalid, the remedy given, or whether any remedy at all is given, may ultimately depend upon the court's view of what is "fair" and "reasonable".

---

[27] Rt Hon. Dame Sian Elias CJ, *The Impact of International Conventions on Domestic Law*, Address to the International Association of Refugee Law Judges, March 2000, paragraphs 10–11 (www.refugee.org.nz/IARLJ3-00Elias.html).

Judges have the power to call a conference of the parties or to give direction to ensure that any application for review can be determined in a convenient and expeditious manner. The grounds of challenge can broadly be divided into three areas:

(a) *Illegality*: The contested decision will be illegal if the authorities making the decision acted outside the scope of their power or based the decision on a wrong interpretation of the law. For example, a decision that is influenced by a legal or factual error or contravenes the legislation will be illegal. Illegality can also arise when the decision-maker failed to take account of relevant matters or took account of irrelevant matters, and also if there was a rigid application of a predetermined policy or the decision-maker was acting under dictation from someone else.

(b) *Unfairness*: Unfairness refers to procedural impropriety. The grounds of review can include breach of natural justice, in that parties were not given a fair opportunity to be heard or have their views adequately considered; bias, where the impartiality of the decision-maker may have been affected, including conflicts of interest; legitimate expectation, where there is a duty to act consistently with the way in which other similar cases have been treated; and substantive unfairness.

(c) *Unreasonableness*: A decision-maker must act in a reasonable fashion and the decision must rely on some reasonable basis.

These grounds often overlap, and decisions are often challenged on a number of grounds. For example, a decision that is illegal may also be unfair and/or unreasonable. An unreasonable decision is almost always either illegal or unfair.

The court will ascertain whether or not the decision has been made lawfully by examining the documents and evidence of relevant decision-makers, as well as interpreting the relevant statutes and case law. Evidence is generally given by affidavit in judicial review proceedings. Typically, the affidavit(s) for the Crown will outline the steps taken and reasons for a decision and will usually include an affidavit from the actual decision-maker. Cross-examination is not permitted as of right in judicial review proceedings. Occasionally the judge may give leave to hear oral evidence where there is a material conflict of evidence and cross-examination is necessary to resolve the issues, but there is a convention that courts will not order ministers or judicial officers to give evidence arising from their roles as decision-makers.

6   Remedies

Judicial review is a discretionary remedy, which means that even if a plaintiff establishes that there has been a breach of an administrative law right, the court can decline relief if it decides it is in the overall public interest to do so. If the court finds there has been a breach of an administrative law duty and exercises its discretion to grant relief, it may:

- make declarations about the way a decision was made or action was taken (e.g. declare that certain things that ought to have been done were not done, or that some matter taken into account by the decision-maker was not relevant);
- set aside the decision as unlawful;
- direct the person who made the decision or took the action to reconsider the matter, and may give directions on how this should be done;
- whether or not relief is granted, also make an order for costs in favour of the successful party.

Decisions of the High Court may be appealed to the Court of Appeal and ultimately to the Supreme Court of New Zealand.

III   Comments and conclusions

Since the entry into force of the WTO Agreement in 1995, there have been no successful court challenges of decisions relating to trade remedies in New Zealand. In one case, an application was lodged with the court, but the matter was resolved between the parties and, in a second case, the application was withdrawn. Prior to 1995, there were four occasions when an application for judicial review went through the High Court process. There has been at least one investigation carried out by an Ombudsman into decisions in an anti-dumping investigation.[28]

---

[28]   Case Notes [W41825], Office of the Ombudsmen (2000). The investigation related to the ministry's interpretation of Article 5.5 of the Anti-Dumping Agreement and its refusal to release details of an application before an investigation was initiated. After assessing the respective merits of the argument advanced by the requesters and the ministry, the Office of the Ombudsmen accepted that the disclosure of the information would be likely to prejudice the international relations of the government of New Zealand, which provided good reasons under the Official Information Act 1982 to withhold information.

The current performance measures which the government expects to be met by the Ministry of Economic Development in regard to the administration of trade remedies, are that the quality of investigations undertaken will be indicated by them being recognized by the parties involved as consistent with the requirements of the legislation, and by the lack of grounds for successful court challenges or successful WTO dispute settlement actions. The ministry has been successful in meeting these measures.

The original grounds for not establishing a separate review process included the relatively limited number of trade remedy investigations initiated in New Zealand and the availability of effective judicial review processes through the High Court. Officials also opposed a separate appeal process on the basis that it could lead to uncertainty and to prolongation of disputes.

The lack of use of judicial review in New Zealand can be seen in two ways: first, the approach taken by the investigating authority has left few grounds for appeal, or second, potential appellants have found the time and costs involved to be too great relative to the benefits they might gain.

The Ministry of Economic Development has designed and implemented its procedures very carefully to ensure that it meets all of the requirements of the law, is fair and reasonable in the way it treats parties to investigations and meets transparency requirements through reports and notices. Under this managed approach, the likelihood of action being taken on grounds of illegality, unreasonableness or unfairness are minimized, and instances of judicial review are avoided.

The cost of challenging a decision will depend on the level of effort the applicant is prepared to put into it, and it is weighed against the benefit to be gained, including the length of time taken. Judges will seek to expedite matters, while an Ombudsman investigation can be undertaken relatively quickly and at no cost to the applicant.

It seems reasonable to conclude that the lack of judicial review action in New Zealand reflects the view of potential applicants that they may not have sufficient grounds, or that, on balance, are unlikely to achieve a level of success that would justify the effort.

The overall conclusion is that, in using existing processes of judicial and administrative review, New Zealand is able to meet the needs of a modest user of anti-dumping and the requirements of Article 13 of the Anti-Dumping Agreement.

THAILAND: A LONG ROAD AHEAD

APISITH JOHN SUTHAM, PATTANAN KALAWANTAVANICH
AND SAKKAPOL VACHATIMANONT

I Introduction

Since the Thai Anti-Dumping and Countervailing Act 1999 (hereinafter AD/CVD Act) came into force, 18 anti-dumping cases have been initiated in Thailand and 13 anti-dumping measures have been imposed. Nevertheless, no countervailing duty investigation has been initiated thus far. As the Thai Safeguard Act (hereinafter SG Act) was only passed in 2008, it is not surprising that Thailand has only initiated one safeguard investigation to date.[29] Furthermore, only two judicial review proceedings have been initiated thus far with respect to the Thai investigating authority's determinations.[30]

The Dumping and Subsidy Committee (hereinafter AD/CVD Committee) is in charge of conducting anti-dumping and countervailing duty investigations, whereas the Safeguard Committee (hereinafter SG Committee) is responsible for the conduct of safeguard investigations. Even though the AD/CVD Committee and the SG Committee are separate agencies, the Minister of Commerce is the chair of both of them.[31] In this chapter, the AD/CVD Committee and the SG Committee are referred to together as Thailand's investigating authority (hereinafter"IA") for trade remedy investigations.

In the Thai system, the actual investigations are conducted by the Department of Foreign Trade (hereinafter DFT).[32] Determinations of dumping, subsidy, injury, or serious injury in the case of a safeguard investigation are made by the DFT. After these determinations are made, the decisions on the imposition of provisional or definitive measures and the acceptance of undertakings are made by the AD/CVD or the SG Committees.

---

[29] *Thai Gazette* website: www.ratchakitcha.soc.go.th/RKJ/announce/newrkj.jsp (last visited 14 June 2011).

[30] These two cases are *Glass Blocks from Indonesia* and *Woven Fabric from China*.

[31] See section 72 of the AD/CVD Act and section 5 of the SG Act.

[32] A governmental agency in charge of conducting trade remedy investigations and acting as secretary to the Dumping and Subsidy Committee.

II Judicial review of trade remedy determinations in Thailand

1 Legal framework

As a general rule in Thailand, governmental actions are subject to judicial review by the Administrative Court, unless provided otherwise in the Law.[33] Exceptionally, the IA's determinations in AD/CVD investigations are reviewed by the Central Intellectual Property and International Trade Court (hereinafter Tribunal).[34] However, this exception does not apply to safeguard investigations. The IA's determinations in such investigations are reviewed by the Administrative Court.

There are differences between judicial review by the Administrative Court and judicial review by the Tribunal.[35] First, the judges in the Administrative Court are generally obliged to follow the procedures stipulated in the Thai Administrative Act. They rarely adopt regulations from other jurisdictions.[36] This is because the Thai Administrative Act already provides procedures[37] on how to carry out the proceedings. On the contrary, the Act for the Establishment of and Procedure for Intellectual Property and International Trade Court, BE[38] 2539 (hereinafter ITIP Act) allows the judges of the Tribunal to take into consideration the provisions of other laws that are relevant to the resolution of a given dispute. Thus, for instance, in a judicial review proceeding pertaining to an anti-dumping or countervailing duty investigation, the judges of the Tribunal may take into consideration the relevant provisions of the WTO Anti-Dumping Agreement (hereinafter AD Agreement) or the Agreement on Subsidies and Countervailing Measures (hereinafter SCM Agreement), respectively, or even the Dispute Settlement Understanding (hereinafter DSU).

---

[33] See section 9 of the Thai Administrative Act and the Administrative Court's jurisprudence.

[34] Ibid., and see also section 7(8) of the ITIP Act. See also Article 61 of the AD/CVD Act, which contains the same language as section 7(8) of the ITIP Act. Apart from AD and CVD matters, the Tribunal is responsible for several other dispute matters. For instance, it has authority to adjudicate various criminal and civil cases in respect of patent, intellectual property and copyright issues. See section 7 of the ITIP Act.

[35] The Administrative Court's authority is regulated by the Act on Establishment of Administrative Courts and Administrative Court Procedure 2542. The Tribunal's jurisdiction, on the other hand, is subject to the ITIP Act.

[36] See section 55 of the Thai Administrative Act. However, where relevant and necessary, they are allowed to do so.

[37] See sections 54–75 of the Thai Administrative Act.

[38] For the legal calendar in Thailand, years are counted in terms of the Buddhist Era (BE), which is 543 years ahead of the Christian calendar.

There have been cases where the Tribunal relied on the provisions of the AD Agreement. In the judicial review proceeding with respect to the anti-dumping investigation on *Glass Blocks from Indonesia*, the Tribunal cited relevant WTO rules as authority. The Tribunal took into account the phrase "upon good cause shown" in Article 6.5[39] of the AD Agreement, even though this phrase did not appear in the AD/CVD Act.[40] In this case, the Tribunal reasoned that Article 6 of the AD Agreement, the AD/CVD Act and the DSU had to be interpreted together in judicial review proceedings conducted by it.

However, the same does not hold true with respect to the WTO jurisprudence. Since Thailand is a civil law jurisdiction, in theory the WTO jurisprudence has no binding status. Consequently, the Tribunal has never relied on such jurisprudence. That said, it should be noted that the Tribunal has occasionally referred to the WTO jurisprudence in an effort to show that its rulings did not contradict such jurisprudence.[41]

Another difference between judicial review by the Administrative Court and the Tribunal pertains to appeal. Interested parties may appeal to the Supreme Court of Thailand from a decision made by the Tribunal.[42] However, appeals from the decisions of the Administrative Court are heard by the Supreme Administrative Court of Thailand.[43]

2 Procedure

Under Thai law, the IA's determinations on the initiation of an investigation, imposition of provisional or final measures, acceptance or rejection of an undertaking and termination of an investigation without measures are all reviewable. Further, determinations made in different types of reviews, such as sunset reviews, changed circumstances reviews and new shipper reviews are also reviewable.[44]

---

[39] Article 6.5 of the AD Agreement reads: "Any information which is by nature confidential ... shall, *upon good cause shown*, be treated as such by the authorities. Such information shall not be disclosed without specific permission of the party submitting it" (emphasis added).

[40] The Tribunal's determination regarding the withdrawal of the AD/CVD Commission's AD determination concerning *Imported Glass Blocks from Indonesia*, 20 April 2009 (BE 2552).

[41] Ibid., note 14.

[42] See section 38 of the ITIP Act. An interested party may notify the Tribunal of its intention to appeal a finding of the Tribunal to the Supreme Court of Thailand.

[43] See section 73 of the Administrative Act.

[44] See sections 56, 57 and 58 of the AD/CVD Act.

It is important to note that the Tribunal has discretion to review AD/CVD issues other than those raised by a complainant in a judicial review proceeding if it considers this necessary on the grounds of public interest, public order or morals. This happened in the case concerning *Glass Blocks from Indonesia.* In this case, the Tribunal reviewed the legality of the calculation of dumping margins, although the complainant had not raised a claim in this regard. Taking into consideration the incorrect definition of the product under consideration made by the IA, the Tribunal found that dumping margins that constituted the basis for the duties imposed were also illegal. The Tribunal then instructed the IA to re-calculate the dumping margins.[45]

Unlike AD/CVD investigations, there is no legal provision that identifies the types of determinations made in a safeguard investigation which are reviewable by the Administrative Court. However, should the case arise, it is likely that the same determinations reviewable in the context of AD/CVD investigations will also be considered by the Administrative Court as being reviewable in the context of a safeguard investigation, to the extent that they are viewed as inconsistent with the SG Act by the Court.[46]

In connection with AD/CVD investigations, any interested party, or any other person affected by the IA's determinations, may initiate a judicial review proceeding. Pursuant to section 4 of the AD/CVD Act, foreign producers and exporters, importers of the subject product, governments of the exporting countries and domestic producers of the subject product are interested parties entitled to file a case with the Tribunal.[47] Under the Thai SG Act, the same parties are considered as interested parties in the context of safeguards investigations.[48] Thus, it

---

[45] *Imported Glass Blocks from Indonesia*, note 14.

[46] Pursuant to section 9 of the Thai Administrative Act, the judges are authorized to review any illegal actions undertaken by governmental agencies. However, according to the Administrative Court's practice and the Thai Administrative Act, the Court will not investigate all concerned issues. The Court tends to focus on the issues raised by interested parties and whether the governmental authorities used their powers appropriately or not, whereas the Tribunal seems to go into more depth.

[47] See section 4 of the AD/CVD Act: a trade association with the majority of its members being producers or importers of the product under consideration, trade associations with the majority of its members being producers of such product or other persons as prescribed and announced by the Minister of Commerce are also nominated as interested parties in this respect.

[48] See section 3 of the Thai SG Act and section 42 of the Thai Administrative Act.

can be seen that the regulations of the aforesaid Thai acts are similar to relevant WTO provisions, i.e. Article 6 of the ADA, Article 12 of the SCM Agreement and Article 3 the SG Agreement.

The time limit to bring a judicial review proceeding before the Tribunal is 30 days from the date of publication of the disputed determination.[49] Judicial review proceedings handled by the Administrative Court with respect to determinations made in safeguard investigations must be initiated within 90 days from the date at which the complainant came to know or should have known about the alleged illegality in the disputed determination, unless otherwise specified in other laws.[50]

There is no legal provision prescribing the time limit within which the Tribunal or the Administrative Court must make their decisions. As a practical matter, the two cases involving judicial review proceedings have taken less than one year each.

3 Remedies

Pursuant to the ITIP Act, the Tribunal may uphold, amend or reverse its determination subject to a judicial review proceeding. Further, the Tribunal has the power to remand. This power was used in the judicial review proceeding concerning *Glass Blocks from Indonesia*.[51] In that proceeding, the Tribunal ordered the IA to recommence the anti-dumping investigation in accordance with its findings. As for the judicial review of safeguard determinations, it should be noted that the Administrative Court, as stipulated in section 72 of the Administrative Act, has powers similar to those of the Tribunal.

Concerning other remedies, anti-dumping or countervailing duties paid and/or a security given by interested parties are refundable. In the judicial review proceedings concerning *Glass Blocks from Indonesia*, the Tribunal ordered the IA to return the anti-dumping duties and securities, in whole or in part as appropriate, to the complainant. Should the case arise, the same instruction may be issued by the Administrative Court in a judicial review proceeding concerning a safeguard determination.

---

[49] See section 61 of the AD/CVD Act.
[50] See section 49 of the Thai Administrative Act.
[51] *Imported Glass Blocks from Indonesia*, note 14.

III   Remarks and suggestions for improving the judicial review system in Thailand

Although Thailand does not have much experience in the judicial review of its IA's determinations, the two judicial review proceedings conducted so far have shown that the review conducted by the Tribunal is an effective one. For example, in the review pertaining to the anti-dumping duty on *Glass Blocks from Indonesia*, the Tribunal looked into the issues of public interest and took into consideration the relevant WTO rules and trade policy implications of the measure under review. In its review, the Tribunal looked at the issues of facts and law discussed in the IA's final disclosures and determinations. The Tribunal drew attention to the importance of transparency in trade remedy investigations and stated that all pertinent issues such as confidentiality, determinations of dumping, injury and causality must be analysed and explained in the IA's final determination. This is encouraging, as it shows that the Tribunal in future judicial review proceedings will pay particular attention to the transparency aspects of trade remedy investigations. This is reinforced by the fact that Thai law allows the Tribunal to review issues that are not raised by the complainant in a judicial review proceeding.

That said, depending on how it is used, the breadth of this discretionary power might also lead the Tribunal to overreach in conducting judicial review. We think this should be avoided and that this power should only be used for the furtherance of the transparency of trade remedy investigations. Anything beyond this could lead to a situation where it is the Tribunal, not the investigating authority, that makes the determinations in investigations. Such an approach might backfire, as it could make it difficult to predict the procedures, proceedings and rulings of the Tribunal.

We consider that the judicial review of trade remedy determinations in Thailand could benefit from two improvements. First, legislation should be introduced to broaden the scope of judicial review by the Tribunal also to cover determinations made in the context of safeguard investigations. This would not only eliminate the ambiguity as to the process with respect to the judicial review of safeguard determinations, but would also contribute to the internal consistency of judicial review, since all trade remedy determinations would be reviewed through the same procedure.

Second, providing the judges who handle the judicial review of trade remedy determinations with adequate training on WTO law in general and trade remedies law in particular would significantly enhance the effectiveness of judicial review at national level. An effective judicial review at national level would, in turn, also lessen the burden on the WTO's dispute settlement mechanism, as foreign producers who complain about the determinations of the Thai IA would have their voice heard by Thai courts, rather than trying to convince their government to bring a case against the government of Thailand in the WTO.

Based on the foregoing, Thailand's judicial review system appears to support the application of the country's trade remedies and to be in compliance with international trade remedy practices. As can be seen from the aforementioned rulings, the Tribunal endeavoured to keep the IA's practice in line with the relevant WTO provisions. Furthermore, the Tribunal attempted to apply the laws in a manner that would enhance international trade liberalization. Such an approach is likely to reduce the number of trade remedies-related disputes filed in the WTO.

IV Conclusion

In Thailand, judicial review of trade remedy determinations by the Thai IA has been used very rarely. Of the 22 anti-dumping investigations and one safeguard investigation completed so far, only two anti-dumping investigations came under review by the Tribunal. Thus, sufficient precedents from court decisions that could shed light on future trade remedies practices in the country have not yet emerged. It should be noted, however, that the two cases handled thus far were useful in terms of paving the way for further future capacity building in this regard. The practical training that may be provided to the judges handling these cases will complement such capacity building.

20

Conclusions

MÜSLÜM YILMAZ*

The previous chapters covered country-specific analyses of domestic judicial review of trade remedy determinations in 21 WTO members that are active users of these measures. This has accomplished the objective of providing the reader with an in-depth description of each of these judicial review systems. As mentioned in the Introduction, each chapter in the book covers information on more or less the same aspects of the judicial review of trade remedy determinations in the relevant country. In this concluding chapter, we will provide a horizontal assessment of the domestic judicial review of trade remedy determinations in respect of each element addressed in the individual chapters of the book. We will then identify the lessons drawn from this study in terms of steps that may be taken in the future in order to improve the effectiveness of domestic judicial review of trade remedy determinations.

I Tribunals

Article 13 of the AD Agreement and Article 23 of the SCM Agreement provide that judicial review may be conducted by "judicial, arbitral or administrative tribunals or procedures". With regard to the tribunals that conduct judicial review, our research has shown that in almost all of the countries analysed, judicial review of trade remedy determinations is conducted by the courts, in other words by "judicial tribunals". Typically, these are the same courts that review other administrative actions of the government. There are exceptions, however. A few countries have special courts for this type of judicial review, whereas others, in

* The author thanks Mark Koulen, Graham Cook and authors of country chapters in this book for their valuable comments on earlier drafts.

addition to ordinary courts, have a special tribunal handling these cases. Further, some countries also have judicial review systems under regional trade agreements which are actively used.

In the United States, there is the US Court of International Trade, a special court dealing with the judicial review of trade remedy determinations, among other things. In Thailand, anti-dumping and countervailing duty determinations are reviewed by a special court, whereas safeguard determinations are reviewed by general courts. Pakistan and India are unique in the sense that they both have dual domestic judicial review systems. In both countries there is a special tribunal in charge of reviewing final anti-dumping and countervailing duty determinations, as well as general courts that have power to review all determinations made in all three trade remedy proceedings. Similarly, in Indonesia, depending on the case's grounds, there are two types of tribunals that conduct the judicial review of trade remedy determinations: the State Administrative Court and the Supreme Court. In the United States, Canada and Mexico, additional judicial reviews are conducted by NAFTA panels, an approach which is very actively used. Finally, the situation in New Zealand is unique in the sense that, in addition to review by the courts, there is also a possibility of review by an ombudsman, which constitutes an arbitral or administrative procedure.

Our research has also shown that the judicial review of trade remedy determinations generally is conducted through the same procedure (such as deadlines for the submission of petitions, standing, powers of the tribunals, the appeal process etc.) that governs the judicial review of other administrative actions.

II Standing

As explained in the Introduction, Article 13 of the AD Agreement does not mention the issue of standing, whereas Article 23 of the SCM Agreement seems to limit members' obligation in this regard. We note that with respect to standing, the vast majority of countries we have analysed take a liberal approach; in principle, all interested parties in a given trade remedy proceeding, including foreign producers or exporters, importers and domestic producers, are entitled to initiate a judicial review proceeding against trade remedy determinations. There is no exclusion for certain categories of interested parties. However, domestic laws do have their own requirements for standing.[1] In a number of countries, the complainant in a judicial review proceeding has to demonstrate, on the basis of the relevant legal requirements, a certain relationship with the challenged measure. For instance, in Turkey, a demonstration of the violation of an interest is required. In Canada, South Africa and Australia, only persons whose legal rights are directly affected by the challenged determination have standing. In the European Union, the complainant has to show that the challenged determination is of "direct and individual concern".

Here, too, there are exceptions. For instance, in Pakistan, as far as judicial review by the special tribunal is concerned, only parties who registered as interested parties in the challenged proceeding have standing to initiate a judicial review case. In the United States, only interested parties that actively participate through written submission of factual information or argument in a segment of the challenged proceeding have standing to initiate a judicial review case.

III Scope of judicial review

With respect to the scope of judicial review, each chapter explains whether the determinations pertaining to all three trade remedy proceedings are subject to judicial review in the relevant country. The chapters then explain the range of determinations that are reviewable in connection with each of the three trade remedy proceedings. In this context, the chapters explain, among other things, whether provisional measures, decisions to initiate an investigation and decisions not to initiate an investigation are reviewable in the relevant country.

In most of the countries analysed, determinations pertaining to all three trade remedy proceedings are subject to judicial review. Typically the review of all three is conducted by the same courts and through the same procedure. Again, however, there are exceptions. In India and Pakistan, the jurisdiction of the special tribunal is limited to the determinations made in anti-dumping and countervailing duty investigations, and does not cover safeguards. Yet the ordinary courts can review the determinations made in all trade remedy proceedings, including safeguards. In Malaysia, safeguard determinations are not subject to

---

[1] Except that in Colombia it seems to be an unlimited right with respect to actions for annulment, which literally may be initiated by anyone. There is no need even to be an interested party in the underlying proceeding.

judicial review. In the United States, anti-dumping and countervailing duty determinations are reviewable on both substance and procedure, whereas the judicial review of safeguard determinations has been limited to procedural issues.

With respect to the reviewability of provisional measures, countries fall equally roughly into two categories: in nine of the 21 countries studied, the investigating authorities' determinations regarding the imposition of provisional measures fall outside the scope of judicial review. These are China, the European Union, Indonesia, Korea, Malaysia, Mexico, Peru, Thailand and the United States. It should be noted that in the United States and Mexico a preliminary determination may be challenged before the courts if it brings the relevant trade remedy proceeding to an end. In Pakistan and India, provisional measures may only be reviewed by ordinary courts, not by the special tribunal.

In the majority of countries analysed, a decision to initiate an investigation is not subject to immediate judicial review before the completion of the investigation. The opposite is the case with respect to decisions not to initiate an investigation. This demonstrates that the situation with regard to the scope of judicial review goes well beyond what is required by the relevant WTO agreement. First, in almost all the countries examined, safeguard determinations are judicially reviewable even though the SG Agreement does not contain such an obligation. Second, with respect to the types of determinations subject to judicial review, in slightly more than half of the countries analysed, determinations pertaining to provisional measures are reviewable although this is not required under the AD and SCM Agreements. Further, other types of determinations, such as decisions to initiate or not to initiate an investigation and decisions to accept or reject a price undertaking, are reviewable in certain countries.

IV   Applicable law

As far as the applicable law in judicial review proceedings is concerned, the first major conclusion arising from the individual chapters is that the WTO Agreement is not directly applicable in half of the countries analysed. In some countries there have been a few judicial review cases where the tribunals cited the relevant WTO agreement on trade remedies, but without giving it decisive weight. Thus, judicial decisions are almost always based on national trade remedies legislation. There is even less evidence of references to WTO jurisprudence. Tribunals in only a handful of countries cited WTO jurisprudence in their decisions, again without attaching any decisive weight to it. One interesting example in this regard is Colombia, where the Anti-Dumping Decree refers to WTO jurisprudence as a potential source for legal guidance in conducting investigations.[2]

V Powers of tribunals

Domestic tribunals have considerable powers which, if used effectively, may well have a significant impact on the investigating authorities' practices. The most common power that the tribunals have is annulment of the challenged determination. In a few countries such as Argentina, Colombia, Indonesia, Korea and Turkey, the tribunals can also order the compensation of damages caused by the unlawful determinations made by investigating authorities. In almost every country analysed, the tribunals have the power to remand. Thus, following a decision setting aside the challenged determination, they can send the matter back to the investigating authorities for reconsideration in light of the judicial decision. Similarly, in almost all the countries studied, the tribunals have the power to stay the execution of the challenged determination pending the judicial review proceedings.

VI Intensity of judicial review activity

With regard to the intensity of judicial review activity, the situation varies significantly among the countries analysed. Some countries have a very frequently used judicial review system while others have very few cases, or no cases at all. What is interesting is that the level of judicial review activity does not necessarily correspond to whether the country at issue is a traditional or relatively new user of trade remedies. Both the group of active users of judicial review and infrequent users of it are mixed in terms of both the number of trade remedy investigations conducted and their level of development.

Countries that have a very frequently used judicial review system are the United States, Canada, Mexico, Brazil, India, Pakistan, Turkey and

---

[2] Article 2 of the Colombian Decree reads: "the case law of the WTO Dispute Settlement Body in respect of the rules in the WTO Agreement on Implementation of Article VI of the General Agreement on Tariffs and Trade 1994 may be considered when conducting investigations". See WTO document G/ADP/N/1/COL/3, p. 3.

Australia. In Argentina, Peru, Colombia, South Africa, Israel, Korea, Indonesia, Malaysia and Thailand, there has been less use of judicial review thus far. China, Japan and New Zealand[3] have had no judicial review proceedings initiated so far. Regarding the distribution of cases among the three trade remedies, in most countries anti-dumping is by far the most frequent measure, followed by safeguards and counter-vailing measures. But there are exceptions to this, such as the United States, where countervail ranks second and safeguards third.

VII   Procedure

In terms of the procedure under which domestic judicial review is conducted, authors addressed three specific issues: whether there is any requirement to go through an administrative review before resorting to judicial review, whether there is an appeal mechanism for the decisions of the tribunals of first instance, and the amount of time required for judicial review. In general, there does not appear to be a prerequisite to go through an administrative review process before initiating a judicial review proceeding. The few exceptions to this include Argentina, Australia, Israel, Mexico, Peru and the United States. All countries examined have at least one court of appeals where the decisions made by the tribunals of first instance may be appealed. Close to half of the countries have two layers of appellate review. The duration of judicial review proceedings looks to be a common and serious problem. In almost all of the countries analysed, the whole process, including remands and appeals, takes several years. In some countries, such as Argentina, Brazil, Colombia, the European Union, India, South Africa, Thailand and Turkey, this can continue as long as four to seven years.

VIII   Patterns in judicial decisions

Finally, the authors were asked to explain whether in their respective systems judicial decisions followed a certain pattern in terms of defer-ence accorded to the investigating authorities' decisions. Half of the authors reported that their tribunals tend to approve the investigating authorities' decisions. They also identified the reasons for this, which we discuss below.

---

[3] In the case of New Zealand, this applies to the period since 1995. Four judicial review proceedings were launched in New Zealand prior to that date.

1   The way forward

The authors of country chapters, after describing their countries' judicial review systems, also identified the problems experienced in their systems and proposed ways to address those problems. In this regard, there appear to be differences between traditional users of trade remedies and the developing countries which have started using these remedies only more recently.

As far as the developed countries are concerned, the authors of the chapters on the United States, Australia and New Zealand do not identify any particular problems with respect to their judicial review systems. However, the authors of the chapters on Canada and the European Union refer to the high level of deference accorded by the tribunals to their investigating authorities. The chapter on the European Union also cites the length of judicial review proceedings as a problem. The authors of both chapters argue that the level of deference should be reduced. The authors of the EU chapter also propose the establishment of specialized EU trade courts to handle trade remedies-related cases.

The problems identified by the authors of the developing country chapters, as well as their suggestions for the improvement of their judicial review systems, have much in common. Almost all of the developing country chapters conclude that their judicial review systems are not effective. The specific reasons for this conclusion are: (a) the length of judicial review proceedings; (b) the high level of deference accorded to the investigating authorities; (c) the tribunals' reluctance to address substantive issues and instead limit their analysis to alleged procedural errors; and (d) the lack of knowledge on trade remedies on the part of judges. These authors' suggestions for improvement are also very similar. They propose the establishment of specialized tribunals to deal with the judicial review of trade remedy determinations and the training of judges conducting such judicial review.

Looking at all the countries analysed in this book, the problems identified by the authors may be grouped into two broad categories. First, in the majority of countries analysed, including some developed countries, there seem to be serious concerns about the level of deference accorded to investigating authorities in the judicial review proceedings concerning trade remedy determinations. The authors of the developed country chapters who expressed dissatisfaction, such as Canada and the European Union, link this problem to the standard of review applied in these proceedings. The authors of developing country chapters, however, link it, rather, to the judges' inadequate knowledge of trade remedies, and consequently, their hesitation to review the details of the substantive determinations made by investigating authorities. Second, many authors complain about the long duration of judicial review proceedings.

IX   Deference to investigating authorities

For developed countries, the reason for the deference accorded to the investigating authorities is reported to be the standard of review that applies in the judicial review of trade remedy determinations. It is useful to recall that the judicial review of trade remedy determinations does not generally differ from the judicial review of other administrative actions of the government in many regards, including the standard of review applied by the tribunals. Therefore, it seems unlikely to expect a change in the standard of review applied in the judicial review of trade remedy determinations independently from the standard of review applied in the judicial review of other administrative actions. That said, it would certainly serve to further the rule of law in the implementation of trade remedy measures if a less deferential standard of review is adopted by the tribunals of those developed countries whose authors have identified high level of deference as a problem.

The deference accorded to the investigating authorities by the tribunals of developing countries appears to be linked mainly to a lack of knowledge of trade remedies on the part of the judges of the competent tribunals. The authors from developing countries propose two ways in which this problem may be addressed: (a) establishment of special tribunals, or special branches in the existing tribunals; and (b) training the judges serving in such tribunals. It seems to us that these two problems are interlinked, in the sense that training judges would clearly focus on acquiring the knowledge needed, whereas holding special tribunals concerns ensuring that the acquired knowledge is preserved and applied to the actual judicial review proceedings involving trade remedy determinations. The central issue, therefore, is how to assist the judges to improve their knowledge on trade remedies.

Training judges on legal matters is a delicate issue and should be addressed with caution. Judges serving in the competent tribunals of their countries are certainly among the best experts regarding their domestic laws and regulations, including those on trade remedies. However, it so happens that in this particular area the judges' knowledge and experience seem to fall short of what is needed in order to conduct a more rigorous review of the investigating authorities' determinations. There are obvious reasons that would explain why judges of developing countries have less knowledge of trade remedies compared with other areas of law. First, in many developing countries, trade remedies are a relatively new phenomenon. Many of them have set up their legislative framework in the last two decades and started using these measures actively in the last decade or so. Second, the number of judicial review cases on trade remedies is lower than cases that arise under other areas of domestic law. Third, in many developing countries, there are not many private lawyers specializing in trade remedies. Therefore, their submissions to the tribunals handling judicial review cases may not be as well substantiated as in other jurisdictions where trade remedies represent more or less a self-standing component of the legal profession. Taking all these factors into consideration, it is quite understandable that not all the judges in developing countries may have acquired the level of knowledge of trade remedies needed to conduct an effective review of the investigating authorities' determinations.

In certain developing countries, the investigating authorities may be instrumental in providing training for their judges. Further, certain bilateral or regional meetings of judges may also be useful in allowing them to exchange views and share experiences with respect to trade remedy cases. The issue of the standard of review would arguably be the most important element of such discussions, and judges would benefit greatly from learning the approaches of other countries' judges with respect to this very important issue. Obviously, each country has its own laws setting forth the standard of review that applies in their judicial review proceedings. Yet explanation of the types of actions which, under the applicable standard of review in various countries, would lead to a finding of violation of the domestic trade remedies legislation would certainly be useful to all judges, regardless of the specific standard of review that applies in their own jurisdictions. If needed, the WTO may also be requested to assist in this type of training for judges.

In addition to the training of the judges functioning in the tribunals that conduct the judicial review of trade remedy determinations, we recall that most developing country authors also suggested that establishing specialized tribunals for this type of judicial review would be useful. Clearly, having a tribunal that specializes in the review of trade remedy determinations would lead to more effective judicial review. In fact, as noted above, some countries already have such specialized tribunals.

Creating a specialized tribunal for the judicial review of trade remedy determinations, however, may face objections. In most countries, there would be a budget issue. It would not make financial sense to have a specialized tribunal for the judicial review of trade remedy determinations in a country where there are only a handful of such cases per year. Therefore, it seems to us that the best approach in this regard may be to create specialized courts that handle not only trade remedies cases, but also other matters such as tariffs, standards and intellectual property. This would make better financial sense and would thus be more acceptable to the governments.

X Duration of judicial review proceedings

A number of authors have identified the long duration of the judicial review process as a factor that undermines the effectiveness of the review. This issue is not easy to resolve, because it is directly linked to the procedural laws of the relevant country as well as to the workload of that country's courts in general. That said, as part of the training activities that we propose, the judges could also discuss this issue and try to find ways to shorten the duration of judicial review proceedings.

With regard to the duration of judicial review proceedings, it is useful to emphasize the requirement in Article 13 of the AD Agreement and Article 23 of the SCM Agreement that judicial review be "prompt". A process that takes several years to complete clearly fails to meet this standard.

INDEX

anti-dumping 2, 4
  Agreement on Implementation of
    Article VI of the GATT 1994
    (AD Agreement) 2
  deadlines (Art 5.10) 130
  evidential rules (Art 6.8) 325
  judicial review requirements 7–8,
    9–10, 318
  length of investigation process 307
  sales below cost (Art 2) 80
  standard of review (Art 17.6)
    61–2, 65
  standing (Art 11.6) 144
  tribunals (Art 13) 150, 296, 311,
    321–2, 357, 366–7, 375–6, 423
Argentina 129–52
  amparo proceedings 137–9, 151
  applicable law 140
  procedural rules 147–9
  requirements 147, 148
  suspension of challenged acts
    148–9, 151
  anti-dumping and countervail
    129–31, 141–2, 143, 144, 146
  concluding remarks and suggestions
    for improvement 151–2
  proposed administrative review
    agency 151–2
  reasons for infrequent use of
    judicial review 151
  history of trade remedies 129–31
  judicial review of trade remedy
    determinations 136–9
  jurisdiction and competent courts
    136–7
  types of judicial review
    proceedings 137–9

ordinary lawsuits 137–8, 151
  appeals 146
  grounds of challenge 145–6
  procedural rules 145–7
  suspension of challenged acts
    148–9, 151
  previous administrative review of
    trade remedy determinations
    133–6, 145, 151
  procedure 135–6
  purpose 134, 135
  procedure 139–50
  applicable law 140–1
  general procedure 139–40
  procedural rules governing
    judicial review 145–9
  reviewable determinations 141–3
  scope of review 149–50
  standing 143–5
  WTO case law 140–1
  remedies 150–1
  safeguards 129–31, 142–3
  structure and functioning of
    Argentina's investigating
    authority 131–3
  organization 131–2
  procedure for trade remedy
    investigations 132–3
Australia 5, 379–98
  conclusions 398
  judicial review 381–2, 390–8
  appeals 393, 394
  correct understanding of the
    statute, decisions based on
    394–7
  merits review, and 379
  nature and scope 379–80